Strasberg at The Actors Studio

STRASBERG
at The Actors Studio

TAPE-RECORDED SESSIONS

EDITED BY Robert H. Hethmon

PREFACE BY Burgess Meredith

THEATER COMMUNICATIONS GROUP

Strasberg at The Actors Studio is published by Theatre Communications Group, Inc., 355 Lexington Ave., New York, NY 10017.

Originally published by The Viking Press, Inc. in 1965. The book is reprinted with the consent and authority of the Estate of Lee Strasberg and The Lee Strasberg Theatre Institute.

TCG gratefully acknowledges public funds from the National Endowment for the Arts and the New York State Council on the Arts in addition to the generous support of the following foundations and corporations: Alcoa Foundation; Ameritech Foundation; ARCO Foundation; AT&T Foundation; Citibank; Consolidated Edison Company of New York; Nathan Cummings Foundation; Dayton Hudson Foundation; Exxon Corporation; Ford Foundation; James Irvine Foundation; Jerome Foundation; Andrew W. Mellon Foundation; Metropolitan Life Foundation; National Broadcasting Company; Pew Charitable Trusts; Philip Morris Companies; Scherman Foundation; Shubert Foundation.

Cover photograph used by permission of the Estate of Lee Strasberg.

Strasberg, Lee.
Strasberg at the Actors Studio : tape-recorded sessions /
edited by Robert H. Hethmon.
Reprint. Originally published : New York : Viking Press, 1965.
Includes index.
ISBN 1-55936-022-4 (pbk.)
1. Acting—Study and teaching—New York (N.Y.)   2. Actors Studio (New York, N.Y.)
I. Hethmon, Robert H.   II. Title.
PN2078.U62N4   1991
792'.028'07117471—dc20   90-29039   CIP

Cover design by The Sarabande Press

First TCG Edition, August 1991

Second Printing, September 1993

This book is re-dedicated to those of you who come into the theatre on the wings of your dream.

A special thank you to Professor Robert Hethmon for his devotion to this book.

As Lee always signed, "With hopes for the future."

—A.S.

ACKNOWLEDGMENT

Strasberg at The Actors Studio could not have been written without the cooperation of many individuals. I am especially grateful for the encouragement, advice, and assistance I have received variously from Lee and Paula Strasberg, Charlotte Hethmon, Cheryl Crawford, Elia and the late Molly Kazan, Helen K. Taylor, T. H. Guinzburg, Alice Hermes, Alec Rubin, Delos V. Smith, Jr., Fred Stewart, Gene Wilder, Gill Crowe, Ned Manderino, Violet Arase, Jeanne DePrey, Matthew Grace, Natalie McCracken, Jean Scharfenberg, The Research Committee of the Graduate School of The University of Wisconsin, and the State Historical Society of Wisconsin.

Lee Strasberg wishes particularly to thank John Stix for his careful reading of proof.

—R. H. H.

Contents

PREFACE BY BURGESS MEREDITH   xi

EDITOR'S PREFACE   xv

INTRODUCTION: THE ACTORS STUDIO AND
LEE STRASBERG   1

PART ONE: THE ACTOR AND THE STUDIO   25

    I. A WORKSHOP FOR PROFESSIONALS   27
       The Studio Stereotype   36
       The "Method"   38
       Working on Problems   43
       An Ideal System of Technical Training   55
       Pragmatism and Idealism   57

PART TWO: THE ACTOR AND HIMSELF   61

    II. THE ART OF THE ACTOR   63

    III. TRAINING: RELAXATION   88

    IV. TRAINING: TRIGGERING IMAGINATION   94
       Beginning Exercises   94
       Emotional Work   107
       Advanced Training   119
       The Logic of the Play   120
       Moments of Difficulty   130

    V. TRAINING: WILL AND DISCIPLINE   143

    VI. PROBLEMS: STOPPING IMAGINATION   170
       Subjective Interpretation of Technical Problems   170
       Too Much Sensitivity and Emotion   171
       Faking and Forcing   174
       The Verbal Pattern   178
       Anticipation   180
       Fear of Being Carried Away   184
       Fear of Not Being Carried Away   190

Demand for Mental Clarity	192
Vagueness	195
Comfort and Naturalness	196
Desire for Originality	204
Ego and Audience	205
VII. PROBLEMS: EXPRESSION	**210**
Cliché	211
The Habit of Inexpressiveness	222
Nervousness	241
Forcing Tempo	244
Fusion	245
The Sense of Truth	249
VIII. PROBLEMS: EXPLORATION	**252**
Conviction of Need	253
Technique for Exploration	264
A Personal Technique	278
IX. APPROACHING THE ROLE	**281**
PART THREE: THE ACTOR AND OTHER PEOPLE	**323**
X. THE ACTOR AND THE DIRECTOR	**325**
XI. THE ACTOR AND THE AUDIENCE	**347**
XII. THE ACTOR AND AMERICAN COMMERCIAL THEATRE	**357**
XIII. THE ACTOR AND THE THEATRE IN THE WORLD OF TODAY	**363**
EPILOGUE: THE ACTORS STUDIO THEATRE	**397**
INDEX	**401**

Preface by Burgess Meredith

Before writing this preface, I had to think back and sort out my earliest memories of Lee Strasberg. I started my career as a teenager, in a totally different theatrical climate from his—working with Katherine Cornell, Guthrie McClintic, Maxwell Anderson, and before that with Eva LeGallienne at her Civic Repertory Theatre. These people, along with the Lunts and Helen Hayes, were the "Establishment," so to speak. Their names lit up the Broadway firmament. A smart kid joined 'em if he could.

Then, as time rolled on, I began to hear more and more about a new movement associated with the Group Theatre, especially from Franchot Tone, a friend of mine and an early participant in this new thrust. Franchot didn't stay around long: he headed out to Hollywood, married Joan Crawford and became a movie star. But before leaving he advised me to investigate what he called "The Method"—he said I would find it useful. "It'll help you to stay sane."

At one point I approached Harold Clurman, one of the founders of the Group, and asked him about joining. He turned me down cold, saying I had too many interests already. "You wouldn't stay the course, Meredith."

I should mention that my friends in the Establishment were, at first, not sympathetic to the idea of a "method" theatre. For them, "method" seemed a derogatory word, a euphemism for bad acting. "Acting is not a *method*, for God's sake. It's an *art!*"

However, time taught me that actors, like athletes, need to keep working. They lose their edge if they don't stay in training. I remember Hume Cronyn and I studied awhile with a Stanislavsky expert, Benno Schneider. It was helpful, particularly the improvisations.

Then, inevitably and dramatically, I caught a glimpse of Lee Strasberg in action. The Group Theatre had dispersed and several of its key members had founded the Actors Studio, with quarters on West 44th Street. One day I was invited there to watch three well-known actors do a short 20-minute scene. No scenery, a few props, general lighting. After they finished there was no applause. The actors sat down on the prop chairs and faced the audience.

Lee Strasberg was in the front with thirty or forty actor-members. He asked the performers if they wanted to tell us, in general, "what their intentions had been" in the scene, "what problems they had faced."

The actors described what they believed the author's meaning was and how they worked to bring it out. Their answers were brief and tentative. There was a short, ritual pause, evidently allowing Lee to get his thoughts together.

What followed was extraordinary. In a concise 25-minute speech Lee evaluated what the actors had and had not accomplished from the audience's point of view. His words were meaningful, unhesitant, precise. His speech had form—as you will see when you read samples in this book. If tape recorders had not come along, there would have been no documentary evidence of his perceptive skills.

He used few gestures, none wasted. Very occasionally he made a kind of click sound in the back of his throat. I learned later this "tic" seemed to indicate his inner emotion or excitement. Otherwise his speech was even, his syntax faultless. No matter how long the sentence, it came out swiftly, nearly perfect. Thinking on his feet, without missing a beat, Lee sized up the effort and evaluated the results. He intertwined humor, praise, reproval, rationale and, once in a while, a touch of rabbinical wisdom.

To be brief, eventually I joined the Studio, was made a member of its Board, directed a production of *Blues for Mr. Charlie,* and became a friend of Lee and his family. Under Lee's tutelage, I ran the West Coast branch for a season.

One day he and I were scheduled to discuss something or other, and I drove to pick him up. He climbed into the car and sat next to me, looking straight ahead, not listening to my small talk. I asked, "Shall we go to the Studio?" He glanced at me and I saw, behind his glasses, he was in distress. Something had happened.

"It's a fine day," I said. "Let's drive someplace." He nodded and I drove aimlessly toward the Pacific Coast Highway. We rolled along the water's edge for an hour or more, saying not a word. I have forgotten what my thoughts were, but Lee's were evidently despondent.

Then, just before dusk, he took a deep breath and said, "All right."
I turned the car around and headed home. By the time I dropped him
off, he was relaxed and thoughtful.

I never learned what had upset him that day. It had something to do
with the Studio. As he left, I said: "Lee, I like your long silences.
They teach me more than your long soliloquies!"

He laughed. "So what did you learn?"

"I learned from you that the best way to solve problems is to shut up
and think."

He smiled. "Yes, that helps, that certainly helps. . . . Where did
we go? Next time, you think and I'll drive."

He gave me a Chaplinesque salute . . . and was gone.

There are not many people who contributed more to our theatre
than Lee.

And then, in his seventies, he returned to acting—in films! He
made a big hit and a small fortune. He probably got more money for
acting in *The Godfather* for 20 minutes than from running the Studio
for 20 years.

I am sure the readers of this book will learn a bit from his critiques.
And smile a bit, too. It is the next best thing to being there yourself.

Editor's Preface

In 1960 I visited Lee Strasberg to suggest that his personal papers and the archives of The Actors Studio be placed permanently on file in the Wisconsin Center for Theatre Research at the University of Wisconsin. My job as Director of the Center was to collect records of our contemporary American theatre that will be valuable to future historians. No person in the American theatre today seems more likely to be of continuing interest than Lee Strasberg, the Artistic Director of The Actors Studio.

I was understandably excited to learn that the sessions conducted by Strasberg at the Studio have been tape-recorded since 1956 and that hundreds of these recordings have been preserved. This is a most unusual chronicle, and it seemed to offer the opportunity of illustrating in book form his philosophy of theatre and methods of working with actors. I offered to undertake the task of converting the tapes into a book, and Strasberg agreed.

These recordings are unique. They constitute a day-to-day record of Strasberg's training of scores of talented professional actors. Many are now prominent performers, as a glance at their names in the appendix will confirm.

The tapes were made either for the use of Studio members unable to attend the sessions or for those who wished to review Strasberg's comments. They cast no self-conscious eye on the future. Rather they embody the creative relationship between Strasberg and more than one hundred and fifty Studio members in the course of hundreds of exercises, scenes, or projects, and in several score general meetings or discussions.

It is true that many writings dealing with the creative process in the theatre—reminiscences, textbooks, criticism, diaries, philosophy—have come down from the past, but it is also true that the achievements of that process have been largely lost. Whereas in other arts—literature, art, music—the masterworks remain, the actor's creation is inherently ephemeral. Even Stanislavski's three books on acting are fictionalized accounts. In historical writings we catch only glimpses of the process whereby the actor creates. Even such detailed sources as Reinhardt's production books and the Brecht theatre's *Mödelbuchs* deal with finished productions. The Strasberg tapes go far beyond such accounts because they record actual work in progress over a period of years.

This book illustrates some of Strasberg's practices in the work of one of the Studio's three units, the Actors Unit. The director's work is included only insofar as Strasberg discusses the direct relationship between actor and director; none of the material comes from tapes made in the Directors Unit, nor is the work of the Playwrights Unit examined. Except for a small amount of material taken from one lecture outside the Studio and from taped interviews with Strasberg, the book comes solely from the tapes made in the Actors Unit sessions. Because the sessions are private, letters of the alphabet are substituted for names of Studio members figuring in the tapes.

A number of problems had to be dealt with in selecting and arranging the material from the tapes. There was, of course, no point in attempting to create a textbook because Strasberg's entire practice is completely antithetical to that kind of approach. He does not promulgate a "system." It is impossible to find in the tapes any extended discussion that synthesizes his various concrete suggestions. In selecting material to illustrate the general ideas that undoubtedly underlie his comments, I was aware of the danger of seeming to present a systematic discussion that actually does not take place. At one point I thought that I might preserve the occasional nature of Strasberg's discussion, while simultaneously presenting his general ideas, by including a series of "case histories" tracing work with individual actors through a period of years, but this turned out to be impractical. Individual sessions in a "case history" might have proved revealing in print, but every *series* of such sessions has so many repetitions pointless to a reader (as opposed to a spectator) that this approach had to be abandoned. I finally decided to excerpt freely from all the available tapes, arranging the material in topical order to show the variety of acting problems that are dealt with. Printed material usually must have a greater clarity and succinctness than spoken language; hence, what appears in the book is almost always the product of condensation. However, in several places extended dialogues between Strasberg and a Studio member have been included to show specifically the kind of give-and-take that characterizes much of the discussion.* The somewhat acerbic tone of these examples merely reflects the fact that opposition often produces Strasberg's most effective and illuminating utterances.

The one virtually insuperable problem I encountered is that the performances commented on are not present to the reader. Not that the reader is incapable of imagining what the actors did; I think he *can* do this from the clues given him. The difficulty is that a book must present serially what an actor can present simultaneously. A book simply cannot say everything at once—even though "everything" is immediately relevant—whereas the spectator is often given revelation by a single comment, not because the comment in itself is profound, but because the spectator has just seen the entire complex subject which the comment summarizes. The dynamic nature of the actor's art has, of course, always imposed this difficulty on the critic and historian, but fortunately has not made criticism and history impossible.

Part One brings together comments on the nature of the Studio and the relation of the individual actor to it taken from many separate occasions. Part Two takes up the actor's work on himself, which is the fundamental work of the Actors Unit. Part Three deals with some of the problems of the actor's relationship with his director, with the audience, and with the commercial theatre. Finally, I have collected some general discussions of world theatre, because they serve the concrete purpose of attempting to relate the work of the individual Studio member to what Strasberg regards as the great tradition of theatre art.

---

* See pages 227-41 and 336-46.

Publishers' Note

Strasberg at The Actors Studio is set in two different type faces so that the reader may distinguish between the extemporaneous comments of Lee Strasberg, as taken from tape recordings, and the written text of Robert H. Hethmon. Strasberg's spoken remarks, which begin on page 27, are in Electra, set to the full measure of the type page. Hethmon's text is indented from the left margin, and is in Fairfield, a slightly smaller type face. This Note is set in the Hethmon style, as are the Editor's Preface, the Introduction, and the editorial commentary throughout the book.

Strasberg at The Actors Studio

INTRODUCTION:

The Actors Studio and Lee Strasberg

BY ROBERT H. HETHMON

In the last few years visitors to New York in search of serious theatre have inevitably been drawn from the garishness of Broadway beyond Ninth Avenue to a modest, two-story, white-painted church building in the Greek Revival style, hemmed in by dingy apartments, set back a dozen feet from the sidewalk, and fronted by black-painted railings. A small signboard identifies The Actors Studio. The visitor must ignore the sandstone steps leading up to a double-door in the façade and enter by a basement door.

Wandering through the lower floor, the guest—students and professional theatre workers are privileged to seek special entree —encounters several busy offices with notice boards and jangling telephones, a quieter greenroom flanked by two doors labeled "Oh, Men" and "Oh, Women" (from the title of a successful production by Cheryl Crawford, one of the Studio's founders), and at the rear a large sunny rehearsal room facing a courtyard where the Studio hopes someday to build additional rehearsal space. On the walls are photographs of Duse and Stanislavski, autographed theatrical posters from visiting European companies, and—a less conventional note—prints of Garrick, Kean, Kemble, and Mrs. Siddons.

A narrow stair leads up to the Studio proper. Once the church auditorium, it still retains the original horseshoe balcony and high-raftered ceiling. The old-fashioned windows, the wooden roof, the narrow balcony, the blue-and-white color scheme—all faintly suggest a Georgian theatre. Where pulpit and choir were is now a playing space backed by a high, sand-blasted wall. This acting space extends out into the midst of the audience, for whom tiers of plain blue chairs line the three walls beneath the balcony.

The visitor arriving somewhat before the starting hour of 11 a.m. will usually find a few pieces of furniture or some battered stage platforms placed about the open space. Drawn shades dim the room. Sometimes several actors are on the stage, perhaps lying down, each concentrating on his own thoughts. Gradually the room fills as people drift in smoking and carrying coffee mugs. They converse in low tones. A technician comes in, adjusts the tape recorder, and places a glass of water and a large alarm clock on the low stand in front of a movie director's folding canvas chair. The audience is mostly young people; they look like an exceptionally attractive and intelligent group of graduate students. Here and there among the informally dressed majority is a fashionably dressed woman. A few famous faces emerge. No one is posing or showing off. Attitudes are casual, businesslike, yet the atmosphere is strangely theatrical. Somehow the *crowd* stands out. The air is charged.

Shortly before eleven a small man in gray, with gray hair and wearing heavy-rimmed glasses, slips in with a crowd of last-minute arrivals, drapes his black raincoat on the back of the director's chair, and sits down. This is Lee Strasberg, Artistic Director of The Actors Studio. He looks around briefly. The audience quiets. Consulting a white card, he announces the name of the first scene. The room lights fade; spotlights "dim up." The stage may immediately erupt into action, sound, music, dancing, laughing, words. The actors may simply continue to concentrate on their own thoughts. Or the scene may begin with movement, the actors beginning to speak only after a long period of paying assiduous attention to various properties on the stage. Finally, whatever the scene, it will be over. The room lights are turned on. The stage manager starts the tape recorder, and one of the performers begins to talk about what he had tried to accomplish in the scene. Strasberg listens, sometimes asks a question, and finally calls on the other actors in the scene, one by one, to explain the problems they were working on. Occasionally the actors will be asked to repeat the scene, so that Strasberg can comment as it progresses. Often the audience is invited to comment. Finally, Strasberg himself begins to speak. He may speak for ten or sixty minutes, but usually his remarks continue for only fifteen or twenty, because a second scene must be accommodated before the session ends about one o'clock.

This is all. Strasberg rushes off to meet another class, and the members disperse to homes or jobs or remain to rehearse another scene. The casual visitor may be somewhat bewildered. "Is this the world-famous Actors Studio? Is this the birthplace and home of stars? Can these rather simple procedures be the famous 'Method'?" Perhaps the visitor has heard an eloquent discourse from Strasberg. Perhaps he has witnessed violent emotions, actors in tears— both in the scene and in the discussion afterward. Or he may have seen what seemed to be mere random horseplay or casual "mooching" about the stage. Actors may have spoken of problems that seem to the visitor utterly trivial or banal. The visitor may very possibly emerge on Forty-fourth Street wondering what all the fuss is about.

The people at the Studio do not in fact care very much what he may think. Many of them have attended these twice-weekly sessions since 1947. For them the Studio is a private workshop; the visitor has been given the privilege of watching the work in progress of professional craftsmen, and reactions are really irrelevant. Every artist requires a place, a "studio," where he can practice his scales, try new colors, botch, invent, test himself. One of Strasberg's guiding ideas is summed up in a favorite saying from Goethe: "The actor's career develops in public, but his art develops in private." But Goethe's apothegm needs to be qualified. The actor really does need other people in order to advance in his art and craft. The Actors Studio provides him with both fellow craftsmen and privacy. There art can actually develop, and the sufficiently sensitive visitor will almost certainly take away from even a random visit a sense of dedication, earnestness, hard work, tough-mindedness, and professional in-

sight. It may well dawn on him that he has been in the presence
of a master teacher.

The Actors Studio exists because it is needed. In America the
actor faces greater difficulties than any other artist. Although we
recognize actors, we do not fully accept acting as a profession.
Very few young people—even those of obvious talent—go into
acting with the encouragement of their families and the com-
munity. There is, in fact, no recognized formal way of entering
the profession. The hundreds of stock companies to which a
young actor could once apprentice himself no longer exist.
America has no official training institutions or theatres comparable to those of France or Russia. Universities, despite magnificent buildings, at best pay lip service to actors' training.
So-called "professional" schools work more diligently, but not
more profoundly. The young American enters acting more often
because of some chance revelation or exploitation of his talent
than through deliberate choice of and education for a career.

The talented young actor can spend years beating in vain on
theatre doors, to say nothing of thousands of untalented people.
The young actor may try for years without getting more than a
small part or two. Meanwhile, the attritions of life, psychological pressures, the lack of opportunity for professional practice
and development take their toll of his essential talent. When
time and experience have carried him to the point where in any
other profession maturity and sureness are usually attained, the
actor's talent has usually been blocked or dissipated. A century
ago Henry Irving spent fifteen years in stock companies training himself in literally hundreds of parts before he "became a
star overnight" in *The Bells.* The American actor rarely has such
an opportunity.

More often—if he gets any chance at all—he is recognized
for some facet of his talent, some physical characteristic or
facility, some useful display of type. He may even find himself
famous—or notorious—overnight, and then the pressures that
beset him outside the magic circle are doubled and redoubled
within. He is basically untrained. He has probably used little

of his full talent—and even that without conscious technique. For immediately the theatre has begun to exploit the talent which chance has revealed. The actor is called upon to repeat nightly, for years, the one role that has brought him acclaim; and he is frequently pushed into a series of repetitions—in movies and television as well as theatre—of essentially the same element of himself that brought him initial success. He begins more and more to use less and less of himself. After a while he is beset by scarifying questions: "Can I do it again?" "Can I do anything else?" "Can I work with a different director—with different material?" "Can I play a different type?" "Do I really have talent? I had it once. Where did it go?"

Often the more brilliant the success, the greater the anxieties that follow. Success does not very often bring power—or even assurance. Witness Broadway's worldly wisdom: "You're only as good as your next show." Witness those who wait—in back bedrooms and luxury apartments—for the call from the agent, the summons from the producer; for winter so they can go south, for summer so they can go north; for the season that never quite arrives to fill somehow the emptiness that was left when the lights dimmed and the posters began to fade and the wise guys started to look the other way, because the Broadway bush telegraph had delivered the message—however true or false— that they didn't "have it" any more.

The Actors Studio is a refuge. Its privacy is guarded ferociously against the casual intruder, the seeker of curiosities, and the exploiter. But the Studio provides far more than sanctuary. The actor of talent will find understanding of the reality of the problems that he faces. Success can be its own enemy and feed on its own vitals. Talent consumes itself. The Studio helps actors to meet the enemy within—those professional problems that derive from the actor himself.

Sometimes an actor may know exactly what he needs to be doing—but cannot do it. Sometimes an actor knows that something is wrong—but cannot imagine what it is. Sometimes he faces the task of repeating himself tonight at eight-forty, when the curtain rises, freshly and creatively—and he finds himself stale, constricted, mechanical, dead, a bundle of mannerisms and clichés. He actually cannot do what he knows he has done many times before.

How does an actor look for whatever it was that he had which doesn't seem to be there any more? A writer can at least write and throw away. A painter can take a month or a year to finish a painting. A pianist knows that his instrument will respond today as it did yesterday. Only the actor faces the uncertainty, the anxious, frustrating, even terrifying moments of difficulty when he wonders if he can re-create—using only himself—what his profession demands that he must freshly create again and again.

Actors come into the Studio well trained, untrained, even wrongly trained. The only common ground is talent and the possibility of improvement. There they find a laboratory to practice elements of their craft away from the pressures of Broadway, to find out not only if they still "have it" but what they can really do with it.

The precise meaning of this opportunity was dramatized for me by another private organization for theatre people located at the opposite end of the same Manhattan street where the Studio is. Going east from Broadway the visitor finds himself at the premises of a sumptuous club. Portraits of past members adorning the walls explain why its name for generations has symbolized the glitter and glamour of the theatre. I visited there a number of times. To me it will always be a sad place. Each time I encountered that utterly conventional novelistic figure, the club drunk—but here a real man: shabby, shambling, red-faced, mumbling, with faraway eyes, a minor annoyance who tried to horn in on conversations. I was told his story. He was once a leading Broadway "juvenile," and then one day whatever he had as a performer was no longer there—or no longer wanted —and he tried to regain it from a bottle. The moral, however, is not why this should have happened, but rather why the club drunk is suffered to go on being the club drunk. Indifference? Perhaps. Pity? Possibly. Eventually I knew. This poor man is essential because every member can come to the club and return to his luxury apartment or back bedroom and there tell himself in the secrecy of his heart, "I'm not yet as bad off as that poor son of a bitch."

Strasberg has a very clear idea of the kind of reality the art of the actor should serve. To him the best theatre art is that which strives most clearly to fill what it does with significance, not with naturalism; to every task and problem that confronts the actor this test is applied. Thus the Studio has a steady continuity of viewpoint that contrasts completely with the fecklessness and mindlessness of Broadway and contributes greatly to Strasberg's utterly pragmatic views on training the actor and solving his problems. Contrary to almost universal notions, Strasberg does not give the members a series of rules that constitute a system of acting. He does employ a systematic approach to *training*. He tries to show the actor the nature of his individual "instrument," so that he can evolve a technique for utilizing and controlling *his* particular resources which will then keep him from being paralyzed by difficulties when they occur. Although much of this approach derives ultimately from Stanislavski, much derives from Strasberg's own experimentation over the years, and it is all used because he has discovered that it works. This tough-minded approach has given the Studio a positiveness of purpose that has kept it alive and growing for seventeen years, that makes the Studio a place of hope, not of despair.

Theatre is an art in which practical considerations are decisive. Artistic problems in theatre always involve concrete problems of human relationship. Actors need other actors. They need training, direction, and management. These problems have been met in The Actors Studio by a minimum of formal organization. The Studio gives privileges. It encourages responsibility. It exacts nothing. Its survival for seventeen years attests the efficacy of this approach.

The Actors Studio was founded by Elia Kazan, Cheryl Crawford, and Robert Lewis in October 1947. Fifty young professional actors, carefully selected for talent, were invited to become members. During the first season Lewis conducted meetings for the more advanced members, while Kazan held sessions for beginners. At the end of that season Lewis resigned, and in 1948 and 1949 a half-dozen teachers, including Kazan, Daniel Mann, and Sanford Meisner, kept the classes going. In the fall of 1949 Strasberg was invited to join. In a short time he became the Studio's sole teacher of actors, and in 1951 he was appointed Artistic Director. In that role he has since been responsible for the Studio's work with actors and its general artistic policy.

Since its inception the Studio has been a nonprofit educational corporation chartered by the state of New York; it has been supported entirely by contributions and benefits. During most of its first fourteen years it was governed by a Board of Directors consisting of Strasberg, Kazan, Cheryl Crawford, attorney William Fitelson, and real-estate expert John Stuart Dudley. Kazan and Fitelson resigned in May 1962, and were replaced by Geraldine Page and Rip Torn.

Actors comprised the Studio's original membership, and the Studio has always been concerned primarily with actors. However, a number of members have discovered or explored talents in playwriting or direction. During the 1957-1958 season the Studio initiated the Playwrights Unit. Earlier Robert Anderson and Clifford Odets had worked with playwrights; the new unit has been headed successively by Kazan, William Inge, Molly Kazan, and Gaynor Bradish. Early in 1960 a Directors Unit was established under Strasberg's leadership. Finally, in late 1962 the Studio instituted a unit devoted to production, The Actors Studio Theatre.

The Studio has been deliberately modest in its circumstances, its essence being the private room where Lee Strasberg and some talented actors can work. The Studio's first meeting was held in a top-floor rehearsal room in the old Princess Theatre. Its first working space was a Sunday-school room rented twice weekly from the Union Church on West Forty-eighth Street. Before the end of its first season it moved, first to a dance studio on East Fifty-ninth Street, and in May 1948, to a studio on the fourteenth floor of 1697 Broadway which it leased until the summer of 1952. The Studio was then given the use of the top floor of the ANTA Theatre, which it occupied until mid-1954 when it was again forced to rent space twice weekly, this time in the Malin Studios on West Forty-sixth Street. There it held out through the 1954-1955 season.

In the middle of that season the members raised a down payment of eighteen thousand dollars to purchase the hundred-year-old church building at 432 West Forty-fourth Street which the Studio now occupies. That spring and summer the new home was put in order, and the first classes held there met in October 1955. By 1961 the Studio held full title. The building, now worth more than a hundred thousand dollars, has been extensively renovated and decorated in the intervening years, mostly by the members themselves.

For the Actors, Directors, and Playwrights Units the Studio employs a full-time secretary and stage manager. In its early years it employed Anna Sokolow to offer dance training. For the last nine years Alice Hermes has given a regular class in speech training, and over half the members have participated in this class. In 1957-1958 Etienne Decroux was brought from France to offer classes for about six months, and the newest special teacher, Sophia Delza, offered training classes in the art of the classical Chinese theatre during 1962-1963. In recent years Strasberg has received a fee from the Studio, because, as Cheryl Crawford explains, "He is giving up prime teaching time [from his private classes] on which he could make a great deal of money to do this for a much smaller amount." Previously his work had been donated, and in fact the hours he spends in the Studio's classes are only a fraction of the time that he devotes to Studio affairs.

The Studio could not have come into existence and could never have continued without the selfless efforts of literally hundreds of people. Nonmembers have served as directors and teachers, and individuals such as Dorothy Willard and Liska March (who has been instrumental in organizing the Studio's annual benefits) have contributed importantly to administration and fund raising. Members have given talent, time, labor, and artistry. Over the years members with special abilities have taught other members through classes in fencing, basic acting exercises, body movement and dance, gymnastics, and classic scenes. Members are called on to do a variety of indispensable jobs ranging from helping with auditions to participating in an annual "big push" to improve the Studio's quarters. However, in the history of the Studio's day-to-day functioning, Cheryl Crawford has played very quietly a pre-eminent role. From 1947 to 1962—outside of her participation in shaping Studio policy—she assumed the most difficult and thankless of all tasks in a theatre organization, the basic responsibility for raising money and taking care of the practical details that constantly arise in the management of any theatrical enterprise. Her contribution has almost certainly meant for the Studio the difference between life and death.

By 1961 the Studio's yearly budget, covering not only salaries but such services as cleaning, telephone, and typing, had grown to more than forty thousand dollars. Since the late fifties film-premiere benefits had raised about half this budget. In 1962, for example, The Actors Studio held a gala benefit at Carnegie Hall for itself and the new Cultural Center in Washington. Studio members have given substantial sums over the years, and many important gifts have come from individuals and organizations, but it is important to understand that all contributions have been truly disinterested. The Studio has been extremely careful not to allow its name or work to be associated with any commercial enterprises.

An important gift to the Studio followed the establishment of The Actors Studio Theatre. In October 1962, the Ford Foundation awarded the new unit a quarter of a million dollars (which was matched by private donors) to carry out its first seasons. The Studio lost no time putting this revolving fund to work. Its first production, Eugene O'Neill's *Strange Interlude,* opened at the Hudson Theatre in New York on March 11, 1963, and had a run of five months.

In fact, a complex series of factors has interacted to keep the Studio in existence and to raise it to its present eminence. Each has been so vital in the functioning of the Studio's organism that it is impossible to assess their relative weight. Could the Studio have emerged without Elia Kazan in its directorate during the years when he has been perhaps the most important director on Broadway and one of the finest American film directors? Could the Studio have survived without the influence of Cheryl Crawford, an outstanding producer, who has worked to maintain its solvency? The Studio's first classes had a dazzling array of talent. Many of its first members were at that moment reaching stardom. Talent attracted more talent. The Studio serves talent on an individual basis. It adheres to its policy of separation from commercial pressures of casting and "showcasing." Membership is a privilege for which the member owes no obligations of any kind in return. The Studio's idealism and achievements have drawn from many sources gifts of time, energy, and money. It has kept its operation confined as much as possible to essentials—a room, actors, and a teacher. If any of these conditions had not prevailed, would the whole structure have collapsed? I cannot say so, but I am sure that every one of these factors is relatively meaningless compared with the Studio's success in coming to grips with the problems of the actor, and it has accomplished that success primarily through Strasberg's very practical work as Artistic Director.

Lee Strasberg was born in 1901 at Budzanow in Galicia, then part of the Austrian Empire. He was the youngest among the three sons and daughter of Baruch Meyer and Ida Strasberg. Shortly afterward Baruch immigrated to New York while his family remained in the home village with an uncle, a rabbinical teacher. The father, who worked as a presser in the garment industry, sent first for his eldest son and his daughter. Finally enough money was saved to bring over the mother and the two younger boys. In 1909 the family was reunited on Manhattan's Lower East Side, where they lived until in the early twenties they moved uptown to the Bronx.

Strasberg had had only religious instruction from his uncle before he started school in New York. He attended two East Side public schools and would have graduated from Townsend Harris High School, which is part of City College, had not the younger of his brothers died in the influenza epidemic of 1918. Instead of going to college he eventually became an office clerk for a manufacturer of ladies' hairpieces, and when the owner suffered a breakdown Strasberg and a friend bought the business.

No other person in Strasberg's family has ever been involved in the professional theatre. His sister married a jewelry salesman. His oldest brother is a dentist. His father worked all his life in the garment trades. In fact, nothing in his childhood gives the least hint that he would become an actor, director, and teacher—and finally one of America's most influential men of the theatre. True, as a child on the East Side he appeared sporadically and quite accidentally in Yiddish amateur productions of playwrights like Sudermann, but he had no sustained contact with play production until the early twenties. "What are you worried about?" he recently asked a young Studio actress very perturbed about her career. "When I was your age, I wasn't even in the theatre. I was in the human-hair business."

Now a man of vast erudition in the realm of the arts, Strasberg has always had intense curiosity about cultural matters. His voracious appetite for reading—which has filled his New York apartment with thousands of volumes—began in high school. One subject about which he read a lot at that time was the theatre, but it was general reading—biographies of actors, history, the early issues of *Theatre Arts* magazine. When in the early twenties a friend invited him to join the Students of Art and Drama, a social group of amateurs that met and performed plays at the Chrystie Street Settlement House, he did join, but without any particular purpose in mind.

Strasberg now looks back on this experience as the extremely important apprentice period when he was able to try himself, as every artist must in one way or another. At Chrystie Street he started playing small parts. He made his first impression on a theatre professional when Philip Loeb, casting director for the Theatre Guild, came to see a friend perform, saw Strasberg as well—he was a blind boy in a Maeterlinck play—and buttonholed him afterward. "Are you interested in acting?" "Not particularly," said Strasberg. "Well, if at any time you are interested," Loeb said, "look me up." And eventually—at a crucial moment in his career—Strasberg did so. As late as 1927 Strasberg continued to work with the "SADs" of Chrystie Street.

The life of the theatre seems so evanescent that most people scarcely realize that the possibility of a living tradition of theatre exists. It is said that Henry Irving's Hamlet could be traced back—actor by actor—to Burbage. It can equally be said that Strasberg's influence on the young actors of the fifties and sixties can be traced back to his theatrical experiences of the early twenties. Certain images haunt his imagination and constantly color his discourse—all dating from that time—Jacob ben Ami in *Samson and Delilah*, Jeanne Eagels in *Rain*, the Theatre Guild's *Liliom*, Chaliapin as Boris Godounov. But the *annus mirabilis* was 1923, the year in which he saw Barrymore's Hamlet, Duse in her farewell performances, and the first American visit of Stanislavski and the original ensemble of the Moscow Art Theatre.

Those for whom Strasberg is the apostle of realism will be surprised to learn that a decisive influence pushing him into theatre was the leading modern advocate of the symbolist theatre. For Strasberg, acting at first was merely a social activity. Gordon Craig's *On the Art of the Theatre*, which trumpeted the theatre's claim to high place among all the arts, catalyzed Strasberg's realization that theatre not only is a place of entertainment but holds the imaginative possibilities of great art. However, not until he saw Stanislavski and the company of the Moscow Art Theatre did he understand that what he had thought of as a dream of theatre art could actually be created on the stage. Finally, his partner in the hair business offered to buy him out at the rate of twenty-five dollars a week for a year. He decided "to take a crack at the theatre."

He enrolled in the Clare Tree Major School of the Theatre, which he attended for three months, feeling vaguely dissatisfied all the while. Then a friend suggested that he look into a new theatre group in Greenwich Village. It was the American Laboratory Theatre, founded by Richard Boleslavsky and Maria Ouspenskaya, members of the Moscow Art Theatre who had remained in New York when the company returned to Russia. Here for the first time Strasberg encountered a concrete expression of Stanislavski's ideas about training the actor. He promptly auditioned for the theatre's school and was accepted.

The ideas introduced to Strasberg at the American Laboratory Theatre have been fundamental to all his subsequent work with actors. He still has the notes taken on his first day in Boleslavsky's class. But it was not a "system"—sentimentally adopted and slavishly followed—that he acquired there. Rather he learned of discoveries about the psychological nature of the actor and ways of training based on those discoveries which Stanislavski had tested for many years. It is characteristic of Strasberg that between 1923 and 1931, when his first Group Theatre production opened on Broadway, he too tested what he had been told, not only by observing professional directors, but more importantly by trying to find for himself the means of using Stanislavski's work in actual productions: plays he directed at the Chrystie Street Settlement House (among others Racine's *Esther,* 1926, and Copeau's *The House into Which We Are Born,* 1927, with Copeau attending the dress rehearsal); off-Broadway productions (Scott Fitzgerald's *The Vegetable*); experimental productions (*New Year's Eve* by Waldo Frank and Padraic Colum's *Balloon,* 1928); finally in the rehearsal and training of the Group Theatre company in the summer before *The House of Connelly* opened in September 1931. No more than any other artist did Strasberg spring full-blown onto the American theatre scene.

Late in 1924 he realized that he had to choose between continuing as a member of the American Laboratory Theatre and striking out for Broadway. Distrusting the viability of the Boleslavsky group and remembering his chance meeting with Philip Loeb, he wrote to Loeb, and some weeks later was rehearsing for the Theatre Guild's production of *Processional,* which opened on January 12, 1925. Strasberg served also as assistant stage manager, and, when *Processional* closed after several months, he was transferred in the same capacity to the Guild's production of *The Guardsman,* which had opened the previous October. Also, that spring he played Ponza in a special Guild production of Pirandello's *Right You Are If You Think You Are,* and his first professional season ended with his singing and dancing in the Guild's first *Garrick Gaieties.*

Except for a gangster part in George Abbott's *Four Walls*

(1927), Strasberg's early professional career—which followed the up-and-down pattern of most minor actors—was in the Theatre Guild. He was stage manager for the second *Garrick Gaieties* (1926). He played a comic role in a Russian import, *Red Rust* (1929), the initial and sole production of the Theatre Guild Studio. In 1931 he played the Peddler in Lynn Riggs' *Green Grow the Lilacs,* and when the show went on tour he went along. That spring, when the tour ended, he came back to New York in time to accompany the new Group Theatre to Connecticut for its first summer of rehearsal and training.

When Elia Kazan, Cheryl Crawford, and Robert Lewis met in 1947 to establish The Actors Studio, they were consciously attempting to carry on a tradition established by the Group Theatre. The founding of the Group Theatre by Miss Crawford, Harold Clurman, and Strasberg had grown out of their association—as early as 1926—as fellow workers for the Theatre Guild. Robert Lewis was a member of the original Group Theatre company. Kazan joined the Group in 1932 as an apprentice and ended as a leading actor. However, the tradition they were concerned with was not merely a personal one.

The Group Theatre made a permanent contribution to our theatrical life. They were the first American company fully trained to perform as an ensemble, and, as Clurman later wrote of their first production, they "succeeded in fusing the technical elements of their craft with the stuff of their own spiritual and emotional selves. They succeeded in doing this because, aside from their native character and habit, they were prepared by the education of their work together before and during rehearsals." Quite apart from the Group's discovery of fine playwrights and gifted actors, this was its gift to our theatrical tradition— the successful realization of a theatrical art which can be achieved only by a trained ensemble theatre. It introduced to the American theatre a vision of reality and truth in acting and production which has served as a standard of judgment ever since.

Although the Group went out of existence in 1941, many of its ideas had become influential, and they were given even greater currency by the widespread activity of former Group members as actors, directors, and teachers on Broadway and in

Hollywood. Cheryl Crawford left the Group in 1937 and in the forties became one of Broadway's prominent producers. Strasberg, who resigned the same year, spent the next dozen years as a director both in New York and in the movies. Clurman, Kazan, Lewis, Sanford Meisner, Franchot Tone, Morris Carnovsky, Luther Adler, Stella Adler, J. Edward Bromberg, John Garfield, Clifford Odets, and Lee J. Cobb were only the most prominent of the Group's alumni. The talent of Group members continued to make itself felt. What was lost in 1941 was the essential fact of the Group's having been a group, a workshop, and a theatre in which professional artists could work permanently together.

Success in the jungle of Broadway certainly did not satisfy people like Kazan or Cheryl Crawford. Nor did Strasberg find any particular satisfaction in the purely commercial theatre. Despite his association with such plays as Hemingway's *The Fifth Column,* Odets' *The Big Knife* and *The Country Girl,* and Cheryl Crawford's production of *All the Living,* Strasberg's career as a Broadway director after 1937 did not contribute much to the vision of theatre art he had carried with him from the twenties, nor could it match the sense of achievement felt in the early Group Theatre days. His greatest personal fulfillment came in the late forties, when he assumed the role of teacher and began to offer both private classes and classes at the American Theatre Wing. He has always been tacitly a teacher. Kazan calls him "one of those people that are by very nature teachers," and the record shows that he has been extraordinarily successful in developing acting talent. It was in a way providential that Kazan should have invited him in 1949 to teach at the recently founded Actors Studio, for from that invitation has stemmed the fruitful marriage between Strasberg's long experience and the youthful talent of the post-World War II generation.

Strasberg's success as a teacher cannot be accounted for by any single aspect of his complex personality. One's initial impression is of a quiet, unassuming man, not especially prepossessing either physically or vocally. Even several visits to the Studio do not fully clarify his particular effectiveness. Only after one observes his work in literally hundreds of acting situations does the pattern become clear. First there are his erudition and the immense experience of the world's theatre observed professionally during forty years. Then one begins to notice a feeling and a passion that are usually held in check by strong powers of concentration and will. One notices too the wit, the humor, and the sentiment. And it becomes obvious that his great personal authority in speaking about and to actors derives from decades of training and directing them.

Strasberg has the great teacher's ability to adjust himself personally and fully to each individual actor with whom he works. This is the central element of his effectiveness. He treats each actor as an individual because he knows that he *is* individual. And he has an extraordinary ability to observe and analyze an actor's work objectively and accurately. This is why all the cant about "Method" is so utterly at variance with the facts. Seventy-five per cent of Strasberg's work is concerned with helping an actor find out how he works individually, what his particular problems are, how he can go about solving them for himself, how he can develop a technique that will take into account the potentialities and the idiosyncrasies of his own "instrument."

Himself a good actor, Strasberg often communicates as much through acting as through logical analysis. Sometimes *what* he says, taken literally, does not make sense. Only when it is understood that he is making his point through a total response to what the actor has done, through a total communication, can one detect his purpose. He is extremely articulate when he wants to be, but he is also aware that a great deal of the actor's functioning is unconscious, that ideas and rules and principles may or may not have any effect on his work. He exhorts, stings, cajoles, incites, denounces, satirizes, worries, advises, praises, encourages, jokes, and inspires. He "lets himself go" with unbounded energy, imagination, and occasionally passion. Only after one has seen in hundreds of examples his ability to bring the full range of his knowledge, experience, personality, and eloquence to bear on the particular problems of individual Studio members can one appreciate the authority he brings to the training of each one. Hundreds of people are able to give actors excellent advice, but Strasberg goes far beyond this and shows the actor how to deal with difficulties often not even suspected. This explains why so many actors are so grateful for his help, so fiercely loyal to his work.

Admission to the Actors Unit is usually by audition, occasionally by invitation. Auditions are open to working professional actors, and preliminary auditions are held by committees of members or qualified nonmembers throughout the Studio season. More than a thousand actors audition each year. The Directors hold final auditions twice yearly, and only they can confer membership. Usually a mere five or six actors survive the auditions each year.

The work of the Actors Unit is directed by Strasberg in a special way. His remarks on a particular exercise frequently suggest specific additional work that the actor may profitably do—either repetition with a different emphasis or an entirely different exercise bearing on the same or a different problem. Sometimes an actor will stay with the same material on four or five occasions, each time using a different approach, or carrying the material through different stages of preparation. Strasberg also occasionally vetoes proposals for work on the ground that it is either irrelevant or actually harmful to an individual. But the Studio member is not obligated in any way to follow his suggestions or, in fact, to do anything at the Studio at all, even to attend sessions. It is the individual member's privilege to take advantage of Strasberg's knowledge and experience if he wants to do so. If he does not, no pressure is put upon him. However, Strasberg's analyses are from the beginning designed to develop an actor's awareness of his special capacities and difficulties, and it is natural that the actor's ensuing work should proceed toward solving the problems that are thus revealed. It cannot be stressed too strongly that the individual is free in his choice of work and that Strasberg considers impartially any work that the actor brings to his attention. Perhaps fifteen per cent of Strasberg's comments are general discussions of theatre art and the relation of the Studio's work to commercial and world theatre.

Actors perform usually alone or with one partner, although frequently "projects" are done and discussed. Infrequently, three or four actors will do a scene together. It is usual for scenes not to have a director. Members use a variety of dramatic material, scenes from classic and modern plays and from unproduced scripts, poems, novels, short stories, or films. They also do a variety of semiabstract exercises, each designed to attack some specific problem. Shakespeare is the author most frequently employed.

During each two-hour session two scenes or exercises are customarily considered; occasionally only one scene will occupy the full period. This schedule allows the actor to work without many of the restrictive pressures of rehearsal or performance. He can prepare extensively before actually starting, can go as slowly as he wishes, repeat, stop, go back, start a second time. A discussion by the actor of his own problem almost invariably follows, and this serves at least two important purposes: it encourages the actor to take an objective view of himself so as to increase his powers of self-awareness, and it reveals to the audience what he thought he was doing so that they can make an objective judgment on how successful he was. The comments of the audience that follow serve the same purposes. They are useful for the performers, and for the Studio members who are present they train those same powers of awareness that are being exercised in the performer. Finally, Strasberg comments on the comments and the exercise.

The extent of the Studio's influence on contemporary theatre, though wide, is impossible to gauge exactly. In some cases an individual's work at the Studio has had decisive influence on his professional accomplishment; in other cases it has been negligible. Perhaps the Studio's inspiration amid the difficulties of professional life has been as important as its help in matters of technique. But its effect on the theatre outside its membership is almost incalculable. Its idealism, its very existence, have aroused interest the world around—yet other studios have not been formed. Certainly the idea of a permanent theatre company has had no appreciable response in the American theatre.

And the question is further complicated because both admiration and criticism have as often as not been based on an entirely false idea of the Studio's activities. How far the professional work of Studio members has influenced the art of other actors cannot be measured, and mere imitation is of little importance.

Nevertheless, persistent achievements cannot be accidental. The thousands of actors who have sought admission over the years and the constant stream of inquiries and professional observers from all over the world testify to an interest the Studio has never sought but has nevertheless provoked. The Studio's international renown must be the result of its dealing realistically with actors in the practical terms of professional life. It has demanded of its members a rigorous professional accomplishment, has worked to bring idealism to theatre business, to combine actuality with vision.

Is it possible to go beyond these self-evident facts? I think not. Certainly Strasberg has often been misjudged. People who first notice his aestheticism often do not see the will and discipline, the vast experience, and the common sense. Those who notice his toughness, his humor, his belligerence, the sharp eye and the Broadway argot, sometimes do not suspect the sensitive artist or the warm human being. Discussions about "Method actors" and other such generalized tags and slogans are mostly causerie, journalism, or pedantry. The only discussion that really matters treats the work of the individual artist, and the Studio is a group of individual artists who have banded together for mutual improvement. A book deserves to be written that will summarize the experience of *each* Studio member, but it is predictable that no picture of a typical "Method actor" would emerge. Lillian and Helen Ross's *The Player* (1962) contains interviews with many Studio members, but the only common element is gratitude to Strasberg for his help.

Statistics provide little real evidence of what it means to be a Studio member. The Appendix lists three hundred and eleven life members, of whom sixteen were admitted to membership on July 1, 1964. Of the two hundred and ninety-five earlier members one hundred did not work at all in the Actors Unit from March 1956 through May 1964, and twenty-six worked in only one scene. But some members, not having worked for years in the Studio, suddenly find a need to return. They know that the Studio is always there for their use. Some who have not worked for years have started to participate in The Actors Studio Theatre. Some have so many professional commitments that they find it almost impossible to work at the Studio. At least a dozen have left the acting profession. Several are dead. Some of the actresses are wives and mothers. Some members have become teachers of acting or directors or writers. More than eighty per cent have formally committed themselves to the new production unit. Some attend the Studio regularly but do not work in scenes. A few work in scenes for the Directors and Playwrights Units but not in the Actors Unit. Some work a lot and accomplish little. Others work little and accomplish much. Some have come to the Studio after years in Strasberg's private classes, and some have entered his classes only after gaining membership in the Studio. Most have never worked in these classes. Some are experienced. Others have only a modicum of professional experience.

But these facts are really random. They provide color but little insight. The artist must be understood individually. The Studio approaches the actor as an individual, and any full evaluation of the Studio's influence or "success" must finally be carried out in those terms.

When The Actors Studio Theatre was organized in 1962,* it was, among other things, a culmination of work that antedates the Studio. As Kazan remarked to me in 1961, "The Actors Studio is obviously a continuation of the acting tradition that was in the Group Theatre, and one of the purposes I had in starting this whole thing was that I didn't want that tradition to disappear." He said at the opening session of the Studio in October 1958, "Here is material to create probably the best theatre possible outside of Russia. I will never feel within my heart that this organization is a success until we have created

---

* See Epilogue, page 397.

from the material here an organization that implements our aesthetic of theatre."

Strasberg pointed out in January 1959 that while the Studio could then put "into the arena of world theatre" an unparalleled combination of talent, "in all honesty it took ten years to create it." He went on to say, "We have here the possibility of creating a kind of theatre that would be a shining medal for our country. By this fortunate accident—it has been an accident, though of the kind that has historical logic—we have created something that certainly we would never have consciously worked for. If we had said ten years ago, 'We are going to start because ten years from now we want *this*,' you would have said we were crazy."

The Studio has, in fact, been active in private production ever since 1947. Its ultimate aim is always to better the actor's professional work, and Strasberg constantly expresses his views of production, not merely of acting technique. The Playwrights and Directors Units were formed to involve the Studio more fully in the total art of the theatre.

Many original works have been performed at the Studio, some of which reached professional production. In its second and third seasons members appeared in a weekly half-hour dramatic series on the ABC television network called *The Actors Studio Theatre*. In 1958 Cheryl Crawford, "by arrangement with The Actors Studio," produced a series of plays at the Bijou Theatre which involved many Studio members. So-called "projects"—fully rehearsed productions—have been privately performed at the Studio from the beginning.* Of two projects in the first season, Chekhov's *The Seagull* was seen only by members, but Bessie Breuer's *Sundown Beach* eventually appeared on Broadway. The projects have continued in this pattern.

The Actors Studio and The Actors Studio Theatre are, in final analysis, the product of a typical and altogether American tradition. It is greatly to the Studio's credit that it was born in the jungle of Broadway, has managed to mature there, and now is firmly established as an organization devoted to "the union of actor and playwright." It has neither compromised its principles nor evaded the realities of the world in which it lives.

This lesson was brought home vividly to me in the spring of 1963. I attended a preview performance of *Strange Interlude,* and as I entered the Hudson Theatre's lobby during the dinner intermission, I saw a small figure in a black raincoat standing by the box office. It was Strasberg, and he was engaged in an exercise familiar to every theatre director: he was listening to the comments of the crowd. I went up to say hello, and I was shocked by what I saw. He was haggard. He looked like a gray ghost. And as I walked on out of the theatre, I couldn't help saying to myself, "The theatre is a mug's game. Here's a world-famous theatre man. Three weeks ago I heard him lecture to a thousand people in this same theatre about his visit to Moscow as American representative to the Stanislavski Centenary. And here he is—driving himself to exhaustion and testing the house like any commercial Broadway director." And then I thought back to all the things I have heard him say about the art of the theatre, the search for truth, the true meaning of reality, the need for discipline, and I realized that he was exactly where he should be—doing exactly what he should be doing. Back of him there stands a long tradition, the Yiddish theatre of the East Side, the Chrystie Street Settlement House, the American Laboratory Theatre, the Theatre Guild, the Group Theatre, Broadway, the Hollywood back lot, The Actors Studio. This is not a tradition of glass and marble palaces, but it is a tradition of the American theatre, tough, pragmatic, and visionary, and it may well have produced a kind of theatre that will be "a shining medal for our country."

PART ONE

The Actor and the Studio

CHAPTER I

A Workshop for Professionals

STRASBERG (*October 1956, the beginning of the second season at 432 West Forty-fourth Street*): We now have a place, you see. That gives us a symbol, a feeling that it's permanent. We don't know what we'll do next year, but we know where we'll be next year. Everything is possible. And so I would like the people really to become a little bit more concerned. (*He hesitates.*) Well, I *will* say it. To hell with it! I hadn't planned to say this, because I don't know how I'll behave when I say it; I don't think it will bother me. But I saw Jimmy Dean in *Giant* the other night, and I must say that— (*He weeps.*) You see, that's what I was afraid of. (*A long pause.*) When I got in the cab, I cried. And it was funny, because actually I was crying out of two reasons. It was pleasure and enjoyment, which is odd, but I must say I cried from that, too. And the other thing was seeing Jimmy Dean on the screen. I hadn't cried when I heard of his death; Jack Garfein called me from Hollywood the night it happened, and I didn't cry.* It somehow was what I expected. And I don't think I cried from that now. What I cried at was the waste, the waste. If there is anything in the theatre to which I respond more than anything else —maybe I'm getting old, or maybe I'm getting sentimental—it is the waste in the theatre, the talent that gets up and the work that goes into getting it up and getting it where it should be. And then when it gets there, what the hell happens with it? The senseless destruction, the senseless waste, the hopping around from one

---

* James Dean, an early member of the Studio, who had become a sensational star through his performance in the films *Rebel Without a Cause* and *Giant*, was killed in an automobile wreck shortly before this occasion at the Studio.

thing to the next, the waste of the talent, the waste of your lives, the strange kind of behavior that not just Jimmy had, you see, but that a lot of you here have and a lot of other actors have that are going through exactly the same thing.

And actually the thing that I cried about wasn't only the waste. It was helplessness, because, while it is something which I feel deeply about, I haven't the slightest idea what the hell to do about it. It isn't temperament. I see other people going through the same kind of shenanigans in one way or another. I hear stories about one person, then another person. As soon as you grow up as actors, as soon as you reach a certain place, there it goes, the drunkenness and the rest of it, as if, now that you've really made it, the incentive goes, and something happens which to me is just terrifying. I don't know what to do. You can tell somebody, "Go to a psychiatrist," or "Go here," or "Go there," but in the meantime there is the waste.

The only answer possibly is that we somehow here find a way, a means, an organization, a plan which should really contribute to the theatre, so that there should not only be the constant stimulus to your individual development, which I think we have provided, but also that once your individual development is established, it should then actually contribute to the theatre, rather than to an accidental succession of good, bad, or indifferent things. But I am very, very scared that despite how strongly I feel, or despite how stimulated you become, nothing will be done. Everybody will feel nice and warm and spiritual, but when we get out, the tasks of life will present themselves and the problems of "What play do I do next?" and "What movie do I do next?" and we will just continue to get so caught up that in a strange way we do not really live our lives.

It is true that when the Studio started it never tried to give any sense of theatre. It started simply to help individuals to use their talent, and certainly it has accomplished that to a much greater extent than anyone ever dreamed. It has been a strange and marvelous experience seeing these things come to fruition as a result of simple, honest work, without any publicity, without anything. I'm not worried about this. This will continue. There are plenty of talented young people. The Studio will not dry up or dry out, but in recent years there has been this feeling of the senselessness of it. What the hell are you working for? The people come. They do exactly what you hoped and what they said they would do, and exactly at that moment it becomes arid. People get involved in big business, Hollywood, this here, that there, and you can't get anybody on the phone!

The individual cannot do anything. He starts with the desire. I know that is true, not only of the people here, but of everybody in the theatre. You have this strange dream that somehow something happens in the theatre. You don't know what, but that is the feeling that you come in with. But the dream has to be fulfilled by some kind of unified effort. And this need bothers me very, very much. I see personal problems here and outside. I wish there were something we could do, but I would feel it an intrusion to call somebody in and speak about it. The only solution is the creation of some effort which could embody the activity of these people, which would not rule out working with other people, but which would at the same time mean that your need to develop, to progress, and to live the kind of artistic life, the kind of career life that we all hope for when we see a talent really bloom and blossom, should have some opportunity to be fulfilled. To me that is the future of the Studio, that a unified body of people should somehow be connected with a tangible, consistent, and continuous effort. That is the dream I have always had. That is what got me into theatre in the first place. That was the thing that got me involved in The Actors Studio. And now that you see the kind of fruition to which individual talent here can come, it becomes time to think a little bit more about our responsibility for that individual talent.

We have had talents before in the American theatre. Jed Harris is an enormous talent. Orson Welles is as talented as any individual you can think of. I could name you a long line of people

whose talents I consider to be first-rate. Still they have not contributed to theatre in any measurable way except when they were
trying to establish themselves. At that time you fight through,
you go for what you want, but once you get where you want to
be, somehow everything becomes a matter of working to have
enough money so you can sometime or other do what you really
want to do. The sometime never comes. Instead something else
comes along and takes it out of you, takes it out in chunks of
heart and soul and talent and mind and incentive and initiative
and in every other way. I saw Jimmy Dean. I had the feeling
about Jimmy. When Jack called me, I didn't cry. I just said, "I
knew it. I knew it." What I felt was the utter waste—and also
the sense of responsibility—but I didn't know what the hell to do.
The talent we can do something about. We can feed it. We can
work with it. We've made a place for it here. But this thing—
I'm stuck. I don't know. And this is really the problem of the
Studio.

The world has never given actors more than it gives them today—monetarily and socially on a world-wide basis. Actors are
among the best-known people in the world. The faces, the images
of actors are better known than the faces of our great statesmen
or scientists. But it is true, too, that the actual conditions of
work are for the actor extremely poor. The actor works, let's say,
on a movie. It takes him months. He works in a disjointed way
that hardly permits his imagination to be aroused. Then he loafs
around because he's glad to loaf around after getting up all those
months at six o'clock in the morning and finishing at six at night.
He gets pretty tired. Then he does another picture somewhere else.
Or, if he goes into a play, he works for a couple of weeks under
the worst possible conditions, much more concerned with lines
and positions than with really working on the play. Then the play
comes into New York, and he has to run through it every night,
the same play every night. The burden of a long run would have
been an impossible task for any actor in the old days. It was the

fact that they played different parts and therefore could revivify their imagination unconsciously that made it possible for great actors to develop, as great actors have developed, in the past. For twenty years they played the same part, but only a few times each year, and at the end of that period they could really mean it when they said, "Now I'm beginning to realize how the part should be played."

Sometimes the acting process is complicated by the fact that at the very time when you misuse your talent you are externally successful. Or at a time when you make an effort to use your talent in the proper way, you may be unsuccessful from an audience point of view. It's precisely at those moments that we need a place with an audience, not only observing from the viewpoint of simple enjoyment but able to perceive work in progress, work that may lead to something. Every time an actor changes from something he is used to to something he is *not* used to is fraught with danger and often with unsuccess. Even if the new thing is not well done, it may lead to a much more successful doing than anything done before. It is in that area that membership here is offered.

The Studio is a place where whatever problems actors have as actors can be worked on, can be solved. Among ourselves we sometimes say this is a place where you can fall flat on your face.

When we take people in, the primary thing we judge is talent, though I must honestly say that we directors have never found a way of defining exactly how that judgment is reached. Nonetheless, it is talent which entitles an individual to come into The Actors Studio. We hope that the people here are not any more deserving than others, but are deserving of our effort to encourage them to find the things within them that will constantly lead toward the further development of their talent. But too many of the members take their admission as a token of being singled out as better than other people, and, while I don't mind anybody on the outside thinking that, it is not really true. The choice is *not* *solely* on the basis of talent. Our vote derives from a sense of what we feel are greater capacities and possibilities in an individual than he now employs. Often we are wrong, but that makes us vote.

I know people who came back for a number of auditions. Finally they got in. The talent had not changed. Our opinions about the talent remained basically the same, but the last time they came around we saw signs of possibilities of progress that appealed to us even more than the talent. We saw a great effort to learn, to progress. That appealed to us because it is that with which we work. We deal with talent in flux, with things that might not be possible but for the existence of a place like this.

Neither life nor talent stands still. Standing still leads inevitably to retrogression. The actor does things that he has done before, perhaps more easily, but without the electrifying spark that usually arises in young people when they do their first productions. We then see the terrifying struggle that in America almost always begins with success, when the actor to maintain his career on a certain level begins to repeat and to imitate, if not someone else, what is even worse, to imitate himself and thus to pay a terrible price in his most important commodity, the very thing that singled him out at the beginning, his talent.

The recent years should have proved that the work done here for people who are already established holds at least equal importance with the work done for people who are completely unknown. These years should have proved the necessity of the professional or craft or technical demands that we make, not just on the actor, but on the good actor. The better the actor, the more the demands.

The work here is not for artistic purposes, for something that satisfies your soul and nothing else. I don't like the kind of separation in which professional work is regarded as practical, but the work at the Studio is done only when you want a little stimulus, when you're a little poor in spirits. "It's not really a necessary part of my career. Now that I've done the work and I've become successful, I don't have to participate any more." I am exaggerating a little, but my feeling is that this is the attitude, conscious or unconscious, that a lot of the people here develop as they come to a certain professional standing. And that attitude is deadly.

With a lot of very good actors here the talent may well come to fruition. The person may go on in theatre, and work here may then cease. But that person's hopes and ideals do not stop. I am referring to a member of the Studio who thinks of himself as a certain kind of actor and wants certain kinds of parts. People don't give him those parts. He insists that he will get them. He turns down things people think he is good for because he insists on other things. But when he decides to do something off-Broadway to show what he can do, his work is not commensurate with his hopes and intentions. That work should have been attempted here first. Problems of growth should be solved here, because by the time you come to the production it is just too late.*

The things I am concerned with are technical problems, and these technical problems are not solved by the correct interpretation of a play. They are not solved by telling the actor, "If you knew what was happening in the play, you would immediately become a better actor." The voice doesn't become any better. The way of behavior on the stage doesn't become any better. The

---

* STRASBERG: He falls into the category of people who went up young, became good actors, reached a certain point, and then somehow stopped. We feel these people, if they've been accepted into the Studio, have further possibilities. We feel they have never really developed general ways of acting, that they fall into sound but conventional acting, and that they don't really know how to go further, how to develop within themselves, how to take the ideas they have and make the carrying out of those ideas as exciting as the ideas are. Often the ideas are very good, but you see on the stage the same performance you saw last time in a different role. We have tried to give this actor a sense of things he hasn't yet done. Usually the real despondency in people like him comes from the fact that they feel they have done their best and "Look. Nobody cares." We have tried to show him he hasn't done his best, that he's hurting himself more than the audience is hurting him, that the audience tells him the honest truth—they're not interested, and that if he feels, "Yes, but I am as good as Laurence Olivier," at that moment he may well cease to know what to do with himself. We try to open the instrument again. We seek new ways to refresh and stimulate the actor's imagination so as to show him that he hasn't yet made full use of his talent.

kind of inner concentration brought about by work equivalent to the singer's voice exercises does not become better by itself. These are all technical problems.

In my running engagement with Actor A here, when I say that I am disappointed or a little annoyed I don't mean there is anything wrong with his acting from the point of view of being a good actor, but that he has a deeper and more intense contribution to make than he has yet made in any of the parts he has done. But work has to be done on his acting instrument, which is composed of his mind, his emotions, and his body. And this work has to be done separately, not just by understanding a part. He must deal with deep, firm things inside himself.

Otherwise the actor often fools himself. He understands the play, and he assumes that he is doing on the stage everything that he understands, when obviously he is not. That is the technical problem in any art: that an individual's understanding does not coincide with his capacity. The understanding reaches out, but the capacity makes for what he actually does. That capacity is established by the technical training to which we have dedicated ourselves.

A violin we make. We pick the wood. We make it a certain size. We put things inside for vibration. We create the instrument for the violinist. The actor too employs an instrument; he brings to his art an instrument already created, and that is the human being himself with the habits, the thought processes, the emotional patterns that are already in him. All these things function in the work of acting without any awareness of them on the part of the actor or the other people in the production.

If the Studio were not here, Actor A would be just as good as he's always been and thereby would never be as good as he can be, as good as he should be in terms of the very thing that makes people say, "Now, there's an actor. What wonderful aliveness! What wonderful sensitivity!" But wonderful aliveness and sensitivity are subject to the laws of human nature. You get a little more tired. The talent gets older. The aliveness and sensitivity don't quite work when you want them to. He doesn't have to worry, of course. He will get parts; he will do television; there is a wide area of work. But he may not get the parts he wants. He may not get the things that he should do. He may not get the roles that people think of him for and yet hesitate. Those hesitations should never arise. They do arise now only because, without a firm, deep technique, acting becomes cannibalistic: we feed on our own goodness. The very moment of success in the American theatre is the moment of defeat, of starting down.

Yet in art there is no age. Actors come into the Studio to find the thing that all people bring with them into the theatre when they are young, when they still hope to accomplish their dreams. In art "older" doesn't mean years. Toscanini, when he died, was younger than most people around him, because he still thought he could accomplish with the orchestra what he heard in his mind. He never doubted that, and he always fought about it, and therefore he was younger than many of the people around him who had lost the sense that their dreams could at some time be accomplished.

Art grows more rich with age, not less. The inner craft, the inner vision, the emotions of the actor can continue to develop because they are not subject to any aging process entailed in the very life experience that enriches them. In every art, even in those arts where physical toil takes a toll and the person becomes actually unable to do it, the capacity, the will, the imagination to do it grow and increase. By the time his voice is gone, a singer sings more artistically, more brilliantly, because he sings not just with his voice. Even a pitcher in baseball, when he becomes an old canny pitcher, pitches more brilliantly than in the old days when he just threw the ball in and didn't care. We can see in Michelangelo a constant increase in skill. The paintings at the end of his life are greater in vision and greater in carrying out; though it took longer to do them, we do not perceive that in the pictures. The older the actor becomes, if he continues his progress, the more fully his imagination works, takes possession of his instrument more completely than it did before, becomes greater as he goes on. The old actors that I have seen have not been less. There's a richness in them as in old wine.

THE STUDIO STEREOTYPE

ELIA KAZAN (1961): There's so much garbage written in columns about backscratching and mumbling that you can't take it seriously. It's all a product of the gossip writers and the nightclub comics. It's really not worth even talking about.

CHERYL CRAWFORD (1961): It's not necessarily nonsense to talk about "Studio acting." Unfortunately many young people whom we took in have not availed themselves to the full extent of learning what the hell that is, or how to accomplish it. The Studio should not be criticized because one member does a poor performance. We would be the first to say it's awful. To that extent there is no Actors Studio fixed image. On the other hand there is a specific way we like to work with actors and specific kinds of results we hope for and expect from them. And when they have taken full advantage of the facilities that we offer, the results can be quite astonishing. It's a curious philosophic point that frequently the most talented people are those most aware of their deficiencies and most willing to work hard to overcome them. I think we would all agree that there is a desired Studio image. It is different from the image of a school that Jean-Louis Barrault might have or that Laurence Olivier or John Gielgud might have.

STRASBERG (1956): Sometimes a lot of you people take tasks onto yourselves unnecessarily. You begin to defend The Actors Studio or Lee Strasberg or the "Method." All you have to say is, "Look at the work and see what other work is as good." There is no need to defend the work as if it were bad. Everybody is talking about the Studio because, without any propaganda on our part, the work that has been done has received a certain amount of acclaim—but not from us. We sit here in high judgment and criticize ourselves, and we are sympathetic, but we are not easy.

Nobody is forcing anybody to work according to Lee Strasberg or The Actors Studio or Elia Kazan or anything else. Nobody's forcing anybody. There are a lot of teachers available. The members come here from all kinds of teachers—good and bad. So we need not be pushed into a kind of self-defense. If somebody is interested, that is one thing. But if somebody sees the work and then argues that it's accomplished by the wrong methods, what is the point of arguing? Let them explain why good work is gotten by the wrong way of doing things. If other people want to work differently, there is no reason why they shouldn't. Good work is accomplished in many ways.

Columnists are beginning to say that you can't get in anywhere except if you're a member of The Actors Studio. We know from bitter experience that the opposite is all too true, that while there are areas where what the Studio stands for is highly appreciated, there are many places where you have to be careful you don't mention that you're a member of The Actors Studio, because if you do, you're not even considered.

We are partially paying the price for something that takes place very rarely in the arts and that has never before taken place in the theatre. Never before has a method of actors' work become almost a burning issue. The other arts *have* been—cubism and the other modern arts. Music has aroused its public to heights of frenzy. Actors have been fought about. Duse and Bernhardt, Kean and Junius Booth, Kean and Kemble, those are classic struggles. But never before has a method or theory of acting become an issue. People in general are discussing the work of The Actors Studio. "Is it too realistic?" "How about Shakespeare?" Till now only sports or movies have elicited this kind of interest. This is the first time that the technical problems of the actor have received public cognizance. Obviously we pay the price. You can hardly expect the general run of people either really to be interested or really to know what they're concerned about. The result is argument on the level of generality.

However, the fact that the Studio has dramatized the problems of acting for the general public is important because awareness that the actor is a technician and craftsman is a prelude to the appreciation of acting. Part of the reason why the remuneration of the actor today is good but appreciation is very low is that the public really regards the actor as no craftsman but still a sort of romantic figure. To the extent that this general concern serves to correct that impression, the contribution of The Actors Studio is significant.

(1959:) When people talk about sloppy dress, I get on my high horse. To argue about artistic things is at least legitimate. But this thing? My blood boils. Obviously these people have all forgotten their youth. I work with young people. I remember that long before The Actors Studio, when I worked at the American Theatre Wing, the boys coming back from the Army set the style because they didn't have the money. If they had nice clothes, those were kept for Saturday or for the holiday. To work in, to rehearse, they wore blue jeans or half army clothes or all army clothes. And for people now in Hollywood to forget where they came from and to forget the time when they didn't have any nickels and to forget that they wore these clothes because they didn't have any others makes me furious. But—just to show you what happens when people from The Actors Studio wear these blue jeans— don't forget that Actor B, who is now a star, wears them with silver buttons.

THE "METHOD"

We are willing to be influenced by anything, to try anything. We have no fear of giving up anything here. Here there is nothing holy. Anything that can help us to become better, to fulfill better the actor's task, to contribute toward a more alive and dynamic theatre is certainly worth trying and working on.

A studio is not concerned with production. Therefore it doesn't matter whether an individual piece of work in a studio is a failure or a success, because it is good or bad only in terms of your own needs, of your own development. In a studio it does not matter whether you agree or disagree. A studio does not need agreement.

It needs leadership—otherwise there is a formless kind of activity —but a studio can exist even without leadership if the individuals in it are avid enough in terms of their needs and their search for development.

Work such as we do can, of course, be done in a school. When we say that we are not a school, we do not mean that there is no schooling here. Obviously the whole nature of training is part of the schooling process. We are licensed as a school based on individual selection. It is not the kind that anyone gets into merely by applying. It is a school that selects the best in a certain area— and certainly we have lived up to that.

People assume the Studio is a school because they are not aware that the results achieved here can be achieved in any way other than some stern, systematic, and long process of study. I always have to explain that we are not a school in the sense that the work is systematic. Our work is only on a very small, part-time level, and the fact that the results we have achieved have been effected on this level only leads us to want to put the work on a firmer foundation.

In a school there are, so to say, no differences of opinion. The school is run by the people who are at the head of it. The teachers teach what they are told to teach. If they don't like it, they get out and are replaced by other teachers. The pupils have no freedom of opinion, judgment, or action. If they wish to remain in the school, they do what they are asked to do. They subject themselves to the discipline which it is the school's province to create. A school has the responsibility of laying the technical foundations for each individual, of prescribing the work, right or wrong, and if an individual disagrees, he has the right to leave. In a school he has no other right.

Although there is no systematic procedure which is here attended to on principle—much as the people "outside" think there is—it is true that I have very definite ideas. Therefore the work in the Studio follows certain tendencies. But it is also true that people work here according to their own desires and initiative.

People who do only what we ask find the work of little value. When the actor does work that he feels like doing, that he feels is important for him, he leaves himself wide open to rather strong criticism. We try to contain that criticism so that it doesn't become too personal, but we do not try to stop it, because it is partly by means of the criticism, or analysis of people who have the same problems as ourselves, that we begin to try to achieve what we are capable of rather than settling for what is easy or easily successful. In these areas we are often rather stringent in our views and in our demands for criticism and self-criticism.

Those of you who were here before the public acclaim started to hit us know in all honesty that there never was any formal talk or discussion of principles of acting or of what we have called the "Method" or even of what we call the Stanislavski approach. As you know, I only began to use Stanislavski's name about 1955. I personally have always deliberately drawn back from using his name or encouraging any idea that we here are addicted to any kind of principle. In the early days of the Studio I was only one of the teachers, and therefore felt it would be unjust to the Studio to do so. I did my own work in the way that I presumed other people were doing theirs. Obviously I have always been clear in my own mind that my own work stems from a certain kind of approach. It has always been fed by those principles that derive from Stanislavski. But I never do anything because anybody else said so, because Stanislavski said so. I do something because I have tried it and think it works. When I have found that it works, I then give credit to the individual who found it. I never take credit for making it work. I am always very careful about saying that what I use is Stanislavski's, because I am liable to misuse it or use it wrongly. I want to give Stanislavski credit, but I don't want him to be discredited with anything that I might do. It is true that the basic elements are Stanislavski's, but I hope I have gone beyond some of it and have contributed something of my own. Nevertheless, I feel very indebted to the work of my teachers and to whatever it is that I understand about Stanislavski's work.

Only when the Studio's work began suddenly to be responded to outside was the word "method" actually first used, and it was used by people outside. Only because other people were saying, "Ah, Stanislavski!" and I could not honestly say the work wasn't his, did I find myself having to temporize and say, "Well, the best things in it I suppose are Stanislavski's. The other things come from me. I don't know." "*The* Method" was first used outside. Emphasis on the article "the" came from other people, who meant to imply that they were referring not to just any method, but to "the" particular method singled out by The Actors Studio. We would simply say "a method" or "Stanislavski's ideas" or "Stanislavski's method," because work in a studio is done very unsystematically—as some of you who come to my private classes are beginning to realize.

The important thing in the Stanislavski method is that it is the opposite of a system. A system implies a theory with precise rules of what to do exactly at each moment. Systems of the past were exactly that. You had specific ways of doing things in different situations. In the Delsarte System, which was very widespread in America, you had pictures from which literally to copy each state of emotion or sequence of emotion. The place for the hands or any of the other manifestations of the body was prescribed. The Stanislavski method is no system. It does not deal with the results to be attained and therefore sets no rules for what should be done. It only tries to show the actor the path to be followed, how he goes about finding what only he can find and what, even when he has found it, cannot be repeated the next time, but must be the next time found again.

No one can explain the mystery of talent. We try to take the mystery out of acting in the sense that we try to give to acting a craft. Nobody can object to that. However, we believe that our craft is not only for the externals of acting, but for the internals. We believe this is a craft in which one can train oneself.

When Stanislavski said, "Don't imitate me. Don't do what I do," he did not imply that he had worked all his life and had written all his books so that other actors should not use what he had found. What he was trying to imply was that he had found principles and truths but that the actor has to know when and under what conditions to use them. If they are not properly used, the work is bad. Thus, his method is not in that sense even a method: it is a procedure. He called it "notes for the moment of difficulty." It is well not to worry about medicine when you are healthy. You need the doctor at the moment when you are ill. But you cannot cure illness and you cannot act by the book. No knowledge is greater than the ability to know when to use it.

Not only is the Stanislavski method not a system, but it's not Stanislavski's. What I mean and what Stanislavski meant by that is that it is not something that he made up by some peculiar process of thought. It is Stanislavski's observations of what actors did. He tried on himself what he thought he saw other actors do, to find out whether or not it would work. As a result he arrived at a kind of comprehension or logic of what takes place in acting, and thus he was able to outline suggestions, areas of training, and exercises for training, so that what actors do can be more conscious, less dependent on things that just happen and that most actors are not even aware are happening.

The Stanislavski method is not as new as we commonly think. The work that we do—what is called the "Method"—is nothing but the sum total of the experiences of many great actors of the past, of the records and statements they have left, and of what we have seen in our own experience. What Stanislavski did—and we try to follow in his footsteps—was to make this material available to the young actor, so that he doesn't have to go through twenty-five or thirty years of grueling experience to find these things for himself. The important things in the "Method" are the things that other actors of the past, great actors of the past, have used to train themselves so as to arrive at the wonderful results which all good actors achieve.

I begin to realize there is sometimes justification for a great deal of the confusion about the Studio. The human being desires rules. He desires something to come down from heaven and to be eternal so that he can hold onto it, so that he can feel safe and secure. As soon as somebody says something—if it is good, all the more so—there is a tendency for that observation to harden into a rule, into a magic thing that is kept and to which no one else is privy. We have sometimes fallen into that tendency and unconsciously have built up among actors outside the Studio a feeling toward us: "They think they've got something. To hell with them! It can't possibly be so good. How did other actors act before them?" It makes it look as if we think an actor can't act who isn't acquainted with Stanislavski's method. No, it's the exact opposite, like Monsieur Jourdain in *Le Bourgeois Gentilhomme*, who was overjoyed and even a little horrified when the man told him he spoke prose, because he hadn't realized that he did. Long before Harvey discovered the circulation of the blood, the blood circulated. The only difference his discovery made was to help deal with problems which previously we could not deal with methodically because we did not know the behavior of this particular organic system. That essentially is what the Stanislavski method does.

WORKING ON PROBLEMS

Problems we are often afraid to face in the professional world we are quite willing to face here, because here we look for answers. People who are getting paid, who have commitments, who go back and forth to Hollywood, who sometimes do not have occasion to come here for many years—these people keep coming. They know that here the problem may not be solved, but people will understand that it is a legitimate problem, that the actor has a right to have a problem, that he is not a nincompoop, not an incompetent, merely because he has a problem. Here the actor learns that he has the problems most actors have. That is where we bring some hope. We feel there is a solution.

This is a place where work can be done on the basis that it will ultimately, even months or years from now, lead to the solution. Together, from our collective experience, from the fact that people approach these problems out of diverse backgrounds and interests—because some people will be able to perceive relationships which another person might miss—we are able to take the unified laboratory approach which is widespread in science but rare in the arts. In professional production the demand upon the actor is that the part be acted tomorrow when the curtain goes up and the critics are there. Under those conditions the problems can't be faced that can be faced here.

We represent a sense that acting problems are irrespective of time and nationality, that the basic problems of the actor existed two thousand years ago in the Greek theatre, as today they are found in the Japanese theatre, in realistic theatre, and as they were in eighteenth-century theatre, in Elizabethan theatre. Actors have always faced the same problems because they derive on the one hand from theatre but on the other hand from the material of theatre, which is the human being.

We are working on varied problems, and our comments have to be angled toward their differences. We are concerned first with the individual's problems, the development of the individual instrument, so that it can carry out whatever task the actor sets for himself. Whether that task is right or wrong makes no difference in the context of developing the instrument. When Horowitz hits the wrong note on the piano, it still sounds just as brilliant, just as live as if it were the right note. Second is the problem of exploration—to see whether the actual task that the actor sets himself, not technically, but from the point of view of how his behavior measures up to what he has set out to do, is so carried out that it begins to give useful results. Third, as an audience of craftsmen, we can be aware of things which the author seems to ask for and which would have led the actor to different conclusions if he had given his attention to them. Fourth is the theatrical problem of the particular kind of play—for example, the problems of Shakespeare. All too often we tend to disregard the first three problems in favor of the fourth, forgetting that the first three are a necessary part of the development which must take place if the fourth is ever to be accomplished.

A fifth stage comes when a director is working on a scene. A director exists in any production for one purpose: he sets for the actor the theatrical tasks that derive from a particular dramatic event which the actor would otherwise not work on. The actor is thus given tasks or commanded to do tasks, and it becomes an additional problem to maintain the level and continuity of his own work and yet to give the director what he asks.

We never criticize anybody for doing a good thing. No matter how contrary it is to what we tell you to do, when it's good, we applaud it. When you steal a good thing, we say, "Good for you, darling." Only when you steal something that isn't worth stealing, something artificial that stops you or interferes with you, do we question it. We question nothing here on principle, only on the basis of concrete difficulties that get in the actor's way.

In looking for the sources of creation, you must realize that they do not come from what the actor intends to do. Otherwise everyone would wish to be Beethoven, Bach, Mozart, Rembrandt, da Vinci, or Michelangelo, and you would have nothing but Beethovens, Bachs, and Michelangelos. You would only have to be an understanding, appreciative, and aware critic in order to carry out your vision. We know that the actor is actual material, that this material is played upon as the poet's mind is played upon, that a lot of things affect the poet or the actor in ways that have nothing to do with mechanical logic. The big experience is not necessarily the one that affects him. Sometimes it is the little personal experience. What happens today does not necessarily affect him. Sometimes it is the thing that happened fifteen years in the past, which seemed unimportant when it happened, that may still affect the actor today. It has created in him patterns of behavior or response which he is most of the time unaware of. We know that the actor's logical knowledge of a part has often very little to do with his experiential knowledge of it. We know that the deep, strong inner responses of the actor often emerge in either irrelevant or conventional ways. Our procedure therefore is to attempt to lead each actor to solve each problem in accordance with the nature of his peculiar individual material —as revealed to us by our understanding of this modern knowledge—so that it is possible, technically speaking, for that actor to become a completely functioning instrument.

An actor is such an instrument when he knows how to get any element from himself that he or you may wish to get. This has nothing to do with the play. Doing a particular run on the piano has nothing to do with the fact that in one part of a Beethoven sonata you make that run. The complete functioning of the actor's instrument implies an ability to make a particular "run" and also many other "runs" so that he can satisfy any demand made by a director or himself. When the actor's instrument is applied to the solution of a particular scene, it is usually too late to work on the technical problems of his particular instrument. Only after the actor has perfected a superb technique is he free to devote himself fully to the problems of a scene. In the Studio, seeing actors' work in various stages is often confusing because it frequently has little to do with solving the problems of scenic material and a great deal to do with solving the problems of the actor's instrument.

I cannot account for the adverse criticism aroused generally by Strasberg's helping actors to understand their own psychological processes. The facts of human conditioning, which begins in infancy and continues through life in patterns of habit and response, are today such a commonplace that their practical application ought not to surprise anybody. Perhaps romantic notions about actors, pandered to by Hollywood make-believe, are violated by the idea that coming to grips with acting problems entails frank and open dealing with very personal matters. Studio members have to be personal. Strasberg is personal. But this is not self-indulgence. It is professional activity. It is a way to offer a kind of help that actors ordinarily cannot find any other place.

Undoubtedly it is dangerous to invade the individual's privacy, but danger must be chanced if the solution of a personal problem is literally a matter of life and death to an actor's career. It is dangerous for a surgeon to operate, but it may be more dangerous for him not to. Strasberg handles these matters with great delicacy and tact, and with great watchfulness to see that discussion does not actually become so personal as to be harmful. But it is not exaggerating to say that a willingness to be personal is a prerequisite to the Studio's work.

(1960:) One of the playwrights attending the playwrights' sessions, who also observes the work here, asked me a question last time after one of the solo exercises. It had to do with understanding the actor's personal problem, so I called him to make sure he would be here today.

YOUNG PLAYWRIGHT: The question was made necessary for me by what had happened that day, but the same thing had happened before almost every time I have been to the Studio. I feel very uncomfortable, and I feel it is unnecessary for someone after a scene to discuss his personal problems as an actor. You don't help him, and he doesn't help himself by that kind of discussion. I would like to hear the actor discuss what he was trying to do with the part and have us judge how well he did the part at that moment. Because he does have personal acting problems which are important to him, he can then translate our comments and make the best possible use of them. To expose himself, and to discuss these problems openly is embarrassing, and I think it's fruitless.

STRASBERG: There must always be special knowledge in approaching any kind of theatre work on a technical level, that is, where the audience is excluded and the people who watch are part of the workers.

YOUNG PLAYWRIGHT: I dislike being put into an attitude of sympathy toward the actor.

STRASBERG: If someone watches an operation and faints away, is that the fault of the doctor? I'm sorry. You go to a theatre to see plays. Here you're seeing operations on plays! If this work was brought to you on a public platform, we would leave ourselves open to your kind of judgment. Here it's different. The presence here of theatre people, even of workers, is based on their willingness to accept the premise that they see work in progress, work on the individual, not work on a production. Don't get worried, because the question, which I will let the actors answer, is a good one.

ACTRESS C: I can only relate personal experience. It took me three years here before I was able to drop my obligation to the audience and really explore the facets of my ability. It is so drummed into most actors that the audience is there and that they've got to get it that you literally buckle yourself up. When you write, I'm sure you let it all come out, and then you edit. The place for an actor to let it all come out is here. This is the only place in the country where that can happen, where you choose what works for you and what is effective for you and doesn't make you keep repeating corny tricks and limiting yourself to doing the same thing over and over again. It's here where you explore and find out. That is exactly what Lee was trying to make me do, but I protested for years until I caught on. "I got to talk loud." "They got to understand what the playwright means." "I got to be effective and cute"—or whatever the hell. Now that is exactly the opposite of expanding yourself. What playwrights can't understand is that we're getting the thoughts to let their words come out in great depth.

ACTOR D: It took me about two years of asking wrong questions and being slapped down to train myself to look and listen and try to understand. No actor ever does any work without involving his personal problems. For instance, I was working in a Broadway show once where the director made us play with such intensity that I was tied up in knots. I had to find out whether it was possible for me to relax as an actor again. I chose a scene and brought it into the Studio and said I only wanted to relax. This would probably not have embarrassed you, but it was quite personal to me. If you had observed longer, you would have noticed from time to time that an actor will start to explain something, and Lee will say, "Stop. That's getting too personal." We have in him a man who can decide.

ACTRESS E: Some of us have watched one another four or five years, some of us ten years. If you waited a little, you would see that it did something. Here we are dealing with our careers. Maybe it does us good to get up and say, "How am I going to change this quality in myself?" Suppose people say to me, "All you're good for is neurotic parts." I don't want to tell people things about neurotic women the rest of my life. Suppose I want to tell things about lovely, happy women once in a while? "Help me!" That's personal, and that is an actor's problem. That's what we're here for, and some of us have watched others of us beat the rap.

ACTOR A: You must understand that when we come in here to work, it's to find a tool. I come here for a specific, personal reason. I disagree with Lee Strasberg a lot of the time, but he represents a catalyst, a conscience, a way to work, a constant finger pointed at me. I've had a taste of this cup of success, and I must say it tastes kind of flat. I've been trying to find a way to flavor it. He knows the formula. That's why I come to the Studio.

STRASBERG: The theatre is the most personal of our arts. All other arts work with an objective material. Only the theatre uses the living presence of the human being. Actors for thousands of years have been aware of that problem without knowing how to solve it. People outside the theatre have never been aware of the problem. When it is suggested that it is a problem, they are unwilling to let the actor solve it on his own time and with his own effort. You find actors seemingly perfectly competent, perfectly able to do certain things, and yet when they are unable to do them, their excuses seem illogical or even silly. An actress of the first rank, a star, somebody who gets ten per cent of the gross, will say, "I can't do that. Please. I don't want to do it. Don't make me do it." She is an actress who should be able to do it. The play needs that value. The author calls for it. The actress cannot do it. From the observation of such experiences over a long period of time, we have been driven to greater understanding of the way the actor works. That is what we try to use here.

We are not here to make judgments based on taste and belief. If you judge on the basis of like or dislike, you are working on the assumption that when good work is done everybody will like it. That's not so. Rubens is one of the greatest painters in the world. I don't like his painting. I don't like his women. I don't even like the wonderful color. I know that the paint was put on by a master. I can follow all the convolutions in which form and shapes combine, but I'm not interested. It does not excite me. I don't like it. But to say, "That's bad painting. He's never going to be a painter that way," is to assume that taste conditions these things.

It may seem that I have very definite opinions—and I do—but a lot of my opinions you actually never know. I rarely tell you what I think about an actor or a scene. We work with each individual in terms of his equipment. We never judge one individual against another. Confusion comes when we forget that ideas here are ideas in use. They are things that have to be tried. The only thing I ever ask is for someone to try it rather than to tell me it can't or it can work. We then point out sometimes that the thing isn't happening because it's not being tried properly. If the actor then says, "Oh, I can do it that way," and does it and then says, "But I don't want to do it that way," that person, technically speaking, has a perfect right to that opinion.

I am also very leery of interfering with anything in the actual process of professional production, because sometimes an inadvertent remark, drawing attention to something we are concerned with but which might not be of significance to the director of the production, may interfere with the actor's work from a purely professional point of view. I shy away from speaking to people in rehearsal. I know how often little remarks made with the desire to help or to flatter draw that person's attention to something, and the performance is spoiled by his attention to that particular moment. After all, we're not going to perform miracles by that kind of comment. Miracles are performed after hard work. Even a saint works very, very hard.

I will not have anybody, including myself, set for any actor or for any other artist what is and what is not permissible in any play or in any other artistic activity on God's earth. It is one of the things about which I am adamant. I do not know what is permissible. Artists have suffered. Tintoretto was called before the Inquisition because Church authorities didn't like the way he made the figure of Christ. Tintoretto is now one of the greatest artists, accepted by the Church, accepted by everybody. Some of you people seem to know what is right. The Church seemed to know what was right. I do not. I can only try to see what the intention of the actor is, to see whether that intention derives from something sound, from a definite need, whether it seems to solve some definite problem that he has set himself. I can then still exercise my own taste and say that the actor's way is not the way I would do that particular thing. But to say dogmatically that this is not the right approach—*that* I will never permit to myself here or in any other place where I am connected.

When you watch scenes here, you must see them in terms of the craftsman's needs. When we see art works, most of the time we see a few works of each of the great masters. El Greco, for example, is one of my favorite painters. We can go to museums and see fantastic works, the *View of Toledo* and the *Cardinal*; the pictures are great pictures. We therefore assume that the great artist is just great. He's born great. He works great. However, if you look at the best book on El Greco, which has all the pictures El Greco ever painted and some of his sketches, you will be startled. Some look childish. Some look primitive. A good many imitate his masters, and some are copied from other people. But in each picture, if you look carefully and have the eye to see, you will see the ingredients of El Greco's art, which become more refined, defined, clearer as the work goes on, and which finally begin to take over.

Rembrandt didn't spring full-blown. Look at the thousands of sketches he made. You see him puzzling over problems. How will the composition be? How should it be—this way or that way? You see an unfinished sketch and then a pencil sketch and then the pencil sketch filled in with ink and then the same thing gone over again. You don't say, "Now, come on, Rembrandt, make up your mind. Are you going to paint a Rembrandt, or are you just fiddling around here? What is this thing? Look at the sketch. You've gone over it fifteen times. If you don't know what the hell you want, then get out. Don't be a painter. If you're going to be Rembrandt, then make up your mind and paint." Well, that *is* the way the artist makes up his mind, by doing, by correcting, by falling on his face.

The playwright is remembered, and the actor too is remembered, but unfortunately in later years nobody knows *why* the actor is remembered. You have the playwright's text. For three hundred years after he wrote people can read Shakespeare and wonder what he meant. In other arts the works live on, so that mistakes in judgment made today can be rectified tomorrow. While we may say today of a particular actor, "This is interesting, but I don't quite understand it," we cannot fifty years from now say of that actor, as people said about Strauss, about Berg, about Bartók, about Wagner, about Stravinsky, about Brahms, about every great composer who has ever lived in this world, including Mozart and Beethoven, "Now we understand him."

In Shakespeare's time people evaluated him play by play. They saw the first play of Shakespeare; it wasn't so hot. They saw the second play of Shakespeare; Dekker wrote a better play. They saw the third play of Shakespeare, but Heywood had written that year a more accomplished one. They saw the fourth play of Shakespeare, but in that same year there were at least four equally good plays by other playwrights. Only after you get to the end of Shakespeare do you say, "Nobody can compete with Shakespeare." There's a wonderful book by Alfred Harbage called *Annals of* *the Elizabethan Drama.** Each year you can see what plays were done. It is flabbergasting. When I went through that year by year, I said, "Oh, Marlowe had already written his best play! He died soon after this." It took Shakespeare fifteen years before his plays began to tower over Marlowe's. When we can see an earlier period in totality, we can then re-evaluate individual artists. In acting we do not have that opportunity. The actor's art dies as he creates it.

Here we sometimes get into the habit of judging everything as if today were doomsday, as if on the basis of this scene it would be decided whether you would get into heaven. Well, even if Stanislavski is one of the judges there, we have to realize that this is not the last time the actor is going to do this scene. So we must be very careful in what we say. Otherwise everyone here would have to heed, perhaps not your opinion because your opinion may not be accepted, but my opinion as to how each scene should be done. That's a terrible onus. I am not willing to bear such responsibility. Such a weight of opinion would be destructive not only to the kind of work done here but to any creative work done anywhere. This is work in progress, and we have to perceive the seeds in that work.

It is my great pride that people who have worked with me, while all working creatively in their own ways, never imitate either me or themselves or each other. Take Kazan, Robert Lewis, other people like that; each has his own style. It is not Lee Strasberg's style, though I hope I contributed to what they do. To say that each scene has to be done to coincide with Lee Strasberg's interpretation is suicidal. It's destructive of the very thing we are trying to do, which is to help each individual to achieve his own creativeness.

When we show a film of Duse, which is torn and the print of which is bad, and someone says, "Well, I can't enjoy it," obviously that person has a right to his lack of enjoyment, but his reaction indicates a poor ability to be a professional observer.

---

* 1940.

Observation here is a responsibility. If an actor sits in a chair in the center of the stage for five minutes and prepares his entrance, you can say, "Well, it is dull and boring." Obviously it's dull and boring, but equally obviously, if this were a production, the curtain would go up at the end of that five minutes and not at the beginning. You are privileged here to see what goes on before the curtain goes up, because those five minutes are when the actor creates what leads to the results you ordinarily see.

The indication of a good operation is not in whether the patient lives or dies but in the nature of the operation as performed. In the case of a surgeon whose patient dies there is no guarantee that the operation was bad. That operation may have been brilliant and adventurous. Very few surgeons might have had the courage or the nerve to try an operation like that. I must constantly emphasize that while your enjoyment of the scene is spoiled by the fact that you may not like the scene, or you may not like certain people in it, or you may not like how the scene is interpreted, that has nothing to do with the ability to observe work.

When our training here has gone halfway through the early stages of work and begins to accomplish some essential elements of concentration, we all too often think the problem of training has been solved. We forget that other artists work years to perfect a technique. Even Heifetz slips up occasionally. Even singers who have worked for ten or fifteen years, who have good voices, still go flat. But if we ask a trained musician to play a slow piece fast, he can do it because he's technically trained. He does not argue with the conductor and say, "But I can't play this fast." He thinks the conductor is crazy to play it fast. He's played it with Toscanini, who always plays it slowly, but if this other conductor wants it fast, he'll play it fast. He has been technically trained. And the technical training of the actor, to which we have here dedicated ourselves, similarly is designed to make the actor able to accomplish any task which is set for him or which he sets for himself.

AN IDEAL SYSTEM OF TECHNICAL TRAINING

In late summer 1960, Strasberg went to Montreal to see performances of the Peking State Opera, the official Chinese theater, which he later described at the Studio's opening session.

It was a tremendously inspiring experience. Never have I seen actors' technique as thrilling. The technique was fabulous. It was not of a kind that we could not do; some of it we could do right now with a little application. Some of it we could not do quickly, but only because it takes time to learn to do it. I have never seen an ease and a security and a strength and a willingness to be easy and relaxed on the stage and an acrobatic facility such as I saw in these actors. These performances were not merely stylized according to the style of their theatre.

We went backstage and met these people. Most of them were young, with very young and fresh faces. So we said, "How long do you train?" They said, "The training takes eight or nine years." We asked one girl who had just done a fabulous thing on stage, "When did you start?" She said, "I started when I was ten. I just graduated. I worked for eight years, and I've just been graduated." One of the men had started at twelve and had trained for nine years. The training takes that long, and it is worth it, because these actors are trained not for an external style as the Japanese are and which the Chinese actor too evinces at various moments, but purely for flexibility. When I saw some of the training work in the Meyerhold Theatre in Moscow, I was very much impressed by the fact that actor's training should consist not of dancing where he learns steps, nor of speaking properly by learning a single kind of speech, but in the flexibility and agility of body, speech, and mind which makes for an almost acrobatic kind of skill. The Chinese theatre is the first I have seen that bore out the Meyerhold approach. In the Chinese actor I saw the full embodiment of this kind of training—one-sided, of course, because it makes the actor ready to act without at the same time making him a good actor, which is the kind of training that our work accomplishes.

Since my return I have given thought to how the two ways of training, the Chinese and the Studio ways, could come together. It would take two or three hundred thousand dollars over a five-year period. I do not start the work that we do by emphasizing the mental and psychologic resources of the actor earlier than eighteen, because the actor before that age is not yet shaped physically, and certainly not mentally and emotionally. To start our work earlier is both valueless and dangerous. Yet the Chinese training in order to get this remarkable facility and agility has to start early. Eighteen is too late. Sixteen is almost too late. The training has to be like ballet training, which starts at an early age.

Perhaps a test could be made by picking people between the ages of fourteen and sixteen—girls of fourteen and boys of fifteen or sixteen—when they are still unshaped and unformed, when it is still possible to give them the ballet-like training which the Chinese actors have. If these young people are then given four years of training where the emphasis is to teach them this acrobatic facility, at the same time they could be given strengthening of voice and of speech—not teaching them to act with the voice, which I think is suicidal, but purely through physical training to create simultaneously strength and sound of voice and freedom and flexibility both of speech and of body. Also during those four years they would have some of the minor elements of training in imagination and improvisation, which is not too much to demand of young people because it still leaves them free. It does not harden into a core, which is the very thing that hurts both the Chinese and the Japanese theatres where they end up in a style outdated for the contemporary world.

After four years of this work the girls would be eighteen and the boys nineteen or twenty. That's when I take people into my private classes. There these young people would have three or four years of solid work, not as we do it here at the Studio, but systematically, as our work should be done. At the end I think I could guarantee that these actors would be, not the greatest actors because you cannot buy talent that way, but actors who would be able to do things which no other actors previously could do in the combination of elements that we dream of. It is possible that a basis might be laid for the creation of those master actors which was Gordon Craig's vision. Unfortunately he misnamed them *über-marionettes,* and that led to a great deal of confusion. Literally his intention was no more than to demand that the actor should have the greatest skill, literally the ability to do anything that can be asked from a human being, mentally, physically, emotionally, or any other way. Of course, the Studio is not set up to perform such training.*

PRAGMATISM AND IDEALISM

There has grown up a view that the conditions of commercial theatre make a systematic or trained approach impossible, that there the actor has no time to worry about Stanislavski or Meyerhold. He cannot afford such a luxury. He must find out for himself. In medicine, in science, in the other arts, to state that each individual must use his own lifetime to find out what others have already found is to be laughed at. In those fields it would not even occur to anyone to make such a statement. And yet that strange idea has become fixed in commercial theatre.

Here we have shown a remarkable ability to work within the conditions of the American theatre. No previous theatre organization of this kind has had that ability. It is peculiar to the Studio. Every other organization has demanded that the surrounding environment be changed to coincide with its needs. "If you want a studio, you have to create a theatre." "Give me a theatre, and I'll give you a studio." "Give me money for the next ten years, and I'll turn out actors." We somehow have managed. We have shown a capacity to work within the actual theatre situation, facing the difficulties everyone faces, not accepting them but sur-

---

* However, during the 1962-1963 season Sophia Delza was employed to offer regular classes in T'ai Chi Ch'uan, the ancient Chinese "exercise art," for Studio members.

mounting them, showing they can be surmounted, that they are not the binding interference they are commonly thought to be.

In my private classes work is very systematic and continuous. Yet it is discontinuous in the sense that people drop out to appear in a movie or a play and then come back. The work we do has been created to meet the conditions of our society—bad as they may be. Sometimes we Americans follow a pragmatic approach and are led thereby to go along with existing conditions, and we sink. But sometimes we surmount them, and even make use of them.

We bear today a responsibility not only for ourselves, but for the American theatre, for the movies, for television, because we have been able to do, without being able to afford it, what they have not been able to do. Today the eyes of America, and really of the world, are upon this unit, and it places before us our responsibility.

Too often in our membership there is a willingness to drift and drown in simple demands. The things each person wants to do are difficult. The demands other people place on us are also difficult. Therefore, it often seems better to fulfill the minimum requirements: about them there will be no doubt, no difficulty, and no trouble. But that is a luxury that *we* cannot afford.

Conditions will never be ideal in the theatre. Therefore waiting for the kind of ideal that Gordon Craig waited for all his life is an empty waiting. Whenever Craig was offered a production, he said, "Yes. Fine. Give me a theatre. Let me work for the next ten years with a company. Underwrite it, and I'll give you productions at the end." But no one was willing to wait ten years to see what can be done.

Among the public there is a great yearning for theatre, the same yearning all of us have when we start in the theatre, this strange sense of magic which little by little becomes only make-up that runs, and lights that are in the wrong place, and scenery that gets in the way, so that somehow this feeling dies. Well, it has not died in the public, and I think that explains the response and the questions and the letters that come from all over the world, even from the dark of Africa, where somebody writes, "I am trying to do theatre here, and the only thing I can think of is The Actors Studio. I don't know whether I can get there or whether I'd be permitted there, but can you help me? Can you give me advice? Because what you are doing is what I want."

Considering how irregular work at the Studio has been, how unsystematic, how many things were not even mentioned here until outside discussion about the "Method" made us mention them, we have shown remarkable results. Certain exercises we have begun to use have produced remarkable effects in the people who needed them. We have not waited for the ideal time and place. We now [1957] have a place of our own. It is not ideal, but it is very much our own and is suited to us. It is not modernistic and not fancy, and yet it is clean and nicely designed and prepared for the future. We have been very careful not to close the doors to the future.

We have been idealistic in keeping the Studio uncontaminated by commercialism. A famous television producer once called up and wanted to visit, and when he told me he was casting, I said, "I'm sorry. Any other time. I cannot permit you to come when you're casting." When a famous movie producer's wife, who had given us a very good donation, said, "I want to see the people," I said, "What for?" She said, "Well, we're casting now. It'll be good for the people." I said, "You can sit in the office and watch the people come in, but I'm sorry. I cannot let you into the Studio. I cannot let the actors get the feeling that they're being watched for casting. I cannot permit this kind of thing in any way to contaminate the work." God knows there is enough pressure when people are watched only by the members, but it is suicide to permit them to feel that they are obligated to work because that will contribute to their careers.

Working at the Studio does contribute to the actor's career— fortunately. But when you start with that, then everything is done on the basis of "Well, what will they think when I do it?" Thank

God we have kept that out! People are willing to come here and take their chance, because they know the spirit is of the right kind. I'm hipped on that because I think it is practical.

Frankly, there are ways we could make a lot of money. There are people who have offered ten thousand bucks to get somebody into the Studio. It was politely put, of course. All we would have to do is take a very nice and talented girl into the Studio. We have never done that. And that's why the Studio has its peculiar flavor. We don't amount to anything, in a sense; we don't have a nickel. We sit here and worry about how to keep the place going while we have all these bright ideas about what to do in the theatre. But don't forget that even those people with millions at their disposal look to the Studio as a place that can't be bought, can't be had, can't be flirted with. They can care about it. That's all. I'm proud of that.

KAZAN: So am I. It's the one clean place in the theatre.

STRASBERG: Maybe it appeals to my youthful idealism which I've never quite overcome. I sort of feel that this way I'm getting back at the world. I wanted to show the value of idealism. And this is it. This cannot be bought. It cannot be sold.

PART TWO

The Actor and Himself

CHAPTER II

The Art of the Actor

The actor is the characteristic element of theatre art. Everything in theatre begins with acting. No matter how brilliant the playwright's ideas or how glittering his wit and language, if they cannot be expressed through the actor they count for little in theatre. Furthermore, good theatre is not achieved merely by choosing between good and bad acting. It is possible to choose among different types of acting, and this possibility must be appreciated not only to train actors and to write plays which use actors, but also to approach the acting of a particular role.

All too often the actor has only a general idea of what actors can do. He frequently does not know what he can specifically do. And the fact that he often is not doing what he thinks he is doing complicates the situation further. Actors today, Strasberg points out, usually use only "the superficial characteristics of their type. Their idea of reality is to be natural, simple, and direct. And they have to be brought to understand that reality means dealing precisely and intensely with whatever the play is concerned with."

In a technological age people unconsciously regard theatre art as an industrial process based on division of labor; they cannot understand how artists can create as a group in any other way. They suppose that after the playwright writes the script the director finds out what the playwright intends, works out a traffic plan to present the story and keep the actors from stepping on each other, and teaches this plan. The actors go where they are told and say the author's words clearly, loudly, and effectively. If the play is Shakespearean, the actor does these things in a classic style. If the play is modern, he does them in a naturalistic style. Finally, the product is packaged and sold.

Not one American in a thousand has ever seen a production performed by great actors working together in an ensemble theatre. Great individual performances are almost as rare. Most of America is served by amateur enthusiasts, second-string Broadway companies, the belt-line shows of television, and the gimcrackery of Hollywood. The subtlety and power of an ensemble art, which can grow only from years of training and working in concert, is simply not a part of the theatrical consciousness of America.

Nor do the conditions of commercial theatre permit the kind of experiment in creative interaction among various artists of the theatre that fifteen years of working together made possible at the Studio in 1962-1963. A director, some actors, and a playwright took one of the playwright's finished, but unproduced, scripts. They worked on it for six weeks—twice the ordinary Broadway rehearsal period—but instead of memorizing words and actions the actors began by improvising the play. Their improvisations were recorded, and from these the playwright rewrote the script. This new version was then rehearsed and performed. This is the exact opposite of an industrial procedure.

More than twenty years ago Strasberg began a description of his work by saying, "There can be no adequate facing of problems in the training of actors unless we possess some sense of values and standards—some sense of the kind of actors and acting we wish to create." Such a sense of values and standards, of course, underlies his comments at the Studio, and to illustrate it a number of specific comments are brought together in this chapter. He admires certain kinds of acting and dislikes other kinds. He admires playwriting that utilizes a full knowledge of what the actor can contribute. He admires Chekhov and Shakespeare because they knew, better than all other dramatists, that reality transcends mere plotting and mere words, however skillful they may be. Chekhov and Shakespeare display "the dramatic faculty," which Strasberg defines as the ability to rise above a literal, superficial, and conventional understanding. The idea of reality encompasses a feeling that "only in nature can such things happen." It involves a sense of things left unsaid or unspecified, and induces the belief that reality itself can never be reduced completely to expression. The actor's ability to present this unspoken and unspecified reality is his indispensable contribution, and he must deal with it "precisely and intensely." Strasberg works to enable actors to "serve" the playwright by creating the full expression of reality that their "human material" makes possible.

During the last sixty years the leaders of the theatre have been seeking a new tone on the stage that approximates expression, thought, feeling, sensation, and behavior to a much greater extent than the previous theatricalized tone which dealt mainly with the problem of effectiveness. Take the notes of the famous dialogue between Gordon Craig and Stanislavski when they discussed *Hamlet*: How are the words of *Hamlet* to be spoken? These were two top theatre people. Craig came from the English theatre, which at the end of the nineteenth century had been on the verge of solving the Shakespeare problem. A way was being found to make Shakespeare more real through the use of ensemble, and a way to character acting, which only great actors like Garrick and Kean had previously found, was now beginning to filter down to many individuals. Craig had played with Irving. He was the son of Ellen Terry. And Stanislavski was head of the Moscow Art Theatre, which at that moment in 1911 was at the height of its powers. It had the top actors in the world. It had probably more first-line actors than existed in any other theatre at one time in the history of acting. And Stanislavski and his wife, Lilina, would read the lines of *Hamlet* to Craig, and Craig would criticize. Then Craig would read the lines, and Stanislavski would criticize. *These were the top creative people in the world!* And they were trying like beginners to capture this tone which had not—and to this day has not—been caught.

A lot of actors using our approach wind up with only one improvement: they use themselves better *logically*. They think better. They may be fed by a bit more of sensation, but sensation and impulse never become fully expressive. We have never really seen on the stage the life of the human spirit—except in those great actors who are able somehow to reach that point by some process within themselves. And even they reach that point only sporadically. They do not do it when they wish to do it. Sometimes when they wish to do it, they cannot. But sometimes when they are not tense, when they have no problems, when they do not feel that "*somebody* is in the audience, so I've got to do it," something happens which enables the impulse to express itself, and they are transfigured. That is what great acting is—not just impulse, but a true relation between impulse and expression; not just a lot of emotion, but the degree to which emotion finds an equivalent expression. Frankly, very few of us are sufficiently free so that body, mind, spirit, thought, and verbalization are able to combine in full and true expression.

I have been fortunate. I have seen this in at least four actors, and I have seen it in single performances in other actors. Duse caught it. Chaliapin had music: to say that he caught it is gilding the lily. Grasso caught it often in his acting. Jacob ben Ami caught it superbly in his great parts. Laurette Taylor and Pauline Lord caught it in their earlier performances. Otherwise there have been only sporadic moments that gave me that feeling. There were moments in the Moscow Art Theatre. We had elements of it in the Group Theatere but contaminated, surrounded, so the life was never quite as fresh, as exciting, as alive, as poetic as we imagined it could be. But I have never seen such expression on the stage as a totality. That is the art of the theatre of which I dream.

Maybe someday we will be permitted to experiment fully with that art here. I am reminded of the experiment we did here quite a few years ago when Clifford Odets brought in a tape on which, in preparation for writing something, he had recorded his aunt and uncle talking. We copied off the words and had one of the actors read them, which he did—very nicely, very simply, very well—and seemingly logically and sincerely. And then we put on the recording. It was a howl in a strange, exciting way, because the sound of human life was so totally different. We heard how real people said those words with fullness of excitement, vividness of response, and sudden poetic leaps of expression. The way in which his uncle could switch from some ordinary remark to (*shouting passionately*) "TEN YEARS OF MY LIFE!" and back to (*chattily*), "Well, I mean, she's an idiot," was fantastic. This was dialogue spoken by an ordinary man with an accent and a choked voice, but that ordinary voice became so vivid and expressive through the coming together of emotion and sound and meaning that it was thrilling. It would be flabbergasting to hear that tone on the stage.

Anything can be seen poetically. If we say that cornflakes in their very nature cannot be poetic, we deny in acting what we accept in other arts. One of the greatest paintings of all times is van Gogh's painting of his shoes. The shoes are depicted very realistically, but from that picture of a simple pair of shoes we receive the impression that van Gogh has imbued them with overwhelming significance. When you look at it, you have a definite experience. That experience is aesthetic. It is poetic. It is tragic. It is whatever you feel—and yet the subject is shoes. The famous apples of Cézanne are obviously capable of transmitting more than the simple external image of realistic apples. It is possible to see anything in such a light and with such an attitude that you can either paint into it or write into it or act into it something which intensifies its significance.

There are times when you pick up your shoes and see through them your whole life. Those are poetic and tragic moments of life. They do not necessarily involve words, but the experience of seeing some aspect of life through an immediate object gives that moment a greater significance. Actually the significance is not "greater." It is the significance that actually exists—but until your attention is directed to it at that moment in a very precise way, it has remained amorphous and vague.

The essential thing with dialogue of any kind—not just poetic dialogue—is to find back of the words the experience and behavior that will give them life, so that they stem logically from the character on the stage. Such a problem is solved more easily with realistic plays than with poetic plays because the connection between word and experience is more easily imagined.

When an actress gets up at night in a realistic play and has to say, "I'm cold," she knows that she has to do something like hugging herself. But if she has an obviously poetic line about the cold, she can easily forget that the poetic line also has no meaning unless the cold is created. And when she then gets back into bed and has to speak about the covers being comforting, that has no meaning either, unless she has previously created the sense of coldness.

When you get up at night with a fever, the fever makes cold very sharp to the senses. You pull on your stockings with an unusual manner because of the cold and the fever. When a sick person gets up in the middle of the night, there is a reason—suppose you need to eat. To a sick person food doesn't taste right. Even so, the body feels a need to sustain itself, so you eat the cornflakes with both great hunger and little taste. And then you feel the coldness, and then comes a need to lie down, and then you can pull up the covers and say, "Oh, what comfort for these to lie against my breast." But if all those things have not been created, who would believe you? I don't care how you say the line. I don't care whether you say it in Latin or Greek. I don't care whether we only hear the sound of the words and not the words. I don't care whether you say it poetically or realistically or super-realistically or surrealistically. What we will respond to and believe is a sound that has pleasure and warmth as opposed to the previous sense of someone suffering from cold.

Words are perfectly logical and believable on the stage only to the extent that they carry the expression of the reality of the moment. Shakespeare's later plays are never undramatic, and yet they have great poetry and sometimes great formality. In each succeeding play Shakespeare's form becomes freer. Some characters begin to use ordinary realistic speech. Others use a kind of free verse. Some use the formalized speech of the early plays, but only because it coincides with their preciousness of thought. Shakespeare finally became able to control his use of these formal divisions and devices, so that we are never aware that they are the author's devices. They are dramatic—not because they are poetic or unpoetic or less formal or more formal or realistic or unrealistic. They are dramatic because they stem from a character in a situation and an event.

People have begun to say, "It is all right to use the 'Method' for realistic plays, because obviously Studio actors are good. But let them stick to their own plays. Keep them away from poetic plays." I cannot accept this split—in life or in art. To me the external is as real as the internal. Just the way you look excites me and affects me. As a human being I can appreciate the exterior—humanly and truly. It is not a false value. The external becomes false only when other elements do not coincide with it.

Do you remember the play in which the girl had only one word to say at the very end? She had to sit quietly through the whole play, and she was so beautiful. She had such a lovely quality that you could think your own thoughts through her being as she sat there, and you could think the author's thoughts through what the other actors were saying. And then at the end she opened her mouth to say—literally—one word, and suddenly the whole external thing was false, because her one word did not coincide with what we had seen.

I cannot separate poetry from life. The greatest poetry has invariably come from life. The vision of a poet as expressed in a play is an intense moment of thought and of feeling that needs heightened expression on the stage because it derives from a moment of life that needed such heightened expression.

The dramatic faculty is not explainable as a thing in itself. Drama implies that something must have happened. Drama implies that there is something we have to know in order to understand what is happening now. The dramatic faculty makes us want another act or another scene, and when we have found out what happens in that scene, it entices us to ask, "So in that case, what happens now?" The dramatic faculty can create a situation in which, even though you know all the facts, you still don't know what is going to happen next. The dramatic faculty involves you in events as they go along.

Unfortunately authors often give the actor the wrong words. They are afraid that the audience will not understand certain things because they are unaware of how much the actor can do by himself, and so they attempt to incorporate everything in words. A significant example is one of our most talented individuals in the theatre, Irwin Shaw. His writing is excellent, and yet he has had great difficulty in the theatre.

We have had the revealing experience here of acting the Irwin Shaw novels and short stories, in which the writing is very crisp, and of finding that they act much more dramatically than his plays do. We have tried to find the reason, and it seems to derive from the fact that in the short stories and novels he gives the characters only lines that people would actually speak, and he puts all the explanatory statements in his own words. He describes what is happening and what the people are thinking as a novelist does, but in his plays he puts all that material in the dialogue. The scenes become waterlogged. The actor is given so many words that he is stopped from doing what he can legitimately do. We don't need to make an actor say, "It's hot today" in order to say that it's hot today. Irwin Shaw does not permit the theatrical and dramatic wheels to turn, because he tries solely by words to make sure we understand. That part of his words which is dramatically viable loses its efficiency because it is drowned in this welter of churning verbalization.

Chekhov had the dramatizing faculty. He gives you logic. It is not ordinary logic, and yet when you know everything, it is a logic that is complete. Chekhov hated obvious acting. He hated obvious writing. He didn't even like Ibsen, because Ibsen openly plotted. Chekhov said, "That's playmaking," and felt Ibsen's plays were made-up plays. Chekhov felt that he in some way represented something else. He never expressed this except in his attitude, but you can see it in *The Seagull* where the young author describes the difficulties of writing. He says that other writers seem to know exactly what to do and when to do it; they put it in, and hang out a flag, and it's all settled. But what this young writer tries to do is very difficult, because he never quite knows whether he's made his point, whether he's caught the moon or just an image.

Chekhov wanted to see actors who did not seem to be acting. He had a sense that the drama in life is undramatic. He certainly did not mean that he wanted drama on the stage to be undramatic, but he did mean that it should not be obviously dramatic. For example, if you wanted to write a play about gambling, you would ordinarily write about a spendthrift who has a million dollars and gets involved in a game and loses the million dollars and goes home and kills himself. That is a movie plot. It's used in every movie about Monte Carlo, and we say, "Yeah. We understand. That's the way things happen, but who the hell wants to see it?" Chekhov had an idea for a short story about gambling which he put in his *Notebooks*. A man gets into a gambling game. He wins a million rubles. He goes home, lies down, and kills himself. That is all, and obviously it is a much more dramatic situation.

You know all the facts, and yet you want to know more. "Why?" You realize that things like that happen. Reality does not always follow the conventional way, and yet there is logic because our sense of life tells us that such things happen. The situation is not completely explicable. We want to know more. Therefore we have the beginning of a play. That is the Chekhovian way.

Chekhov had an idea for a story about a man who goes to a doctor and is told that he has a bad heart and has to be careful because he may go at any moment. He has to take very good care of himself. He goes home and lives very carefully for about eleven years. He is always expecting to die, so he enjoys every moment. Everybody gives him sympathy. He has a wonderful life. Then he goes back to a doctor, and the doctor tells him, "You're perfectly all right. There's nothing the matter with you." The man's

life is ruined. What is he going to do? He has no reason for existence. That is a dramatic moment. That is Chekhov's peculiar
way, but it is the real dramatic vision.

Chekhov was insistently opposed to fake dramatic vision. He
didn't like sentiment. He didn't like the actors to be too aware
of acting. He didn't like points to be made too emphatically on
the stage—or for that matter off the stage. And if Chekhov's
vision is the true vision, as I think it is, that means we have an
artistic reason, and not just a technical reason, for what we are
trying to do. Only by the approach that we follow can we possibly
attain the kind of evanescent reality which Chekhov sensed. Somebody once described Chekhov very well. "Chekhov," he said, "is
like something you see reflected in water." I understand what was
meant. Chekhov has the strange throb of real events. He has that
sense of "more-ness" that life has. His writing seems always about
to move into a different kind of meaning and significance, and
yet somehow it retains its shape. The shape is there. It's simple.
It is, after all, just water. It is not a cascade. And yet somehow
we catch in it a reflection of something else.

I saw the Moscow Art Theatre productions of all the Chekhov
plays except *The Seagull*. I saw the people who played the parts
originally. Those performances and those productions were like
good wine that is aged, and I will never forget them. And yet,
impressive as they were, so much so that even now I can describe
characters and entire scenes, I felt that those productions were
not quite Chekhov as he wanted to be seen. Chekhov was seeking
a certain kind of simplicity, a strange significance through insig-
nificance, poetry that was not poetic, emotion that was not sentimental or obvious. There still remains something to do for people
who wish that they might capture what Chekhov sought. I don't
think it has ever been caught.

The Moscow Art Theatre was superb in its own terms. It can
only be criticized on the ground that something else is possible.
Call it the lighter touch that we see in the wonderful Dutch
artists, de Hooch and Terborch. You almost want to touch their

paintings to see if they are real. They have a very sensuous sense of materials. And do not forget that Chekhov was really part of the impressionist school and that he admired impressionists like Liebermann and semi-expressionists like Israëls. He liked the kind of painting which is simple and easy and yet has a texture through which something less obvious shows. That was what he was trying to get at in his plays.

It is possible that the technical work we do here, which strips the actor of obvious theatricalities, can lead to the fulfillment of Chekhov's intention. Chekhov did not want the actor to be concerned with giving the words the colors they should have. He did not want a concern with anything obvious. So we can at any rate promise that the kind of exploration we do here holds forth the possibility that we can really discover the way in which Chekhov should be done. After all, he liked some actors better than others.

On a few occasions I have seen young people in classes solve scenes from Chekhov in a way I have never seen on a stage. I once saw two young untrained people who had been given a simple technical problem to work on, and they did the last scene in *The Seagull* in a way I guess I will never see again in my lifetime. Perhaps they would never have been able to do it again. These were just two young people in a class. I don't even remember who they were. When they started, they did not create even the simplest reality. I stopped them. I said to the boy who was doing Treplev, "Now, wait a minute. If you are writing, write. Next time really try to write." I didn't know where that would lead him, but it was a simple task for his concentration. I gave the girl a similar task. The things those simple tasks led to were horrifying. I remember vividly that he would write something and tear it up, so that when she came in, he had papers scattered around the room. His whole concern when she entered was that she shouldn't see his inability. The way he tried to pick up those papers and get them out of the way or into the fire was heart-rending. And suddenly you realized that this boy thinks of himself as a failure, as someone who cannot put down on paper what he sees and wishes other people to know and understand. You realized that he envies the ease and security of Trigorin even though he doesn't really want it. I remember that he watched Nina as she was speaking about the affair with Trigorin and that he walked away from her because it was tough to take and then sat down and watched her like an animal. You've all seen a beaten animal after you've told it, "Stay in the corner," and the animal just stands there and watches. This boy made you feel, "Somebody better watch this guy. He's a suicide. He's going to do something." These were just two young people in a class, but the things that happened in that scene and on a few other occasions have shown me what can be found in Chekhov.

The Moscow Art Theatre had a totally different quality. The emotional power of their acting was so great that watching them was like being bathed in emotional life. I remember when Stanislavski as Vershinin came to say good-by to Masha in *The Three Sisters*. They have tried not to show their love for each other, but the band was playing, and they looked at each other, and then they grabbed each other. I'll never forget that grabbing. I remember literally holding onto the seat. The simple reality of that good-by, of the two people holding on as if they wouldn't let go, of both literally clinging to each other, will stay with me always. The Moscow Art Theatre productions were rich and full, but Chekhov never quite liked that kind of thing. He was searching all his life for the sense of reaching out and capturing life but holding it like a bird. When you hold a bird, you have to be careful. You hold it, and you feel that strange trembling. The bird is there, and you can almost feel its fear, but yet it stands there. As long as your hand is confident, the bird will remain. But as soon as your hand twitches even slightly, the bird flies away. Chekhov was getting at that sense of reality. I would like to see an effort made here to capture that on the stage. If we caught only a little of it, I would be very happy.

The extraordinary thing about acting is that life itself is actually used to create artistic results. In every other art the means only pretend to deal with reality. Music can often capture something more deeply than any other way, but it only tells you something *about* reality. Painting tells something *about* the painter, *about* the thing painted, and *about* the combination of the two. But since the actor is also a human being, he does not pretend to use reality. He can literally use everything that exists. The actor uses thought—not thought transcribed into color and line as the painter does, but actual, real thought. The actor uses real sensation and real behavior. That actual reality is the material of our craft.

The things that fed the great actors of the past as human beings were of such strength and sensitivity that when these things were added to conscious effort, they unconsciously and subconsciously led to the results seen in all great acting, the great performances accomplished by people who would say if asked, "I don't know how I do it." In themselves as human beings were certain sensitivities and capacities which made it possible for them to create these great performances even though they were unaware of the process.

The actor's human nature not only makes possible his greatness, but also is the source of his problems. Here in the Studio we have become aware that the opposite is also true, that an individual can possess the technical ability to do certain things and yet may have difficulty in expressing them because of his emotional life, because of the problems of his human existence. The approach to this actor's problem must therefore deal first with relieving whatever difficulties are inherent in himself that negate his freedom of expression and block the capacities he possesses.

All actors who have worked at their craft have found it hard to describe what they have done. Stanislavski had difficulty because he didn't think abstractly. But this was wonderful because it kept him from arriving at the abstract conclusions with which most people had previously satisfied their minds. Most people suppose they have really solved something when in fact they have only made an impressive formula. It means something to them but is not cogent or concrete enough to mean anything to anybody else.

The clearest and most precise statement about acting to be found is a fifteen-page essay written by the great French actor Talma—one of the greatest actors of all time.* In it he states everything you need to know about acting. For example, sensibility without control or intelligence is wrong; there must be a unification of inner and outer resources; intelligence and intellectual control must be involved to insure a proper use of all elements. Talma's essay is the best ever written about acting, but nobody can understand it who has not already found out what it means. It has made no impression on the theatre because it is abstract.

One of the most brilliant descriptions of the actor's problem comes from Jacques Copeau. He describes the difficulties the actor has with his "blood," as he calls it. The actor tells his arm, "Come on now, arm, go out and make the gesture," but the arm remains wooden. The "blood" doesn't flow; the muscles don't move; the body fights within itself; it's a terrifying thing. To someone on the outside this sounds like verbalization or poetry. But we know, because we have often felt what it means to stand on the stage and know that what you are doing is not what you mean to do, that you meant to move your arm differently and you meant to come over to the audience with ease and warmth, and instead you're standing there like a stick. Copeau calls it "the battle with the blood of the actor."

Copeau was also the first to bring to my attention the marvelous phrase Shakespeare used about acting. Remember where Hamlet says, "Is it not monstrous that this player here, but in a fiction, in a dream of passion, could force his soul so to his own conceit . . . ?" Isn't it monstrous that someone should have this capacity? The profession of acting, the basic art of acting, is a monstrous thing because it is done with the same flesh-and-blood muscles with which you perform ordinary deeds, real deeds. The body with which you make real love is the same body with which you make fictitious love with someone whom you don't like, whom

---

* "Reflections on the Actor's Art" (Paris, 1825).

you fight with, whom you hate, by whom you hate to be touched. And yet you throw yourself into his arms with the same kind of aliveness and zest and passion as with your real lover—not only with your real lover, with your realest lover. In no other art do you have this monstrous thing.

The basic thing in acting is what William Gillette calls "the illusion of the first time." It must seem that this has never taken place before, that no one has seen it before, that this actress has never done this before, and that in fact she's not an actress. Even in stylized forms of theatre, unless you feel that what you are seeing is somehow at that moment being creatively inspired, you say, "Well, he's repeating," or, "It's very good, but seems mechanical; it seems imitative," or, "It seems as if he's getting tired of it." The conditions of acting demand that you know in advance what you are going to do while the art of acting demands that you should seem not to know. This would appear to make acting impossible, but that is not so in practice. It is just that there is a slight confusion about the problem.

A piano is a precise instrument. It exists outside of yourself. When we say that the pianist is doing something real, we mean that he knows the music, that with a definite finger of a particular hand he will hit a certain note, and that he knows he means to hit it with a certain amount of energy and a certain amount of feeling, and therefore not only of physical pressure but also of rhythmic and mood pressure. However—and this is what preserves the illusion of the first time—when his hand comes down on the piano, because it is a real instrument and cannot be misled by the pianist's intention, the sound that comes out is the precise result of the amount of energy that he employed. But the actor has no piano. In the actor pianist and piano are the same. When the actor attempts to hit on some key of himself, on some mood, thought, feeling, or sensation, what comes out is not necessarily what he thinks he should have hit, but what he actually hits. He may consciously follow the same procedure which he employed on a previous occasion to evoke the desired response, but instead some unconscious pattern may well trigger an entirely different and unwanted response. There is no such situation in any other art.

On the violin I don't care how wonderful I feel and how great my passion, when I scrape that note, that note scrapes—and I know it. It's a real violin, not a trick violin. It's a trick violin when I pretend to play but somebody is really playing a record behind a curtain. It's trick acting when I pretend to be experiencing something for the first time but really am only imitating what I did in rehearsal or what some other actor does in a part like this. In acting, the danger is that the actor can fool himself into thinking that what has happened is what he thinks should have happened. If the actor were a piano, he couldn't possibly fool himself, because he could know, "It sounded false."

Edwin Booth was an intelligent actor though never an actor of passion. One day he was playing Hamlet. His daughter was sitting in a box, and as he started to speak about Ophelia, thoughts of his daughter's being trapped in Ophelia's situation came to his mind, and he was very moved. He became emotional. Tears flowed. And he was shocked and surprised when people at the end told him, "It was a very bad performance you gave today. What happened?" He assumed that it should have been a good performance.

The human being who acts is the human being who lives. That is a terrifying circumstance. Essentially the actor acts a fiction, a dream; in life the stimuli to which we respond are always real. The actor must constantly respond to stimuli that are imaginary. And yet this must happen not only just as it happens in life, but actually more fully and more expressively. Although the actor can do things in life quite easily, when he has to do the same things on the stage under fictitious conditions he has difficulty because he is not equipped as a human being merely to play-act at imitating life. He must somehow believe. He must somehow be able to convince himself of the rightness of what he is doing in order to do things fully on the stage.

When the actor comes off the stage, he often knows that some-thing went wrong, but because of the ego that is involved in acting he is usually ashamed and afraid to ask what people are referring to when they say, "What the hell happened today?" It is not merely that the actor fears he was bad. He is much more afraid that he will find out he was fooling himself by thinking that what was bad was really good. That would mean that he literally doesn't know what is happening on the stage, that he goes on without knowing what is going to happen. He is then in a desperate situa-tion. To go on then, he must have either an absence of ego—which is impossible—or a degree of faith that is equally impossible.

In the modern theatre we have begun to be aware of the in-trinsic relation between the capacity of the human being and what happens to that capacity when he starts to act. The things that affect the actor as a human being condition his behavior and his achievement on the stage to a much greater extent than is com-monly recognized.

Children at play have a wonderful naïve quality which lasts till they're about eight or nine. They play, and they don't care. When you come into the room, they say, "Hold the baby," and "Here is the tub," and your presence doesn't matter. They take you into their belief. About the age of nine you see them start to close the door. They say, "Let's go and play," and they go into another room and close the door. And when you open the door, they say, "No, no, no, get out." Their faith is beginning to be broken.

This process continues, so that by the time the human being decides to be an actor he has inculcated in himself many habits that are wrong for acting. The naïve faith of going with the im-agination which is so wonderful in the child has been knocked out of him. The relation between "what I think" and "what I say" has been inhibited. The child has learned to behave as a human being, but not as an actor. You take a child to a teacher to learn to dance when he is five or six. Then the child begins to dance at home all the time, and you say, "Don't behave that way." But when company comes, you say, "Dance for the people." However, when the child then wants to act for them as well, you say, "Please, don't do that. Please, go to your room."

Thus the manners and needs and customs of society create a hindrance that in later years interferes with the actor's freedom of expression or freedom of response. Do you remember Actor F? He comes from an academic environment. One day we did a very interesting exercise here in which he admitted that in that environment certain words were never used and that one of the most difficult things he has to do as an actor is to use dirty words on the stage. But that awareness was for him already an advance, because most of us do not even know that we have these difficulties. There is nothing terrible about this process of social conditioning. The actor still has to be a human being, which means a social being in part. But when at about eighteen he wants to train himself as an actor, he too often finds only a kind of training which is a continuation of the social process of telling the child how to behave. The training does not free the instrument for the process of creation in acting.

In life, life itself is a sure standard, because if you deal with life unreally, it reacts in such a way that it forces you to correct. On the stage, and in art generally, mistakes are never noticed unless somebody is sensitive enough, willing enough to think. The audience comes into the theatre inactive and becomes active only as a result of what the actors do. Therefore, the basic problem for the actor is not how he deals with his material in terms of his audience, but how he begins to make his material alive to himself. Once he has carried his understanding of the play beyond conventionally conceived textures and experiences, he must then meet the problem of how to evoke and create these fuller and more real textures and experiences on the stage.

In regard to this problem there are two schools. One solves the problem by very good observation; this is the French school, which was dominant in the training of the actor until modern times. The actor of the French school at its best recognizes what is going on in the scene and then tries to find out how he should behave accordingly. He asks himself, "What must I choose to do?" The best French acting and the best German acting are quite superb. The details are finely arrived at. They can differentiate between a girl's being half excited and her half not knowing what she's excited about and her being half frightened. They are able on each line to do something—a flicker of the eye, a movement of the hand, some little look, some breathless little heaving —which manages to capture the image of what they are trying to create.

The other school, our school, starts basically the same way. In all good acting the actors perceive the reality of what is to be acted, but the ways of arriving at it differ. When it is a matter of suggesting and demonstrating, we can do that as well as anyone else, because that is easy. But we believe that the actor need not imitate a human being. The actor is himself a human being and can create out of himself. The actor is the only art material capable of being both the material and the reality so that you almost cannot tell the two things apart. Only in theatre do we have the emotions, soul, spirit, mind, and muscles of the artist as the material of art. We believe that a greater fusion of all these elements with the reality of what is to be acted can take place than is accomplished by the French school. We therefore have ways in which we advise you to work. Basic to these is a recognition of the great difference between conventional reality, which most good actors settle for, and the kind of reality envisioned by our school.

Conventional reality makes no sense. It does not excite the audience. It does not tell the audience what the scene is really about. It is willing to be effective, but nothing beyond effectiveness emerges. We believe that art has the function of giving the audience something without which it would be less—less human, less alive, less excited, less amused and entertained, not on a light level but on the topmost level of which theatre is capable.

Once when two people worked here on a scene from *Macbeth*, an observer from abroad came over following the session and with great sympathy said, "Now if you really want to work on *Macbeth*, I can recommend some books for you to read." And I said, "The books should have been sent to Shakespeare; obviously they would have helped him a great deal." The actor is constantly being interfered with by the idea that if you send him a couple of books and give him the right ideas and explain the scene to him he will be a great actor. Whereas, what we try to come to grips with here is the basic process of creation, which exists in all the arts, which is the same in all the arts, and which has always been the same.

Mrs. Siddons, who was probably the greatest Lady Macbeth of all time, has told how, when she had to play certain parts, she would stand backstage and watch the entire play before she made her entrance; otherwise she could not act the scene. She didn't know about getting into the scene the way that we pretend to know. She didn't know about the psychology of imagination. She didn't know about concentration as a definable element of consciousness. She didn't know any of the things that Stanislavski and others have brought to our attention. She knew only the actor's problem of appealing to his imagination. She, one of the greatest actresses of all time, had the same difficulty of whipping herself into a scene, of getting herself in the mood, of starting herself in the play that we do. Yet she understood what the play was about as well as anyone.

The appeal to the imagination, to the unconscious and the subconscious, is the strongest lever in artistic work. The essentials of the creative mood or moment, when something begins to happen, when the actor unconsciously begins to work, are relaxation and the presence of something that stirs the actor subconsciously. This something is not the kind of mental knowledge that gives the actor answers that have no meaning for him. This something is not the kind of answer that tells him why he does what he does. It is the kind of subconscious answer that brings him alive, feeds him, makes his imagination work, makes him feel, "I can now get up and act. I would like to act. Things are working for me now."

I am not talking about not knowing what one is doing. I do not mean hysteria or hypnosis or anything like that. I mean employing the unconscious or subconscious knowledge that we have, the experiences that we have stored away but which we cannot easily or quickly put our hand on by means of the conscious mind. I mean employing in acting the knowledge which functions in dreams, where we often come up with things that seem to make no sense, with things that happened many, many years ago but which we have long supposed to be forgotten.

Unconsciousness does not mean lack of consciousness. It means a consciousness which is subterranean, which has been pushed very deep within you as a result of living. Sometimes the actor says, "A thing like that never happened to me," whereas, if you happen to know his life, you know that it actually did happen. How could he possibly have forgotten? Usually the things that are important, especially if they have painful or certain other connotations, are pushed back into the unconscious; otherwise life would be too difficult. Nonetheless these deep-seated things are active, so appealing to the subconscious does not mean involving something of which one has no awareness. It means dealing with an area of consciousness that is not easily or quickly evoked, but which we must find ways and means of getting to.

However, if I need to work for everything I do on the stage, either I am not an actor or I am so untrustful of myself that I have not permitted the impulse to act to develop in myself. The actor deals with the leap of the imagination. The actor's imagination may have its strengths and weaknesses, but essentially it must be there in the same way that there must be a voice in order to train someone to sing. The actor must be active in imagination. He not only must be willing to make the initial leap, but his imagination must be willing to follow through. You cannot take someone whose imagination does not leap, whose imagination does not go forward, and say, "That's all right. I'm going to train him to act." It is impossible.

I know that when you jump with a parachute it will open. It can be an automatic parachute. You need not worry. You can arrange everything in advance. It can all be figured out. But no amount of figuring could get me to leave something solid and jump into empty space. Therefore, a parachute jumper I will never be. (*Laughter.*) Somebody would have to throw me out. I do honestly think that no matter what the circumstances were, no matter what the logic would demand, I could not get myself to jump. Therefore, in that profession I cannot get off the ground. I can't start.

If there is not the willingness to conceive, to go, to take the imaginary thing and see what can happen, all the actor's work, no matter how good it may be, will stop short at a certain point.

The essential thing for the actor is to use himself, to be willing to trust and to go with the scene, himself, and the audience. On the stage the actor cannot be one-third actor, one-third critic, and one-third audience. He must be ninety-nine per cent actor and a little bit critic and a little bit audience. If he is one hundred per cent actor, that is no good. He does not know what he is doing. There has to be one little bit left that makes him aware of what he is doing. The actor never permits himself to go out of control —though the point at which the actor goes out of control is usually much beyond the point where he begins to fear he will go out of control.

The actor must guard against a search for perfect solutions. Neither on the stage nor in life do we find perfect solutions. However, often when you know that something has to be there to move you and you are still willing to go on the stage without having found that something, although you say to yourself, "Isn't that funny? I can't find an experience that really moves me that strongly," the audience will often see you creating exactly the right kind and degree of experience. An actor need not do a thing one hundred per cent in order to do it. A little coffee is coffee. A little of anything always contains the ingredients of the whole. A drop of blood contains all the elements of blood. On the stage, if we are willing to concentrate on and give ourselves to a prob-

lem, we are already dealing with that problem. The willingness to
go step by step without worry about whether you have the hundred per cent is the big secret in acting.

In the human being there is expression when he is least concerned about it. The actor is an instrument that pays attention.
Something happens to him as a result of paying attention which
is pure expression. It is happening even when he thinks nothing
is being expressed. I'm not talking about energy. I'm not talking
about loudness. I'm not talking about *strength* of expression. I'm
talking about the expressiveness which is part of the fundamental
equipment of the human being—and therefore of the actor.

Acting exists in every human being. Its extent differs with different human beings; that makes for the degrees of talent. Inspiration is within the actor; something starts it off. If you push
a button and no electricity is attached, nothing happens. Electricity only comes from where electricity is, not from where the
button is. In the actor both electricity and button are usually
unconscious. Often the button seems to be external to the actor,
but it is not. When a lot of people are watching the same thing,
and only one is inspired, the inspiration is not in the thing being
watched; otherwise all the watchers would be inspired. Inspiration
—the appeal to and functioning of the actor's imagination—is
within the actor. The problem of creation for the actor is the
problem of starting the inspiration. How does the actor make himself inspired?

Other artists are free as to when they create. In them inspiration
can take place spontaneously, even accidentally. They can wait
for it. They can recapture it by correcting what they have already
done. We can't. Fortunately the human being is built with a
natural need to repeat. He wants to repeat, and he sets himself to
repeat, but unfortunately the second time he repeats coldly what
he did the first time out of impulse. So in acting we not only
need to repeat, but we have to watch that the impulse stays fresh.
If the impulse does stay fresh, the response and expression that
it gives rise to will invariably tend to repeat. Little by little the

repetition conditions the actor, so that whenever this particular impulse comes, the need for the associated expression comes.

ACTRESS G: Can you contrive an impulse?

STRASBERG: That's what we constantly do. The central thing that Stanislavski discovered and to a certain extent defined and set exercises for was that the actor can be helped really to think on the stage, instead of thinking only in make-believe fashion. Once the actor begins to think, life starts, and then there cannot be imitation. "Make-believe thinking" is a mental idea of thought, a paraphrasing of the character's lines rather than the kind of thought a human being really thinks. Before Stanislavski, actors were criticized as conventional or mechanical or imitative, but no one had ever set himself the problem of defining exactly what that means. The actor obviously wants to be good, original, and striking. Stanislavski was the first to realize that the cliché, the conventional idea of what is to be accomplished in a scene, satisfies a very strong need both in the human being and in the actor; that the cliché functions as an habitual response; that it is at best a caricature of what really happens in life; and that once the habitual response is interrupted by something the actor does not expect, the cliché vanishes because the actor then really has to think on the stage.

When Actress H was doing *The Millionairess* here, and she stopped and I said, "Don't throw her the line. No line. Go on," at that moment something happened. Earlier she had forgotten a line and had asked for it and had gotten it, and nothing had happened. She walked around. She was just acting, but the next time, when she was forced to stop, and thus something in her had to take hold and think, with that real thought something then began really to happen. Wonderful things came from her, a freeness, a looseness, real laughter. A whole new range of colors was released in her and therefore in the play.

The actor must have full belief in whatever he thinks and says on the stage. A good deal of routine acting work merely consists of finding substitutes for that faith and belief. But when the actor can really believe, when he allows himself really to think, when his imagination really functions, he does not need clichés and preconceptions, because this natural process of acting makes him feel, "I'm working," and something begins to happen in him, and from that he gets the certainty and security to go ahead.

Stanislavski's basic point is that his training work is not intended directly for production on the stage. The training work teaches the means by which the actor incites this imagination, this thing that takes place and makes him feel, "I think I know what it is. I can't quite put it into words. Let me do it." Then the actor wants to act. He does not quite know what he wants to do, yet he's impelled to go ahead. He is creative. Stanislavski's entire search, the entire purpose of the "Method" or our technique or whatever you want to call it, is to find a way to start in each of us this creative process so that a good deal of the things we know but are not aware of will be used on the stage to create what the author sets for us to do.

CHAPTER III

Training: Relaxation

THE first thing Strasberg does, both in his private classes and at the Studio, is to check the actor for tension. Very few of us are fully relaxed in life, but we are not usually aware of tension until it becomes extreme and shows itself through pain. Tension can be so habitual that when relaxation is induced we feel actually as if a great weight had been removed, as if the pull of gravity were somehow lessened. Strasberg's highly developed powers of observation enable him to point out the manifestations of tension in actors' bodies, voices, even in the expression of their faces.

Long ago Strasberg enunciated his belief that "when there is tension, one cannot think or feel." But he also constantly emphasizes the opposite and positive sense of this idea: the human being is naturally expressive. When he is relaxed and really thinking about or paying attention to something, or even when random thoughts move through his consciousness, impulses pass without interruption into pure expression. The voice changes. Distortions in the way the body or the head or the arms and shoulders are held disappear. The expression of the face changes. The person actually takes on a new appearance.

Strasberg knows that calling the actor's attention to his tensions is merely the first step in dealing with them. In the long run the actor must be reconditioned to function in a state of relaxation. This is accomplished by making him aware of the particular causes of tension in himself. Relaxing the tensions acquired in a lifetime and in years of wrong acting may take further long years of conscious hard work in which deliberate relaxation plays a part in all stages of activity. Relaxation is worked at as a separate activity, but it is also made a conscious part of all acting work. And as he comes to understand what causes his particular tensions and the extent to which he can naturally respond when relaxed and concentrated, the actor's belief grows, and belief in turn encourages further relaxation. But it cannot be emphasized too strongly that tension cannot be eradicated by paying lip service to an idea.

Tension is the occupational disease of the actor. Relaxation is the foundation on which almost all actors' work is based. Stanislavski posited that relaxation is an actual professional activity for the actor. When you see good performers, one of the things that makes them good is a certain amount of relaxation. We may not always be aware of exactly what they're doing. We may refer to their sense of ease or authority, but in fact it is relaxation that we are noticing.

The ordinary actor sometimes achieves relaxation by himself as a result of working on the stage, but that takes about twenty years—literally. If you watch the development of an actor, you see that as he starts off he is young and energetic—and tense. After about ten years he begins to overcome some of the tension, but nothing really takes its place. After about twenty years a wonderful thing begins to happen. It has almost nothing to do with whether he is good or bad. He simply feels that when he comes on the stage he is there to stay. And he gains the wonderful ease that is part of the medal you earn by being in the theatre a certain amount of time.

Stanislavski stressed relaxation as the essential first stage in almost all acting work. Without relaxation a lot of things an actor may rightly want to do will be deformed as they enter his instrument, because the instrument itself sets up resistance through tension. When that happens, the actor cannot achieve a real relation between what he is thinking and the expression which should be part of that thought or experience. The expression becomes contaminated.

Stanislavski said that a lot of actors think they are doing what he recommends but that actually because of tension they continue acting as they did before. The actor may think the opposite and even speak of himself as changed, but the impulse coming into the body merely takes on the same aspect as before and can't really quite get through as a fresh impulse and response.

Recently, having reread Stanislavski's emphasis on relaxation and being reminded of the extent to which he begs the actor to make the effort to relax, I have tried in my private classes to stress relaxation with certain people who were having difficulty. Their work was coming along, but slowly. The results they obtained were somehow not commensurate with what they seemed entitled to achieve. To these people I said, "Now, wait a minute. Let us take a longer time to relax. We have told you to relax, but obviously you are not yet relaxed. So take all the time allotted to the exercise if necessary, just to relax. If you never get to the exercise, I don't care."

I have been amazed to find that in certain cases the tension had been so strong that nothing, no matter how real and vivid, could come through. Sometimes when the actor just starts to relax, the release of impulse is so strong that we could swear that the actor is deliberately expressing. Yet at the end when you ask him, "Well, what did you try to do?" he confounds you by saying, "Nothing. I just tried to relax." Simple relaxation permits a lot of things locked in the instrument to come out.

Tension is both physical and mental. Physical tension is exactly that. Stanislavski urges the actor to use a highly particularized way of dealing with physical tension. He says that the actor has to learn to control each muscle separately. The actor picks out one muscle at a time and learns to control it. Well, I think he is right, but we would never get to acting if we really went into it on so detailed a level.

I have found a more convenient form of training in relaxation. It takes quite a lot of time but not so much as Stanislavski recommends. Wherever the actor is, sitting or standing, he finds a position for the body in which he could go to sleep. For example, if you take an overnight ride in a car or on a train, it is not easy to fall asleep, and yet somehow you fiddle around until you get in a position in which the pressures are taken off the body so that it can begin to relax physically. Only then can you begin to fall asleep.

We ask the actor in training to try to find such a position. We don't want him actually to go to sleep, but we want him to get to the point where he begins to be convinced, "Yes, I've got it. If I kept this up, I could, if I wanted, go to sleep." This is difficult to do, but it tests the actor's physical relaxation very well.

We then proceed to the second phase of dealing with tension. Whatever relaxation is not thus accomplished on the physical plane, we try to accomplish on the mental plane. To me mental tension is an even worse enemy than purely physical tension. Physical tension is more or less easily observable. Mental tension is not so easy to observe. I have found that three areas are indicators of mental tension. This discovery does not stem from theory or scientific observation but purely from practice.

The first of these is at the temples, where you find the so-called blue nerves. When people are tense, you find them pressing the finger tips to these areas without knowing they are doing it. Headaches come here. Here a lot of nerves and blood vessels feed into the brain. We simply ask the actor to become aware of this area and to permit these nerves to relax. You will be surprised how a real weight will lift if in life you will simply say, "Wait, let me see if I'm tense or not," and begin relaxation in this area. However, we do not encourage the actor to do anything with his hands, because he cannot in the middle of playing Hamlet rub his temples in order to get relaxed. He has to be able to control the relaxation through inner concentration.

The second is from the bridge of the nose into the eyelids. Only recently have I realized that this area is involved in life with a great deal of automatic response. It is so responsive that if somebody's hand suddenly comes close to my eyes, the eyelids will close. I don't know that that hand has any bad intentions, but the eyes protect themselves so automatically that they close before the mind can even examine the potential danger. On the street as soon as a particle of dust touches an eyelash, the eyes close. This defensive mechanism is so active and so automatic that a great deal of tension builds up. The tension is relaxed simply by permitting the eyelids to droop. As the lids come down, here again you can feel weight actually leaving. Sometimes when you relax this area, you get a strange feeling that you are losing control. You have gotten so used to tension as your personal state of equilibrium that when you relax, the muscles momentarily cannot find their own level.

The third is around the mouth. Early in life one of the most important of the human being's automatic processes begins to manifest itself here. Thought is immediately reduced to words. Before the child knows what his next word is going to be, it has already been said. Imagine how active these muscles are. Imagine how alive they are. They know what you're going to say before you know what you're going to say. They are so active and automatic that again a lot of tension builds up, because as you grow older there are a lot of things you feel like saying but don't say. The price you pay for that is tension. You have to relax the mouth area by releasing the energy there just as when you are drunk and don't worry about how you are speaking.

Thus, to the actor here at the Studio who really wants to find out what relaxation can do, I say, "Let's do the exercise for pure relaxation." We take half an hour or forty minutes. We do nothing. The actor does everything. First, he relaxes physically in the way I have described. After he is physically relaxed, he then goes through these three areas. He tries to relax the temple area. Then he tries to relax the eyes. Finally he tries to relax the whole mouth area so that the tension is as much as possible reduced. That is an exercise in itself, and we have found extraordinary results from it.

Sometimes the talent of the actor reveals itself for the first time so fully and so unexpectedly as to be startling. The actor becomes completely responsive. His instrument gives forth a new depth of resonance. Emotion that has been habitually held back suddenly rushes forth. The actor becomes real—not merely simple or natural. He becomes fully concentrated. He unveils totally unsuspected aspects and elements of himself, but with such a degree of ease and authority that he seems literally to have taken off a mask, to have emerged from a disguise that previously had smothered and concealed his true personality. Yet all he did was relax.

CHAPTER IV

Training: Triggering Imagination

In acting, imagination has three aspects: impulse, belief, and concentration. Impulse—"the leap of the imagination"—may be conscious or unconscious in origin, but it is useless without belief, which is the actor's faith that what he is saying, doing, and feeling is both interesting and appropriate. Concentration both causes and results from impulse and belief. The actor who has enough belief and will to follow his impulse is usually concentrated. On the other hand, much of the actor's work consists in making himself sentient, in creating experience, and this involves a deliberate search for the proper objects or means of becoming concentrated. In turn, a state of concentration leads to impulse and belief. In other words, the actor cannot really think on the stage unless he is concentrated, and he cannot be concentrated unless he is really thinking on the stage. Imagination thus operates in terms of these three interacting factors, and only when all three are operating does imagination in acting actually function. Training the actor to be really alive involves his being conditioned to receive impulses from imaginary stimuli, to make these real—that is, believable to himself—and thus to awaken the proper sensory, emotional, or motor responses.

BEGINNING EXERCISES

When the actor gives up what he is doing in the face of the audience, or when his natural desire to affect the audience starts to run away with him and lead him to do things regardless of their appropriateness, he has problems of concentration. Concentration is an essential requirement of the actor's technique. When concentration leaves or tension comes in, the actor is lost.

Stanislavski's two basic early discoveries, primary in the suggestions he makes to the actor, are the importance of relaxation and concentration. Stanislavski found that the only sure thing the actor has in order to combat and do away with tension is concentration. Tension, outside of what can be done separately to relieve it, is most effectively eradicated by concentration on some task which does not seem to be directly connected with the play, but which arouses the actor's belief and sense of freedom, and therefore releases the actor's creative spirit. The actor feels, "I can do anything I want, because I somehow feel relieved of tension. Nothing bothers me." His heart and soul, his senses and imagination, are opened to what is happening.

It is important that the actor have concrete things on which to concentrate. Concentration cannot be abstract. If I just say to myself, "Concentrate," on what am I going to concentrate? Concentration implies that there is an object in which the actor is interested. The concentration in which he tries to have faith in order to begin to act is only make-believe. That approach leads to phony concentration. True concentration implies a real object, one that impels concentration from the actor—that kind of concentration always works.*

To Actor J: You, for example, are constantly making an effort to see the thing outside the window, but you never quite see it. I never know whether it convinces you or not, whether you do see something or whether there are some things you can't see. You always behave as if "I don't have to work, because I know what I'm supposed to see." Well, anybody can do it that way:

---

* Concentration comprises several kinds of attention. Involuntary attention results from an objective stimulus and requires no effort; this is the kind of attention that characterizes everyday life, and the actor tries to avoid it in acting, where it becomes mere distraction. Voluntary attention requires effort to maintain. Spontaneous attention is aroused by something which has a personal interest or appeal. Concentration in acting is a combination of voluntary and spontaneous attention.

"I don't see a damn thing. I just see the crisscross things on the window. I'm not making any effort, but since I have an idea of what I should be seeing, I don't need to do anything else." No. If you have to see something outside the window, you have to make an effort to do so. (*Demonstrating.*) At this moment I have to see the Statue of Liberty outside the window. All right. I have to decide exactly how high I am going to see it within the first two panes there. But my concentration is a little blurred, because the middle section of the window for some reason attracts my eyes, and I cannot now see the Statue of Liberty out there. I would like to create for myself the Statue of Liberty outside that window, but my eyes keep going back to the middle section. Thus, even though I do not succeed in putting the Statue of Liberty outside the window, I do begin to make an effort to deal with my concentration. I really try to see if I can bring alive to myself what I wish to see. Maybe I get it, and maybe I don't.

What you do is to define the object, but your thought never goes beyond thought. Concentration on an object implies believing in it, seeing it so precisely that you really do become convinced, so that the senses come alive as they do in life when you see a real object. In life the object is really there, and seeing it is enough to bring my senses and emotions alive and to make my imagination work. But you merely define the objects in your mind so that they belong to a logical sequence. That is not true concentration. Those objects do nothing to you. You do something to them.

To Actor K: On the other hand, while you have physical relaxation, your mental attitude toward your concentration is, "Do it or else." But our senses don't work that way. For example, in the exercise, you worked to get the sensation of putting soap on your hands. You held your hand in a particular way to try to get the feel of the soap, but obviously you weren't getting it. Although you have put soap on your hands hundreds of times in life, here, when you have no actual soap, you have difficulty in creating the sensation. But if you are not getting the sensation in one way, you should try other ways. You should say to yourself, "Wait a minute. Do I have the weight of it at least? Do I have the shape of it? What have I got? Wait a minute. I have a little something there. Now I'm getting a little something. I don't know quite what I'm getting. Well, I'm getting the shape now." Thus, you try to get the feeling of an actual bar of soap. Your concentration was in fact very strong, but you put your hand over the imaginary soap as if you were saying to your senses, "Either you'll do it my way, or you won't do it." That kind of ultimatum causes the senses to function only halfway. In order to work fully, the senses must always feel partly free to do or not to do, to be or not to be. Senses you are not thinking about often work unconsciously for the actor, but they do not work if you are too set upon getting the exact thing about which you are thinking. If you do not try too strenuously to feel the weight of the soap, you may not get the weight, but you may get the color or the shape or the odor, or even the peculiar wetness or "soapiness" of a bar of soap. Although you are free from physical tension, I see a battle of will between you and the senses. But there should be no war or competition. Your senses are perfectly willing to work for you if you appeal to them in the right way. The process of appealing to the senses is like boring a hole. The drill must go round and round. If you pound on it like a nail, it sticks and won't go in.

As soon as I ask myself simple questions to which I do not know the answers, I am forced to spend effort and attention. "Here is a table. Concentrate!" Well, it's an ordinary table. What should I concentrate on? That kind of generalized approach cannot lead to concentration. But concentration begins as soon as I say, "Now, wait a minute. How wide is the table this way? How much is the width the other way? How tall is it? These legs are how much? They're about three inches wide at the top—I think. I'm not quite sure. It may be less, but I would say at least three inches. But it may be more. They seem to narrow down to about an inch and a half at the bottom. Wait a minute. Maybe a little bit more. The height is about thirty inches, but not the over-all height, just to the top of the legs." As soon as I ask myself questions, the answers to which I do not know, I am thus encouraged really to look and really to think, and true concentration ensues.

True concentration always works. Even though I may not be particularly interested in the object at this moment, nevertheless the concentration will work. The actor may look a little bored or tired, but his concentration will not thereby be less. Its quality may be less energetic or emotional or involved. Yet if the concentration is rightly approached, it always works.

The object and the concentration that results from attention to it is the basic building block with which the actor works. It is a basic unit in the same way that the notes of a piano are the basic units of the pianist's art. The pianist always gets the note he wants when he places his finger on the appropriate key of his instrument. The objects on which the actor concentrates similarly work and thereby produce a sense of belief and of faith and involvement in what he is doing, and this in turn leads to unconscious experience and behavior.

Objects are, of course, of different kinds. They can be imaginary physical objects. Or they can be remembered sensory objects like the feeling of heat or cold or the quality of a particular sound. These are nonmaterial objects on which the actor can concentrate, and thus he can actually re-create on the stage the sensation that they originally produced. Objects can be mental or thought objects, or fantasy objects. They can be situations, or events, or relationships, or characters—or elements of these things—as created by the playwright. Through concentration the actor brings these things alive for himself.

There does tend to be more reliability in a real object as opposed to a fantasy object in repetition. Real objects tend always to induce belief. They produce true concentration—if they work at all. The actor must remember that these various kinds of objects or devices for concentration are needed only because he cannot depend on one magic key to unlock every scene. Especially when he knows that the scene must somehow be "big," but he doesn't know what to do, the actor uses objects instead of attempting an inflated, vague, general approach that merely confuses him. The properly trained actor learns to depend not just on technique or approach but on a variety and sequence of objects. He has more than one string to his bow.

The definition of an object can never be absolute. What serves one actor's concentration will not work for another. A simple material object may serve at one moment, while a more complicated nonmaterial object may be required at another. The reliability of an object depends not only upon the degree to which it works for a particular actor in a particular situation but upon whether or not it works whenever it is required to do so. An object that works at only three performances out of eight can scarcely be considered reliable. Also, an object that serves an actor's concentration in one play may not work in another. That which convinces the actor in one characterization may not do so in another. However, once the actor has been trained so that his senses respond readily to imaginary objects or stimuli, he is then equipped to search out for himself the particular objects that will serve to arouse true concentration in an imaginary situation created by the playwright.

We believe that concentration is fostered by exercises dealing with objects in sense memory, that is, without the actual objects' being there. This process begins with such simple tasks as seeing the Statue of Liberty outside a window, washing the hands with soap and water, combing the hair, or putting on make-up. We know that these simple exercises arouse and focus the actor's impulses, that they actually engender the actor's faith in his ability to respond to properties or elements that are not physically present.

In these elementary exercises, the actor does not try to imitate an action or to convey his reactions to the audience. Rather, his effort goes toward recapturing the stimuli and the muscular efforts involved in such ordinary acts as putting on shoes and stockings, picking up a cup and saucer, listening to a familiar composition, or tasting a lemon. The actor has encountered these simple realities many times in his everyday experience. They are clear and objective and unemotional. No profound insight or act of imagination is required. And yet working with these simple realities increases the capacity of the actor's imagination to deal with the far more difficult and complex realities that he must customarily face on the stage. They test whether the actor will ultimately have difficulty in creating emotional and other realities which can never be present except through his imagination.

Many tasks which the author calls on the actor to perform—to die or to murder someone—have no counterpart in the actor's everyday existence. These realities are never actually created on the stage, but a sense of their taking place is conveyed to the audience by the actor's *imaginative* use of his various mental, physical, sensory, and emotional resources. This means, in effect, that the actor uses concentration on objects to achieve these desired results, because only concentration will unlock all these resources and place them at his disposal. Thus, elementary exercises in sense memory have as their goal the actor's ultimate possession of his essential equipment—the kind of sensory apparatus able at will to act out an event.

Every human being has sensory memory. In some people it easily leads to strong responses. In others it works less easily. Exercises in sense memory using objects that have a real, material existence, such as soap and water, cause the actor to grow more aware in life, and this leads to his growing more aware in memory, which in turn leads to his senses' becoming more responsive. The senses are thus trained to remember more and to remember more vividly, and they respond to the actor's concentration more vividly. But if the actor tries to by-pass the work with material objects and to proceed immediately to objects such as pain, which involve only memory, he will find that the sense memory is not really trained. He will have no objective means of judging the effectiveness of what he is doing. Instead he will remember what he remembers, but what he doesn't remember will simply not be recalled. He will be no better off than before.

On the other hand, while I do not mind the actor's occasionally bringing to class a few actual properties to stimulate his imagination toward the fictitious realities he has to create, too many such actual objects have an opposite effect. They simply make him dependent on them. They become the reality and thus fail in their purpose, which is to incite in him a belief and a far greater reality than can be created on the stage by any medium other than the actor himself.

If the actor wants to bring a kettle from home because it has a special, definite meaning which makes it real to him, that is fine, but I do not want a prop kettle. I want to see his imagination work with a kettle that has some meaning for him. I want to see him bring it alive. That is the actor's job. He brings nonexistent things alive on the stage. He first makes them real to himself in order to convey that reality to the audience.

Prop kettles and other literal objects not only stop the actor's training by blocking real imagination, but make him revert to ordinary, literal habits of behavior. In life those habits do not matter too much. In life we are surrounded by real objects which continuously stimulate our emotion and unconscious expression. On the stage there are no real objects—except these literal stage properties—and thus there is no strong and real continuity outside the actor to bring him alive. If we rely only on these literal objects, we tend unconsciously to use literal habits of expression. The very thing we are trying to create dies, because after all it is not actually real. It can only be made real by the kind of concentration which it is the peculiar power of the actor to employ.

> In the very early stages of training his concentration, the actor must do the exercises again and again until they have been mastered. Strasberg does not permit an actor in training to tackle a more difficult task until he has laid the proper foundation for it.
>
> Strasberg's private classes follow a logical progression, from the recall of simple, habitual, and external sensory experiences to exercises that begin to explore the individual's emotional re-

sponses. For the first exercise Strasberg specifies the actor's regular breakfast drink, such as coffee or orange juice. The second exercise begins to awaken the actor's awareness of himself as a physical object: girls put on make-up and men shave, but the essential is seeing oneself in the mirror. The third exercise— sunshine—again uses an external stimulus, and the fourth— sharp pain—tests the actor's ability to re-create a sensation that does not derive from an external source. The fifth, sixth, and seventh exercises deal successively with sharp taste, sharp smell, and seeing or hearing. The kinesthetic sense is tested by a rather complex exercise, number eight—taking a shower or bath— in which the actor can experience over the entire body such sensations as hot or cold water, the feel of soap, or the feel of getting dressed or undressed. Any sensory exercise may result in emotional response, depending on the previous conditioning of the individual actor, but the ninth exercise is the first of the series that seeks emotional response directly: the actor must find a physical object that has some marked personal association or meaning. In the tenth exercise the actor works on two objects —one inner and one external—simultaneously. The eleventh exercise, the private moment, is described later in this chapter* and is used only to help actors who are not responding satisfactorily to the earlier exercises. The final exercise, which has no fixed content, deals with individual problems in the area of emotional response by beginning to work with the technique of affective memory.**

This kind of systematic training is, however, more characteristic of Strasberg's private classes than of his work at the Studio. In the Studio he generally deals with problems of exploration, of expanding the actor's capacity, of challenging him to use himself more fully. This is done most frequently through improvisatory work on scenes rather than in pure exercises. Also, work at the Studio is initiated by the members rather than by Strasberg as a teacher. Nevertheless, the Studio member's problem is often revealed as a lack or loss of training at the most elementary levels. He has difficulty doing even very simple

---

* See pages 114-19.
** See pages 107-14.

things on the stage. Many such members have undertaken work in Strasberg's private classes, although a few have been able to carry out this training work in the actual Studio sessions, and some of the older members have held special exercise classes for the younger ones. But the Studio's special conditions make it difficult to train the rank beginner systematically—no matter how talented he may be.

All the early concentration exercises are performed individually, from using well-defined objects such as shoes and stockings to less well-defined objects such as heat or cold or pain, through putting two objects together, such as listening to music while combing the hair. The actor may work individually on a scene based entirely on sensory elements, such as a person's poisoning himself. In "The Art of the Actor" Strasberg describes an even more complicated type of scene built around the actress's creation of cold, fever, hunger, warmth, and night.* Finally, the single actor is asked to create a situation based on sensory objects which the teacher arbitrarily changes during the exercise. For example, a person who is preparing a tête-à-tête meal receives word that his guest will not arrive, and he must finish preparing the food just for himself.

Meanwhile, as the actor's concentration develops and he becomes more proficient in using objects, he starts exercises with other actors. The very first thing that two actors learn together is to "start from where they are"; that is, they are encouraged to assume that they are "real." Their concentration then goes on to what each is really doing, thinking, and feeling; thus they immediately lose their self-consciousness with each other. These group exercises then proceed from simple scenes based largely on sensory objects (an eating scene), through scenes in which each actor must create a simple, but individual, relationship to a central situation (a dinner at which one guest is hungry, another bored, a third drunk, a fourth impatient); to scenes in which each actor creates a character based on a single, carefully defined characteristic (a committee luncheon with one member very elderly, another chronically ill, a third morbidly suspicious). Finally, the actors do an exercise in which they de-

---

* See page 68.

vise a situation that is dramatic in nature, but which has no fixed outcome. Each actor tries to create for himself a sense of who he is, what has happened to him previously, what his special characteristics may be, and what his relationship is to the present situation. Thus, the actor's concentration is gradually attuned not only to simple objects but to the more complicated objects of situation, character, and event.

Another individual exercise, which Strasberg first encountered in Maria Ouspenskaya's class at the American Laboratory Theatre, is usually employed after the actor completes the group exercises. This is the animal exercise.

The animal exercise has a simple training result. The actor, when he comes to play a character, usually says, "Well, he's a man; I'm a man," and therefore behaves as himself, without trying to find out the differences between himself and the character, just as many of the girls, when they come to play Juliet, say, "I'm Juliet," and when they come to play Lady Macbeth, say, "I'm Lady Macbeth," and then go ahead and merely say the words in the play. But when you say, "Play an animal," immediately the actor says, "How can I? I'm not an animal." He is then forced to use observation to single out the qualities of a particular animal, and to find out how he, the actor, can accomplish them. Thus he learns that he can and must accomplish much more as an actor than what he initially conceives as the simple embodiment of feelings and responses.

Because he has to choose definite elements in order to create the animal, he finds that the exercise becomes an entrance into the problem of physical characterization. He varies his normal being, takes on characteristics he does not normally have—in walk or ryhthm or behavior or attitude. The exercise thus gives the actor elements he would have difficulty finding as vividly within the human sphere as he can more or less easily in the animal sphere.

Another stage of the exercise passes over into the area of emotional training. Here the actor uses the emotional or mental rather than the physical characteristics of the animal. However, the animal exercise is basically used to help the actor learn to control his muscles, so that he is capable of completely carrying out purely unemotional tasks. Such tasks have to be done by muscular control. They cannot be done by feeling.

> The exercises that have been described so far train the actor's concentration perhaps more than his fantasy or impulse. However, other exercises are aimed at increasing the actor's "mental, physical, and emotional agility." They emphasize the impulsive element of imagination through forcing the actor to improvise in such a way that he cannot rely on conventional or habitual patterns.

In the Group Theatre we did a lot of work to show the actor what he can do in imagination with a scene, or even with a word. When we were working on *Men in White*, we did two exercises, one right after the other. The first was for mood, for the specific mood or rhythm of the operation scene in the play. To stimulate ourselves we did it with the second movement of the Beethoven *Seventh Symphony*: dum dum da dum dum, da-da dum, da-da da dum dum. You know? We did the scene in pantomime with objects of concentration, but with an operation—unlike the one in the play—in which the patient died. It was very sad and moving. Immediately afterward the same actors did the second exercise, which was a *commedia dell'arte* version of the same scene. The actors cut the patient apart and sewed him together again, and after they sewed him together, they found that all the instruments were inside. Neither exercise had any direct connection with what was actually done in the play, but they helped to stir the actors' imaginations and thus to enable them to get behind the words of the play and into the event that was taking place.

Another exercise, the one-word improvisation, is usually done with a single individual. It is an exercise for an immediate impression rather than a sequence. You give the actor a word and a minute of time. At the end of a minute he is supposed to act out the word in pantomime, not naturally, but sharply, vividly, and theatrically. Sounds can be permitted, but not words. The idea is to encourage the actor's body somehow to develop a clear idea of things.

I remember vividly two of the one-word improvisations that were done in the Group Theatre. The word was "America." One was done by a girl who got up and did the Statue of Liberty. That seemed rather ordinary, but it was all right, and she held it for a while, and suddenly—the light in the Statue of Liberty began to come down little by little, and the torch turned into a cocktail glass, and the Statue of Liberty got a little bit drunk. That was "America."

The other improvisation was one of the early playwriting efforts of Clifford Odets. He is asleep. Suddenly the alarm rings. He gets up. It's late. He gets dressed very quickly, rushes out, rushes into the subway, pushes his way into the train, rushes out, rushes into his office, takes his coat off, puts everything in place, gets set, sits down in the chair—and then leans back and takes out a cigar. That, too, was "America."

The one-word improvisation trains the actor's imagination to perceive possibilities of thought and meaning and to be stimulated to immediate behavior. The exercise forces the actor in this direction, because it can only be carried out by behavior.

Another kind of improvisation used in the Group Theatre was designed to show that any statement can be made to mean anything, depending upon the circumstances that surround it and the characterization that is brought to it. Words do not have as fixed a primary meaning as we customarily assign to them. The same words in different situations and spoken by different characters wind up having totally different meanings. This exercise develops the actor's imagination by showing him that words derive their meaning from what the actor is doing. Bobby Lewis, for example, took the words of "I Sing the Body Electric," Walt Whitman's famous song of love to man's body, and he did a little clerk who is always cold when he gets up in the morning but nevertheless always takes a cold shower. When he got into the shower and said the words of "I Sing the Body Electric," of course the result was completely different from Walt Whitman's intention. It was, in fact, hilarious.

The three-word improvisation is usually done with two people. They are given three words and a minute of time. They go off, and in that minute not only must they choose a basic situation but they must also give to the three words interesting and unusual meanings which are totally different from their ordinary ones. Then they come back on the stage and act out the situation. Obviously neither knows what is going to happen. For example, a girl and a boy are given "candy," "music," and "whisky." They might decide that he is going to assassinate someone, that she is an agent of the FBI, and that "candy" really means "poison," "whisky" "explosives," and "music" "the plan of operations." The whole point is to learn to see behind words, to learn not to think of words as a safeguard, but always to look for imaginative comprehension which will extend the actor's own avenue of thinking. The improvisation trains the actor's willingness to act without knowing the end result and at the same time to permit fantasy. The actor's imagination is trained to perceive possibilities of thought and meaning.*

EMOTIONAL WORK

All the training up to this point has been concerned with preparing the actor's instrument for the requirements of emotional work. Obviously, a great deal of acting is concerned with emotional response, but Strasberg is careful to point out that much is also nonemotional, and to insist that nonemotional must precede emotional work in a proper course of training. However, at the proper time the actor is permitted to start working on affective memory.

Mrs. Siddons had a husband and children. She had to feed them and to perform other family obligations in addition to acting, so the only time she had left to work on her parts was late at night

---

* See also Strasberg's description of the gibberish exercise, pages 213-15.

when everybody else went to sleep. Sometimes she would start at midnight, and, because there was no other place, she would go up into the attic. So when she started to work on Lady Macbeth, that's where she went. She later described how she started to read Lady Macbeth's lines late at night in that quiet attic and how she became scared. The lines took possession of her. Something happened to her. Suddenly she started to run out of the attic, and as she started to run, the candle went out. She was petrified. And that, she said, is how she learned to play Lady Macbeth.

Edmund Kean said that when he played Hamlet, which was not one of his good parts, in certain passages he had to seek excitement outside the lines of the play, because in those passages Shakespeare's words and situations did not move him. However, there was one moment that always worked for him, and that was when he picked up the skull of Yorick. Tears would always come into his eyes. And he loved that moment, as an actor loves, because it meant something special to him. Every time he picked up the skull of Yorick, he thought of his own uncle who had first introduced him to Shakespeare and had taught him to act. And therefore, he said, that moment always worked.

But he never drew conclusions from that experience. He never sought the law of how a human being responds, so that he could use it at moments when the play didn't work for him naturally and unconsciously and, therefore, when he needed it most. Actually, as we go through the history of acting, we can find loads and loads of such wonderful experiences, which show that actors of the past clearly understood how the proper responses could be aroused. But they always found this out play by play. They never asked themselves, "How can I carry on what I found here into the next play?" The discovery of how that can be done is, of course, the great and abiding contribution of Stanislavski.

An actor may work on the emotions in a play unconsciously. They may come to him easily without any conscious work, but the fact remains that tomorrow night he has to repeat them. The purpose of doing emotion on the stage is not to do it once. The actor must be able to repeat it at will.

Affective memory is not mere memory. It is memory that involves the actor personally, so that deeply rooted emotional experiences begin to respond. His instrument awakens and he becomes capable of the kind of living on the stage which is essentially reliving. The original emotional experience can be happy or frightening or fearsome. It can be concerned with jealousy or hate or love. It can be illness or accident. It can be anything that your mind immediately goes to when you ask yourself, "Has anything strange, unusual, or exciting happened to me?" If your mind does not immediately go to such an experience, that is usually a sign that the experience has taken place but is built into the unconscious mechanism and doesn't like to be remembered. Such things happen to human beings all the time, especially when we are young. They condition our subsequent behavior through the rest of life.

If the actor is just starting to use affective memory, it is wise to go back at least seven years to find emotional experiences. In fact, the farther back the memory goes, even to childhood, the better it functions for the actor. The older the pattern of conditioning, the greater its tendency to function continuously and without change. And the closer the experience in time, the greater is its tendency to change with use on the stage.

Emotional response induced by affective memory cannot be determined in advance. A human being does not function with machine-like precision. The actor must explore the original experience abstractly—as an acting exercise—and see what will happen. Sometimes nothing happens; although the actor remembers the experience, it did not actually make the kind of impression he thinks it did. Sometimes when the actor thinks that not much is going to happen, a lot happens. He has to find these things out by experiment. We never permit ourselves to say, "I don't remember." We make the effort, because very strong things have usually happened to a person who says, "No, nothing has happened to me." He has merely tended unconsciously to put them aside. They are often stored up in secret, but the actor must learn to face them, because it is only through himself that he can experience on the stage.

The important thing in using affective memory is to maintain one's concentration, not on the emotion, but on the sensory objects or elements that form part of the memory of the original experience. This is why the actor must master the concentration exercises in sense memory before he attempts work in emotional memory. In affective memory you try to see the people that you saw. You try to hear the things that you heard. You try to touch now the things that you touched then. You try to remember through your senses what your mouth tasted and what you wore and the feeling of that garment against your body. The emotion you try not to remember at all.

To ACTRESS L: If you say, "I remember standing in a room when that experience happened to me," that implies that your feet touched something. What did they touch? Can you remember what part of your foot touched what type of carpet? Can you remember the feeling that carpet injected into your foot? "Standing in a room" implies a room. Is there a light? Can you see where it is coming from? Can you see a pattern that it throws on the wall? Can you see the color of the wall? Can you see various objects in the room? If you can't see a particular thing that you remember was there, don't worry. Go on to the next object, but make a determined effort to see that. "Standing in a room" may mean, "I remember wearing a dress. It itched in the back. I was hot. I was sweating, and the sweat ran down just here, and at that point it itched. I remember the way it itched right there." You must go on trying to recall and re-create the sensory objects and realities of yourself and the room in which you stood. If nothing emotional happens, you should not worry about it. But if the experiment works, you can say to yourself, "This is one of my golden keys."

Out of a hundred affective memory experiments six may work,

although all may work to some extent. But some emotional conditionings are permanent, and the conditioning strengthens with time. When an affective memory seems to wear out, that results almost invariably from the actor's anticipation of what should happen. He pushes too energetically toward the objects, and tension intervenes between him and the emotion.

If that happens, we ask him to sit down, to relax, and to go through the affective memory. It then works. Once an affective memory has worked, it is theoretically capable of working always.

However, even if the actor performs the affective memory correctly, it may not work the first time. This means that a counter-conditioning has somehow taken place, and the original experience has lost some of its emotional force. Moreover, the emotional value of the experience may have changed. You may start by remembering a happy experience and wind up weeping because the happiness is now gone. You may remember something sad which suddenly strikes you as a joke. Nevertheless, by attempting a lot of affective memories, the actor gradually obtains a stock of memories that are permanent and become easier to invoke as he continues to use them.

After the actor has discovered an affective memory that is really serviceable, he still faces the problem of bringing it into the scene he is playing. He must fuse his personal emotion with the character and event he is portraying. For example, when the actor's partner is speaking, he listens and answers naturally, but at the same time he tries to concentrate on the objects of his own event and thus to fuse his material with the author's. The actor will find as he goes on, especially if he does not have lines, that the memory process becomes faster so that the performance of the affective memory actually takes no more than two minutes. In the Group Theatre, where we worked with affective memory in production, we would set a definite amount of time. We would allow the actor a minute before the emotion was needed to carry out the affective memory. When an emotional response was needed at a point in the middle of a scene, the actor knew that he had to start the affective memory sixty seconds before and that the emotional reaction would be ready exactly on cue.

Vakhtangov has described affective memory as basic to an understanding of the entire process of reality in acting. The common understanding of such reality supposes that the actor says, as it were, "Hit me. Come on, hit me, so that I feel anger toward you. Really do something to me, so that my response will be real." But that is not acting. Anybody when hit will feel a response; that is depending on real emotion, and real emotions are undependable on the stage. They vary. The actor doesn't quite know what they are. Vakhtangov said, "We never use real, that is, literal emotion in art, only affective memory emotion, only remembered emotion." Only remembered emotion can be controlled. The emotional things used in the craft of acting are things that can be remembered, because that offers a way of repeating them. They preserve the actor's performance from being accidental. Remembered emotion, which has continuity and logic and therefore can be dealt with, is the only emotion that can be the basis of art. Wordsworth called it "emotion recollected in tranquillity." Somebody else said that a thing must lie in the mind until the memory cools before it can be used in art. Vakhtangov summed it up for the actor by saying that all emotion in acting is affective memory emotion—true and real, but not literal.

If the actor tries to push the emotion or give it a helping hand, before he knows it his acting is all tension. The emotion is gone. Emotion is caused by itself and continues in the way that water continues if you open the faucet.

Emotion is like a little child. If you go toward it too quickly, the child will run away. So you take out a lollipop and say, "Oh, I just bought myself a nice lollipop." The child will stop. You then say, "You like a lollipop? I have another one." Little by little the child will edge toward you. But if you then say, "Come here and take the lollipop," the child is going to run away, because it has to be affected by its own volition. Even when it wants the lollipop, it will say "No!" The child resents being made to do it.

Sometimes an actor tries to impel himself toward the emotion in a scene by directly trying to remember the emotion in some personal experience. We do not want him to do that. The human being cannot compel emotion within himself. Emotion cannot be directly pushed or pulled. It arises as a result of doing a different order of things. For example, a lot of times when we are emotional and try to stop the emotion, we cannot stop it. We have to do other things, take a pill, lie down, take a long walk or a shower—things which ease us and thus exercise an indirect control over the emotion.

If you tell yourself to think of a certain place, you can do that. If you tell yourself to think of a certain event, you can do that. You can even think of yourself at a time when you were emotional, but that will not produce an emotional response. You cannot order yourself to feel a certain emotion, because emotion is brought about only through concentration on the objects with which it is connected. That is the process of life. We like certain places; they have that effect on us without our knowing exactly why. Obviously things must have happened in those places to make us feel that way. Other places have the opposite effect. These are not intrinsically different, but we say, "A-a-ah, I don't like that place!" When people argue, "But that's a wonderful place," we still say, "I don't know. I feel uncomfortable there." Obviously in that place some forgotten thing happened whose memory continues to stir a feeling of discomfort.

Emotional response is conditioned response. It can be evoked by concentration on the factors associated with the particular conditioning process. When you experience emotion in life, it is real. It is part of a real life process. When you approach an emotional passage on the stage, the situation of which it is a part is fictional, a product of fantasy. Therefore the actor feels that he must do something special to create the emotion. His tendency is to anticipate the desired emotional results. He says, "What I want is *this* emotion. Come on, emotion!" And the emotion immediately disappears. No matter how hard he works, nothing happens. But frequently when he stops working, suddenly the emotion is there. In working for emotion the actor must create a sense of "I don't really want the emotion. I don't care whether it happens or not."

Affective memory is the basic material for reliving on the stage and therefore for the creation of experience on the stage. What the actor repeats in performance after performance is not just the words and movements he did yesterday but the memory of emotion, which he reaches through the memory of thought and sensation.

> Exercises for affective memory begin with the actor's verbalizing his remembrance of the sensory objects associated with an emotional occasion. This is done only to test the correctness of the actor's procedure. Then Strasberg asks the student to stop verbalizing his memory, but to continue concentrating inwardly while performing some simple task. This leads to using simple dialogue while trying to retain the affective experience. It is then simply a question of talent and continued work as to how far the actor can go. He begins to use progressively more difficult material so as to expand his ability to fuse himself in all respects, including the emotional, with the role.
>
> However, there are certain actors who have talent and emotional capacity but in whom emotional response—or any true concentration—simply does not take place on the stage. They seem to relax, but never really quite do so. They work very hard. They seem to have no special difficulty in willing the carrying out of prescribed tasks, but their hard work does not pay off. In concentration exercises, they have difficulty "going with the object." They always "act out" the results to a degree. When they attempt an affective memory, whatever response they get is always somewhat conventional and "untrue." And yet these are actors whose talent has impressive possibilities, who have often spent years of arduous labor in training themselves. They do everything that should enable them to act, but they remain deficient in the one essential of good acting—the ability to use oneself.
>
> For this actor Strasberg has devised an exercise that often

produces remarkable results—the "private moment." * This tool enables him to go directly to the unconscious region in which impulse is permitted to become overt. Thus, it deals with the fundamental process of imagination, and also reaches into the next stage of the actor's work, expression.

To some actors with this particular difficulty, Strasberg allows the exercise quite early in his private classes or even in individual work at the Studio. For other actors, especially those few in need of psychiatry, he is adamant in refusing permission to attempt it at all.

The private moment is a variation on concentration exercises I began to use in 1956 and 1957. For certain people I have found it highly useful. It has great value for the actor who has difficulty involving himself completely so as to permit reactions without worrying about acting for the public. For others the private moment has no value. People who love to do things in public have no difficulty in this area, and for them the private moment is senseless. For people who love to do emotional things, the private-moment exercise means continuing to eat sweets when they are already eating sweets. It has no value.

The exercise came from simple logic, and only after I began to use it did I discover its full value. I was rereading Stanislavski's books, and I came across the statement that the basic problem in acting is to learn to be private in public. Obviously I had read that many years ago, but it had made no strong impression. That is truly what we try to develop by the various concentration exercises, but when I reread that phrase—"to be private in public" —it suddenly leaped at me that I had not done something in the exercises which could perhaps emphasize what the exercises were intended to accomplish. I said to myself, "That really is the important thing. I know many actors who develop concentration, and yet the audience never gets the sense of 'going where they are.' These actors are always coming out to join the audience."

---

* See also "the song-and-dance," pages 161-69.

That is the primary difference between two kinds of acting. One kind comes out to you and shows and affects and demonstrates. The other kind demands that you go where it is going. Even when you don't like it and resent what is being done, that kind of acting takes you where it is going. As a result you experience not only joy and pleasure, but the things that the character is experiencing.

Although we have many exercises from Stanislavski, I could not remember any that tried to deal directly with this need to be private in public. So I asked myself, "What would happen if I asked these actors to do something that they do in life, but which even in life is so private that, although they do it and it is real, when anyone comes in, they have to stop doing it? These are people who even in life can be private only in private. What would happen?"

We started to do this as an exercise, and two things happened. The exercise produced wonderful results in the actor's belief in what he was doing, and it led to a releasing of emotion and a degree of theatrical energy I had not previously seen in these particular actors. Somehow the objects of the exercise, drawn as they were from the individual's peculiar privacy, were strong enough to incite this kind of concentration. At the same time the improvisational nature of the exercise left them free to follow through with what they were impelled to do.

We found an additional thing, and this I had not foreseen. People do things in life on a much wider and more vivid scale of expression than they will permit themselves to use on the stage, even at a moment of good acting. People who were inhibited in moving on the stage did private-moment exercises in which they behaved with startling abandon. One girl had worked with me for two years. She had made slow, steady progress, but nothing really happened to her on the stage. Before she came to me, she had worked with practically everybody in the business. For those two years her work was sound and simple, but it was always mental, always precise. It was a banknote that merely looked genuine. Her reality seemed hidden under a veil.

I asked this girl to do a moment of privacy. The first thing she brought in was private and revealing. She did things girls don't like to reveal. She plucked hairs and other things like that. It was private, not too personal, but still personal enough to be a kind of behavior not usually talked about or seen on the stage. Something very good began to happen to her. We saw an aspect of herself totally different from anything she had brought onto the stage before, so we said, "Continue. Think about it."

One day she came in and said she had another private moment, but she didn't know whether she'd be able to do it. I said, "Fine." She brought in a Victrola and a Turkish record she had once used in an exercise. Then she did just a moment of being by herself. She was lying in bed in her room all alone, because she only does this when she's by herself and in a mood everybody gets into sometimes. Then she put on the Turkish music and started to dance. You have never seen such abandon as this girl had on the stage. It was what I call hot dancing, and it was exciting, thrilling, and shocking in the sense that you just didn't think of this kind of thing with that girl. She hadn't seemed that kind of girl.

It acted like a tonic. From then on her work changed. There was a real break in the continuity of her acting. Her voice actually began to alter. Many more vocal colors began to come through. She began really to think on the stage, and the thinking began to take possession of her. We encouraged her to pick scenes in which something like this private moment could be done, and we began to get from her an ease and a fullness of response, and finally in one scene she was going along, going along, going along, and—wham!—she burst out as in the private-moment exercise. Thus we were able to counter her long-induced habits of not expressing as fully as she could what in fact she did feel.

Some actors confuse the private moment with just being alone or just being personal. That is not what we mean. When you are alone, it doesn't follow that you are private. A lot of personal things are not private. We don't mind talking about them or anybody's knowing about them. They are deeply personal, but we don't mind sharing them. We say, "Well, it's difficult to talk about, but sometime I'll tell you." And we do tell. That is personal, but it is not private. We do private things when we are alone, and we know they are really private when we cannot continue them if somebody comes into the room. Whereas if somebody interrupts us when we are doing a personal thing, we become shy or a little embarrassed, but we go ahead and do it anyhow.

A private moment is precise and concrete. The actor watches himself and says, for example, "Well, I have noticed that I have moments when I'm thinking not just about myself, but of this particular thing about myself. When that happens, I usually do this and this—which I would never admit to anybody except in some kind of indirect way. I know this happens to me. Therefore I know that I can do it. I have no difficulty doing it privately."

The actor then takes that kind of experience and follows a simple process. First, he tries to create through sense memory the room in which the private experience usually happens. He tries meticulously to bring his senses alive to the existence of that particular room, hoping to increase concentration and belief in the private *activity* through establishing belief in the *place* associated with it. For that reason we permit him to bring here things from his own private environment—books, records, and other small physical objects. These strengthen his sense of being alone. He tries to create the room until he can say to himself, "That's the couch, and that's the table," until he can see and touch and smell the objects in that room, until the room has for him the kind of reality that any reality on the stage should have.

He then says, "I am going to choose the moment in this room when I think this particular thing about myself, when I worry about my job or my home life or my relationship to people, when I carry on long speeches to people who aren't there, or dance wildly or sing or dress up or undress." He then does that moment as fully as he can, but he does not imitate. The doing is left to happen as easily as it can. He says, "I am going to see how far I can go in that direction. I will not do things that good taste obviously will not permit on the stage, but I will try to get close to my moment of privacy. If I get too close to a part that good taste does not permit, I will walk off stage. I'm not sure I'll reach that point, but if necessary I'll walk off and complete that part off stage and then come back. I will see what will happen. I will see if I can create it here as fully as if I were not being watched."

A made-up privacy would not have the same results, because there would be nothing to encourage the actor unconsciously. But a real private moment consists of something the actor knows he can do, and the real acting problem then consists of whether he can actually do it in public. In the real private moment the fact that the privacy is real stirs and incites the imagination.

The private-moment exercise is particularly useful in training because it obviates questions of interpretation. You cannot say, "You should have done this" or "You should have done that." That would be nonsensical. There is no sequence or plot, only the essential acting problem. We come down to the rock bottom of acting—the conviction of a certain thing and the way it makes the actor behave. It carries Stanislavski's idea into exercise form, and the actor can retain in the public eye a kind of behavior that not only is private, but often exceeds in vividness anything that he would create by ordinary good acting.

ADVANCED TRAINING

Once the actor reaches an ability to respond emotionally, he has arrived at the stage of training where he can begin work on fusing himself in all respects with the role. This is the stage where most of the training at the Studio and in Strasberg's private classes begins.

To enter this advanced training is particularly difficult because the actor must commence by reversing the premise on which he has heretofore worked. In his early training, the actor in effect asks himself—in Stanislavski's formulation—"What would *I* do if *I* were the character in this situation?" *His* senses are invoked. *His* impulses are stimulated. *His* emotional response is sought.

Now he must learn to lend these resources to the role. He must ask himself— in Vakhtangov's formulation—"What would I have to do in order to do what the *character* does in this situation?"

The line between emotional response and fusing the response with that of a character is one of those invisible boundaries the actor must cross. He does not cross it by understanding the idea that he needs to do so. Nor does he cross it by achieving a mental image of the character. He must learn "in the body," and until this is somehow accomplished the actor never moves beyond a certain level of promise.

However, once that invisible boundary has been passed, the actor's training ceases to deal only with himself. It becomes twofold. The actor must concern himself both with evoking his responses and adjusting them to the demands of a role.

THE LOGIC OF THE PLAY

Eventually the actor has to concern himself with mental objects that derive directly from the logic of a particular play. These—like other objects—may or may not produce the necessary response in a particular actor. If they do not, he can resort to various devices suitable for attacking such "moments of difficulty." * But these objects cannot be ignored. The actor's imagination must deal with them in one way or another, because they are the skeleton of the thing he is trying to bring to life.

Every play has a complex unity of logic, but among objects deriving from the logic of a play it is possible to separate and distinguish the logic of previous circumstances, the logic of character, the logic of essential sensory objects, the logic of situation, and the logic of the particular event. Examples of each are given below. However, Strasberg—as always—warns that the logic cannot be mechanical.

The antibiotics seemed to be a wonderful discovery because

---

* See pages 130-42.

they appeared capable of wiping out a number of the serious and widespread illnesses about which we have worried for a long time. Yet they already present problems, because the antibiotics are creating strains of viruses that are not subject to themselves. That is the logic of life. That is real logic, not mechanical logic. A deluge of rain should be great for a place dying for want of rain. Yet the deluge easily becomes a flood, and the very thing that should be great destroys the country. The logic of reality differs from mechanical logic which says, "We have prayed for rain. How can rain be bad?"

In reality each thing has a real manifestation. A real cause has a real relationship to a real result, and that relationship—if not perceived—can play havoc with our understanding.

If the answer to every actor's problem began with the play, there would be no difficulty. What actor ever thinks of anything but the play? What director ever starts work without saying, "This is my interpretation"? If we think mechanically, we suppose that an approach that concentrates on the play should lead invariably to creative, sound, worthwhile, excellent work. It doesn't—not because it can't or shouldn't. The difficulty comes from misunderstanding the relation of actor's work to the scene.

When you ask a great actor about a role that he plays very well, logically he should be able to explain it very well. If he doesn't understand the role, how can he play it greatly? Nevertheless, if you ask a lot of great actors about their roles, they tell you, "I don't know what you're talking about. I don't know anything about relationships. I just go on the stage and act." But if you ask ordinary actors who give bad performances about their parts, they explain in great detail the philosophy and the background and the intention of the play. In the history of the theatre I can remember only one great actor who left a great description of a part. Mrs. Siddons left a brilliant descriptive interpretation of Lady Macbeth—totally different from the Lady Macbeth she really played.

Creation does not come merely from what the actor intends to do. The sources of creation lie in whatever it is that stirs the unconscious and conscious powers of his imagination. That is the real logic of the actor's creative life.

To ACTOR M: We have worked very hard to get you away from what was a terrifying concern with the play when you first came to the Studio. Nothing could be seen except your concern with the scene. Actually, it was not truly concern for the play, but rather with, "What am I going to do to let that damn audience know what I want them to know about the scene?" You have made continuous progress away from that attitude.

Today that progress paid off wonderfully in the first half of this scene. You were really involved. As you sat there, your face changed; that is one of the moments of pure belief I have seen from you. Something was happening. The acting seemed continuous until the moment of outburst. But in the second half there was unconscious reliance on cues, on all the things by which you used to act. After that you didn't quite know where to go, so you decided that the character would just go to sleep. You tried to stick to the cues, because, actually, disbelief in your own logic throws you. The things that bothered you are things in the scene and character that you had not solved. You did not have a sense of your own line. After the outburst you had no solutions.

M: I didn't see any logic.

STRASBERG: You mean you tried to make the best of it. But acting is not a matter of making the best of it. A doctor doesn't try to make the best of it. For any technically equipped individual a problem is a test of his skill.

> The logic of previous circumstances was the issue when Actress N worked on the scene toward the end of *Summer and Smoke* in which Alma Winemiller is finally rejected by Doctor John.

To ACTRESS N: You were sufficiently aware of the problems to make concrete some of the things that would help you, such as watching his house from your house, and watching his situation build up so that this visit from you became necessary. You told us about other people in the play. You showed us through yourself what was happening to him, and therefore what made you come to his office. But you left out what he would have seen if he had been watching *your* house.

What would he have seen? What did you go through before you came to his office in this scene? You had not expected to come here. What had you gone through? You had gone through something quite unusual. You were ill. Is this scene a continuation of the illness? Or have you come out of the illness? It seemed to me that you did not ask those questions.

This girl actually had had a breakdown. For months she sat and did not speak to anyone. She was mentally disturbed, but now she has come out of it. What did she come out of and with what attitude? You did not create in this scene the quality that results from the experience she refers to when she says, "We are weak, but sometimes find the strength to look truth in the face." That's what happened in the illness. She burned up all her previous feeling. She has gone through something and come out purified. She had been quiet and inward, but as she was convalescing, she was looking herself straight in the eye for the first time. That is why she said to herself before this scene begins, "This is what I want, and this is what I must have."

I was aware of the absence of this prior experience from the moment you came on the stage. Even though you were here in his office, it was obvious that the decision to come had not yet been made by you; whereas Alma Winemiller had taken six months to make this decision. There can still be the doubts and worries and concerns which you did wonderfully today, but there must also be the other thing which made her face herself and makes her face him in this scene. I don't know what it is. I don't know whether it's strength or something else. You find out. Your way of doing it, your imagination, your awareness, may be different from anybody else's idea. But what has happened to you before is a vital part of this scene, and that I did not get.

Strasberg discussed the logic of character with Actress O after she had worked on the fourth-act scene of *The Three Sisters* in which Tusenbach tells Irina farewell before his duel:

What does this girl want more than anything in her life? Never mind whether she's young or old.

O: She wants love.

STRASBERG: That's right. This is a girl who is still looking for love. Anybody that still has that is young.

O: But she doesn't really want Tusenbach.

STRASBERG: Please! Forget about that for the moment. The father of the three sisters died some time ago. Some of the life that went on when the father was alive has stopped. Problems of life annoy and involve the sisters, but this girl, the youngest, is looking for love. She is sentimental. She feels there is something like love, that she hasn't found it, that maybe if she didn't give up, she would find it. Unless that quality is created there can be no scene. In order to create a girl looking for love, what would we have to do? You don't have to answer exactly, but you can imply what you would do.

O: She is constantly thinking of that.

STRASBERG: That's right.

O: So when she hears the voice calling, she thinks of Masha and her husband and of Masha's emptiness of feeling—

STRASBERG: No. Don't think of Masha. Only of yourself. Don't worry about the play. I don't want any philosophy. I don't want any mystery stories.

O: She's dreamy.

STRASBERG: Do you know what that means? We've all had that mood in which we walk around and people constantly say, "What's the matter?" Sometimes we say it's spring. Sometimes we say it's something else. That's the kind of quality that has to be created on the stage in order to create Irina; that quality makes you into a person like her, still young, still looking, still dreaming. She's gotten up early in the morning, and people are leaving, and so there's more of a little stir in her heart rather than less, because the moment we give up something and accept something else is the very moment when the first thing gives a dying gasp and flares up before it goes out. Her unconscious mood pervades her being. You need to work for it, because there is nothing in the scene to inspire that directly. Only the things Irina is going to accept are here, not this other thing which she still desires and thinks she is going to give up.

O: It is obvious to me. I always make this mistake. I have that need to deny the obvious thing.

STRASBERG: It isn't simply a matter of denial. It is also a matter of creating.

> "Logic of character" refers both to an awareness of a character's qualities and to the degree of experience needed to produce those qualities. Strasberg discussed this with Actress P after a scene in which she worked on Nicole in *Tender Is the Night*:

This is a very difficult monologue. You proved that by saying you had to leave out some of it because you couldn't find any logic with which to start it. However, the scene that you did in no way carried out your actual knowledge of that scene.

After the scene you told us that this woman is supposed to be a little upset mentally. This monologue is the kind of utterance that comes out of her at moments when she experiences this kind of thing. Now, what did you do to create that? You said, "Well, when she is mentally upset, she has a headache. Therefore, I will give myself a headache." It simply does not follow that having a headache will cause you to be mentally upset. You have to look more imaginatively and find something that will arouse in you some kind of upset. In other words, you stopped too soon. You presented the idea of the problem to yourself, but in your choice of things that might affect your imagination and thus solve the problem you stopped short.

In the scene you actually gave up the headache, not only because your concentration went elsewhere, but also because you
didn't really perceive any logical connection between headache
and mental upset. The headache didn't start anything in you related to mental upset, so the headache actually hindered your
concentration.

Let's see whether you can bring your own imagination alive by
questions. Don't leave that to me. What happens when a person
is alone, and that aloneness starts fears of something being wrong
with her, fears of something she has done to and with somebody
else? You cannot be satisfied to choose a thing like headache to
create a large thing like schizophrenia. The headache helped you
to do something more concretely, but it did not lead to finding a
logical solution. This woman's experience cannot be created in
separate moments. It has to be created from the core, from the
fact that she is, to begin with, in a certain state of mind.

Technically it is sometimes possible, by the choice of one simple
object, to find the key to a whole house. Other times you need
separate keys for each room. Although you may not have the over-
all ability to create the central experience in a scene like this,
nevertheless you have to see the relevance of each separate element to the central experience in order to create them separately.

> The "logic of essential sensory objects" means simply this:
> certain things that are part of the environment of a particular
> event are not emphasized by the author, but they must be cre-
> ated imaginatively by the actor in order to play the scene. Actors
> M and Q illustrated this need when they worked in Heming-
> way's "Three-Day Blow."

This was a good example of a scene which can be worked on
by means of the actual physical objects in it, but both of you left
out one object which is essential because the author himself calls
attention to it. This scene is not called "drinking" or "Scotch" or
"a girl is lost." It is called "a three-day blow." That means the
author—unless he is crazy—is drawing our attention to some-

thing which, if left out, causes the scene to remain just drunkenness. The characters just wobble around, and little else comes over.

You must take the image the author gives us and look for two things. You must try to create people who are stopped from outside activity because of a three-day blow, but you must also try to create the sense of what kind of storm it arouses inside the people. For instance, when you went outside the cabin, I saw no difference between outside and inside. Yet the whole point is that while outside it is stormy, inside it is calm and warm and they get drunk. When they stand outside, it is storming and they get annoyed and aroused at the world. The three-day storm is the author's symbol of what is taking place in the lives of these young people.

I did not get from you the simple sensory creation of the three-day storm. I did not get the boy running through a blow which is more than a little hectic. I did not get the sense of their being constantly surrounded by elemental forces. In Michigan these blows on the lakes come suddenly. Even in Chicago the lake sweeps into the city. I was there once when the lake looked so nice, and suddenly the wind was whipping it up, and the water really went round and round. This is obviously what the author is getting at. These two people are involved in the emotional equivalent of a three-day blow. When they go out to find the father, it's an adventure. They take the guns. They brave the world. They get rid of their aggressive impulses. They get rid of the things that stifled them.

In the scene it seemed as if all the reality was in the cabin, and outside there was almost nothing. Actually it's the other way around. These boys are going to show that they're big. They have more than just young people's problems on their minds, and yet they're treated as just young people. One has had a girl, and that relationship has broken up with a force that for the first time in his life is equivalent to a tragic experience. Superficially this experience seems over. Though the author does not stress it, it is not over; the three-day blow is still there. It is not easy to get over that kind of experience.

By not investigating the physical task of creating the blow, you left out what makes this scene necessary. The fact that it's blowing inhibits their normal activities and encourages other activities, and this makes for the semi-introspective, semi-drunken quality. If you had created this one essential object, it would have led to a greater sense of unconscious drama with both of you—not just to a character scene, but one in which we would have recognized the personal elements as the really germane part of the scene.

When Actor M worked on the first scene of *Liliom* and succeeded in finding a personal logic, as he had not done before, he still did not succeed in dealing fully with the logic of situation or event:

This is the most logical carrying out I have seen you do on the stage. I have not previously seen so great a willingness to abide by whatever logic you were using—regardless of whether it is right or wrong for the scene.

It is true that, in terms of things you had to find, you found perhaps the wrong things in the scene. You left unsolved the basic problem of the transition. Obviously there is something in Liliom and between him and the girl which has never occurred between him and another girl. Equally obviously, the solution lies in something that he feels about himself in relation to his environment.

He knows what he is. He thinks well of himself, but the woman he works for has tied him down. He's got to be there when she calls, and he doesn't like that. He knows that he's a bum. He knows that he takes money from the girls, but something in him wants more from life than that. Yet nobody he meets wants more. When a girl goes out with him, that's what she wants—she wants it now, and she doesn't want anything else. She doesn't care. That's all that people want from him.

Yet here tonight is a girl who doesn't seem to be concerned with that. At first he doesn't believe her when she says she doesn't want the usual thing. Her answers are all wrong. And little by little it grows on him that she is a different girl, that she has a deeper feeling for him and yet somehow is not angling to catch him. The answers she gives are naïve—she didn't stay for that purpose; she stayed for something else; she doesn't quite know what—but they're the real answers for her. She has been locked out. Usually a girl would say, "I've been locked out; it's your fault," but, no, he almost drags it out of her. He came in and said, "You see, I just lost my job on account of you," but the girl doesn't say anything, so that by the time she does say, "I can't go home now anyhow; I've been locked out," he is the one who draws the conclusion that she's lost her job on account of him without saying anything about it.

Something happens in this scene to arouse in him a feeling long dormant, hidden from himself. When he says, "What if I said I'd marry you?" he really means, "You would never marry a guy like me. Even if you would make love to me, you'd never— I mean, I can see the kind of girl you are. You are a respectable girl trying to build a family. You'd never marry a guy like me." But this girl, although at first she responds in a way to make him say, "Uh-huh. That frightened you, huh?" actually says, "No." And you see that something is happening which isn't fright. The whole last part of the scene, all the talk about acacia blossoms, is an effort on his part to describe what he feels—which is something that he has never felt before. In this kind of experience he has no way to speak to a girl.

By speaking of acacia blossoms, they tell each other things they cannot otherwise say. She cannot say, "I love you." She says, "I'm not going to marry; I don't love anybody." He has the same difficulty: "What do you mean, love? Bah! Nobody loves. You get what you can." If somebody asks, "Do you love her?" he never admits it. He always says, "She needs me."

You were aware that you hadn't found the key to the logic of the scene. You picked various objects just to help your belief, whereas you should have sought your belief in the logic of the scene's basic situation, not just in what he does and says. Because you did not do that, you had difficulty, although your behavior was easier, and a simple thing like the headache was done very well.

Some external elements of the character were also missing. You did not need many external elements, because physically he could be big and strong like you. But he's a barker; therefore, the speech, the sound of the voice, the sitting, and the walk would not just be yours. Your own walk comes out of a recognition that you are tall. You try to shorten yourself by not standing up straight. He has to call to people and stands above the crowd and is seen by everybody, all of which colors his behavior. Today the character needed more of those colors.

MOMENTS OF DIFFICULTY

Suppose an actor has spent several years in training. Can he now act? And if he can, is that solely a result of training? Great confusion can arise at this point if Strasberg's basic ideas are not firmly kept in mind. The actor runs the danger of trying to use his training as a "system" of acting instead of using himself as a trained instrument to act.

Strasberg's major premise is that training does not confer talent upon an actor. Training develops talent. It helps the actor to get rid of bad habits. It teaches him ways of controlling his talent. It helps him to develop a personal technique. But technique does not enable the actor to act any more than breath control enables him to breathe. Technique can lead him to real experience on the stage, but that experience springs ultimately from his talent and his human nature, not from the technique itself.

Strasberg has many definite ideas on how the actor can approach a role—some are expounded in Chapter IX—but the "Method" is not a system for acting. It is true that the "Method" offers—in Stanislavski's phrase— "notes for the moment of difficulty," but if the actor has not been thoroughly trained, many

of the devices developed by Stanislavski and Strasberg are useless at these moments.

A variety of devices—of which I cite a half-dozen examples
—should be ready in the trained actor's arsenal for "moments
of difficulty." If he has trouble with a particular emotional response, he can employ an affective memory. If his work on a
role is vague, general, and lacking in belief, he may employ a
personalization or a particularization. A personalization is a
technical device that gives the actor concentration through remembering carefully and concretely an actual person as a model
for the character the actor is portraying, or is talking about, or
is reacting to as played by a fellow actor. In particularization
the actor defines the things that he speaks of so they have for
him the significance that the author dictates.* For example,
Strasberg instructed Actress R in this technique by suggesting
to her a repetition of an exercise based on John O'Hara's
Butterfield 8:

You have chosen ten objects. The behavior involved in each is
relevant to the moment in the play when you wish to use that
kind of reality. You are to discover the reality behind each object.
At home you are to work separately on each of the ten. Take five
hours on each one. Take a whole day. Take a week. Take whatever time is necessary to explore for yourself the kind of reality
involved in each object. From this you come up with material for
the scene.

The next stage is to limit yourself to a definite amount of time
in which to create each object. For example, you may say to yourself, "I will do each thing as much as I can for five minutes."
Perhaps you will give yourself a little more time on the first object
in order to get your concentration going, but once your concentration comes into being you should create each object in no more
than five minutes. For example, if the object is "boredom," you
should be able to create that sense in five minutes. You may use
any sensory elements that you have discovered to have significance

* See pages 125-26.

for you in relation to "boredom," but no more than five minutes should be needed to create that sense. You should work as quickly as you can.

This whole process is like learning to dress as a child. First it takes us hours to get dressed. Later, when we have to go to school, the time begins to be stripped down. We can respond to external cues not set by ourselves. We can make sudden adjustments. You have been taking three quarters of an hour to get dressed. Today you wake up late. You have only five minutes. Well, you make it, and you make it just as well in five minutes as in an hour. Once you are capable of doing whatever has to be done, the timing can easily be accelerated or slowed. But everything depends on finding the elements that will incite the kind of reality or significance that is associated with each of the ten objects.

When you bring the exercise into the Studio, give me a list of the objects numbered one through ten, and a word or phrase that will indicate to me the nature of each—that is, the sense of what it means to you, whether it's dramatic or lyric or just passing the time or dreaming or whatever it is. We will have you do only about five of the objects in the scene. We will give you about ten minutes on the first so as to get started, and then as you go on I will steer you. I may ask you to skip to number eight because something suggests the need for a lyric thing. Thus, I will show you and the audience how putting the objects, whose significance you have thoroughly explored, together with the scene can lead to the staging of the scene.

When the actor has constructed a good foundation and two floors of a building and somebody says, "Let's add another floor," the actor can say, "Fine." The foundation can take it. He can add ten floors if the foundation can take it, but if the foundation cannot take it, even the first two floors will collapse.

Preparation is a technique of concentration for the actor who has a problem of inciting his imagination at the very beginning of a performance or a scene.

Preparation incites in the actor a logic of thought and feeling and behavior so that he is not limited to the conventional tone or characterization that tends to arise from too immediate an expression of what mere words seem to suggest. If the material is dramatic and theatrical rather than merely rhetorical, preparation puts the actor, whether he is playing Hamlet or Macbeth or a character from Thomas Wolfe, into the vital sequence of which these words are a part. Preparation makes sure that the peas go into making the kind of soup you are concerned to make. The purpose of preparation is to help the actor's faith by adding an emotional velocity to the words, and also to create the continuity of behavior characteristic of a living being—a continuity out of which the words of the playwright may logically arise.

Great actors of the past have unconsciously used preparation. When Mrs. Siddons stood in the wings for an entire performance up to her entrance and listened to the other actors, she was using preparation. When Macready chopped wood in the wings before entering as Macbeth, he was using preparation. When Salvini played Othello, he would come to the theatre about six o'clock and walk around inside. Then he would put on a little make-up and walk around some more. Then he would put on part of his costume and walk around again. That is not crazy or stupid. It is a very logical method of getting into a very difficult character.

Nonrealistic actors also feel the need for preparation. In the Japanese theatre the process of preparation is done unconsciously, but nonetheless definitely. The Japanese actors follow a ritual in which the stages of make-up are carefully prescribed and in which they cannot be interrupted. Then come the tea ceremony and prayer and other traditional elements. We can see that these things have little to do with religion but a great deal to do with heightening the actor's concentration, his feeling that "what I am doing is important," that "I have to get rid of my ordinary awareness and acquire a heightened awareness," with his fullness of response and keenness of reaction—all those things that comprise acting on the stage.

Preparation should be kept to a minimum. When the actor is not fully trained, there is no reason why he should not take a long time in a place like the Studio to see what preparation will do for him. If it does good things, he should use it. But as he goes on he should be careful to use less and less time in preparation rather than more and more. Actually the less time employed, the fresher and more spontaneous is the response. The actor should learn not to rely solely on conscious preparation to get into character and the scene. The technique should actually be so quickly and skillfully used that, no matter what the scene, the actor needs no more than five minutes, and actually he should be able to start the preparation two minutes or even a minute before curtain time. However, the actor may unconsciously start the preparation when he enters the theatre and starts to put on his make-up. Thus, a new conditioning is gradually built up quite apart from the conscious technique.

Conscious preparation is especially important when the actor has to enter in a state of high emotion. Too often he assumes that using a lot of energy and tension gives the sense of something happening, but the only thing happening is that he is yelling and screaming and the audience is saying, "We don't know what is going on, but it looks like something must be happening." But if he knows how to excite his imagination quickly through preparation, he has no difficulty coming on the stage sufficiently aroused.

At the Studio, actors who tend toward caricature or stereotype or false theatricality are encouraged by Strasberg to carry out a preparation before the audience. For example, Actor S and Actress O played Richard and Lady Anne in the funeral scene from *Richard the Third* and were asked to do a repetition of the scene preceded by a preparation.

To ACTRESS O: *Take* your time, and do the preparation. Sit in the chair, but bring it out a little so that we can see you. Try to build for yourself the sense of other people being in the scene. Let us see what would happen if you can find the reason why Lady Anne really stops here. What are you really doing in stopping? The emotion you create will feed your mourning for your husband, but the reason for stopping will feed the logic of your behavior.

To ACTOR S: I want you to start in the chair. The chair is for preparation. Once you get up, you have started the scene. The curtain has gone up. When you are in the chair, you can do whatever you want. It's a hot day, and if you've been walking, I don't want you to be— Atta boy! That's what I want. Wait a minute! Wait a minute! I want the hand. I want to know exactly what's wrong with that hand, to what extent there is real disfigurement in the body, what the deformity actually is. Till now you have hidden the hand, and while my imagination worked well, I never knew what *you* were doing.

S: I have taken it that the fingers are like this.

STRASBERG: I know you have taken it, but I am afraid you have taken that first of all because other people take things much more literally than you do, and therefore you have decided to be original. But I'm not sure that in being original you're helping yourself. Later there is a line in which you descant on your deformity. A hand in which the fingers are a little thinner is hardly so deformed as to deserve a whole Shakespearean peroration in which you tell the sun to shine out so that you can see the shadow of your disfigurement as you pass by. I want you to find something to start your sense of yourself working to such an extent that it feeds behavior.

You now come on the stage to do everything for the scene and for your partner and nothing for yourself. You do interesting and good things. We are not trying to rob you of that. But if that is all you do, it means you are serving the food before it is cooked.

One of the actor's greatest handicaps lies in the very fact that he has to do the scene. That is what all his work is for, but too often anticipation enters in. He then finds himself merely doing the scene instead of doing those things that will make the scene possible by propelling him into it. So take your time. I will tap my foot when the scene should start. Take your time. It will give you a good long journey.

> Yet another technique for "the moment of difficulty" is the use of an "action," a device Strasberg described following a scene from Noel Coward's *Private Lives* in which Actress T played Amanda.

Let us say that a director looks at this sort of scene and says to himself, "This is fine, but I would like this actress to give more the sense of a woman concerned with her looks no matter what goes on." He won't quite know why he wants this. He'll know that he wants her to show a little more flair and to be a little more alive, but since he knows she's been trained by Lee Strasberg, he'll be afraid just to say that, because he knows she'll probably answer, "Why? What the hell for? What's my motivation?" and that will put a crimp in him because he really doesn't quite know the answer. So he'll end up by not asking her and by getting sore at her or Lee Strasberg or himself.

How could he present that kind of request to the actor? How can the quality he wants be obtained? In a case like this, instead of arguing with the director, the actor can help him by using an "action." This word is frequently used but sadly misunderstood. People think it means only one thing, a literal paraphrase of the author's words, a synonym for what transpires on the stage or a logical analysis of the scene. But we know that concentrating on the logic of the scene very often does not create the necessary colors. An action that does not differ very much from the conventional or mechanical way of performing a particular task does not add anything. Actions are valuable only when they define areas of behavior which otherwise the actor would not create.

For example, if I were the director, I could say to T that her action at the beginning is to find out whether she has changed too much to get her former husband back. That is an action. It has nothing directly to do with the words of the scene. It doesn't come from the words. She would never play it unless it was deliberately given to her, unless somebody, for example, says to her, "Until you pick up the telephone, your action is to find out how much you have changed, to find out whether you can stack up against the young girl he has picked, to find out what you would have to improve in your looks to make on him the impression you want." That is an action.

An action is a deliberate activity, although not every action is as physical as concentrating on your looks; some actions involve only thinking. Some of *this* action must involve thinking, about yourself, about how good you are in certain areas of life, how much of that has changed since the old marriage, how dull the new marriage has been, how much you have or have not enjoyed that sort of thing with the new husband, and how much you used to enjoy that sort of thing with the old one. You have to be thinking how the old husband must be missing a good deal of that, and how he won't be getting that from just anybody that comes along.

But along with that thinking, the action must involve a real examination of yourself. You must really look to see how much you've changed, to see how your dress looks, so that, when you are saying the author's lines—"My God, I think I'm dying. Oh, my nerves are going. If I don't get out of this, I think I'll—" you would really be doing things derived from the action, things which are completely outside the words.

If the director merely says, "Just be concerned with yourself," it implies that the actress should do something mechanical or artificial without knowing why she is doing it. An action gives her some real thing to play and to think about. It gives the director the quality he wants, a quality the actress would not create except in the most accidental way.

Occasionally the director can give the actress an action by establishing for her the circumstances from which the flair or aliveness he seeks can proceed. He may say, "Let's do an improvisation in which you are getting dressed the night after the second marriage. I won't tell you what to do. I'll just say that last night you found out that the second husband wasn't quite as good as you thought he was going to be and you don't know whether it was because you didn't arouse him, or because of something else. You are now in this scene with your first husband trying to find out." That improvisation of an entirely fictional given circumstance would impel her toward an action without the director's even having to tell her what the action is. Thus, the idea of action is at times an important clue to problems which otherwise the actor could not define because the lines themselves do not lead to them.

Each of the techniques so far explained—affective memory, personalization, particularization, preparation, and actions— when used in a "moment of difficulty" is actually an application of the Vakhtangov formula, "What would I have to do in order to do what the character does in this situation?" The last technique to be explained differs in that it derives from the Stanislavski formula, "What would I do if I were the character in this situation?"

Sometimes the actor finds himself in one of two difficulties. He has tried everything, and yet his imagination does not work. Or he does not know what to try, and therefore he cannot start to trigger his imagination. Both difficulties are remedied by a similar process. When the actor has tried everything fruitlessly, Strasberg recommends that he "start from zero." When the actor does not know what to try, Strasberg recommends that he "start from where he is."

To ACTRESS U: Working without knowing is not necessarily an unwise or wrong thing for actors. On the contrary, Stanislavski advises that very thing at certain moments of difficulty, moments when the actor is doing all the correct things, when he feels that the actions are in the right places and the adjustments are appropriate and he has prepared himself and the part is all worked out—but it doesn't go. The actor has done everything that he should do, and yet the part is dead. At such a moment Stanislavski advises the actor, "Forget about it. Don't do anything. Just sit for five minutes. Start from zero, and then try to be logical, simple, and direct."

Whenever you come to a play, a lot of thoughts go on. You are not an empty vessel. You have picked up a lot of ideas, a lot of things you wish to do, a lot of things you know about the relations between a man and a woman. In a scene like this all of those things can and do feed your imagination; therefore, you need not be too worried about feeling dead at this moment—so long as you are making the effort to make contact with your partner, so long as you are trying to carry out the logical behavior of this character. The result of leaving yourself alone will very likely be the freeing of the unconscious mechanism which will begin to pour forth all the material that has accumulated.

To ACTOR M: When you do a scene, you tend to be concerned both with what you are doing on the stage and with the audience's response. We are trying to engender in you a sense of being completely involved so that you cease to be thrown by audience response. Of course, nothing wipes out the audience. The actor is never unaware of the audience, but at least it should not throw him so that he is unable to do what he is doing to the full extent of which he is capable. The exercise was in this sense not bad, except that you were thrown on some of the minor sensory tasks that have to be created.

M: It was my fault. I did the whole thing in a purely superficial manner.

STRASBERG: A little bit so, but not as much as you pretend.

M: I wasn't really thinking about the things that I had set. I wasn't able to think real thoughts.

STRASBERG: Now, wait a minute. There's no such thing. There is no such thing as "I couldn't relax enough to think real thoughts." You can always think real thoughts, even if you only think, "Gee, I can't think of anything at this moment." We can overcome any "insoluble" problem so long as we face the fact that it is not insoluble.

If we come on the stage and say, "At this moment I'm supposed to be jealous, and I'm trying now to think of the thing I'm supposed to be jealous of. Well, goddammit, I can't think of it. Jesus Christ! Why the hell can't I think of it? I can think of it at other times when I don't even want to think of it. I get jealous. What's the matter with me now? Why at this moment am I not really jealous? What is it? Is it that I'm thinking about the audience, that I'm worried about the audience? Or am I shy? Or am I embarrassed?" As you start to think of these things, you will find that you will thereby become able to think, because you are starting off on the basis of the reality that you have.

If I sit down at a piano and hit a note, and the note is bad, and I say, "Gee, that key is bad; I have to fix that piano," I am assuming a perfectly proper attitude. If I do not fix that piano, I can never make that note better. Anybody coming in and seeing me concerned thus with the bad note would conclude that I was acting perfectly logically. However, if I sit down at the piano, and the note is bad, and everybody knows that it is bad, but I say to myself, "Gee, that note is bad. I can't help it. I'm stuck," and I keep playing, everybody will start laughing and say, "He doesn't know the note is bad. He doesn't know not to play it. He's just fake," and I therefore demean myself in their eyes. But if I say, "What the hell is the matter with this note? Who the hell fixed that piano? Oh, the hell with it, I'll play anyhow," that attitude will register with the audience as plausible: you cannot at this moment fix the piano.

If the actor is not even aware that something has to be fixed and therefore cannot go through some normal process of dealing with it, he becomes unreal, unconvincing, illogical. He acts in a false sense rather than in our sense, which is creation on the stage of logical steps and believable sequences, not only in terms of what the character is doing but in terms of that leaven of belief and experience which the actor actually has at that particular moment. Doing and belief must fuse, and in every art and craft they do fuse.

If I am a violinist, and I am playing, and the string slips, and

I blow up in the performance and don't fix the string, people say, "What's the matter with him?" If I go on playing that way, I lose that audience. But if I correct the string as soon as I have a chance, the audience says, "Something slipped. That is perfectly plausible." That is what we mean by the actor's learning on the stage to "start from where he is." Without that knowledge the actor becomes only a fake, an unbelievable thing. We see two things that do not fuse, as in color printing when two plates are not properly superimposed and we see two outlines where we are only supposed to see one.

The important thing is not that the fusion should always be perfect. Perfection is a goal that is rarely achieved. But at the moment when the goal is not achieved, the actor must know that, and correspondingly make that effort which thereby makes him superior to the audience. But if the audience is aware that he has not achieved the fusion but behaves as if he had, then they see that he is a false actor, that he is doing something that is not believable, not convincing either to himself or the audience.

If the actor thinks always in terms of perfection, he will invariably be led only toward an imitation of things, because imitation is the only way he can invariably repeat something in exactly the same way. But if he is not afraid to start from a moment of "Here I am. I'm trying to concentrate, and I'm not concentrating. Where am I tense? Where am I relaxed? What should I do now?" then he begins from the actual moment of reality that he has, and he begins to harness and use the resources that are actually transpiring within him. This becomes a stage in creative work that leads to proper results.

So there is no such thing as the actor's ever having to be unreal because his imagination is not working strongly enough. At a moment of uncertainty the reality may be a little less high or less keen, but in life, too, it is true that we sit down every day to eat, but not every day are we equally hungry. The way we eat is always adjusted to the degree and amount of our hunger. We say, "Well, I should eat. He makes such a wonderful meal. I'm not really hungry, but I should eat a little bit. Hmmmm. It doesn't taste bad." In the same way we little by little begin to convince ourselves on the stage so that our imagination begins to work.

A lot of the time what throws you is the recognition that the scene should be truer or realer or higher but that you can't quite get it. And at that moment you give up the reality that you have for a phoniness which is unnecessary, instead of building on the reality that you have, safeguarding it, nurturing it, and developing it so that it is almost as good as what you need. You become able to control more and more. The imagination strengthens in belief and concentration. You become able to create anything that has to be created, whether it is an object or a thought or a sensation, in the same way that the pianist can create any tone that is needed in any sequence and relationship. That is when we call him technically trained. Therefore the difficulty that you call attention to is the thing that we regard as an essential starting place.

CHAPTER V

Training: Will and Discipline

To ACTRESS V: The actor can do a great deal of training by himself away from the Studio and in the privacy of his own life. Every day is for the human being a sequence of real events. Real things happen to him, and the ability to repeat real things is the actor's essential craft. Just as a writer makes notations for future reference, so the actor usually finds that everyday happenings deserve to be marked down in his ability to repeat.

At the end of every day go through that day to find things you would like to recapture and ask yourself, "How can I recapture it?" In looking for the answers, you will be prompted by the impulses you experienced and by the objects with which you came into contact, which therefore have for you a peculiar aliveness.

The actor can do a great deal of that work, and he can actually do it every day, and after a couple of years it can become second nature. As a result, when you start on a scene, things will rush unconsciously into your mind. You don't even have to ask a question.

Unfortunately, sometimes the light flashes on, and then it goes out again. If you have not worked at repetition in various ways, inspiration fades, and you cannot really make use of the impulse and experience that you have.

Until modern times the conscious work of actors has gone mainly into external means, but the work that really motivated great actors and made them great was done subconsciously, when they were walking around or sitting, when they were in the privacy of their rooms and of their own minds. They did that private and unconscious work because they were actors, and acting was their profession.

Today acting is hardly a profession. Many actors seldom act, or act sporadically. In the old days acting was a daily routine, and that routine provided a constant reassertion of and communion with the actor's problems and needs. Each night your skill was activated. Each night new problems and areas of concern called out your full amount of skill. That skill has to be used in order to be aroused, and it has to be aroused in order to be used.

I am flabbergasted by the way some of you sit around and think that your professional development will be helped by other people. You do not have the initiative to find out "the parts that are mine." You do not ask yourselves, "What is my repertoire? What do I want to play?"

There is a good kind of actor's ego that makes him find out for himself. He says, "Boy, the Hamlet that *I* will create no one ever saw! Never mind Garrick. Wait till they see me." That is the right kind of ego so long as he doesn't just sit around and say, "When somebody gives me the chance, I'll show them." He must show himself. He must work at home in the privacy of his own room. "What would I really do in this scene? I'm going to be so great in it. Well, what would I do? That's a tough son-of-a-bitch, that scene. What is really happening?" You just let your mind go. You may be in a taxi or on a bus or at home, but the ideas you will get will surprise you. Yet that is the way every artist gets what he is looking for.

I am appalled at how little you people read about the theatre. I never went to college; I didn't finish high school. But by the time I came to the American Laboratory Theatre, which was the first time I came into real contact with the technical work we do here, I had already arrived at the essential principles. I say that only to show that such a thing is possible. I had read lives of actors. I had read all the books about acting. The only thing I didn't know was how the hell you do it. I already knew everything, except I didn't know what I really knew.

At that time Boleslavsky said in his first talk, "There are two kinds of acting. One believes that the actor can actually experience on the stage. The other believes that the actor only indicates what the character experiences, but does not himself really experience. We posit a theatre of real experience. The essential thing in such experience is that the actor learns to know and to do, not through mental knowledge, but by sensory knowledge." Suddenly I knew, "That's it! That's it!" That was the answer I had been searching for. The point is that I had already read Freud and already knew the things that go on in a human being without consciousness. I had already picked up everything Boleslavsky said, but he showed me what it meant.

Suppose a Studio member has sufficient resolve to enrich his "material" in this way. It is also true that he must simultaneously develop his power of self-discipline. Without that he cannot unlock the doors of his storehouse and use what he has there.

Every door to the storehouse of an actor's imagination is protected by two locks. Relaxation opens one. The other is opened by the actor's ability to define for himself precisely what he hopes to accomplish in rehearsal or in training. Defining what the actor hopes to accomplish is a process of self-discipline. If the actor waits for his teacher or his director to do it for him, it is often too late. It's as if the lock has rusted, and the key will not fit or turn it.

However, the actor must understand the vital distinction between defining a scenic difficulty, which may be purely a production problem, and defining an individual difficulty. Either of these can cause problems in any production in which he is cast, and he must distinguish between them and solve both kinds if his acting in general is to improve. There are always two elements in any production problem, the actor and the play, and both must be taken into account.*

But in solving his individual acting difficulties, the actor's self-discipline must enable him to keep certain other consider-

---

* See pages 120-30 and 281-322.

ations in mind. Setting an exercise to correct a difficulty that has been defined does not require emotion. It cannot depend on inspiration. What is to be accomplished must be clear and concrete. The individual must really have a difficulty and he must really need a solution to it. And above all, he must not confuse his individual problem with the problem of getting scenic results.

The precise value of what an actor does to help himself depends upon what the problem is and whether or not it is explored by properly chosen means. If either the problem or the means of dealing with it is imperfectly defined, what the actor does has almost no value. It is like doing work because the actor has nothing else to do.

Nothing that a human being does is wrong if it is part of an experiment. When a scientist says, "I'm going to see what happens," and then blows two fingers off his hand, it is bad because he has lost two fingers, but scientifically it is good if the scientist learns something. If a scientist learns nothing from an experiment, it was wrongly conceived. And if what the scientist learns is already known, the experiment was unnecessary. He need not have risked blowing two fingers off his hand.

As an actor starts the process of finding his own way of work, he has a tendency to approach every problem and every scene as if it were difficult. But an actor needs to learn when to work and when not to work. He must have sufficient faith and confidence in himself to realize that certain things are simple. Only when what he has to do becomes difficult should he become concerned with helping himself. Otherwise he often gets in his own way.

Also it is sometimes true that the actor thinks he has no problems in areas where in fact he does. He tends to be satisfied with results that are not good enough, not convincing enough, not exciting enough. But he must be careful not to carry these problems away from the area of training and into the area of taste. An essential purpose of training is to make the individual precisely aware of his own technical needs. He learns what *he* has to work for. An actor who is tough and robust and earthy does not work to be tough and robust and earthy in a scene that calls for a person with those colors. He works for sensitivity, for things other than his natural roughness and toughness, which are already there. But if an actor playing that part is not the rough and tough type of person, that is what he works to get. To the actor who already has sensitivity, sensitivity is no problem.

In the individual's progress we are concerned with whether or not he is able to deal with any task he sets himself. If the actor gives himself tasks here which are not carried out, there is no point in his going on to new tasks. If a violinist has difficulty playing the notes and you tell him, "This has to be played faster," his playing will get worse, not better. It is already difficult for him to play slowly. When you are able to throw one ball up, then two balls, then three balls, then four balls, and to keep them going, that means you are gradually developing the skill. After you have learned the skill, you can do it even if you have other things to do at the same time.

In fact, it is the nature of an acting exercise—or any exercise—to be abstract. When you play a run from a sonata as an exercise, you do not worry about conviction or feeling. You try to play that run as fast and as definitely as you can so that later you will be able to play it under any conditions. Otherwise—if you try to play it with feeling—you train yourself to do it only that way, and when you have to do the same thing with another feeling, the fingers do not respond.

Thus, there is a stage in training—and also usually in working on a part—where you do not help the actor by setting him tasks related to final results in the scene. At this moment you do not worry about whether the problem is logically right or wrong in relation to the scene. At this stage you help the actor by setting him tasks that help to encourage in him the kind of response which he has to be capable of giving in any play under *any* conditions. Once he is able to do those things, he can then become concerned with whether the things he has picked are right for the scene or whether he could have picked a different or more logical approach which would have aroused both a greater degree of conviction and immersion in the scene and a fullness of behavior.

Some of the inner techniques taught at the Studio produce such marvelous results that they tempt the actor to apply them to every situation. Strasberg constantly warns against this temptation. He is stern in pointing out to Studio members that self-discipline in speech and in technical facility is indispensable to an actor's training. I can find no evidence to support the often-repeated charge that Studio actors are encouraged by the Studio to be highly undisciplined in rehearsal or performance. On the contrary, Strasberg is rigorous in his warnings and demands.

Awareness of our technical defects and flaws is even more important for us than for other actors. They are either not trained or make no effort to work in the area of inner technique, and consequently they do not suffer from some of our difficulties. An actor who always remains cool and calm and collected, who never permits his imagination really to soar or his emotion really to flare, has not too much of a problem. He learns what he has to do. He does it with a certain amount of skill that rarely varies. There are no sudden stops. There are no sudden impulses that destroy his ability to maintain his muscular facility and control. We do suffer from these difficulties because we do permit emotional and imaginative things to happen to us that are actually difficult to control.

But we often take much too glib and offhand an attitude toward technical problems out of the general feeling that something else is more important. On the contrary, these technical things are the least we should be able to do, because doing them is only a matter of superficial skill. It takes only time and effort. It does not take intelligence. It does not take talent. It does not even take ability. It just takes practice—literally. Technical skills are not a sign of anything except that the work on them has been done.

The actor must never evade a problem on the ground that he can only solve it by purely technical means. If the play says, for example, "The person has to choke her," there's no point in saying, "I don't feel like it." No. An effort must be made to carry out the task as simply and as well as the actor knows how. Don't forget that if I put my hands on someone's windpipe and pretend to choke, the simple physical effort will give a fairly good imitation of what you have to do even when you are not completely convinced. Being convinced one hundred per cent on the stage is very rare for any actor. Often the actor only needs to make the proper effort.

Actors come to the Studio with localized intonational patterns, with speech that definitely says, "I come from a certain place," with voices that are unused to speaking in public, that lack resonance and strength, that lack the facility to keep breath in the lungs and throat and to keep making the tone even when the actor is aroused by some passion that simultaneously burns a lot of oxygen and requires additional breath. These are abilities that are required on the stage, not in life. A singer may have a good voice, but when he has to get up on the stage and make sudden leaps with the voice and hit the note precisely and maintain it for a certain length of time and do these things to the rhythm of the music, it is difficult to do without a trained voice. The singer's training is concerned with strengthening what he already has. In the actor these are technical problems.

The kind of exercises Sarah Bernhardt permitted herself in order to learn to speak as quickly as possible and yet to be understood were technical. Those skills cannot be achieved by emotional means. They can only be achieved by practice, purely external, technical practice, which enables the organs of speech to be controlled quickly and precisely. (*To* Actor W:) For instance, when you try to do certain things, the lips are tense. They can't quite function. They can't make the sound as quickly as it was being, so to say, propelled from the lungs. That creates tightness and even a certain amount of nasality. I think you should go to the speech class that is offered here at the Studio and see whether some of that can be worked on technically and precisely. (*To* Actor X:) You have set yourself very deliberately and correctly the problem of moving away from the localized way of speaking that you have. As a problem that is perfectly plausible, but it is not an acting problem. It is a speech problem and is therefore correctly worked on as a purely technical problem in a speech class. As soon as you make an acting problem of it, you double the difficulty: you have to work on the scene and at the same time keep the speech less close to your natural speech.

External skill becomes a matter of aesthetic principle only when it is dissociated from inner technique. External skill by itself cannot be judged in terms of right or wrong, but only in terms of skill or lack of skill. But we think there is also an inner technique which can serve to combat difficulties every actor faces. In fact, all the actor has with which to combat these perfectly normal difficulties—the sense of embarrassment, the sense of "things are not going right, so I better give up"—are his will and concentration. Only by means of will and concentration can the actor control his imagination. Once he gives up will and concentration, he is lost. The top stars, the greatest actors in the world, are more subject to these fluctuations and difficulties than the ordinary actor, but their extreme sensibility and sensitivity make up for their greater difficulty by functioning for them unconsciously far more than for the actor of ordinary talent. Yet when their sensibility and sensitivity do not function, these great actors often do not have an inner technique subject to the control of will, and they literally do not know what to do.

The one thing we do not permit at the Studio is for things to happen without the actor's will being thereby strengthened and emphasized. If I am working on muscular development and I say, "Well, I think I'm now strong enough to pick up this weight; I couldn't do it last week, but I'll do it now," and I try but can't pick up the weight, I then say, "Okay, I'm sorry. I'll do it next week. In the meantime I'm going to practice." I do not give up. I take more time and effort to do what I want and need to do. Otherwise I train my will to give up in the face of difficulty.

The circus performer never stops when he has done a thing badly. He will never just bow and walk off with his mind contaminated by the idea, "I may not make it next time." He will immediately redo it. I have seen this many times. The audience is satisfied and applauds; they understand the difficulty, but the performer does not. To him giving up would become a hazard. The will cannot be left in that kind of tenuous and unsettled condition, and therefore actually the circus performer struggles until he does it.

The same thing should be true in the training here, especially in the work that the actor does on himself before the audience in the Studio. For example, when the actor is having difficulty, he should always say, "I am having difficulty. I am going to take as long as half an hour to do just this. I'll not let that get away from me. If I want to listen to the other person, I will try to listen. I know I can do it. If I am not able to listen, something in me is pushing to go elsewhere so that I cannot control what I am doing." And the essential thing to the actor in controlling what he does is will.

The most common misunderstanding about acting is to suppose that what the actor ought to do he can invariably do if only his attention is called to it. And the misunderstanding is doubled when it turns out that the actor does not actually do what he is supposed to do and what his talent presumably ought to permit him to do.

The actor must develop the ability to initiate and control what he does on the stage. Otherwise he cannot work with other people, and he cannot carry out the actor's professional task of repeating the play for an audience. The real question always is whether or not any particular individual has developed the kind of will and discipline that enable him to do what is individually required of him. The actor is very much like a machine in this respect: no amount of exhortation or pride of craftsmanship will help him to perform tasks and to express impulses if the condition of his instrument precludes that performance or expression. It is like exhorting an automobile to run when it has some mechanical flaw.

On the other hand, sometimes the actor is lazy or uninformed, and all that is necessary is practice, or correcting his mistaken idea of the task.

What is called "will" is often confused with persistence or with exertion of energy, but it is in fact a much more complicated phenomenon. We have already seen that forcing the organism to exert energy usually results in tension and frustration of the very thing that is desired. In fact, "will" cannot really function as an isolated element in acting, nor can it be trained in isolation from other elements. That is why Strasberg insofar as possible begins the training of the actor with simultaneous work in relaxation, in imagination, and in will as it relates to those elements and to expression. The word "willingness" might be more accurate, because training the will means training the actor's readiness to follow the expression of his imagination more than it does pushing his instrument to express. So much of the functioning of imagination and expression is unconscious that "will" may properly be described as that which first leads the actor to the use of his unconscious resources and finally allows him to permit these resources to flow through his instrument. Much training of the will is actually training in self-awareness. It involves expanding the actor's consciousness of how his organism functions unconsciously, what impulses rise under what conditions, what happens when he tries to feed these impulses into expression. He must be particularly aware of any tensions in the instrument. Thus, he does not will expression, but wills the readiness to permit expression and to continue it once the instrument becomes expressive. Especially when the actor is working at exploration of himself is it essential that he be willing to take time and to keep going. Will is seldom the engine. Much more often it functions as the master control station that starts the engine and directs its power in the proper channels.

Thus, Strasberg does no work with the actor that is solely devoted to will. Instead, will enters every phase of training from the beginning. Nothing is allowed to happen "without the actor's will being thereby strengthened."

A single example will illustrate Strasberg's concern with will in the day-to-day work of the Studio. Actor Y is a "very interesting stage type who can readily be used for many little parts. He obviously has a greater talent than he shows in these parts; yet he doesn't really quite know how to use it. He tends to go toward the type for which people have cast him. But the training work that would be most valuable for him, work in which he really learns to concentrate and to harness the various elements of his instrument, he is unwilling to do. He always tries to expand by climbing impossible mountains, and he inevitably falters. Thus, he excuses himself in advance for his failure. Yet when he tries to do very simple personal things, he literally does not know how to get started."

When Strasberg made the following remarks to Actor Y during a scene from *Mourning Becomes Electra,* he was not exhorting or driving him to obtain results useful to the play. Rather, he was encouraging Y to maintain his concentration, to keep going, and to become aware of his impulses and tensions during the scene, so as to train his will to deal consciously with his difficulties on the stage.

To ACTOR Y: You are beginning to deal with the problems that you really face, which at the moment are entirely of your own making. So far, the problems that I see do not relate to whether the scene is difficult or to whether or not you understand the problem. Last week you understood the scene very well. You simply refuse to make an effort to carry out whatever tasks would deal with the solution of the problem you understand. And the reasons you refuse are almost unrelated to acting, although they affect the acting result; they relate to your insecurity, your lack of concentration, your doubts, your self-consciousness, which comes from how you think you look and impress people, and from a sense that certain things are taking place in you at the moment you start to act: you wonder and become scared that perhaps we see the feelings that you have and that we misinterpret them. At such moments you have to have objects that are simple and yet sufficiently convincing to keep your concentration going. You need a mental picture that unconsciously incites more than a mere memory of the picture, a picture not chosen accidentally, but somehow related to yourself so that your subconscious can thereby be started to work.

Today you started with such a picture, and your subconscious did start to work. By having such a simple little net, you were able to catch very delicate animals, which you can't go around trying to catch with your hands. And even if people look at you as if you're crazy and laugh at you, I'm sorry—that's the only way to catch butterflies. You have to be willing to follow through, to go in your concentration with the things that you decided for yourself.

Obviously you did work a great deal to define the significance of the things you spoke of in the scene so that they would have for you the significance that they're supposed to have. But the important thing was that at the beginning you sat there for five minutes. I could see you fight with your concentration, and I could see you begin to get the concentration and then kind of slip back, and then start over again and then think, "Well, maybe I should start to speak," and then suddenly say to yourself, "No, no, no, it's hard to speak; I'm getting scared; it's gone," and then go backward and build up again. Then I saw a very good concentration begin to work—perhaps things fused, and the picture began to incite you—and then, as you started to speak, the mouth went a peculiar way, as if to say, "Hey, hold it; I don't know; I'm not sure I can make it." And actually the first sound didn't come out, and I thought, "Oh, he's gone back," and then you seemed to say, "No, it's time to speak now; I'll go on with the thing; I better keep going," and you kept going and the sound came out.

At the same time the sound came out, I saw a terrific tension, a fight with the muscles of the mouth which indicates a great inner struggle taking place. In the future I do not wish to see any of this. I do not wish to see any of the struggle. The struggle must take place inside. I want you to sit and to feel, but not move. Suffer. I don't want to see any little movement. Now when something happens you lick your lips. In the future, nothing. Suffer. With these hesitations and involuntary manifestations all that happens is that the impulses escape.

At the moment of expression I don't want any effort on your part to will the words where you wish them to go. Believe in your own thoughts, not in what you're going to do with the words. Otherwise, you somehow feel, "I'm not doing enough." Today you did plenty. I watched very carefully to see if you would be able to go higher from a simple start. When it came time for the really aggressive part of the scene, would you make it? Well, each moment where you wished to get a rise out of yourself, you got a rise. You got it simply. The voice came out. I have never before heard you speak as clearly and precisely and with as interesting voice colors. But it is not the criticism you have received here that brought that about. It is going on the stage and saying, "I'm going to follow through. I'm going to go through with it come hell or high water. I will not let myself slide back at the moment I feel insecure. I will go on. I will make vague things definite."

We are concerned with giving you the fullest possible control over your equipment and therefore the fullest capacity to create what you wish to create when you wish to create it. What I would like to see is the work done even more emphatically. Sit in the chair. Don't move. Really find out, "Where am I tense? Relax! My—this is quivering here; my chin is tense—relax!" This is for you the most important kind of work. When the audience hears Heifetz, they are concerned only with the result, but Heifetz is concerned with whether or not the violin is properly tuned and with whether or not the bow has enough resin on it, because he knows that's what is going to help him make the beautiful tone you hear. He knows that if the violin is not in tune he can play his goddamned heart out, and it will sound terrible. The result is inconclusive. So I can only encourage you for the moment to begin really to face your problem and to work on it.

It is valid to distinguish between problems of "will" and problems of "discipline," that is, between tasks the actor wants to do but somehow can't, and tasks he can easily accomplish if he determines to do so. But this distinction is seldom clear-cut. If an individual has a problem of will or discipline, which is it? Or is it partly *both?* Often only repeated observations permit Strasberg to decide.

The unconscious mechanisms affecting will operate in devious ways. Even before the actor reaches the stage they can control his choice—or lack of choice—of a problem or a task. Sometimes, the actor's problem is that he literally cannot define his problem.

Actor Y protects himself from coming to grips with his problem by choosing "impossible mountains to climb." Other actors unconsciously protect themselves from fear of self-revelation or failure by picking very simple tasks without really relating them to their own needs. For example, Actor Z "started at the Studio when he was young. Sometimes, you literally don't know what a young actor will develop into, what his métier will be. He starts with the generalized idea that 'John Barrymore worked; I'm working. If John Barrymore worked, and if I work, I can be just like John Barrymore.' But it takes time for people to find out what their material lends itself to." Thus, after a while Strasberg had to point out to Z not that he was on the wrong track but that actually he was not on any track. "You have set problems," Strasberg told him, "in an effort somehow to satisfy our requirements. You have picked things that have no meaning for you, because you thought they were problems that we wanted you to be concerned with, simple objects for concentration and things like that. It is now about time that you concern yourself with finding the things that must actually take place in you before you can solve the problems presented by a scene."

Actress G is a person in whom "the relation between personal life and what she does on the stage is very marked. And when her personal life and her acting are not sufficiently divorced, or, on the other hand, when her personal life is not sufficiently used in her acting, she winds up in unconscious conflicts which make it difficult for her to function." Despite the fact that her talent has permitted her to make some progress, G has had difficulty defining the work she has to do at each stage of development—a fundamental problem which Strasberg has tried repeatedly to clarify for her on such occasions as the following.

Toward the end of her life Eleonora Duse was much concerned with the mother-and-child relationship, and she performed roles that evoked the maternal quality. Also, something about the sea affected her, so that any play that involved both the sea and the mother-child relationship especially intrigued her. That is one way the personal things which an actor is often unaware of affect his relation to artistic material.

Personal things affect you in a different way. On the one hand you are trying to do simple exercises, and on the other trying to win the war in a single battle.

I understand what you are trying to do, but you are also trying in one moment to solve your whole personal problem. That is impossible. It takes time. Work has to be done continuously and consistently so that you get away from making everything a judgment on yourself and begin to develop a professional attitude. A doctor tries to alleviate suffering, but he knows what he can and cannot do. That same professional attitude must be developed in the actor's work. Therefore you must be much, much simpler, clearer, and more logical in the way you define problems, so that you have a real reason for doing a particular exercise. The reason cannot be that "It occurred to me; therefore, I decided to do it." This haphazard attitude has always dodged behind you but nevertheless has continued on with you. You have a way of facing problems but not really facing them. You don't want to face that just this single thing has to be done. You say, "But a lot of things are wrong with me, huh, doctor?" You seem to say, "Just give me the pills. After all, I can't do anything about everything." That is the unconscious attitude which now diffuses and hinders the very thing you are now making a fairly good effort to do.

> Actor AA presents a far more terrifying example: whereas Actress G tries to solve all her problems at once and therefore solves none of them, Actor AA sometimes cannot define a problem at all, and so he faces the situation of going on the stage without actually knowing what he is doing. In exercise after exercise at the Studio, of which the following dialogue is but one example, he is unable to clarify what he is trying to do. In his case, defining the problem is far more a problem of "will" than of "discipline."

You can't just say, "Since everything is impulse and since I don't really know how to begin with what I want to do, therefore I'll do anything and just see whether I can do that." Nothing is achieved if you do not have in mind what is supposed to be achieved.

AA: What should I have in mind?

STRASBERG: Well, I don't know what you're trying to do.

AA: I just wanted to see—I wanted to see if I could not freeze up. You know. I just wanted to kind of be—be—to go with what I felt like doing.

STRASBERG: But then you have to set yourself something difficult to do and see whether you can go with it and do it. But just to set yourself anything— It may be difficult for you. It may involve personal things, but they may not be of much use to you. You still may not gain anything from that.

AA: Well, what could I have—I don't—

STRASBERG: I don't know what you are working on. You say, "I want to work." What you really mean is that you want to climb walls. I don't know what you hope to get when you climb the wall. If you will tell me, for example, "I want to build a building," then I will tell you, "Stop climbing the wall, and do this and this." But if you say, "I want to do something that will be an impulse," I don't see what is to be achieved.

AA: Well, isn't a private-moment exercise this kind of thing? I was afraid to label it a "private moment" because I have never done one.

(*Strasberg shows him at length why he has not done what Strasberg calls "the private-moment exercise."*)

AA: I certainly kind of thought in those terms.

STRASBERG: That this was a private moment?

AA: No, I meant in regard to the concentration. Something that I—

STRASBERG: Everything is concentration! Everything involves concentration! The kind of concentration you use has value only in terms of the problem. Now, if you will please tell me the problem, I will tell you what to do. I don't know what you have in mind. You wanted to do something. What did you want to do and why?

AA: I wanted to—uh—I—I—I think I wanted to—I wanted to gain control of the impulses, to find out what they are: whatever I feel like doing I'm going to do. I'm going to go with the impulses. I gave myself a simple task, to come to this place and revisit it. And first I set myself to kind of make this place as much as I can, you know—

STRASBERG: You mean that this place that you talk about is a real place? Just a minute! Please, just answer me. Don't outguess me, and don't answer me things I don't want to know, which only confuses me. This place is a real place? Yes?

AA: Yes.

STRASBERG: Don't worry about what you did with it. First, give me the facts, please. This is a real place, a place that you have not been to for a long time. Now, the place has some special meaning for you? Is that what you mean? In that place certain things happened, and since that time you have not gone back. Right? Now, you wanted to see what would happen if you went back to that place through imagination. That's really what you are saying. Yes? Without knowing in advance what would happen or what wouldn't happen or whether it would be interesting or whether it would be exciting. It was to be an improvisation, an exercise to see what would happen from this object of concentration, from this place. Now, had you any reason to assume that something would happen?

AA: Well, as I went over it in my mind and I would catch myself, I would be carried away at certain spots, and I would stop myself.

STRASBERG: "Carried away"? I don't know what you mean by "in your mind."

AA: I would go into certain kinds of areas, and then I would just kind of, you know, I would become kind of—kind of—emotionally involved. And I would say, "Now, wait awhile. I don't want to do that yet." You know. "Wait awhile. Just wait." And I'd stop myself from thinking that, just walking the streets.

STRASBERG: This was after you had chosen to do the exercise?

AA: That's right.

STRASBERG: Forget that! Please, don't speak to me about the exercise. I'm talking about the real place. I will— Please, just listen to what I ask you. I ask you things, and you tell me other things. It doesn't help me. I'm trying to find out about the real thing and not about the acting thing. Please, don't confuse yourself and me. You had reason to assume that this place, this real place, had some meaning for you. You didn't know what the meaning was? No, no, not after you decided on the exercise, before, before, before.

AA: I knew even before.

STRASBERG: You knew what the meaning was. Yes? It aroused certain emotional—

AA: Yes. Yes.

STRASBERG: Well, then what did you want to do the exercise for? If you know what the meaning is, you can do an exercise in emotional memory and create the emotional response. What did you pick this thing for? In all your work, in *all* your work till now, there has been this terrifying looseness where you climb walls, and I don't know why the hell you are climbing. I have not seen in your work a willingness to go step by step toward the accomplishment of things that you see in your imagination. You make deductions that are not based on what we have asked or on what we have said, but that go away off into your own idea of how something is to be done, and you then set it up, and even when something is accomplished, you have defined the problem so vaguely that it does not accomplish what you wish.

The exercise that has proved most successful in dealing with will as a separable area of training is the "song-and-dance." In the early stages of an actor's basic training—particularly in the highly systematic work of his private classes—Strasberg typically calls on the actor during a single class session, first, to relax, second, to carry out an exercise to increase his concentration, and third, to perform the song-and-dance. This exercise has two parts, and each has both overt and internal elements.

The actor stands before Strasberg and the audience. He must try to be completely relaxed, physically and mentally, but he must also maintain concentration on what he is doing and contact with the audience. It is not necessary that he work to "put something over," but he must also not evade the audience. He starts to sing any song with which he is so familiar that he need not worry about his ability to carry the tune or to remember the words. As he sings, he tries to remain completely relaxed. He does not deliberately move his feet, legs,, body, hands, arms, or head.

He sings the song one tone at a time. Each tone is initiated in the chest with complete fullness and freedom of expression, is maintained fully, and is ended without diminuendo. This is the overt element of the exercise's first part, and obviously the actor's will, concentration, and expression, as well as his relaxation, are involved. The inner element is the actor's attempt to be aware of his own feelings and impulses as he performs. Because the material is an abstract series of tones he can keep his attention both on what he is commanding himself to do and on the nature of the impulses that simultaneously arise.

This first part of the song-and-dance is also a useful tool by which Strasberg can turn his uncanny insight onto diagnosing the specific difficulties that afflict the actor's will or ability to express. Any tension, stoppage, hesitation, or involuntary expression reveals to Strasberg's practiced eye some problem or hindrance of which the actor should be aware, but of which he may actually be completely unconscious until his attention is called to it.

In the second part of the song-and-dance the actor continues to sing as before, but simultaneously he moves or dances in a succession of different rhythms. He does not know in advance which rhythm will be used at any particular moment. He may move in a circle, leap, throwing arms and feet wide, swing the torso from side to side, change directions, do jazz rhythms, or combine several of these. To insure the spontaneity of the actor's change of rhythm, Strasberg himself often gives the commands.

This second part provides further opportunity for self-awareness. Afterward, Strasberg usually discusses what he has observed and frequently asks a series of questions to clarify further the actor's awareness of what happened to him while he was performing.

We have found that there is a difference sometimes between people who are sensitive and can't express themselves because they're inhibited, and people who are sensitive and can't express themselves and are not inhibited: they simply have not found in life a power of expression to match the strength of their response. Often, by channeling the sensation and then at the moment of feeling or impulse permitting the actor to do things he's never done before without knowing in advance what he's going to do, you help him to break away from his set pattern. He begins to find new ways of expression which deal with strong responses which have been, not inhibited, but simply not expressed.

In training we have exercises, such as the song-and-dance, which deal with this problem and often accomplish extraordinary results. The song-and-dance makes it possible to go directly to the basic areas of human effort, to deal with them more precisely than we can in general acting or scenic problems in which these areas are hidden.

The song-and-dance came about purely practically. It started because I had some students who were singers as well as actors. In singing, the emphasis is set so strongly on the musical pattern that it becomes very difficult for singers to break out of it to act. A singer invariably sings in the rhythm and with the pattern he has been taught. We simply wanted to train these singers in acting by breaking up this verbal-musical pattern. So I said, "Instead of doing things with words, let's do things with songs. But instead of singing the song, let's separate the sounds, so you can simply learn to do what you want to do, regardless of whether it's right or wrong. You will train your will by making it accomplish something which goes against the grain."

When we started, we found first that it wasn't quite so easy to do. Then some actors tried it, and we found a very strange thing. Some had peculiar difficulty. They were actors who seemed to be unmoved and in whom nothing seemed to be going on, so that you would have assumed that they would be perfectly capable of controlling this rather simple demand to separate the tones, but they had difficulty. And they had similar difficulty in moving their bodies to different rhythms without knowing in advance what each rhythm was going to be. On the outside they gave the impression of being perfectly controlled, perfectly poised, perfectly capable, and yet they were not able to carry out what seemed essentially rather simple things.

It then became evident that somehow through this exercise we were able to see farther inside than we had ever seen before. Actually these rather simple exercises turned out to be an X-ray into the problem of will and the relation of will to consummation, that is, to the ability on the part of will to carry through what the actor is trying to perform.

Thus, we became much more concerned with this problem and added certain adjustments, such as "making contact with the impulse." As the actor stands before the audience, he begins to feel things happening within him. These are things which rarely have outward manifestations, although sometimes we do perceive something. Sometimes these veiled impulses reveal themselves by the fact that parts of the body start jerking or moving: in other words "involuntary nervous expression" takes place. The actor then learns to "make contact" with these impulses, which is done without words. That simply means that while this is happening he asks himself questions: "What is this? What kind of a sensation is this? What kind of experience is this? What is it really? Is it one kind of reaction or another kind? Is it fear or embarrassment? Or is it shyness? Or anger? What am I angry about?" Actually all that the exercise does is to permit impulses, which obviously have been going on in the actor's sub- or unconscious, to express themselves more readily than they previously have been permitted to do. Such expression is usually prevented by censoring, one of the automatic processes of human conditioning and behavior.

In the song-and-dance the actor permits his impulses to take their own course. Very often in ordinary rehearsal you see things start to happen inside an actor, but that he fights against them. For example, an actor has the feeling that he's going to cry, and he doesn't want to cry, because you don't cry in the middle of a scene for no reason. At those moments you can actually see the muscles start to be active on the basis of habitual response, and in the song-and-dance we try to relax these muscles so the habitual responses come to the surface. Then the actors sometimes start to laugh or cry or react or break up in certain ways. They don't really know why, but it means that the actor is then induced to be a more expressive instrument, like a piano which does not censor the pianist.

When the pianist hits a note, the piano responds to that note; whereas when a human being hits a note there is a whole process of conditioning which often interferes with its expression. A human being thinks something, but knows he shouldn't say it. Sometimes by the time he grows up he doesn't even know that the censoring process is working. Therefore people come to acting with strong incentives *not* to say and *not* to behave in ways contrary to the needs of the scene and sometimes contrary even to their own desires. They do not realize that by the time they are ready to become actors they are already fixed instruments and that this instrument has to be retrained—reconditioned—to enable it to do what you want it to do.

This is, in fact, one of the greatest discoveries in the work I have done. Usually we think that if the actor is a good actor and understands what he wants he will carry it out. In so doing, we haven't really understood the difficulty with this problem, which every actor describes. And what makes it particularly hard to understand is that the greater the actor, the more often he has this difficulty, whereas it seems as if the exact opposite should be true: the greater the actor, the less difficulty he should have.

An actor often does not do everything he wants to do. His intentions are deflected by habits of which he is unaware most of the time. Instead, he often does things of which he is equally unaware because they are mannerisms—automatic and unconscious behavior. The essential part of the actor's training tries to make him aware of what he is doing at the time a thing is happening. Otherwise, he doesn't know whether to do it more or to do it less. That is the difference between acting and life. In life it is perfectly possible for the human being to be unaware of what is happening, even at moments of top intensity. But for the actor it is absolutely essential that he know all the time "what I'm doing while I'm doing it." This split awareness, which Stanislavski calls "the feeling for truth," must develop as a kind of sixth sense, and yet it cannot do so at the expense of the actor's belief, his concentration, his involvement in what he is doing.

It is usually assumed that if the actor is involved in what he is doing, then he is not aware. Or if he is aware, then he cannot be involved. But we know from our experiences as human beings that that's entirely possible. At moments of high emotion, we are often quite aware of what we're doing and say, "My God, look what I just did! Isn't it strange? I never would have thought I'd behave this way." Yet that doesn't stop what we're doing, because the impulse or incentive in life may be very strong. But on the stage, what we do may often stop, because the incentive is an imaginary one and therefore isn't strong enough.

One of the most serious misunderstandings of actors is to assume that to act truly and believably means to forget what you are doing. But that's hysteria—in life as well as in acting. When a person forgets, it means that he has gone beyond the point where he is willfully doing something. Art is always willful creation, though at times it has results which you could not predict. These results stem from many levels of the human being besides the conscious and willful ones. Yet in order to repeat, which is the ordinary professional requirement of the actor, there must be some element of awareness working. And this level of awareness is not, despite the common misunderstanding, opposed to the possibility or the need for the actor to fuse himself with the character or to give himself fully to the part. On the contrary, the awareness is essential if he is to accomplish that fusion and involvement.

Breaking the song into single tones and changing rhythm at command in the dance is valuable in dealing with the actor's ability to give himself to the carrying out of a command freely and flexibly, which means without knowing in advance how he will do it. Most people don't do that. They do only what they are accustomed to do. If they know in advance that they want a step, they seem more or less free in doing it, but actually they are not free at all. They are simply bound to the habit which the body has learned. The body can do the habitual thing easily, but if you give the actor a command to do something which is not practiced and habitual he may go to pieces because his body is not really trained to express the impulse induced within it.

In this respect the song-and-dance exercise deals with another essential problem in acting: the actor has to know what he is going to do when he goes on the stage, and yet he has to permit himself to do it so that it seems to be happening for the first time. This means that the body, the voice, every facet of expression, must follow the natural changes in impulse; even though the actor repeats, the strength of the impulses may well change from day to day. The actor starts the song-and-dance at the very beginning of training. At that time other exercises deal with the creation of reality for the actor, whereby he learns to give himself with belief to the object, event, or experience that he's trying to create. The concentration exercises and many other exercises deal with the problem of creating impulses. The song-and-dance deals with the other side of the medal. When the actor tells himself to change the dance rhythm, or when he obeys a command from me, he doesn't know what the new rhythm will be. Yet in doing the very first movement he recognizes the rhythm and can continue it. Thus you train the actor's peculiar ability to be free and yet to will the freedom. He gives himself a definite act, deed, or object. He is aware of what he is doing while he is doing it. Thus, the impulse pours, is permitted to come out in expression. We used to do the concentration exercises without the song-and-dance, and the actors would create impulses, the imagination would begin to work, but somehow the acting wasn't improved. In other words, the instrument was not free to respond to the very strength of the impulses which the concentration exercises succeeded in creating.

The song-and-dance is not an exercise which helps by being done once. It should be done over and over, because you are dealing with habits, and we have found that while habits can be broken, it is not easy to do so. I had a girl I permitted to stay in my class for a very long time. At one time her problem seemed insurmountable. She seemed to have little possibilities for the theatre. She was not prepossessing. She had sensitivity, but so locked up that her personal behavior was almost deformed or grotesque. But I let her stay as long as she wanted, because I wanted to see if habits, which in her case had been rooted from childhood, could be changed. Her voice was a childhood voice, a squeaky little voice, high-pitched but not quite dead, which indicates a lot of nervous energy held back. Her body was always in a state of contraction, in a panic reaction, wanting to do but not able or afraid to do. To change those habits seemed an impossible task. Sometimes I simply got annoyed, but I kept at it. And we got nowhere, but nowhere.

One day, after she had been in the class for several years, I was just talking to her, and I said, "Has anybody ever told you anything about your voice?" "No," she said, "nobody ever did." So I was stuck. "Oh, except my mother," she said. "Oh, your mother told you something about your voice? What did she tell you?" "Oh," the girl said, "she didn't say anything. She just said not to make sounds. She didn't really say anything." I said, " 'Not to make sounds'? Why did she tell you that?" "Well," she said, "there was a relative visiting us, and my mother told me not to make these sounds, because they didn't sound human; they sounded like animals, like wild animals." I said, "Your *mother* told you not to make these sounds?" She said, "Oh, yes, she didn't mean anything. She didn't mind. She told me later it was all right." Even that didn't seem to explain fully, so I said, "Well, what's so important? Just because your mother told you, so what?" She said, "Well, she told that to my father, too." Now, beyond that I didn't go, but you could obviously see there the formation of a fantastic pattern. The mother had come into the child's room and told her she sounded inhuman, like a wild animal.

After that day the girl started to make progress, but the problem was tough, because the will just wasn't there. I would push at her. The teacher can substitute his will at certain points—as in the song-and-dance—by kind of badgering the actor to activate energy he has simply never permitted himself to use. Well, she would do it, and the next time she wouldn't do it. But you have to keep fighting, fighting for relaxation and will and energy, and she would try and try to get away from the previous habits.

Finally, after she had been with me for about three years, working regularly on herself and presenting the results of that work at intervals to the class, she was able to do a scene, and, though it wasn't great, it was believable. She was real and human, and her voice was beginning to be normal. And after five years she made sufficient progress so that when she did, for instance, a scene from *The Rainmaker*, she was lovely. Not only could she create reality and believability, but her peculiar visual aspect began to take on a shining quality. She could get up on the stage and give a very good account of herself. Though she could never carry out completely, she could carry out to the point where impulses began to happen to her on the stage which she could allow to come into her acting. It was a very stirring thing.

CHAPTER VI

Problems: Stopping Imagination

Acting is an organic activity that calls upon the actor's entire physical and psychological resources, and any difficulty—however trivial—tends to afflict and poison the entire organism. Impulse is blocked. Concentration is deflected or divided. Belief is shattered. The actor often does not know whether his trouble is a "cold in the head" or a "mortal" affliction. And if he does not know what is the matter he cannot take steps to correct it. He becomes progressively more paralyzed. His imagination falters, and, while this, of course, does not bother the mediocre actor, if it begins to happen to the actor of talent, he becomes panicky. The panic stifles imagination further. And so the downward spiral goes on and on.

Perhaps even more important than Strasberg's uncanny ability to observe an actor's "moments of difficulty" and to diagnose their cause is his ability to do so without harming the good and actively functioning elements of the actor's talent, just as the physician knows how to cure without using drugs or techniques that have harmful side effects. With his long experience, Strasberg has the objectivity of the doctor who stands outside the body he is treating. He realizes that general approaches to acting have no value in solving such individual problems as the following.

SUBJECTIVE INTERPRETATION
OF TECHNICAL PROBLEMS

You learn to swing a bat when the pitcher isn't throwing the ball. After a while you say, "Gee, I swing the bat well. Wonderful! My God! I could hit some home runs one after the other."

Then the pitcher starts throwing the ball. You then say, "Gee, there must be something wrong with me. I was so good before." No, there is nothing wrong with you. You have encountered an actual difficulty. You learn to swing the bat, but when a new element comes in, you cannot maintain the natural ability. In other crafts you have an external medium or instrument which can be controlled by itself. In acting, the medium and instrument *are* the actor, and the instrument is subject to any ailment of the person. When the actor's training has progressed only halfway through the early stages of work and he comes to a scene and has difficulties, he invariably assumes that there is something the matter with him. He has a tendency to think of any problem as an impediment, as a sign of incapability, as an insult to his talent.

Acting is too often surrounded by a kind of mysticism or by a kind of fear that says, "Now, wait a minute. If I start asking myself questions, I'm going to be unable to act. I can only act when I act. If I start asking myself about this problem, I won't know where I am, and I won't know what I'm doing." Or, if the actor asks questions, they are not real questions; they are doubts. Or the actor asks himself or somebody else a question because he is afraid to get up on the stage and test his doubts. The acting instrument is so close to the actor's own subjective feelings that the actor cannot differentiate between the two. He is stifled. His imagination is blocked. But the solution to the craft problems of the actor is essentially the same as in any other craft. The technique has to be prepared and heightened and trained for the exact problem—whatever it may be.

TOO MUCH SENSITIVITY AND EMOTION

Sensitivity is the capacity of an organism to respond to a stimulus. The response may be emotional or nonemotional, and the stimulus may be external or internal, conscious or unconscious, volitional or accidental. Talent in an actor means that he is endowed with sensitivity. If he cannot respond, he cannot be an actor. However, sensitivity or emotional response can be present and yet be a problem because the actor cannot control it. The very thing that should be good for the actor is a hindrance.

To ACTOR BB: You have great sensitivity, but almost too much. Your sensitivity does not yet have a base. You are very young. You have lived in a localized environment where there has been little need or use for your particular sensitivity, but it is obviously sufficient for theatre purposes because it has got you into The Actors Studio without very much previous training or experience.

In this scene your sensitivity was very keen in a purely physical way. For example, when an impulse came and your hand rose, the movement did not complete itself. As the hand rose, the fingers were already closing. Your sensitivity goes this way and that way, this way and that way. It is not full and easy and relaxed. Once the impulse starts, the muscular response is not willing to go completely to the point and to come down at ease when the impulse is spent. The impulse shoots, and at that very moment, either because you are not used to allowing the impulses to go through or because you are not used to behaving as a result of emotional responses, the impulse pulls back. It's like pushing a door against the wind. The wind is blowing so hard you cannot open the door far enough even to slip through. Yet you say, "I tried to open the door. What's the matter with me?"

Nothing is the matter with you. Nothing is wrong with the results you are now getting. These results merely indicate that you need to learn more about handling the sensitivity you undoubtedly have.

Take a batter at bat, very keyed up. The pitcher is a fast-ball pitcher; therefore the batter must be ready to swing when that fast ball comes in. One of two things usually happens. Either the pitcher throws a change-up and crosses up the batter so he swings late, or he throws the fast ball, and the batter is so anxious to hit that he swings too soon. The batter is so keyed up, so ready, that he has exactly that extra aliveness and readiness to respond that he needs, but his nerves are too quick, too active, and therefore he misjudges.

Your problem is not one of sense memory and not one of choice of objects. Your problem is that in responding you are constantly criticizing the thing that is happening. Your energy spurts but never quite keeps up, never quite keeps going where it should go to fulfill itself. Therefore, we don't want you to work on scenes or exercises involving emotion. Your sensitivity is strong enough so that you do not need to worry about that. You need to worry about your ability to take a simple object, to work for it, to take your time in working for it, and when you have it going, to look at us and say whatever you have to say unemotionally, without dramatics, without anything. You must learn that in doing and saying anything you thereby create reality. The best work for you would be to participate in the pantomime class in order to learn pure physical control without any emotional involvement.

> Actress 'I' has "great talent but a problem of literal hysteria. She thinks the feeling of the role is the only thing that is important, and, unless something operates to draw her away from feeling, she becomes hysterical. Hysteria on the stage is not emotion. Emotion on the stage must be deliberately created. Hysteria is emotion which takes over and does what it wants without regard to the character or event."

To ACTRESS T: You have too much emotion, and it functions at times when it is not needed. Today the effect was a little disturbing, because the emotion seemed to be in a vein different from what you were doing. The emotion was too real and convincing in the sense that its visual expression did not match the emotion's reality.

If I am not mistaken, I have asked you not to concern yourself with any exercise that has to do with emotion. You are to pick objects that are either logical or simply objects for concentration. You are to prove to yourself—since you are very emotional—

whether or not the emotion will come by itself. You are to prove to yourself that you need not work for it.

T: But I didn't work for it.

STRASBERG: You told me you had chosen an object from which the tears came, although you did not expect the result would be so great.

T: I chose the wrong thing.

STRASBERG: Not only the wrong thing. The exercise should have been an illustration of what can be achieved from this one simple object. You mixed it with so many other elements, we did not know what came from what.

T: I didn't want to rely just on remembering a physical object.

STRASBERG: It is very good for you to rely just on one thing. It will teach you to have faith in yourself. It will teach you that emotion is not your problem, but that the control of emotion is your problem. At times, of course, there may be a problem of getting the particular emotion you need, but you already know how to use affective memory to do that. The more you give yourself to working just with a physical object, without worrying about what it will do in the scene or where it will lead, the more you will gain faith in your ability to direct your will toward the solution of problems that either you or your director may set.

FAKING AND FORCING

Technically speaking—that is, without reference to the play—an actor is real so long as expression matches imaginative impulse. Actor BB and Actress T actually had plenty of impulse. Another kind of actor merely pretends to have impulses; he manufactures out of whole cloth the responses he thinks the pretended impulses should produce. This is faking. A third kind of actor may in fact have a functioning imagination, but he feels compelled to distort it for the sake of an exaggerated response. This is forcing. So long as the actor fakes, his imagination cannot work. So long as he forces, his imagination cannot work either fully or truly.

The basic elements of any acting problem are always known, but how that problem can be solved no one knows. It can only be predicted that the problem will be solved to the extent that the actor does his work well. These working premises are taken for granted in all fields of human endeavor.

I once saw an elaborate television program on the history of a missile. You saw the scientists working, top scientists with millions of dollars to spend. Everything was made ready. The right person touched the right button—the rocket didn't go off.

The scientists said, "We'll start all over again." They didn't kill themselves. They didn't leave their profession. They weren't kicked out. They didn't lose their union cards. They knew something had gone wrong, they didn't quite know what. They were going to check everything to correct the error.

That is what happens in all human activity. The only place we're not willing to accept that limitation is in acting. In acting we want to be able to do all the work and to push the button, and when the rocket doesn't go off, we still want it to go off. So what happens? The rocket doesn't go off. We go off. We try to make the rocket go off by pretending.

When that happens, the rocket will never go off. That's the point. Once you start to go off instead of finding out what is wrong and building another rocket, you are not creating the kind of activity that will lead to another rocket's going off. You are not creating the kind of imaginative activity that will ultimately lick the problem.

However, when an actor approaches a scene or an exercise here in which he's trying on the stage to work as honestly as he knows how and to explore the particular personal thought, sensation, or experience which he has set himself to explore, what happens often is that he doesn't even push the button. He doesn't trust himself, so he doesn't push the button. Instead he uses a phony rocket, a convention or a cliché.

We say that in technical training the actor must be content just to follow the correct process of work. In production, when an audience is waiting that has to be given its money's worth regardless, you can fake for the audience, if you wish, because the audience will be satisfied with faking. But as a scientist you will ruin yourself if you are fooled by your own faking. As long as the actor knows that he faked today and therefore prepares himself for doing it properly tomorrow, he's all right. But if the actor ever starts to take faking for the truth, he eliminates the possibility of ever making the creative kind of development and progress that every actor wants.

To ACTOR CC, *following a scene from "Henry V"*: What did you have in your hand?

CC: A sword.

STRASBERG: Yeah. Take the sword. (*A pause.*) What are you going to do with that sword?

CC: Right now?

STRASBERG: No. (*Laughter.*) I don't want to tempt you right now.

CC: In the scene? Or with myself right now?

STRASBERG: What can you do with that sword?

CC: A few things with it.

STRASBERG: What?

CC: I can clean it.

STRASBERG: What can you do with the sword that would fulfill its purpose?

CC: I could cut. I could stab. I could kill. I could—

STRASBERG: Yeah, but that's a general thing. You couldn't do any of those things now.

CC: I could stick.

STRASBERG: No, you couldn't do any of those things now. That's all play acting.

CC: Oh, I couldn't—uh—now—but I couldn't do anything with it now.

STRASBERG: Why not? Why not? You can't hold the sword in your hand?

CC: Well, I thought I was.

STRASBERG: No. I don't think you're holding a sword. You're holding some kind of prop that you're waving around. That's no way to hold a sword. You didn't show the slightest awareness that you had a sword and that this sword had a purpose. If I gave you a baseball bat, you would know how to hold it. Would you hold it this way? I don't think so. Something in the handling of the thing would have been indicative that you know how to deal with the object. You say, "Well, I don't know how to hold it." Fine. If you don't know how to hold it, then why hold it in a way that implies that you do know? If you don't know how to handle it, keep it out of the way. That you can do. Then you are not pretending to do something and thereby indicating that you do not know how.

> DD is "an actress of very great talent who just didn't know very much about herself. Her work as an actress was fresh, an assertion of her own personality. Had she continued that way, she might have wound up with her freshness becoming only a seeming freshness, a mannerism, so that everybody would have said, 'Well, that's all she can do.' At the time she came into the Studio, she had no proper technique for using her great talent and flair. The Studio tried to show her to herself, to get her away from her fears, to give her new tasks and problems, and thereby to make her feel she was not just a girl from the Bronx and that she was not limited solely to that."

To ACTRESS DD: We are trying to make it unnecessary for you to exert so much effort to express what is already going on inside —as if you didn't quite believe either that it is going on, or that, if it is going on, we will see it. We are concerned to take away this extra, unnecessary effort in order to leave you free to do more with other areas of yourself.

I want you to gain the confidence that every craftsman must develop in order to be able to do what he wants to do as fully as possible. You cannot do that if you worry, "But is it now enough for the public?" That comes later in the stage of production. The food must be cooked before you start worrying about the dishes.

Expression does not need to be pumped. The basic capacity of a human being is to think, to experience, and to express. The actor uses that basic capacity. He sets up and creates resonances in another watchful human being who has paid his money and is determined to get his money's worth.

The strongest audience response comes when the actor is himself involved in what is happening and at the same time possesses a good instrument. A good acting instrument is so interestingly developed that it responds like a good piano to every impulse that goes through it. On a bad piano you have to pound the tone to get it out. On a good piano you can put the hand down very easily, and yet the tone comes out with resonance. You say, "My God, almost like Horowitz! Boy, I sound so good on this piano that I ought to be a piano player!"

The scene can be just as convincing when you don't push yourself into fabulous effort. After all, in life it's the other way around. Somebody says something, and while we make great effort to behave very calm and collected, nonetheless the emotion goes on.

The flower is the inevitable result of the seed. You plant a little seed. You water it. You keep the earth moist. The flower itself grows. If you try to pull it to accelerate its growth, you pull the roots out and ruin the flower. The flower has to come up by itself; it may be large, it may be small, but it will grow by itself if the basic things are properly done.

THE VERBAL PATTERN

All of Strasberg's work is directed toward helping the actor find the reality of character, situation, and event that lies beneath the words of a play. But the actor's imagination is never aroused if his effort remains fixed on the level of the words. Strasberg calls this "adhering to the verbal pattern."

To Actor M, *following a scene from Tennessee Williams'* "*Mooney's Kid Don't Cry*": There were often moments when what impelled you came more from the words than from your own imagination, that is, from the conventional color of the lines rather than from the real meaning of the lines. If we talk about the St. Lawrence River in life, we say, "Gee, what a great river it is. It moves there, and it's a blue just like the sky. It's so blue and so terrific." But in the play the line says, "It's blue like the sky," so you said (*intoning and gesturing vaguely upward*), "It's the St. Lawrence River, and it's blue like the sky!" I'm sorry. The St. Lawrence River cannot be blue in the way that fake tone implies. That's not a river you were pointing to up there—that's a sky. The river when it is blue is blue in the river. That vague gesture toward the roof shows that at that moment you were being fed by a conventional impulse that came solely from the line.

To Actress G: The human being is often pushed by unconscious patterns associated with words. Especially when the words are not your own but have been given to you by an author, they immediately give rise to a conventional way of intoning or speaking or even to a sequence or an unconscious meaning.

For instance, on two occasions in this scene you had four words in sequence, and they were said as—four—words—in—sequence. You said something about having your first contact with—a husband—with—a friend—with—lover—with child. The words were actually—done—that—way. At the end of the fourth word the tone dropped. Obviously in the back of your mind you knew there would be four words and no more.

G: How can you not know that?

STRASBERG: Either an actor knows, or he tries to think. If he knows, he says, "There are going to be only four: a husband, a friend, a lover, and a child." When we hear him, we know there are only four. When a person is trying to think, as you seemed to be doing, then obviously he doesn't know there are going to be only four. He's trying to think how many there are. He says, "The first time you come in contact with your husband or—with a friend, or—with—I don't know—with a lover, of course—it is even truer to a certain extent—and then even with a child, although that's different, you see." Actually these four things that he eventually thinks of exhaust all the major relationships that a human being has. But that's how thought goes. Thought doesn't go in advance. If it did, obviously the four words should come out unconditioned and continuous. But if the words come—out —the—other—way, then obviously the meaning is only acted, is presupposed, and no real meaning is engendered. Words fall unconsciously into these verbal patterns. We all have them. As soon as we reach a sequence, unconsciously we recognize it as that sequence.

As you know from my private classes, an individual will do a scene whose lines he hasn't memorized very well so that he skips words or even whole lines, and yet every punctuation mark will be in place. Obviously he has not intended to memorize the punctuation. He scarcely knows the lines. If you ask him how many punctuation marks are in the scene, he will look at you as if you are crazy. Yet every punctuation mark is in place as he speaks. It must be that our first impression of lines is reached through punctuation; therefore we unconsciously create a stencil of the punctuation which thereafter unconsciously serves as a guide. This first impression is very strong, and it frequently hinders the actor.

ANTICIPATION

Stanislavski was probably the first to recognize clearly the significance of the actor's disease called anticipation. No matter what he tells himself and what the director tells him, the actor knows that he is out there on the stage to do exactly what he did yesterday and exactly what the director wants him to do and exactly what he himself hopes to do. The actor knows things the character cannot know and therefore tends unconsciously to act upon that knowledge. He tends to act the result rather than to make the result happen.

The character does not know what is going to happen. He has not read the play. The play is about him. The author is going to write the play from him. What we always advise is that the actor ask himself, "What would be going on here if this scene never happened? What would I really be doing?"

> Strindberg's *The Stronger* takes place in a ladies' café in Stockholm on a Christmas Eve. There Mrs. X, a married actress, comes in from Christmas shopping and encounters Miss Y, an unmarried actress. In the play Miss Y, who was performed at the Studio by Actress DD, has no lines.

To ACTRESS DD, *after the exercise:* What are you interested in our seeing? What are you trying to tell us? The actor is constantly telling the audience things. Even if the actor says, "I don't want you to know anything at this moment," he says so so deliberately that we know he is really giving us some mysterious kind of message. There is no such thing as the actor's not wanting the audience to know anything even in an improvisational exercise like this.

DD: Okay. What should I say? I don't want you to know anything except that I'm here.

STRASBERG: The play posits a basic sequence: no matter what happens through the first part of the play, Miss Y is the stronger. She's supposed to be the stronger at the beginning in the simplest dramatic terms. The play is called *The Stronger*. Some point is made about that. Obviously, if you are the same at the beginning as you are supposed to become at the end, there is no play. That means that from the simplest point of view you have at the beginning to appear as one thing and at the end to be recognized as another thing. Whatever you do at the beginning should not give away the end.

DD: But I didn't intend to.

STRASBERG: I'm sorry. If Mrs. X comes in and looks at you and says something and you pay no attention, something is off. What was that for?

DD: Well, I don't really care about her. I'm invulnerable at the moment. I have something to eat and my drink and my newspaper.

STRASBERG: But you've read the newspaper. You've been sitting here for hours. You haven't just come in?

DD: No.

STRASBERG: No. You've been sitting here most of the evening. You've read the paper at least fifty times. How many times can you read a newspaper?

DD: I didn't think that.

STRASBERG: That's because you are now starting the scene as a scene and as an acting problem without trying to separate the acting problem from the concern with yourself. You are not relating the acting problem to something in the scene that you discover by means of yourself. See what I mean?

DD: No. (*Laughter.*)

STRASBERG: All right. Now, here's what I want you to do. Instead of hiding your face behind these newspapers and hiding behind any of the other things that you now unconsciously hide behind—

DD: I see.

STRASBERG: Okay. Since I have to put it on the line for you, I'll put it on the line. Instead of doing that, I want the exact opposite. When the curtain goes up I want to see your face. I want to know that you've been sitting there and thinking of personal things, some interesting and some not so interesting. That's right—just what you are doing now. You don't need the beer to help you, and you don't need the newspaper to help you, and you don't need the director or anybody else, because there's plenty inside of you to deal with this problem which is serious to this character.

Miss Y feels all right. It's just that on this kind of evening she pays the price for what she does. But otherwise she gets everything that she wants. All the men who go home to their wives on a day like this are really hers. It's true that tonight she has to give them back to the family, but otherwise she is "the stronger." She thinks so at the beginning of the scene and all the way through until suddenly the tables are turned because through Mrs. X she finds out one thing that shows her she is not really the stronger.

What you are thinking now as you sit there is what I want on the stage. This you have not yet done on the stage. Do you know what you're doing now? I don't know what word to call it. You have a sense of yourself now. You realize we're talking about you, and that kind of intrigues you, but at the same time there you're on icy ground. And yet you don't mind skating. That's right —what I see now. That is what I would like to see in the scene.

She thinks she has this power. She is sure of that, even though tonight it isn't being used. She's sure of a hold over the very people she hasn't got tonight. So don't give the end away. When Mrs. X comes in and talks, be ready to answer whatever you want to say. Try to answer. When you try to answer, remind yourself, "Well, the damn author doesn't give me the words. He made a stunt out of this, so I guess I won't, but I could if I wanted to," so that you constantly feel the need and the desire and the willingness to speak. Now you unconsciously get into the idea, "She never speaks throughout," which holds you back from any but a certain type of reaction. You hold everything else back, because you know that in the play it is never going to come out.

If Mrs. X comes in, and you want to smile at her, go ahead. Think to yourself, "People busy themselves with all this kind of nonsense on these holidays—running around, buying presents. People buy presents for me. I don't buy presents for them. People make themselves busy for their husbands—he's not even her husband. I mean, he doesn't really belong to her." What you are doing now is what I want in this scene. That's right—Mona Lisa. This is the secret of Mona Lisa. You're sure, strong. You know your power. And all through, when Mrs. X talks and describes things, I want to see that you know what *really* happened with her husband. You're certain of that. Any time you want to, you could crook your little finger, and he'd be back. You could have him if you wanted him, but you don't want him. You have plenty of other people. There must not be too much awareness of what we will ultimately become aware of. This is where unconscious anticipation plays a great role and often depletes and stultifies and to an extent destroys the actor's work.

FEAR OF BEING CARRIED AWAY

ACTRESS R, *following a private-moment exercise:* The first moment bothered me because something was—what I wanted to use was very personal.

STRASBERG: That's right.

R: And I was so afraid!

STRASBERG: That's right. Of what?

R: Well, you know, I might get carried away.

STRASBERG: Yes. And what would happen?

R: Well, I didn't want to do it fully, just enough to—to get on that subway and make all the local stops.

STRASBERG: Yes.

R: I didn't let it go purposely because— (*a pause*) I didn't want to confuse the work with my own thing—

STRASBERG: What does that mean? What the hell does that mean? If I am a painter, and I'm seeking a model for Venus, and I fall in love with somebody, and I paint her as Venus, and then I say, "I don't want to confuse my own feeling with—" What the hell does that mean? How can I paint unless I am willing to confuse my own feelings with what I am doing? I then have to have the skill and the means to make *my* vision, *my* feeling, *my* thought apparent to other people who don't have my personal attitudes. But I can only work out of my personal attitude. How else can I work?

That is something that I admire so much in Gadge [Kazan]. Whenever it comes to a certain kind of situation where I might expect him to argue, he doesn't argue. I get violent. I argue about the play as if argument were actually going to cause something to happen. Gadge says, "I'm sorry. This is what I think. I may be all wrong. I don't know. After all, I can only do what I think.

You're probably right, but I have to do it my way." He lets it go at that, and from that comes achievement and creation.

How can anybody who tries always to meet somebody else's specifications possibly achieve anything except on a conventional level? For the audience that is all right, but for the artist nothing of any importance is ever achieved that way—never. It's impossible. When you go up there on the stage, it is with the idea that you will give *your* life to this character. There is no life in her. There is only a sequence that the author demands of you, but the life is your life. That's what you give. You give it to her.

> Actress C "has enormous talent but also severe emotional problems as to how to use that talent. A good deal of the time her talent spurts like lava and destroys her rather than being channeled to create something in the play." Strasberg has tried "to give her the plumbing—concentration, will, the simple elements of acting that are commonly taken for granted—so that the impulses which are pouring can be contained. The little screws have to be tightened, or the car racing at two hundred miles an hour falls apart."

To Actress C, *following a private-moment exercise:* Acting with you is always compulsive because the feeling shoots up that if you stop for a moment, "Where am I going to be?"—as if something will disappear unless you keep doing things for us. Nevertheless, your entire attitude of work in the movies and on the stage is toward an unconscious use of yourself. Even the purely superficial and mechanical work has been predicated on the hard-pounding something going on inside. That's the kind of person you are. That's what makes for the intensity and the veracity of your acting. In your case there is no problem of ability, but the compulsiveness comes from a fear which every actor of deep intensity is subject to—the fear of revealing more than you think should be revealed.

For the actor there never is more. What the actor reveals is always in terms of what he is creating. He reveals the things that are related to that particular object or event. He must say, "Yes, I'm willing to give you one hundred per cent. I may give you seventy-five per cent today. I don't know. But I want to give you everything I've got." The actor never actually gives one hundred per cent of himself, but he does give one hundred per cent of his willingness. In you the willingness to conceive, to live, to take the time to let the thing happen to you and to go with it is not offered to the extent that you are able. You can always manage to make a little bit seem like more. I want the opposite. I want it to *be* more.

I can think of two men who had no fear of revealing on the stage. I cannot think of a woman. With most great actors it is the opposite. Duse had that fear to an unusual extent. She died a thousand deaths before each performance. At fourteen she played Juliet, and afterward she was so filled with it that she ran through the streets. She ran away. She couldn't see anybody. She was highly sensitive and peculiarly strong in going with what the actor is creating, and that she maintained for the rest of her life. For that precise reason she could not act for several years after the love affair with D'Annunzio. When she got up on the stage, she felt the audience was thinking of what D'Annunzio had written about her, and she was so sensitive to that that she could not act. She would be ready to go on, and something would throw her, and she would actually call off the performance.

The craft that we discuss here is often more necessary for the great actor than it is for the lesser actor, because the great actor has these fears and worries and doubts to a greater extent. The smaller actor, the ordinary actor, the superficial actor, the mechanical actor doesn't have them at all. To him acting is very simple and easy. "You move from here to here, and when you get here, you say the line, and this is the way you say it. What is so difficult? What are you making such a fuss about?" He has none of the problems of the sensitive actor who is somehow touched by what really goes into acting.

Actress EE "came into the Studio with a very interesting quality, so shy, so inhibited, so unable to use herself except in her shyness, that it was almost like a quality without a body to contain it. Work with her has been almost purely training and has consisted of making her aware of herself as a woman and as a person." Strasberg "demanded that she make the effort to dress differently and to use her body in unaccustomed ways. Therefore she has enormously widened the range of parts she might possibly play. This work has also led her to an intensification and deepening of her experience on the stage. In her previous acting, reality had been simply being natural, doing nothing too forcefully, which is only negative goodness, an absence of the wrong thing, but not yet the presence of the right thing."

To Actress EE, *after she had performed Eurydice in a scene from Anouilh's play:* The honesty and directness that you have keeps you afloat under any and all conditions. No matter how far-fetched the character, you do it with such ease and simplicity that actually it becomes highly theatrical.

At the moment I would like to encourage from you bad results. I want you to let yourself go. I do not want the correct playing of any one scene. That is what now holds your talent in fetters.

Talent is like a fire. No matter how controlled a fire is, the sparks have to get off, and the flames have to leap. A fire which has no flames and no sparks is an electric fire, a mechanical fire. To be a real fire there must be that spurt, that burst, even of smoke which chokes a little but which shows it's burning, that it's about to flare up.

The work we are encouraging you to do is not just good work. Good work you are already doing. But the instrument you have is now a little too bound by habits, customs, manners, and behavior that you have encouraged in yourself and that end up in just a quietness and a simplicity. Here we always see work that is very sound, very good, very nice. It has reality. It has conviction. It is wonderfully modulated. It has great taste. Part of this I would like to overcome. I would like your work to be raw and bad.

I would like you to wallow a little bit in your behavior. There is now great impulsiveness, great sensitivity, which is too locked up. In the scene I saw little things you wanted to do at a moment when some lines were rather suggestive, but you didn't do them. You didn't quite show us what those lines meant.

I would like you now to go to town on any of the things that you work for in order to find out how far you can go. You have very much the sense that a lot of the girls have, which is, "I will be sincere. I don't want to fool you. I don't want to put on make-up that will make me look prettier than I am. I will not put on any clothes that will make me look more attractive. I just want you to realize that I am sincere, and I want you to like me for myself." Well, that's very good, but even sincerity can be served up handsomely, and therefore I encourage you to be sincere, but also to go to town a little bit.

In this scene you are talking about whatever it is you remember in your romantic behavior with him. I want to see that moment, how you really were with him, not just a stage enactment. When you start to remember the first night, you say, "You remember? You took me. You came to the room and you took me then and there." Well, that's nice, but I really don't know from that what happened or how it happened. Anouilh adds "in doublet and hose," which is something to get you over that spot, so that you don't really have to do anything. He implies some theatricalized kind of activity. At that moment I would like from you a fuller giving of yourself to the kind of things that we know exist in life, but that we never see on the stage—even when they are called for. Today when we see on the screen in the French movies even a like image of that, we say, "It's great." When the Lunts as partners used to handle each other not like actors but like people who were not afraid to handle each other, even that made the situation electric or comic or inventive. But even they—except in one scene I remember—always stopped short.

I remember one scene in their production of *The Seagull* that was fabulous. It is the scene in which Arkadina fights for herself against the younger girl. He has told the girl, "I'm coming back," and then he goes inside the house, and Arkadina won't let him go. At the end of that scene she has him groveling at her feet and saying, "I'll stay." Now, I don't know after all these years whether I really saw it, but I remember that as the one time I have ever seen Lynn Fontanne do something suggestive on the stage. It was not done in a vulgar way, because she has extreme good taste, but it was something that suggested the wiles of an older woman who knows how to get a man excited. She did startling things. Somehow she got him toward her and aroused him, sort of made love to him without seeming to, so that by the end of the scene he was completely befuddled by this woman who was more skillful at this than a young girl and therefore had him groveling like a man in heat.

You very rarely see this kind of behavior, because it takes place in private. On the stage we have to be careful how behavior like this is done. But, after all, in novels and in paintings we describe behavior like this. If the playwright deals with it and if it is to be convincingly portrayed on the stage, the actor has to commit himself to a knowledge of what happens.

So what I want to see from you in scenes like this is how this character behaved with this other character. That is what I mean by letting go. I don't mean throwing things or just being externally easier. I mean being easier inwardly. Permitting a greater degree of belief. Coming up with solutions that are not just acting solutions. Showing the imagination of the artist, the recognition of this kind of event, the awareness of how two people make love. In a novel the author would put these things in the descriptions. Here the actor speaks the lines but also creates the entire complex of experience, reality, and situation that the lines suggest. On the stage two actors must act in such a way as to get from each other what the author desires to happen. That is what I mean by letting yourself go. When there is something in an actor's experience that makes him afraid of a particular kind of event, that is a sure sign that there exists in him wonderful material for dealing with that event.

FEAR OF NOT BEING CARRIED AWAY

To ACTOR FF: At the moment you confuse acting with excitement, with doing a lot of things on the stage, but a good deal of the time that is not needed. We should not confuse the excitement which audience and actors share with any necessity to work ourselves up to that pitch of excitement which we sometimes mistakenly suppose an actor must have. We should remember actors like Macready who felt they had to do that kind of thing. Before Macready made his entrance in *Macbeth*, he used to chop wood and flail around backstage and actually wind himself up. Well, that kind of excitement is physiological or muscular excitement. It has a certain aura of emotion, but it is only generalized emotion. It leads to the actor's confusing his own emotion with the character's. The two things are not necessarily the same.

You don't have to work that way. You have a good instrument. Your imagination is good. You give yourself well and easily to the stage. On the contrary, I would like to suggest the simplest, most ordinary kind of exercise in which you do not have to excite or involve yourself too much.

FF: I'd get bored.

STRASBERG: Well, that is true. Nine-tenths of every profession is very, very boring. Unless someone wishes to go through that boredom, he will never become a professional. To achieve the skill that makes for a Heifetz or a Stern, you stand for four hours each day, very bored, but you keep going up and down that fiddle, up and down that fiddle, doing a lot of boring things. The moment you perform is based on these seemingly endless boring hours that you spend every day. Geniuses keep working even though everybody says, "Well, why are you spending your time doing all this for nothing?" They plug away and keep going up and down, up and down, this way, that way, the other way, until suddenly somebody says, "You know, he's a genius."

You have not been close to the theatre. You have very little professional experience. Every time you appear at the Studio is for you an important event. You act for us. You test your wings. That has a value, but the specific value of an exercise depends on individual need. Therefore I want you to be bored on the stage. I want you to learn to bore us and enjoy it. Until you can do that, acting will always be a strange challenge and a fear. You will never be able to take enough ease and time to do on the stage what you have to do, because you will be scared that either you will be bored or—even worse—that we will be bored.

The greatest moments on the stage are moments when the excitement germinates from within, when something very simple and pure and easy comes out and somehow captures for us the complete nature of the play. One of the most memorable events in my theatregoing life was a moment when Duse stood on the stage and smiled. She did literally nothing but smile. The critics, who had come to be excited, had written reviews saying, "Well, we can't quite understand. This is good acting, but a lot of other actors have been more exciting." And I must say I shared their feeling. When I walked home after that performance of *The Lady from the Sea,* I was a little bit let down. I too had gone expecting to be bowled over, and I had watched her perform very simply and very easily. But as I started to think of what she had done, I said, "My God—it's funny, I never quite understood that play, but when she smiled, for the first time I knew what this woman is about. She doesn't really want to leave when she asks her husband to let her go. She only wants the freedom to make her own decision. When the husband finally said, 'All right. If you want to go, go,' at that moment the most beatific smile came over her face. It started in the face, but it actually took in the whole body. She doesn't want to go. She only wants the freedom to make the choice. I think I finally understand the play."

Then I said, "What the hell am I saying? I told myself I wasn't thrilled or carried away. I'm now saying that by means of just a smile I understood more about the play than I ever had before from either reading it or seeing it." This little thing had been a revelation, and yet she had done it very simply, with no muscular strain, and no emotional fervor.

You have now to learn the labor, the boredom, the professionalism, and the technique that belong to the craft of acting and to discover that what you are doing now, just sitting there with your heart pounding and your mind thinking, can be for us the most exciting thing on the stage.

DEMAND FOR MENTAL CLARITY

To Actress DD: We have to remember an interesting anomaly in the theatre. The great actors and actresses have not been obviously intellectual persons. They have been people who somehow understood. They have been people who worked hard to a much greater extent than we ordinarily recognize, but they have not been people who puzzled out their parts.

Edmund Kean came to London at twenty-eight to appear as Shylock. The people who saw him go through the usual half-hearted rehearsal of those days said, "Don't do it. You'll be hooted off the stage. No one has ever done Shylock that way. It's never been played with a black wig. Everyone plays him in a red wig. They'll think you're crazy." The people pleaded with him. He insisted. In some way that he could not explain he had worked on the part. He had to have the black wig, and yet he could not say why. He could not give the kind of analysis that Hazlitt, who saw him in all his parts, was able to write about him in wonderful critical descriptions.

Very unimportant things can and often do stimulate the actor to an extraordinary extent, while a coldly, philosophically, and correctly laid out interpretation often corrupts, stifles, inhibits, and constipates him. The actor knows everything about the part and nothing that he should do to play the part. He binds himself with a lot of ideas he cannot carry out. They do not affect him. They do not lead to behavior. They do not incite him. They do not appeal to his imagination.

Actress GG has "unusual talent and ability. She should be able to generate the power of an Anna Magnani, but she hasn't quite been able to do that because the personal problems of her being hold her back. She has difficulty subjecting herself to the discipline of training or even of work on scenes or roles. Only work that leads her to penetrate more deeply certain experiences, to deal with them, to go further in searching for what is real, will enable her to get what she is entitled to. She is good now, but not as good as she should be."

To ACTRESS GG. I would like to help you define for yourself those basic tasks that you need to concern yourself with in order to be left free to function, those things that have to be conscious so that you can arrive at results which are unconsciously achieved, results which need not be known in the head even though you want to know in order to have that kind of security. Your concern with knowing now ties you down to things that might happen but which are not happening and therefore prepares you for the worst rather than for the best.

You say you have to jump out of the way of the car. You say you want to know which way. Does it matter whether you jump this way or that way? Not at all. The problem is not how you jump or where you jump. The problem is only, Do you stand still or do you jump? Once you decide to jump, jump. You'll find different ways, and you'll find that they are all right so long as they carry you out of the way of the car.

You now say, "Wait a minute. I should jump. But should I jump this way, or should I jump the other way? I don't know." Then you stand still and get hit. Obviously that's bad, but you have a tendency to do that because you are concerned with the wrong end of the problem. Which way you jump makes not the slightest difference. The problems you are concerned with are legitimate problems, but you get involved in seeking the answer in thinking rather than in doing. The two then begin to struggle and fight so that you can't quite solve what needs to be solved.

I am very proud—and I very rarely use that word—that there is an Actors Studio that can serve the purposes of people like you. An Actors Studio that just helps actors develop you can have any time. A lot of people need development. But it is not quite so simple to have an Actors Studio that should serve the purposes of first-rate talents, where the work is not just a matter of saying, "Oh, we know what to tell you. We just tell you one, two, three, and you go up and do it, and you'll have the magic word." No. Talent such as yours is not simple to deal with. It will run away. It will get confused by the very fact that there are more answers than one. It will get confused from its very richness of response.

In you are different kinds of answers. All the answers are right. Not just one answer is right. Which is right at any given moment depends upon the way in which the instrument is responding. You have fifty answers, and all the fifty answers are right, and all the fifty answers are possible.

Which answer will you do today? That depends on how strong the motivation is and how strong the instrument is. How fast will you turn the corner today? That depends on how fast you drive up to it. If you're a good enough driver, you will make the turn, you will somehow get around that corner. But to worry about what might happen if another car should be coming so that you say, "I better go slow"—that is the very thing from which we would like to discourage you. You discourage yourself by thinking about things that stop the solution.

Which answer you will give in a particular scene will depend on the director, on his willingness to leave you free, on his ability to perceive the details that he wants, on his helping to stimulate one area or another, on the partner, and on many other things. What I would like you to learn is to use yourself fully and completely without tying yourself down to a contract in advance: "I will supply five pounds of this." You've got a lot. Just tell me you'll bring me something from the garden. What do I care what you bring me? Today you'll bring me one thing, tomorrow another thing. There are a lot of things there.

VAGUENESS

To ACTRESS N: You are now working more freely and more personally, and yet, even as you are more personally touched and involved, you somehow hold back from drawing conclusions or from making distinctions and from coming to ideas, and therefore from being able tomorrow either to do the same thing as today or to change it if need be.

I don't care whether you can tell us here in the Studio what you did in the scene in the terms in which you think we are asking you to speak. I care only that you should tell yourself. If you can tell yourself whatever conclusions you came to or whatever experience you think you had, we are then perhaps able to share that experience. We are able to see whether our observations coincide with yours. We are able to bring to bear some amount of disagreement or agreement as to the path that you followed. Then we serve a purpose for you, but you serve an even greater purpose for yourself.

When you tell me that you are simply confused, I don't quite know whether it comes from one thing or another thing or from totally different things which you're not even mentioning. Therefore, I sometimes push you to answer me, and whenever I push anyone here, the assumption always is that it's a combat, that I'm putting you on the defensive. No, I'm asking in order to find out. Sometimes the people literally refuse to tell me. You think I'm asking something else, and you keep telling something else that you think I want to hear. When I keep on asking, you then say, "I'm confused." I say, "Yes, I understand that you are confused. At what moment?" You say, "Well, I don't know." I say, "That's impossible."

When I tell you that it is impossible that you don't know when you are confused, you feel that I am calling you a liar. Well, I am, that's right, because it is an impossibility not to know when you are confused if you know enough to know that you are confused.

There is an unwillingness to say, "Wait a minute. When really was I confused? I wasn't confused all through the scene. It was that moment when he put out his hand to me, I don't frankly know what happened. In fact, I'm not sure that was the moment when I was confused." I don't care. If you will tell me as honestly as you can, as a result I am sometimes able to define for you the nature of the confusion. I may have seen something at that particular moment which I can relate to your statement, and thus I may be of some help.

Acting is a profession where the doing and the awareness of the doing must go hand in hand—and not after the doing, but during the moment of doing. This awareness is essential, because the actor carries out the play by means of commands derived from it.

The actor defines the problem; the work is left free. Those are the two sides of the actor's coin. It is a definite coin with a definite significance and value, but to an extent the coin can vary a little bit. The die can slip a little bit, but the coin has to remain the same coin. It will not be legal tender if there is too much of a difference. It will look like a phony coin.

The actor must accept the responsibility of knowing what he is doing. You've got to put the ice-cream soda together and stir it up a little and put it on the counter and give me a bill so that I'll know I'm being served. But if the ice cream is here, and the soda is there, and the cherry is over there, and you say, "Well, there it is. Get it," it's very disorganized; I wouldn't come in here again.

COMFORT AND NATURALNESS

Many loose comments are made about the supposed casualness, sloppiness, and literal acting of so-called "Method" actors. They imply that training in the "Method" is somehow calculated to produce such acting. Nothing in Strasberg's teaching encourages in the slightest degree casualness, sloppiness, or literalness. If actors in Strasberg's classes or the Studio have this problem, it is one of the first things that he tries to attack. It is an attitude toward which he is very antagonistic. These are difficulties that have always afflicted actors; they are in no way engendered by the Studio.

"Method" actors, it is said, are "unreal" and "untrue." Obviously, reality and truth are ideals to which all actors, "Method" or non-"Method," pay lip service. But what is "real" in acting? What is "true"? These makeshift words constantly creep into talk about acting, but they have no unequivocal meanings. It is certainly clear that no group of actors can claim to have a monopoly on reality and truth.

An actor is "real" in the technical sense when his overt response neither exceeds nor falls too short of his imaginative impulse. However, he faces the added problem of becoming "real" in the sense of creating the character, situation, and event which the author has conceived and demands from him. The difficulty with just being natural is that while it enables the actor to be real in the technical sense, it does nothing about meeting the demands of the play. In that sense naturalness is unreal and untrue.

Sometimes the play itself may be so absurd in terms of ordinary experience that what the actor is doing seems somehow spurious. It is often difficult to tell whether an actor is doing a good job in a bad play, or whether a good play is being spoiled by bad acting. There have been many instances of inherently silly plays which were brought to life by good acting to such an extent that the audience thought it was really seeing a good and truthful play. But if good acting can do this for a bad play, good plays must be dealt with on levels of acting quite beyond that of just being comfortable and natural.

When the actor explores fully the reality of any given object, he comes up with greater dramatic possibilities. These are so inherent in reality that we have a common phrase to describe them. We say, "Only in life could such things happen." We mean that those things are so genuinely dramatic that they could never be just made up.

This is not a discovery of mine or of Stanislavski's. Quite a few

years ago—about 1789—there existed in Germany the first dramatic academy, not for students, but for the principal actors of
the Mannheim National Theatre. Baron Dalberg, who was the
head of the theatre, set the actors problems about acting. The
actors would discuss such questions as which is the better recompense, applause or no applause, and which is better for historical plays, contemporary or historical costume? One of the questions that was brilliantly answered was the problem of what is
nature. Among these actors was a romantic actor of great temperament named Johann Friedrich Fleck, and he said that we
must make differentiations when we use the word "nature." Usually when we say a thing is natural, we mean it is ordinary and
common, that it is less than something else. On the other hand,
when we say that "only in nature does such-and-such a thing happen," we mean that only in nature do things of such terrifying
proportions or of such an intense reality occur.

The true meaning of "natural" or "nature" refers to a thing so
fully lived and so fully experienced that only rarely does an actor
permit himself that kind of experience on the stage. Only great
actors do it on the stage, whereas in life every human being to
some extent does it. On the stage it takes the peculiar mentality
of the actor to give himself to imaginary things with the same
kind of fullness that we ordinarily evince only in giving ourselves
to real things. The actor has to evoke that reality on the stage in
order to live fully in it and with it.

To ACTRESS HH: As an exercise, it was a good exercise, but
could have been a little fuller. It is true that the heat you were
concentrating on creating could have been more full.

HH: Well, this dress is soaking wet.

STRASBERG: I didn't get that. No, it wasn't soaking wet. I didn't
get that. The dress was acting well, but you weren't. It was soaking
wet, but I didn't get that from you.

HH: What do I do if it doesn't always show?

STRASBERG: I'm not worried about showing. I'm just talking
about where the concentration was. The concentration accepted

that wetness but didn't really work on it to see how wet it was. No, never mind that it's wet. The question is how wet is it? Is it as wet as you want it to be? Should it be wetter?

HH: Well, you don't do that in life, do you? You know what I mean.

STRASBERG: But in life the reality exists with or without the awareness of the participant. On the stage it has to be created. This is an exercise. You are an actress. This is not in life. You are doing this deliberately to act. The more you will recognize that objective part of the work, the more it will help you and lead you to conclusions that you are entitled to because of your sensitivity. Now these conclusions are often destroyed by your own subjective worry and concern, by your knowing what to do and losing faith and then not knowing quite what to do. Things that seem to you sound, simple, and clear become confused in your own evaluation.

Actor Q has had "very strong and serious blocks." Strasberg has never found out exactly what they are, but Q has "very strong adherence to mental ideas; everything is colored by the meaning of words, so that he really doesn't do anything he means to do. He only associates some gesture or intonation with the intended meaning and effect of words. The Studio has presented to him in a rather roundabout way the need to get away from the scene or anything else in which the mind is involved and to open up his reactions and responses." Only recently has this begun to happen.

To ACTOR Q: My God! You have enough stuff in this scene to make three Greek tragedies, but your tendency is to make everything fall nicely into its place.

True, today the emotion seemed easier. There was a wider gradation of responsiveness and a wider scale of emotion than we have seen from you before in a scene like this. You went ahead, but you actually didn't go anywhere.

You did not say, "Now, in this scene I'm going to find out really what these things mean to me, what really is my relationship to this woman I love and of whom I am jealous. What will happen? What will I feel? What will I experience? What will I do?" It seemed to me that you were willing to settle a little too easily for good results, nice results, but essentially for comfort, and that is not good for you. It retains a sense of noncommitment, of not being willing to go.

An actor should go, even if he goes only with the voice. If that's all that he does, at least that's acting. Bad acting is still acting. But sometimes a certain kind of acting is not yet quite acting. The actor is confusing his own sense of comfort with the search for ease and relaxation, and he is confusing the search for relaxation with what it should lead to. Sometimes the problem of relaxation is basic. In your case I feel that the essential thing is the breaking down of general patterns of behavior. Once you are touched, once the idea comes to you, and once you sort of affirm, "Yes, I've thought of it," you say, "That's real. That's enough now." And therefore there is no revelation.

That's what acting is—acting is a revelation. It's telling us things that in a way we know about people, but we forget about them until the actor tells us.

Even in an external technique there can be this search for reality, but then the actor simply settles for details of reality, how to behave or how to drink or how to burst out. It is an imitative kind of reality, but still it is based on reality, on an awareness and an observation and a recognition of reality.

The approach you used today simply becomes a kind of seeing, "Well, how far can I go and remain relaxed? How far can I go and not force myself and not tense myself?" Well, we don't want an actor to tense or to force, but we do want the actor's concentration really to work on those tasks he has set himself.

If someone wishes to be comfortable, he stays home and doesn't do anything. He doesn't go climbing mountains. When someone climbs mountains, he gets out on the mountain. Obviously he cannot say, "I've got to climb the mountain, but at the same time I can't let myself be uncomfortable." In that case he doesn't go mountain climbing. He stays home. When you go mountain climbing, you go for something you get out of it, some satisfaction, some sense of conquest, the very sense of danger and excitement. You do things dangerously. You do things which may lose you your life. And that conquest leads to the real sense of ease that comes from undergoing that kind of experience.

Today the idea most of us have of reality is casualness, but casualness is only casualness or, at times, naturalness. A lot of times amidst the casualness of life we can't see what's really going on in people, yet we are able to perceive these things on the stage because the actors show us not merely the natural elements necessary to put the play into time and place but what is really happening. Essentially acting means going toward those things that have to be created.

To Actor X: In life there is behavior—sudden movements, sudden gestures, sudden things that people do—which indicates that they are thinking. Stand at Forty-second Street and Broadway for half an hour one day and watch the people walking by. You will see that at least twenty-five per cent of those who are alone are talking, are moving their lips, are occasionally ejaculating words. Others will make gestures with the hands or the head. People act, move, behave. They do not just walk. Some are rushing to get ahead. Some are looking for something, but what it is they don't know. Walking is not just walking nicely and easily so as not to get in each other's way.

Our understanding of these simple things is much too literal. In even simple behavior on the stage, we absolve ourselves from what such behavior would be if we really observed people.

Lift your head for a moment, and look at all the people sitting here. Everybody is sitting differently, differently turned, differently twisted, some people back, some people forward. There are almost no two positions the same. On the stage people sit and listen. The director says, "Come on, show a little life," so the people lean forward a little. That's how they show life. Well, everybody here is showing life, but very few of them are doing so in the conventional way. There is in these little areas that we commonly think of as just natural, as having no possibilities for expression, a much greater degree of responsiveness and behavior than is ever seen on the stage.

JJ is an actress of long experience in the theatre. She had a lot of excellent training as a young actress, and yet "She never really learned to use herself. She shows that training cannot be taken for granted. It has to be maintained and continued to retain its efficacy. Otherwise, the actor settles into natural and believable forms of conventional behavior. When she came into the Studio, the first problem was to make her aware that she was really following an exterior pattern that was believable and natural but not yet accomplishing whatever the character has to accomplish on the stage. It was a ticklish problem to try to stimulate the use of additional areas without robbing her of the facility she had already gained as a result of long, hard work. That experience is ultimately very valuable. It cannot be replaced. It is sound and serves a theatrical purpose. It cannot be cut away too quickly in order to make the actress aware of what should and will finally happen."

To Actress JJ: We do not always say the same thing. The world does turn. But the very thing that some people here referred to so lightly when they said, "Well, of course, you can do this. Therefore, why don't you do more?" is the thing that for two years we have tried to get you to do. Today it was done. Today in that area we have no more criticisms. We are disarmed. The acting *was* simple. This was the first time that almost all the things you did, even the wrong things, coincided with what at that moment was happening to you. That problem seems to be on the road to solution.

However, it is true that we are never satisfied. As we begin to perceive solutions in this one area, we then become very concerned that you should not misunderstand us and assume that all we want is simplicity. You are much too rich. You have much too vivid an imagination. You have much too great a theatrical experience to be limited just to simplicity. We want all things to be fed by one organic kind of impulse. We want to see you share with the character, rather than only demonstrating the character to us like a salesman. This element that we call simplicity is an essential stage in that work.

What we want now is that out of the simplicity, out of the essential concentration that has been developed, there should be concern for the scene rather than concern for yourself in the scene. The purpose of simplicity is to make it possible for you to explore the scene as fully as your own response and imagination and feeling for the possible truth of this kind of event can incite you to do. Unfortunately that was not done, and you now settle for what you did today. But even so this was a great thing for you. As you know, we have never said that to you before.

JJ (*with great dignity*): I want to say something. I understand that, but I was afraid.

STRASBERG: That's right. That is exactly why I am telling you.

JJ: I also have to tell you that the first time I rehearsed this part, I personally kidded this old woman, this character. I'm as vigorous as I can be. I don't know what to do to be sleepy and age myself. Many times I did not feel this truth of myself in the play. My experiences are not the experiences of this woman. And so I decided, instead of doing that which is really perfectly unfamiliar to me, because I am inclined to be savage, that I would do what you saw, the simplicity. That would be easy for me.

STRASBERG: You seem to assume that that is all bad. A good deal of that is good, but I felt in you the fear of doing more, and that's exactly what I do not wish to be responsible for encouraging in you. If the simplicity, which is the real honesty of response, now begins to carry you into areas where you begin to think, "That's melodramatic," you will have to chance that. Otherwise you will ruin a very healthy and good and normal theatricality in order to get something which is also good, but which is unfinished without the other. I made the point that I did because what you did seemed to come out of a fear, and an actor should not ever work out of fear.

I felt myself responsible partly for frightening you in this. At certain times that is necessary in order to get you to do this work. Now you have done it. Now the other things that you have, and have wonderfully, should continue to be done with the same conviction and the same reality that you now bring to these simple tasks.

DESIRE FOR ORIGINALITY

To Actor S: You are now struggling to achieve the things you perceive the author intends. When the actor perceives this, he is always quickly impelled to do the conventional thing. You are trying to go away from this. However, you do not search for the correct and impersonal things to be concerned with so as to develop the logic of the character and situation so that you can give your individuality to the doing of it. Instead you make a subjective choice. You perceive the separate moments of the scene, and you go simply with the color of each moment.

You have contradictory impulses that make you search for originality so that you slide over what is necessary. You look for what is necessary for the scene, and then you get a contradictory impulse, and then you say of what is actually necessary, "Well, yes, that is possible, but it is not necessary now." You stay too close to your own reality. You respond immediately—and then you say, "Well, that is the reality in the scene." Whereas, it may be only *a* reality on a certain level within you and may not have any necessary relation to the scene.

If you wish to be original, say to yourself, "I will pick two moments in the play where I will follow just my impulse." You like to be original. You do not like to do just what anyone else might be inclined to do. Fine. Settle for those one or two things. Do like Hirschfeld, who draws the opening-night cartoons for the *Times.* In some place in every one of those cartoons he puts in his little girl's name. People who know look for that first. They say, "Now,

wait a minute. Where did he get it in this time?" That's his little
bit of originality. If you cannot make up your mind, if you give
in to your desire to put everything in, this unconscious striving for
originality will make you lose the very thing that is necessary for
the scene. Then the knowledge and the sensitivity and the originality that you have will be of no value.

EGO AND AUDIENCE

Only rarely does an actor remain unaffected by the audience.
The presence of the audience may terrify or exhilarate—or both
—but it seldom leaves the actor untouched. Along with will
and concentration, the actor needs the kind of ego that will
sustain him in front of the audience. He also needs the kind of
ego that will carry him through the trials and uncertainties of
the acting profession. Healthy ego in the form of belief is an
essential ingredient of imagination. But ego can also be a hazard.
Sometimes—as the following examples show—ego can lead or
drive the actor into nervousness, complacency, self-disparage-
ment, contentiousness, or an attempt to overpower the audience.
As a result the proper functioning of imagination is suppressed.

M is an actor "whose very strong personal problems stop him
from facing himself." When, for example, Strasberg had occasion to "mention the difficulties he has outside the Studio," he
flared up: " 'Who's having difficulty on the outside?' " Yet "he's
been fired from five parts, and he's walked out of five others,
but 'Who's having difficulty? Nobody's having difficulty on the
outside.' " Strasberg has found it necessary to "lead him a little
easily. Unless the actor himself is willing to face his personal
problem or somehow faces it in his work, it is very difficult to
deal with it."

TO ACTOR M, *after learning of M's quarrel with his partner in
preparing the scene:* The work was sound. The fact that you held
your own against what she wanted is good, except that part of it
comes a little bit out of ego. Often you will do something and
give a good reason for it, when actually it's just as easy to do the
other thing, but to do the other thing means for you to give in,

and you don't like to give in. Please, watch yourself and examine your motives, because at times your real reason for doing certain things has nothing to do with the rightness or wrongness of what is going on on the stage, but rather has to do with a personal psychology of your own.

To Actress KK: All through the scene I felt an inner nervousness which is still your basic problem. Unless you get over that, none of the other things we tell you will have much value. They will not help you to arouse within yourself the many elements you have. Those elements cannot come out until this nervousness is removed.

That kind of nervousness comes essentially from ego. Ego is good for the actor insofar as it makes him want to go on the stage and do something, but ego also has a dangerous aspect, because it implies, "I have to be so good that obviously I cannot possibly be that good."

In life you cook meals. The meal cannot always be perfect. If every time you cooked a meal that was a little less than perfect your husband walked out to the restaurant, cooking a meal would become a terrifying experience. If every time you are less than great on the stage your concentration and belief walk out on you, that too can become terrifying. We are not asking from you just a greater willingness to be free on the stage, but a greater willingness to ask yourself questions different from those you now ask, questions that derive only from your emotional needs, from an effort to create great things on the stage.

To Actor LL: In the back of your mind is always an idea of how a good actor should play this. You are always judging yourself. "Am I good enough to play it the way a good actor should play it?" Well, I don't know whether you're good enough to play it the way a good actor should play it. I only know that you're good enough to play it the way *you* should play it if the things in this scene are vivid, real, believable, and convincing to you. It is true that you have to eradicate certain muscular, mental, and emotional difficulties and inhibitions which now get in your way. However, you have no difficulty in eradicating these things when you are not under pressure. When there is no pressure to act like a good actor, you can make things in a scene believable and convincing to yourself. The difficulty comes only when you face the problem of acting on the stage.

> If Actress H had not been taken into the Studio, "she would have remained just what she was, a secondary actress. She would probably have ultimately settled for doing bits and funny parts. The Studio pushed her to deal really with her talent. From that she began to play small parts wonderfully well, and she started to get better parts. Finally she has become an actress who can play any part she is given very well."

To ACTRESS H: The sense of truth within you now comes from ego which you're struggling with rather than from any real awareness of something on the stage. Forget about that. When you think what you are doing is terrible, when you think it is awful, suffer—but go on. Get the suffering somehow into the scene. Make it part of the character rather than part of yourself. You may find it very valuable; it may be the very thing which, if you go on, will feed in you the beginning of a sense of security which I can never promise you fully because of the peculiar person that you are. But the suffering may get less and less. (*Laughter.*) "Peculiar" is the wrong word. Because of the interesting person that you are. (*Laughter.*)

H: That's worse.

STRASBERG: Well, let's say complicated. That includes all things.

To ACTOR MM: When you get before an audience and desire simply to impress the audience and not to play what should be played, you begin to judge what you do by the way you feel. If you feel good, you think you are getting somewhere. If you don't feel good, then you think you are not getting somewhere. Your judgment of goodness or badness is not related to what is being accomplished. It is related only to a subjective sense of actor's feeling and not to an objective sense of actor's doing.

In some of your recent work there has been an unconscious effort to solve scenes for some kind of self-gratification, for emotional ego gratification. That is a dangerous thing. It leads to reliance on a subjective emotional process, and when that goes nothing is left. There is no logic. There is no actual concentration. The imagination is not really working.

> X is an "actor of great talent and developed as an actor out of ego and desire to attain the top quickly. His energy has been so forced that he literally came over as the opposite of the heroic image he tried to create. He came over as villainous and negative. Eventually he undertook two kinds of work here. The first was pure relaxation. The second was to learn to make contact with his deeply introverted but very strong emotions. They propelled him. Often he could not hold them back. They made him do things on the stage he didn't know he was doing, but he didn't even know what they were. As a result of this work, his type actually began to change. As he lost the forcefulness and harshness and tension, a totally different individual and actor began to develop."

To Actor X: You are beginning to seek the reality of the scene rather than the means of doing it so that the audience will applaud and say you are a great actor. In Grade 6-B I read one of Hawthorne's stories that has been very influential in my life. It is the story of a man called Ernest who lives near a little town in New Hampshire, and opposite the farm where he lives is a mountain whose structure resembles a face. When he is a little boy, his mother tells him the legend that someday a great man will come into the town who will look exactly like the Great Stone Face, and his mother's story makes a great impression. As he grows up, Ernest sees the face every day, and every evening he watches it and dreams of the time when the legend will be fulfilled. Over the years a kind of secret understanding grows up inside Ernest. On every occasion when an important person comes into town, the townspeople flock together hoping that the legend is about to come true, and sometimes think they see the resemblance in some particularly famous man, but Ernest always has to shake his head and say, "No, he doesn't resemble the Great Stone Face." And then he would go back to his farm and wonder why the great man did not appear. And then one day, when Ernest has become an old man, another famous man, a poet, comes to the town, and Ernest introduces him to the crowd. But when this great poet gets up to speak, suddenly a murmur runs through the crowd, and the poet turns and sees what has struck the people: in the setting sun Ernest's face is revealed as the likeness of the Great Stone Face. And so the legend comes true—though not in the way that anyone expected.

The actor creates with his own flesh and blood all those things which all the arts try in some way to describe. Goethe said that an actor's career develops in public, but the actor's art develops only in private. The Studio exists to encourage that private process of creation. I do not know what plays you are going to do, or what parts you are going to get. I am only concerned that you should find your way toward not pushing, not leaping, not almost breaking your neck to get from us, "Ah! what a wonderful leap! What a great actor!" We want you to work at certain moments easily and soundly and simply, and at other moments to work more within yourself, because we know that out of that work done in quietness comes little by little a greater thing, the art of the actor. Finally, as he looks deep within himself, the actor finds in that communion knowledge beyond what is explainable in words—which is the knowledge that all art aspires to reach.

CHAPTER VII

Problems: Expression

Acting problems—distinct from those of imagination—can appear at the level of expression. The magnitude of these problems is one of Strasberg's most important discoveries, though actors and directors have always been aware of them. It was not until Stanislavski found out that healthy acting works through stimulating imagination rather than through emphasizing expression that the separate identity of these two kinds of problems became clear. An active imagination does not necessarily guarantee proper expression. Most of the problems described in this chapter can hinder actors who have no difficulty in stirring their imaginations. Often the cure for problems of expression is simply to make the actor aware of them. Ultimately every actor should develop the full awareness that Stanislavski calls "the sense of truth." But before the actor reaches that final stage, he must often depend on other people—teachers or fellow craftsmen—to inform him of the quality of his expression and to suggest remedies for his problems.

Cliché or conventional acting is, of course, the sign of a mediocre actor. But very talented actors may also be plagued by their full, ready impulses' being transmuted into mannerism or convention when they emerge as expression.

Other actors are afflicted by the problem of inexpressiveness. Their imaginations seem dead, because they either have been conditioned not to express their impulses or have simply never created channels through which their impulses can complete themselves on the expressive level.

A third kind of actor is troubled by involuntary expression that stems from nervousness. Often these actors are not even aware that it is happening; at other times, though aware of it, they cannot help themselves.

A fourth problem, distorted expression resulting from forcing, is related to imagination. Forcing emotion must usually be dealt with at the imaginative level, but forcing tempo is peculiar to the level of expression. The solution—relaxing the tempo—works because it frees the actor's instrument to respond to his imaginative impulses.

The final problem discussed is the result of a split between imaginative activity and expression: when the actor's imagination is working, he does not express; when he is expressing, he is not fed by imagination. A solution to this problem is especially important with Studio actors, because the Studio's ideal of acting calls for a greater fusion of impulse and expression than is common to the ordinary actor who seeks only effectiveness.

CLICHÉ

The actor comes to a scene—whether he knows it or not—with strong conscious and unconscious ideas of how the scene should be played. That basic situation was first pointed out by Stanislavski. Other people had criticized actors as conventional or mechanical or imitative, but no one before Stanislavski had ever really set himself the problem of defining what that means. Why should an actor act that way? He doesn't want to be good? He doesn't want to be original? He doesn't want to be striking? An actor wants to imitate? An actor wants to be mechanical? Obviously not. Then where does such acting come from?

Stanislavski tested his ideas on himself, watched himself, verified, changed, and expounded, and thus he realized that this kind of acting satisfies a very strong need for security in the human being when he goes on the stage. The actor comes to a scene. Before he even starts to work on it, an idea of how the scene should be done is already clear in his mind.

Where can such an idea stem from? Obviously from the human being's inclination to habitual response. And habitual response in acting leads to what Stanislavski called the cliché. I call it the "verbal line" and other things, but those are simply different forms of cliché. I am terribly concerned about the cliché, because it means that the primary impulse to creation is lost and that work on a scene goes into unconscious patterns—all the worse because they are unconscious. When you are conscious, you say, "Oh, look what I'm doing. It's all wrong." But when the actor does not know how to solve some acting problem, these unconscious patterns assert themselves, and he says, "Well, I have lines. Okay. I will just say the lines with energy and effectiveness." As soon as he does that, acting becomes impossible. I constantly see the situation where the actor has reality inside, the instrument is working, the imagination is working, the emotions are working, and yet all these things are completely stifled because, as the actor starts to act, it all comes out in conventional expression.

It is difficult to realize how much the sense of "I'm doing, I'm acting" can commandeer the mind. It is difficult to realize how strong and animal-like the adherence to a verbal pattern or convention can be. It is difficult for the actor to perceive how ferociously the cliché holds on to him.

The conventional mold holds out to the actor the attraction of security. After all, a convention becomes a convention because it has proved its effectiveness. It has taken years to develop. It is both acceptable and impressive. It may be phony, but it gives results on the stage. That's why bad acting is always acting. Even if it's bad, it still deals in performance with some of the problems that have to be accomplished in the scene.

In wiping out conventional routine the teacher is of great importance. The destruction of cliché is his central task for the pupil. The actor, after all, can practice training exercises at home. In fact, actors' work is mostly done at home. But this work will not be fed into expression with the conviction of reality and truth without breaking the cliché, because the actor is very often completely unaware of the cliché pattern. Keeping the actor away from the wrong thing is the decisive area in which the teacher works.

Strasberg occasionally employs abstract exercises in dealing with the problem of cliché. One is an exercise in permissiveness. Another, the gibberish exercise, is designed to place the actor in a situation where he is forced to avoid cliché.

I have a crazy exercise to accomplish what you call the sense of "Here we are, and let's see what will happen." It is called permissiveness. The actor chooses any speech or monologue. He says to himself, "I'm going to sit and work with these words." He does not prepare *how* he is going to say the words. He does not worry whether or not he will get emotional. The purpose is to see whether or not the actor will permit whatever he is really thinking to come into the words. The exercise is designed to make the instrument completely free to respond to whatever impulses are fed into it. And since the impulses in the exercise are spontaneous, they may go in any direction.

For example, the first line may be, "I have to tell you something. I don't know what I have to tell you because I—" At that moment there may feed into the line the actor's feeling, "My wife. You don't like my wife." This has nothing to do with the line as such. Nobody has said anything about his wife. Sometimes these banal phrases come out with meanings and connotations that are hair-raising. The exercise is very difficult to do, because the lines the actor says have no meaning in themselves. He can only feed into the lines the meaning of whatever thought is actually transpiring—no matter what it may be. If he can do so, it means that at this moment he has been able to rid himself of those preconceptions which unconsciously lead the actor to imitate the conventional idea of how a thing should be done.

To Actor NN and Actress OO: Words are not speech. Words are action. The word does not begin with speech. The word begins with an object which it seeks to define. The word originates in the effort to communicate to another person. The gibberish exercise teaches that the word itself, which we commonly take for granted because it is so familiar to us, should not be taken so easily for granted.

Although we are today very free in life, yet there is great in-expressiveness. When we have to say something to someone, about all we can do is say, "How about it, baby?" We are not really quite able to express what we want to say.

The gibberish exercise forces the actors really to understand each other and to make themselves really understood. For ex-ample, if he says something to you, and you don't know what he's talking about, you say, "Uh-huh." He then has to make clear what he is saying and yet continue to use gibberish. Or she may come in and do something and then say something, but you don't know what she says in words because she is using gibberish; nevertheless she's supposed to make you understand. Thus each of you learns to listen freshly and also learns to expedite the sense of expression in the words. But each must hold the other to strict account so that the exercise calls for more convincing acting than the actors would give without it.

To ACTRESS OO: Did you understand everything that he said?

OO: Not everything.

To ACTOR NN: Did you understand everything that she said?

NN: No, but a good deal.

STRASBERG: Yet you both went ahead as if you understood each other. The exercise was excellent in that both of you seemed fluent and flexible and colorful, but I doubt that you understood half the time except generally what each of you was saying. What she was really saying and what you were really saying was at many times unclear. And yet we all noticed how much more expressive the voice becomes in the gibberish, how the thought that is really being thought gets into the tone.

I used gibberish in the Group Theatre for a specialized purpose. I found it most helpful in dealing with actors who had an emo-tional problem in that they could feel, but expressing the feeling was difficult. In one play I had great problems with an actress, but also with my backers, who wanted the show to be finished so they could see what was going to be done. However, because of my difficulty with this actress, I didn't wish to finish the production.

There were scenes in which she had to cut loose emotionally, but they had no real lift. They were cloaked in conventionality. I wanted her constantly free and improvising in the hope that what we were working for would break through. Fortunately in the last week the break-through came, and it came through gibberish. She had to keep doing these emotional things and talking about them in gibberish, and in using sounds and words that broke away from her conventional and habitual tightness, she exploded.

When Actress U came to the Studio, "she was already well established. The audience thought of her as a top actress, but they had rightly begun to think of her as mannered. She had continued to act in the very ways she had acted in her first parts. What had seemed natural to begin with began after a while to appear as the mannerisms of an actress rather than the characteristics of a part." The Studio has attempted to "rid her of these mannerisms," has tried "to make her aware that they were mannerisms that have nothing to do with reality. Although she was perfectly capable of dealing with the reality of a character, she simply had not gone far enough in that, and no one had pushed her to go far enough."

Strasberg also tried "to deepen the intensity of her reaction. She tended to take her emotions very easily and quickly, but lightly. Her acting was hit-and-run—which intrigued the audience and seemed very good. It was very good, in fact, but often it did not deal with what had to be accomplished in a situation or a character. She was quick in response. Therefore, she assumed that whatever happened happened, and when it didn't happen, it was difficult and nothing could be done about it." Strasberg tried "to suggest that there are ways and means of stirring the actor's 'rise-ability,' or creativeness, or simple willingness to live on in the kind of experience that the author demands, so as to go beyond what the actor previously thought he could do. The real flair of her temperament has not yet come out. The audience has seen her sensitivity and the mercurialness of her response, but the full depth of her response has not yet quite been seen."

To ACTRESS U: I like you too much, and I like the work you do, and yet somehow I feel that it is not good in your case to be kind, and yet we cannot stop ourselves. Your work always has this wonderful ease which amazes us and shows us the working of your sensitivity. The unconscious nine-tenths of your sensitivity works wonderfully. The conscious one-tenth does not work as fully as it should. You take yourself as if you could afford to be vague— and fortunately you can. Even when you are vague, these wonderful things come along.

I have a feeling that you are not as vague as you describe. I have a feeling that when you come to a scene, the scene is often just too rich for you to make a decision. Well, you need not worry about what you will do, but you do need to worry about that part of the work which is in your conscious control.

U: What *is* that?

STRASBERG: I don't want you to work with apples, darling. I don't want you to work with all these props. If *you* do not know what to work for, then, goddammit, come on the stage and find out. I think you know. You just don't want to come to grips with it, even if it's no more than saying, "Lee, I can't give up the apple. I must hold onto it. I need it." Fine! But I want that apple to be an abstract instrument. I can get an actress that will peel that apple and look natural and real. But if you come in with that apple, I want you to say to yourself, "This apple is going to be peeled so that I will take off the least skin that I've taken off in my life. I will be so careful about this apple that I will not take off an unnecessary jot—only the surface!" I would like this apple to be a net that catches in you the elements of this character.

In this scene there was much less fooling around and fussing around. There was much less using those few simple things that an audience will always accept from you, but which I will not accept because they are throwing you off. I want you to come in with no help—sink or swim. You don't need water wings, but you always come in with a little well-tested water wing on the side. I'm sorry. You're a strong swimmer; we will not let you hold back.

We will not let you encourage this vagueness in yourself, this mannerism which has become a little joke that we like. It's wrong of us to encourage you by liking that. We like these things. They show you're human. They call out our sympathy. I do not want you to put us in a position where we should sympathize with you. You do not need our sympathy.

> Actor QQ is "a perfectly capable actor. He can go on at a minute's notice and give a very sound, clear, good performance, but it doesn't move him, and it doesn't move the audience. When he explains a scene he has performed at the Studio, it is brilliant. But you ask, 'Now, wait a minute, why didn't you do that on the stage? Where was that in the part?' He thinks he has actually done what he has only described." The Studio's problem is to make him aware that in him the actor's thinking does not lead to doing on the stage. He has very strong habits, very strong patterns of behavior, very strong verbal patterns, very strongly inhibited emotions which he doesn't quite know how to deal with. He did a wonderful Hamlet at the Studio, which "gave him for the first time a sense of his problem. He now realizes that he is in a shell, that the actor's problem is not just conception, but making his conceptions somehow grow within him until they ignite and motivate his being, his behavior, his thinking, and his experience. He now has a sense of that." How far he will go, Strasberg does not know.

To Actor QQ: You say that you work on parts in professional production more than you work on parts at the Studio. You then say that although you work less hard here, somehow you often get better results. From that you must draw a conclusion.

We understand something that people on the outside do not understand. They think that when the actor does something bad on the stage, it's because he's a bad actor. We know that bad work on the stage often comes from the finest intentions of a mind working with wonderful brilliance, but then something takes possession of you. You say, "I want to stop"—and you can't. You say,

"I don't want it to come out this way"—and you can't stop. You say, "Jesus Christ, what am I doing? I don't want to do this phony business with the pipe"—and the pipe goes on and keeps making you do it. That's what we mean by clichés. That's what we mean by the conventional way of doing it, the thing you think should be done because you have seen people—usually bad actors, but sometimes good actors—do it that way. You just will not accept the evidence of your own senses and your own experience. Why?

It is easier to do what Guinness has done because the audience has already put the stamp of approval on it. But not even the audience has put the stamp on it to the extent that you think, because there are a lot of things that we forgive Guinness. When he does something on television very poorly, we say, "It's just another of Guinness's kind of things." But he should do it well. He's a good actor. Why not do it as well as he can? No, he too begins to settle after a while for the way Guinness would do it—not the way Guinness would do it if he weren't Guinness. You begin to see not Guinness acting, but Guinness giving an imitation of the way Guinness acted. And that you see with all actors. That is the price they pay for success, and that is why success does not pay off. If it did, we would make a technique out of that.

I hope it is becoming clearer that when I say these things, I mean it in simple Broadway terms. I don't mean it in arty terms. I am talking about something that will take a talent as good as yours and make it usable on Broadway. Today, as you know, certain people say your talent is good—but you don't get the part. Why is that? There must be some reason for it. It's not something that we're doing; it's the other way around. I am trying to get you the parts you are capable of playing by making you able to use that talent which is yours and which is therefore special to you.

You have driven yourself into a blind alley from which your present work cannot lead you forward to a use of all your mentality, your imagination, your awareness. Whatever you now do, you wind up giving somebody else's answer because you see too quickly how someone else would do it. But they do it because they are themselves. They have found their way. And you have to find your way.

When Actress O worked on the funeral scene from *Richard the Third* * she was using preparation to overcome cliché. Strasberg asked her to repeat that scene at several Studio sessions so that he could comment on details as she was actually performing. Such an "interrupted rehearsal" is one of Strasberg's most effective "tools" in attacking problems of expression, particularly cliché, inexpressiveness, and fusion. Impulse passes into expression unconsciously to such a large extent that only by making the actor aware of what is happening at the moment it happens can Strasberg hope to break habitual patterns and strengthen the actor's will in this area. Strasberg has used the "interrupted rehearsal" technique—a sample is included in the next section, "The Habit of Inexpressiveness"—over a period of years in working with Actress O. Following is his description of her cliché problem. In working on it, Strasberg never permitted her to settle for the first performance of a scene, because her habitual patterns of behavior always asserted themselves first.

To ACTRESS O: You are now able to arrive at a very wonderful and strong inner reality. We have been very excited by your recent work. The quality is very far from the pale quality of the conventional image of yourself that you used to create in the movies and from which you suffered and died. However, you have not yet made sufficient use of that inner reality on the stage so that you feel free and easy, and you have not yet evolved your own way of expressing these deep emotions, these real things which are the truest and best parts of yourself.

A lot of your acting has tended to be on the external side. A long time ago you formed unconscious acting habits. Now, when you start with something as fresh and exciting as your actual re-

* See page 134.

sponse on the stage today, you have difficulty in letting this response feed the words.

As you start to say Lady Anne's words about Henry, the words have for you a conventional mourning quality. In fact, in the middle of the scene if you listened carefully to yourself, you could hear the sound go up, each note a half-tone higher. Fielding in the eighteenth century described this in the acting of King, who played with Garrick, "Oh, and now," and *"Oh, and now I will,"* and "OH, AND NOW I WILL," on and up, on and up, the conventional lyric tone used for speaking this kind of words.

But then what happens inside you is that you need to express your wonderful inner sense. Something wants to come out and do a completely different thing from the conventional. And this something which is not satisfied tries to do what is needed only through the tone. You are always making the external effort to convince us that you are doing and saying what you are obviously already doing. That comes from the actor's unsureness and leads to a certain kind of restlessness. However, what also happens is that what is in front of you takes over and convinces you more than what is inside.

When I watched what was happening inside, I saw something which could have come out in a real and human kind of expression instead of this theatrical carrying-out. When you started to cry, after the scene here, you did not say, "I have to cry now because this is for the scene." No. You turned your face away. You seemed to say, "Please, I don't want to, but I have to cry." If you had done the scene with the ease and naturalness that you used when you thus turned away and afterward when you spoke to me, you would have shown a logical and human behavior. What you actually showed was the behavior of an actor who thanks God and Stanislavski that the emotion is working and says, "Okay. Now I can go to town. Last time it didn't work, but now it's working. It's so wonderful. I can really let it go." So what happened were things that make me as a human being cringe.

When you threw yourself onto the dead body, I cringed— hu-

manly, not theatrically. Theatrically I like it. I have *seen* people
do that, but the sense of deadness is so clear that they do not treat
the body simply as an object which is lying there. An *actor* does.
The body is simply an object that receives his theatrical impulse
and emotion. That is not the way a human being deals with a
real body. When he becomes aware of what he has done and finds
his hands holding the clammy body—I went through tortures as
you were acting that, because I have great difficulty even looking
at that kind of thing.

To me it is always exciting to see theatrical things come alive
—not just to see theatrical things. For many years I had a fear of
going into churches because of certain things in my background.
Well, you can't be in Italy and not go into a church, because after
all the art is all in the churches, so naturally I went in. But what
was wonderful was what we saw in Venice. When we were there,
they brought back to rest in the cathedral at Venice, which was
his place, the body of a pope who had been beatified. They had
the same kind of festival that you see in the Bellini paintings
where they bring the body from the boat into the cathedral. And
the whole thing, colors, sound, everything, was brought alive for
me by one thing. There was all this panoply, all this wonderful
color. There was this procession of priests with the little acolytes
walking in back, and at one moment one of the priests walking
in the procession saw somebody he knew in the crowd, and he
suddenly lifted up what he was carrying and waved it at his friend
—and somehow the whole occasion came alive. The spectacle was
magnificent; it was picturesque; it was theatrical, but it was that
little bit of reality that somehow made it alive.

When I later went into the cathedral in Venice, the thing that
won me so that I felt, "Now I can go in," was that I saw a typical
Italian woman, dressed in black, and she had her lunch in a little
bundle, and she was tired. So she sat on the base of one of the
pillars, and she took her shoes off and started cleaning them out.
And I said, "This is a temple of God, because human beings are
here." If we tried to stage scenes like those, we would try to be

theatrical, and we would tend to become so abstract that it would be only obviously theatrical and therefore phony.

Your emotions and thoughts and ideas and intentions are beginning to work powerfully; the sense of what is going on is being permitted now to a much greater extent, but your previous encouragement of a theatrical way of behavior sometimes causes your impulses to come out theatrical, not human.

THE HABIT OF INEXPRESSIVENESS

Inexpressiveness is perhaps an even more serious problem than cliché. After all, cliché is an attempt to give meaning to the play, though it does not succeed beyond a superficial level. But the inhibited actor is often blocked unconsciously from even attempting to give meaning through expression. Consequently a continuation of such inhibited patterns is literally the death of the actor's talent. Strasberg is extremely concerned about this problem and goes to great lengths in dealing with it.

He tries to make clear to the actor that his lifelong patterns of nonexpression are carried over into acting. Sometimes he attempts to isolate in the actor's past the experiences and situations that have set up such inhibited patterns, and works at strengthening the actor's concentration and will. However, he deals with the problem principally by attempting to induce the actor really to express himself before an audience.

Since expressiveness is natural to the human being, inhibition is likely to result not in mere lack of expression, but in a log jam of emotions that the person needs and desires to let out but cannot. This is likely to result in tensions and frustrations. The actor may then try to overcome the block by forcing, which makes for distortion and further frustration. A log jam is alleviated not by keeping logs out of the river, not by removing all the logs in the jam, not by digging a new river channel, but by dynamiting the key log in the jam. If the key log can be removed, dramatic results ensue.

By using gibberish to force the Group Theatre actress to unprecedented expression, Strasberg was able to elicit such dramatic results. His experience with the private-moment exercise and the song-and-dance, which permit the inhibited actor to show and do things that he knows he can do, illustrate the sometimes dramatic release of a key log-jamming expression. Sometimes the problem can be alleviated simply by getting the actor to relax.

Strasberg's firmness with actors who are afflicted with inexpressiveness derives from a recognition, based on long experience, that the actor cannot temporize with patterns of behavior that literally kill his talent.

To ACTOR M: Many people are unable to carry a melody. We have experimented and found that this has ramifications beyond singing. It is tied up with emotional response. The vocal mechanism is very strongly tied up with early training and therefore with the entire responsiveness of the human being. Overcoming the inability to carry a melody has a great deal to do with acting in that it helps free the actor from certain unconscious drawbacks in the area where whatever is going on within himself transmits itself to the outside.

I have a girl in my classes, for instance, who has difficulty with melody. She is able to carry the tune, but at times her concentration or energy is not sufficient. Her energy retreats because it is afraid to make a mistake; therefore, instead of hitting the tone, the energy gets panicky, and then flies away. This fluctuation is completely illustrative of the emotion going on inside.

In almost every case the difficulty is related to emotion and not to an actual physical disability. Almost invariably a person who doesn't quite remember whether as a child he could sing or did sing or how he sang can still remember the time when he was discouraged from singing.

Oddly enough, women are more subject to this difficulty than men. We try to explain that men are less susceptible because boys go through the voice change, and at that period the onus is taken off the individual. Every boy goes through that period. Therefore, no matter what has happened to a boy previously, at that age he begins to consider difficulty in singing not as an individual lack of accomplishment, but as a sign of manhood, of growing up. And most men do grow out of it, so don't worry. You're in a select group. This has nothing to do with singing.

M: I'd like to blame my family. My sister can't sing at all.

STRASBERG: No. Sometimes it's the other way around. Sometimes in the family there is one person, a brother or a sister, who sings very well, and so that leads to the difficulty.

It is true that family elements are very important, because they are the first major conditioning factor for the young human being. The next important factor is the school. Usually the first memory of people with this difficulty is being told to stand aside. The teacher goes around and listens and smiles and says, "Why don't you stand over there? Just listen." I remember one person who told me how he tried to steal back, and the teacher went around and listened and picked him out again.

Now, I will tell you what to do in this exercise* in order to work on this problem. Sing the song easily and simply. Do not stop. If you forget the words, don't worry. Go on with the melody. Try as much as possible not to stop. Sometimes there builds up a great desire to stop so as not to fail, but try to keep singing easily in the rhythm of the song.

Stand completely still. Try to watch so that there will be no movement outside of singing the song. Keep a little of the mind free to watch for movement. If you feel a little tense in any area, don't do anything. Get rid of the tension mentally.

Sing with normal actor's energy, that is, with the energy that is usual for the actor but higher than the ordinary individual energy in life. Sing so that the tone is firm, simple, and definite. But don't worry about the melody. Rather pay attention to the sense of resonance, the sense of feeling in the whole body a certain vibrancy.

As you go on, strange things, emotional annoyances, feelings that "I'm gonna bust if I don't let go," may happen. Or nothing like that may happen. If it does happen, continue to sing with good energy and definition. Don't worry whether you go on or

---

* This was one of Strasberg's early experiments with the song-and-dance.

off. Don't try to correct too much. If the emotional thing happens, ask yourself, "What the hell is this?"

Don't hold on to yourself. Stand free. Stand solid. If anything happens, I'll give you a command, so don't worry. Okay? All right. Let's hear it.

(*M sings "My Country, 'Tis of Thee."*)

STRASBERG: Your tone of voice is excellent. There's absolutely no reason why with that quality of voice you can't sing. Usually the tone itself is inhibited. There was no lack of resonance, which would imply a definite break between the individual and the voice. That means part of you is functioning very well, and some other part related to volition and consciousness has for some reason been inhibited in the area of singing, and therefore you have never practiced it.

Now, let's try this. Without thinking ahead of what you're going to do, start to move in march rhythm and then sing the song. Like this (*Strasberg sings "My Country, 'Tis of Thee" loudly and stamps his feet to the rhythm.*) Whatever you do, maintain that simple continuity of rhythm. Start to move, and then sing out. Yell. Try to sing the melody without worrying where it is going. Do it with full energy and real effort.

(*M sings again.*)

STRASBERG: Actually, you know the melody. The tune simply goes a little off and on. If there were a real physical difficulty, it should have gotten worse because by making you stamp your feet we took away the possibility of your paying attention to the melody. It's a strange thing—you slide off a little bit, you come back. Actually, it comes more from a lack of will and following through of effort than from any actual difficulty.

Let's try another exercise now. Stand completely still, and this time sing the song not for us but for yourself. Almost hum it, but as slowly and evenly as possible. Stand absolutely quiet. Even though I didn't stop you before, you were moving the head. This time I will tell you, "Stop moving," and you will have to make an effort to stop. During the exercise, you may find that a time comes when you've got to move. At that moment, move—but really full. Not little involuntary movements where the hand twitches. I don't care what you do, just so you let the impulse out. If necessary, stop and look at us. Really look at us. Don't just make believe. Really see us. Make clear to yourself that you're real and we're real—regardless of what's happening to the tone. Make sure that the tone's a reality, not a fake. There's no acting. You're not pretending. You are really here. Right? Okay.

(*M sings.*)

Strasberg: You repeat the same form. In other words, you repeat the same wrong note. Well, that shows that you can carry a tune, but you're carrying the wrong tune. (*Laughter.*) It's flabbergasting, really. You get something in your mind, but you don't really pay too much attention to it, because you've given up the idea that you can sing. Therefore your effort in singing is a little lamed and inhibited. When you repeat the wrong thing, it's always the same wrong thing. That means you are fooling yourself. The voice is good, but you are afraid to let go. When you do let go, things come out suddenly, and you catch yourself. You are trying to be conscious of that. Be conscious of it, but don't worry about it. Let it come out. And it cannot be done if you're not going to make the effort in life, too. The habit was created in life and now lingers on the stage. So it has to be dealt with in both areas.

A break-through for the inhibited actor cannot be hoped for except in improvisation. If the emotionally bound up actor merely rehearses and performs, almost inevitably he will merely continue his patterns of inexpressiveness. One technique requires the actor to prepare both a private-moment exercise and a character and scene that are closely related to himself. He begins with the private moment, which is, of course, improvised. When his inner reality has been sufficiently stirred by the private moment so that impulse, concentration, and expression are full, he begins the scene—which is sometimes but not always improvised—and tries to carry over from the private moment the fullness of impulse and freedom of expression. Expression during the scene is further stimulated by commands from Strasberg.

Actress RR came into the Studio "very young and showed up wonderfully well. She seemed to have a very free, natural talent. Her first few exercises were excellent." But from the very beginning it was predictable that "there was a price she would have to pay when she had to do a definite thing rather than only what just poured from her. And when it came to making use of herself to carry out a definite problem, such as a director might set her to do, she did have trouble. Her very tough acting problems obviously go back to and are related to deep personal problems. She has trouble following through a task without becoming involved in something that has nothing to do with it, some feeling or emotion or extraneous difficulty. Yet it is generally supposed that an actor should not have the problem of being stifled psychologically, that if he has this problem he shouldn't act. It is not realized that the actor acts out of these peculiar sensitivities. Every artist works out of peculiar sensitivities. His sensitivity to the things he comes in contact with produces the responses and attitudes and expressions that make him an artist."

Actress RR worked on Juliet's scene of waiting for the Nurse to return from arranging the marriage with Romeo (Act Two, Scene Five). She began the improvisation with a private moment which included recorded music. Then, before she repeated the improvisation, Strasberg questioned her about her methods of private preparation at home.

To ACTRESS RR: Don't tell me exactly what is involved. The point is that the private activity does give you something inside. From then on you go more or less with the lines of the scene, and these lines suggest certain meanings or moods to you. You seem to be tearful at certain moments because the idea of what is happening in the scene affects you. Right? Now, as a part of the private activity, do you use anything definite? Like preparing with music?

RR: You see, sometimes, when I'm getting dressed and I'm putting my make-up on, sometimes I just say these lines. Especially after I've had a bad— (*Mumbles.*)

STRASBERG: What? I can't hear a word you're saying, darling.

RR: After I come home, and I'm either taking off make-up or putting on make-up or washing clothes, and I'm conscious of something, and I just say the lines then, and then—and then after that, then, the nights that I actually rehearse it, I do something like I did here.

STRASBERG: Yes, darling. I'm trying to differentiate between two kinds of work you do when you are alone. One kind you choose deliberately because it incites you to create something that you feel is desirable in the scene. The other kind is accidental, when you practice the lines while doing something else, in the hope that practicing at that moment, easily and without pre-setting, will give you some way of doing the lines. Basically this second kind of activity is accidental. It is not related to creating for you a mood or some definite relation to the scene. It just makes you feel natural and real and therefore helps to induce a certain sense of conviction when you say the lines, so that certain emotional things happen. But they happen accidentally, and, as you say, today it didn't happen.

However, your use of music is not accidental. When I stopped you, you were starting to say that the music you used is somehow related for you to a sense of the scene, to a mood, to the start of the imaginative condition or state in which Juliet should be when the scene starts. That is a necessary thing. The other activity is accidental. Right? Okay. Now, when you start the lines, you then have moments when you feel it isn't going right. What do you do at those moments?

(*RR mumbles.*)

STRASBERG: What?

RR: I cuss and start over again.

STRASBERG: Yeah. But what do you do? You stop. Right? Now, if you have enough mood and emotion to curse, why don't you do that with the lines? Juliet's pretty annoyed in the lines about what is happening. You always stop. When you criticize yourself, you stop. That is deadly for the actor, because at that moment the motor *is* turning over. You know what you do with a motor as it starts to turn over? You catch it at that moment and give it the gas. If you stop, it won't keep going. The actor can never on the stage afford to lose his will to be, to do, to go on and not stop, but you always stop. Even when the thing is not going badly, you stop. Today when you spoke the lines the first time, you came to a line that started to make you weep. At that very moment when emotional things started to happen to you, you said, "Oh, hell!"—you used another word—and you broke off. Things at that moment were beginning to happen.

RR: But—

STRASBERG: But what?

RR: But they only happened because I couldn't do it. The impulse came like that (*snaps fingers*) and went.

STRASBERG: What do you mean "went"?

RR: It came when I couldn't do it, and I said—a cuss word, and then—

STRASBERG: Nope! I'm sorry. You were crying before then. You started to cry from the lines. In fact, you are invariably moved by that moment in the scene. Now, my interpretation of what happened is the opposite of yours. My interpretation is that something emotional starts to happen. You then don't know what to do with the lines to fulfill what is happening. You feel that there is a split between something that you're beginning to feel and the expression of the feeling through the words. You feel pulled both ways, and then you stop. And that is the very thing that you cannot do.

There are many, many moments throughout the work you are now doing when you are ready to take advantage of your impulses, and you don't do it. Almost every time in this exercise, when you were ready you didn't do it. You would always delay, go on, lessen whatever it was you felt, go on to something else, and then finally you said to yourself, "Well, now it's time to speak the lines," and you spoke. But at the moment when something was happening, you did not speak. At the moment when you had tears, you wanted to stop. At other moments when you were quiet, but something was beginning to take place inside of you, you never used words. That means that you do the opposite of what you should do.

The problem is not just the problem of how Juliet should be played. That will vary with different directors; each will have his own interpretation. But after that your basic problem will remain —how to get yourself to do what you want to do so that you are both convincing for the audience but at the same time have belief in yourself.

You criticize yourself so much and stop so much that you do not catch your impulses and make use of them. The expression is stultified. Thus an interesting thing happens. You know that emotional things happen when you are quiet, but as soon as you start speaking, you stop the emotion that you have. So, when you do stop that way, you then have to try to find some other emotional thing to give you the desire to start the words again. This is not just a stage problem. As you very well know, even in life you have very great difficulty telling us what you think and feel. It's basically a problem of your instrument, and therefore we have to approach it through often devious devices.

In a play a director would get expression from you by his own devices. But after you had finished that play, you would not necessarily know how to express yourself in another play. What we do in the training of the actor is to help him learn to create by himself so that he can give a director the kind of things he asks for. Then the actor does not have to be constantly supported by the director and told what to do.

What I want to try now is partly the same exercise and partly a different thing. Can you sing the music without playing the record?

RR: Can I just hum it? Do you mean sing the words?

STRASBERG: Why did you say "just hum it"? You don't like to sing it without the music? You're afraid you won't know it? Or what?

RR: I'm just wondering— I don't know that I would know the words without the music.

STRASBERG: All right. Well, it won't bother me, so if it won't bother you, we can try it first with the music. I want you to try the scene with the position you had in the chair.

RR: In the chair? Upside down?

STRASBERG: Upside down? Yeah. I don't know. You know. Hanging over.

RR: Let me tell you something first.

STRASBERG: Yeah. Tell me.

RR: I feel so tied up.

STRASBERG: Yes, I know, darling. That's what I'm going to work on with you. That's exactly it. No—

RR: Besides, I can't feel anything.

STRASBERG: I don't care about the feeling. The "tied up" isn't a matter of feeling. You cry and you weep and you curse, darling. Therefore you're not tied up. And you use dirty words here, so you're not so tied up as you pretend.

(*RR starts to speak.*)

STRASBERG: Wait a minute, wait a minute. I mean you're not tied up inside. You can't get the inside outside.

RR: But I have a feeling that I can't have anything inside.

STRASBERG: But, darling, if you cry, if you weep, if you are able to feel vicious enough to use curse words, then obviously something is going on inside. Your evaluation of what you think and feel is obviously completely erroneous. The basic thing that we have tried to make you realize is that you fight with yourself, that you fight with your partner, that you take all the struggle from the scene onto yourself. We have tried to make you realize that if you would *express* these struggles within yourself, the scene would begin to live for you. The very things you wish to inhibit are the things that can feed your expression on the stage. It is not that nothing is going on inside that makes you feel stifled, but it is true that you are stifled. Do you follow what I am try-ing to say? You are stifled in a very simple way. When anyone is tied up and tries to untie himself, what does he do? Show me. What does he do? (*Pause.*) I don't mean realistically.

RR: Untie himself.

STRASBERG: Yeah. But how? Where does the energy go? Which way does the energy go?

RR: Into untying.

STRASBERG: But how can you untie yourself, darling? You're tied. If you have to try to get out of this thing, what do you do? (*Pause.*)

RR: I don't know.

STRASBERG: I'm not going to tell you. (*Pause. Walks to her.*) If someone holds you this way, and you try to get away, what do you do? (*Sharply:*) THAT'S IT. COME ON! COME ON! OH! COME ON. OH! Look at what you did. You just did that, and then you stopped. Now I'm not going to be so nice. All right. Now, pull, and really —fine! (*Sharply:*) COME ON! COME ON. COME ON. REALLY PULL. NOW, LET YOUR HANDS PULL APART. No, darling, you stopped. You get so far, and you stop in your mind. You say, "I'm finished al-ready. That's enough." No, you're not finished; I let you up. You could never have gotten up. I'm stronger than you. You took the energy and pushed, but you didn't follow through. Your energy stopped. That's what you do with your impulse and your move-ment, and what I want is that your energy should continue on. In other words, when you want to untie yourself, you have to send out of you whatever energy is going on. Okay. In the ex-ercise I will tell you things to do at certain times, and I want you to do those things as fully as you can—not as simply as you can.

RR: What do you want me to do?

STRASBERG: Start with your own sequence, darling. Put the record player on when you want it. When you put it on, I want you to wind up in the chair hanging over. Then you start the singing. And with the singing you did some kind of association, yes? That's what I want. After that I will tell you what I want. Right? (*A long pause in which she carries on the private-moment activities.*) When I speak to you, try to continue what you are doing without being disturbed by what I say. Just take the direction. (*The music, a romantic popular song, starts.*) Oh, that one? Okay. Start your own way. If you want to start from there, I don't mind. Fine. (*Music.*) Take your time. Don't rush it. When you feel like singing, what I want is that you should be leaning out of the chair. Till then, even if you feel like singing, don't sing. Hum, but don't sing. (*Music.*) Now you can start the song from the beginning, sweetie. But earlier you placed yourself in that chair as if you had picked that position and knew that you were not going to move out of it or do anything else. If you don't want to sing, move your body as if your body, and not the voice, was singing. (*Music continues.*) When you really feel like singing, go into that chair. Then do whatever you do with the song—some kind of association. (*Pause. Music.*) Stretch out your hands, darling. Stretch out your hands. Take it easy. Take it easy. (*Pause.*) Keep moving the hands or some part of the body. I don't want the body quiet. (*Romantic music stops. A rock-and-roll record plays through, and a second rock-and-roll record begins to play.*) I'm waiting for the song that you sing, darling. (*First rock-and-roll song starts again.*) Now, try to do what I asked you without thinking. (*Pause. Music continues.*) Now, throw your arms out, and start the words. Throw your arms out wide. No. Throw them out—but, darling, really wide. Don't just give a little gesture. Do it! Now, try to do it. My God! You're a young girl. You've got energy to burn. What is the point of just putting your arms out that way? Put them back against you. Hold onto the chair. Put 'em out. Throw 'em away. (*Music continues.*)

RR: "The clock struck nine when I did send the nurse. In half an hour she promised to return."

STRASBERG: Now, get yourself against the chair. Move. Move against the chair. You had a movement with the legs. Don't think. You remember—no, no—when you got up and you put your legs around the chair. Quick, quick, *quick*, QUICK, QUICK! DARLING, WHAT—WHAT IS THIS? WE GOT FIFTEEN HOURS? No. Oh, come on, sweetie. Now what is this? Now, forget about it. I mean, if you don't want to do it, then forget about it. The hell with it. I asked you. I told you. I told you very simply, "Do it as quickly as you can without thinking." And you don't do it. You don't make the effort. You criticize yourself. You don't do what I ask you to do. Do you understand what I'm telling you?

RR: I understand.

STRASBERG: Now, is there some reason why you don't do it? (*Pause. Music continues.*) It isn't that you cannot do it. Right? (*Pause.*) Why don't you do it quickly? What is the thing? You can't get from the one thing to the next, or what? But, darling, you obviously don't try. Now, you must learn to abide by the sense of actor's truth and not just by the kind of things that you tell yourself, the sort of thing that you see here constantly when the actor says, "I didn't do it," and everybody sees that he did do it. We understand what that comes from. The actor is not aware. That's right. We understand that. But if you are not aware, and yet you think that you are making the effort, then you are never going to make the effort. You know darn well that you are not moving quickly. I mean, I stopped you and said, "Please, do what I ask you to do as fully as you can without thinking." Now, do you want to start it again? (*Music continues.*)

RR: Yes, I would like to—

STRASBERG: Go ahead. Tell me, darling. Go ahead. What do you want to tell me?

(*RR mumbles.*)

STRASBERG: You mean you cannot obey an order when it is given? You are so resentful of a command that you cannot obey an order when it is given?

RR: I mean about that first line.

STRASBERG: I don't care, darling. That proves my point exactly. You stop doing what you're doing, because you say, "I don't re-

member the line." Therefore you don't do what should be done
sufficiently. If you did the movement sufficiently and then went
on with the lines, you might forget for a moment, but when the
line did finally come out, it would be a little tormented. It would
come out like a shot. But no. You start and you stop, and you
start and you stop, and you start and you stop, so that in the
scene you are using more energy in criticizing and stopping yourself than you would ever need to get beyond this ease and simplicity you had when you started acting because you didn't know
what you were doing. Now your emotion is richer and fuller, but
you still want to work the way you worked at the beginning
when you didn't work. You follow what I am saying?

RR: I understand what you are saying, but I have a feeling that
I can never connect this with me.

STRASBERG: You again prove my point, darling. I said to obey
what I was asking you to do. Now, what do you mean? What
am I asking that has to be connected with you? (*Music continues.*)

RR: I don't know how to explain it.

STRASBERG: Well, try to explain it, darling, because I don't understand what you are talking about.

RR: I did it. I—

STRASBERG: No, no, you didn't do it. What does it mean,
"Throw your arms out"? Show me now. (*Pause.*) No, I don't
mean that. Throw your arms out wide and back. That's right.
The arms are now out. Now, just yell as you do that.

(*RR yells.*)

STRASBERG: That's right. You see that you can do that. But before you only did a kind of gesture that didn't mean anything.

AUDIENCE MEMBER: She once mentioned to me that she has to
think of gestures and movement before she can do them—as in a
ballet.

STRASBERG: That's right. Notice that she has a flair for picking
wonderful theatrical attitudes, but in those attitudes there is not a
flicker of movement. (*Music stops.*) As a dancer she is used to

following out movements that have been supplied to her. She has not yet found the expression of her own individual body and self. The movements she makes are deliberate, indicative of dance movement. (*To RR:*) Whenever you can make that deliberate kind of movement, you move very fully. Whenever you don't have that kind of movement to do, you feel stifled. But that is exactly my point. The stifled feeling does not come from a lack of emotion. You feel stifled now, but there is emotion. Do you know why you feel stifled? Because all you are doing to get the emotion out is to make a little twisting movement with your ring, and that is not sufficient expression for the emotion of a girl like you. You want to yell. You want to scream. You want to jump. Right? Why don't you do it? Go ahead. COME ON. COME ON. Yell! Go ahead. (*RR is half-weeping, half-laughing.*) But yell. That's no good. I'm not interested in that. Yell! Go ahead.

RR (*yells*): NO!

STRASBERG: Now, with your body. Yell with your body.

RR (*louder*): NO!

STRASBERG: No. I mean with your body, with the hands, with the feet. Yell!

RR (*very loudly*): NO!

STRASBERG: That's right. That's it. That's right. Now, do the same thing, and start your lines, and kick that. Go ahead.

(*RR, weeping, screams a few words incoherently and kicks over a chair.*)

STRASBERG: But let's hear the words.

RR (*weeping*): "Perchance she cannot meet him."

STRASBERG: Now, pick up the thing and put it back and keep the words going. Pick up the chair and put it back. Fix the chair. COME ON. Put it down and say the line. (*She throws down the chair.*) COME ON. If you don't know the line, don't worry.

RR (*weeping*): No, I don't know the line. (*Throws something and breaks it.*)

STRASBERG: All right, then say the next line. COME ON. What is the word that you say? What is the thought? COME ON. What is the thought?

RR: "The hour from twelve is three (*throws something*), and yet she is not come."

STRASBERG: That's right. (*Pause. She weeps.*) Now, throw yourself in the chair, and kick your feet and say whatever comes next, whatever line. Come on. But kick the feet. COME ON.

RR (*still weeping*): "Had she affections and warm youthful blood, She would be as swift in—" (*Weeps incoherently.*)

STRASBERG: But let's hear it, let's hear it, from the chest.

RR (*weeping and angry*): "She would be as swift in motion as a ball." (*Weeps hysterically. A moment's pause.*)

STRASBERG: Now, pick up what you have on the floor. Throw it at the chair, and say the next thing. Don't worry. That's right. That's right. (*RR sobs.*) But with words or with a song. Yell. Do something. It has to be with sound, darling. I don't care if you say a different speech. Come on. Come on. SPEAK.

RR (*weeping but clearly audible*): "Had she affections and warm youthful blood, She would be as swift in motion as a ball."

STRASBERG: That's right. Now your next. COME ON. Do something, and say the next.

(*RR starts to speak.*)

STRASBERG: No. No. You have to do something before you say it. Come on. But a definite thing. Pick something up and throw it. This thing here. Come on. (*She throws it.*) Come on. Come on. Come on. Quick. Come on. Now, say. SPEAK.

RR (*half-sobbing*): "My words would bandy her to my sweet love, And his to me." (*Slight pause.*)

STRASBERG: Now, throw yourself in the chair. Go ahead. Throw yourself. Go ahead. COME ON. COME ON. COME ON. And kick your feet. And come on. Speak.

RR: "But old folks, many feign as they were dead— Unwieldy, slow, (*sobs*) heavy, and pale as—" (*Breaks down.*)

STRASBERG: Don't worry about the crying. Let's hear the words.

RR (*loud, angry, still half-sobbing, but clear*): "Unwieldy, slow, heavy, and pale as lead." (*Sobs.*)

STRASBERG: Now, open your arms wide, and say the next line. I think it's something about the sun.

RR: I've skipped everything.

STRASBERG: I don't care. I don't care. Come on. I don't care. Just use the words. Come on. It's an exercise, darling. I don't care about the sequence.

RR: ". . . is the sun upon the—" (*Sobs.*)

STRASBERG: Let's hear. Let's hear.

RR (*loud and clear*): "Of this day's journey—"

STRASBERG: Let's hear your voice from the chest.

RR: "And from nine till five—till—from nine till twelve Is three long hours, and she's not come." (*Sobs.*)

STRASBERG: But on each line I want something that you do. Jump. Run. That's right.

RR: "Had she affections and warm youthful blood, She (*breaks down, continues half-sobbing*)—she would be as swift in motion as a ball."

STRASBERG: Let's hear it.

RR (*half-sobbing, clearly audible*): "My words would bandy her to my sweet love, And his to me. (*Sobs. Pause.*) But old folks, (*sobbing, half-audible*) many feign as they were dead."

STRASBERG: Let's hear it.

RR (*clearly audible*): "But old folks, many feign as they were dead, Unwieldy, slow, heavy, and pale as lead."

STRASBERG: Arms wide. Hold on to the chair. That's right. You have good hands. That's right. (*She sobs.*) That's right. But kick with your entire body. Not just with the feet. Let the whole body do whatever you do. That's what you're not using in your speech now. Okay. All right. That's enough. Now, do you see where you stop yourself so much? You see, you haven't really found your own expression. When you do something like this, what do you feel?

RR: What do I feel?

STRASBERG: Yeah.

RR: I just feel like Hades.

STRASBERG: Yeah, yeah. I understand. But do you now feel more frustrated?

RR: Yes. More frustrated.

STRASBERG: Why?

(RR *half laughs, half cries.*)

STRASBERG: Do you feel more hate or more frustrated?

RR: Right now? Both.

STRASBERG: That means that the frustration comes only from the fact that you are not letting it out sufficiently in relation to the strength of the feeling. Right? Well, what do you want to let out? What do you want to do?

RR: I don't even know what I want to do.

STRASBERG: No, you want to let out the hate. Yes?

RR: Yeah.

STRASBERG: Yes. What do you want to do? What do you do when you let the hate out? Yell? Scream? What do you do? Nothing?

RR: Sometimes I hit my head against the wall.

STRASBERG: Yeah, well, that we don't advise for actors. Only for non-actors. For actors we advise better things that serve the same purpose. You do not have a problem of an absence of emotion. When you feel frustrated, you can always be sure that it is because you have emotion.

RR: I don't know how to get it out.

STRASBERG: How to get what out?

RR: Frustration.

STRASBERG: I don't care how you get it out. Look. You broke a chair. You almost broke your knee. You were weeping. You couldn't stop. You threw yourself all around. You threw the coat. You almost broke the tape recorder. If you had done a little bit more letting out, we would all have had to leave the room. There is so much inside that you haven't let out that you feel stifled. Therefore you cannot go by that feeling as such, because it will tell you, "It's not enough. It's not yet real. It's not the way I want it." That feeling will tell you the wrong things now, because it will tell you in terms of its need to be expressed. Full expression will not take place in a sudden leap. That will take time.

RR: Sometimes I have an impulse just to throw things at people, but I don't ever do it.

STRASBERG: Well, there again, if they are actors, no. If they are not actors, yes. But not policemen. And I'll tell you what you do. Buy something very soft—(*laughter*)—some little thing. Keep it in your pocket, and when you have to throw, take that and throw. But really throw it. You think this is a joke. I know one very sensible, intelligent, sensitive girl. She has in her room especially for this purpose things that can be torn up, things she has discarded. She doesn't throw them out. She keeps them in the closet. When this kind of moment comes along, she goes into the room, she closes the door, and she takes these things, and she *rips* 'em. That's right. You have a lot of frustrations, but the basic frustration comes from an oversupply of emotion, and the emotion is so held back from going into expression that you can honestly say, "I don't feel," because you have no feeling of releasing it.

RR: I have released it before. And it's terrible to release it.

STRASBERG: You mean in life?

RR: Yes.

STRASBERG: That's what art is for. If the person who doesn't like something you did to him in life sees you do the same thing on the stage to your partner, he says, "Gee! Terrific acting! I know it's just the way she behaves." On the stage it is likable because it is art. It is controlled. You do it at your will. You learn to express fully, and therefore on the one hand you get expression, but also we get art. That is the basic need for art in life, not self-expression, but rather a saying and doing of things we cannot completely say and do in life but which have to be said and done. We transmit these observations and experiences to other people by the very vividness of our response to them, and thereby we become artists. We become people who create in imagination what other people go through in life.

NERVOUSNESS

LL came into the Studio as "a young actor who had not really had any training. A lot of young actors come into the Studio without systematic training, and the Studio does not really supply it. It encourages it. It suggests it. In cases where a door has to be opened, the Studio opens the door, but it doesn't build the building. It is up to the actor to follow through. LL was a stubborn case. He has talent, but he refused to accept the fact that he was not doing on the stage what he thought he was doing. Recently he has started to accept that fact, and his work is changing. He is beginning to come through in unusual ways."

To LL, following an exercise: As you have been sitting here, you have been straight, simple and easy. You have what seems to us security. No?

LL: But I'm not secure.

STRASBERG: Now, wait a minute. By "not secure" you mean, "I'm scared, but nobody must know it." That is great security. It is not being scared that makes you say you're insecure; it is the fact that "nobody must know it, because if anybody knows it, I'm gone."

When somebody says, "Yes, I'm sick. It may be very serious," that is a kind of security. Don't forget that some people refuse to go to the doctor to find out what is wrong. They know they are sick, but they will not go to the doctor because he may tell them that they're really sick. If they're really sick, it is important to know that. Maybe something could be done. Yet they stay away. That's insecurity.

Who is willing to admit an error—a secure or an insecure person? A secure person says, "That's right. I'm sorry I made a mistake." An insecure person makes a mistake like any other human being, but he then is unwilling to admit it and so makes a double mistake. But mistakes, falls, stumbles happen to anybody.

Recognition of nervousness is already a way of dealing with it. The actor has both to do what he wants to do and to be aware of what he is doing. The more real he tries to be, the more he has to be aware, because the more he is real, the more he uses elements of himself which are usually left purely to the unconscious or automatic functioning of his instrument. Therefore, in a moment when he is real, he has a lot of awakened energy that is unwanted and that can lead to mannerisms and deflections of impulse if it comes out as involuntary nervous expression.

When your heart pounds, that means there is terrific stimulus. There is terrific emotion, enough to make the whole scene go round if that's what you need. It becomes a matter of "connecting the pipes." If the pipes are connected, the water flows through them. If they are not connected or the connections are weak, then what happens? The water spills out. And what happens when water spills? It's a mess.

You must begin to realize that your fear does not have to inhibit your work. Fear inhibits and stops your work only if it functions without your knowledge. You have unconsciously made a fetish out of fear. You have in effect told yourself, "I'm going to control the audience if it's the last thing I do," but we see that you really don't. You have excellent expressiveness. The very thing that makes you sensitive also makes you expressive, and that is why you are vulnerable. We want the sensitivity, but we want it to rise in response to things that you present to your imagination, rather than to things that are presented to you unconsciously.

To ACTRESS SS: If you are nervous, then the character is nervous —not you. Nervousness is wrong only when the actor says that the character is not supposed to be nervous and then tries to hide his nervousness. Once you try to hide any real and true thing, it becomes even more obvious. The audience sees the nervousness and sees that you are being hurt or constricted by it. Therefore the first thing the actor can do in dealing with nervousness is to say, "Well, if I'm nervous, that's fine. There's nothing wrong with it. The character could be nervous, so what's wrong with it?"

With some actors that is not enough. They cannot have faith in that conclusion. Therefore it is essential for them to say at the beginning, "All right, I'm nervous. I'll try to do it as a nervous character, but at the same time what can I find to become concerned with?" That search will take your mind off yourself. Essentially nervousness means that we are concerned with ourselves rather than with the things we have to do.

It is important to realize that the actor as a human being works on various levels and that not everything that is going on in a human being is expressed. On the stage only those things are expressed which fit into an objective scheme. Actually, where your concentration goes the rest of you goes, and all the other impulses of which you are aware are not seen by the audience. We have previously seen your nervousness, but not today. In fact, I was going to say to you that your work today was the clearest and most definite that you have done. It was the least rattled that I have seen. And then you put a spoke in my wheel by saying, "I was nervous."

It is the fact that you do not panic at these moments that saves you. Once we were driving with someone in San Diego, and we made a sharp turn, and there was a car coming straight toward us just as fast as we were going. Somehow we went around that car into the other lane and stopped, and we said, "How the hell did we get out of that?" Nobody knew, but the driver had held onto the car. If he had panicked, we would have been gone.

When the actor panics, he says, "What's happening to me now shouldn't be in the character; I'm wrong." Then the subjective impulse takes over and becomes separate from the character, and we become aware of it. But if the actor makes the proper effort to do the objective tasks, most of the time he will accomplish the objectively necessary results.

FORCING TEMPO

Forcing hinders imagination and distorts expression. It prevents impulse from following through naturally and completely, and it lies at the root of the question of tempo. However, right tempo and true expression are related to the demands of the dramatist's material as well as to the technical reality of the actor.

TO AN ACTOR AND ACTRESS: Most of the work in today's professional theatre is affected by a very simple premise. If a thing is boring, make it faster: it will then become more interesting. If a thing is boring, make it louder: it will be more exciting. Well, it doesn't become more interesting and exciting. It simply becomes emptier. If you say an uninteresting thing quickly and loudly, doesn't it become more boring, not less boring? When you make the show fast and loud, the only thing the audience gets out of it is to get out of the theatre a little bit sooner, and that, I suppose, is a consummation to be wished for, but hardly one to be greatly desired.

After Shaw had watched the Japanese Nō theatre, he made a very interesting comment. He said that it is very slow, and at the beginning it's so slow that you almost push forward. You want to make it faster. Your muscles push to get the actors going. Instead as it goes on they become even slower, and by the very fact that it becomes slower and slower, before you know it you are completely caught up; whereas if it went in the way you first wanted it to go, you would remain on the outside as an onlooker.

Even the things that you both did not do for the scene were excellent. When you first read a scene like this, you think you have to scale the heights. You think that the play should come out in some obviously poetic manner. You drive for the peaks, and the play becomes an ostentatious, semi-poetic, driven play. But today you permitted the play and the event and the situation to ride along, and the play itself came through much better than if you had made everything emphatic. You did not force.

I liked the ease and continuity. You did not seem to be saying to yourselves, "This has to be terrific." Once you stop asking for it to be terrific, I am willing to accept it as real. Once it is real, I go with it.

I liked the simple way in which you came in and were impressed by what you heard from each other and sat down and quietly listened and permitted the play to permeate us. You did not make the kind of effort that says, "Now comes the big scene where my soul is bared and my body cries out."

To ACTOR LL: At the final moment it was rushed. As an actor you knew, "This is really my exit because the author has not given me any more lines." But that moment is actually what Stanislavski calls the "star pause," because the actor is at that moment perfectly capable of continuing on and having lines of his own that he desires to say. An actor can take his time, especially in plays like this one, where the writing is not vivid and where the actor is not caught up in the dynamics of verbal progression as in Shakespeare. In Shakespeare the verbal progression is so wonderful that when the actor stops it to put in his own little details, he has to be very careful to do so only at the elbows, the transitional moments. In plays like this one it is taking one's time that makes the play vivid and alive. It brings out the texture of the play. The audience goes with the event and the situation, and the words do not seem empty, melodramatic, and obvious.

FUSION

To ACTOR X: Your expression divided itself unconsciously. You didn't mean to, but nonetheless it divided itself into moments in which you were really expressing something that was going on within you, and then into other moments in which your manner seemed to say, "Now I speak," or "Now I speak to be heard." In these moments when you felt unconsciously the need to maintain and impel the words, you fell into two ways of performing the words. One way followed the conventional method of exertion of energy. This would continue until you reached a high point, when a shift would come and you would relax because you either couldn't go further vocally òr something happened to you inside. As soon as you relaxed, you hit a tone that seemed to us to be just right. At one moment in the middle, the flare of the words kind of impelled you so that you had a little bit more faith that you were at least doing something real—even if you didn't quite know what you were doing. You sat down. You relaxed. The tone eased, and you started to speak, and we understood you. It was not that the dialogue is any clearer at that point. It was clear because you were thinking and not just saying.

You are now working on your difficulty in the wrong area. It does not matter what you are doing. It may be right or wrong. It may be some physical action. It may be sitting quietly. It may be looking around. Whatever it is, you must be able to continue it and at the same time be able to say the words so that they express whatever thought at that moment needs to be conveyed. Otherwise, you fall between two stools. You start to do something, but when the words come along, either they are dropped and the thought does not go into the words, or the words begin to take over and disturb what you are actually trying to accomplish.

To AN ACTOR: It is true that you took time, but I do not know why you took time before you started talking. I can understand why you might want to take time before you started acting, but to do that and then to say, "Now when I have to start talking, there's something special," is to make the kind of split between doing and speaking that I hate to see made. A lot of you people have a tendency to do inner work where it is not necessary.

To ANOTHER ACTOR: You created the behavior. You wound up with good emotion and good inner sensation. You were relaxed. Your thought was feeding the basic image or meaning which you saw in this material. All you needed to do was to start the words when that activity was going on. Then we would have known what the activity meant. But when you arrived at the point where the words needed to begin, you felt that the words had a different meaning from the sequence of which they are a part. Therefore when you started the words, they were separated from the previous inner activity, and the verbal continuity or literal logic of the words became stronger than the inner logic that you had created.

There seemed almost a separation between what you were doing for yourself and what had to be done with the words. That is exactly the thing that we deny. Words are part of what a human being does on the stage. They are in themselves action. Words are thoughts and feeling. You had sufficient faith to say some of the things with a meaning that you somehow felt they had, but you were unable to behave with the consistency and continuity of the character you had evolved. This demarcation robbed you of the value of what you had done.

In the second part you did not rob yourself. Your concentration fed only emotional things in the scene. You gave us the sense that this was a speech that had to be said. An actor never plays a speech. He always plays a scene, an event, a situation, an occurrence. Words are part of the occurrence.

Separating action from words is a characteristic problem with people who try to work as we encourage them to do. Since concentration is required to create inner life, the actor's very awareness of this process makes him afraid to throw the words into the caldron of what his concentration is creating. He thinks, "No, no, no, I have to have special awareness to say the words. I can't, because I'm concentrating on the other things. I'll hold back, because otherwise I won't know what I'm talking about in the words." We see constantly, not only here at the Studio, but in rehearsal, in actual production work, that people who are trying to work properly work first for themselves and then work for the play: "Now I do the work for myself; now I come back to the play." They do not fuse the two things.

That is why a lot of professional directors are kicking about members of the Studio. They think you are perfectly all right, and yet you say, "No, I'm not all right. I'm not ready yet." To the director you look completely ready. Even when you say that

the work is not quite ready, to the director it is perfectly satis-
factory. You wait unnecessarily for the moment when you are
completely at ease instead of going on with what you are doing
and thus concentrating yourself and fusing the expression.

This problem comes not from real difficulty but only from a
fear of difficulty and therefore from a fear of going on. The batter
who stands up at the plate to hit the ball knows that it's going
to be difficult to hit the ball, but he does not say, "Okay. After
he throws the ball, I'm then going to hit it." The batter has to hit
the ball when it is thrown. Otherwise, all the batter's shenanigans,
warming up and swinging bats, doesn't mean anything. The
batter does these things only to prepare himself to hit the ball.
If he prepares very well but swings at the ball when it isn't thrown
and then stands there when it is thrown and says, "Well, I'm not
ready now," all of his work is for nothing.

The way we are trained in everyday life makes a slight discon-
nection in all of us between what we feel and the ability to express what we feel. It is very important in social life or in life
generally that you should always speak and behave nicely no matter what you feel. Today we keep away from a lot of realities. In
Elizabethan times somebody had to put his cloak down or Queen
Elizabeth would have stepped in the mud. Today there are auto-
mobiles and canopies, and you can ride around all day and literally
never touch ground. If you were Sir Walter Raleigh, you rode
on a horse. You rode through mud. You rode through rain. You explored. You went to strange countries. You lost your head on the
block. People in Raleigh's time still had very much a physical
contact with life.

Today we are more separated from the things around us. We
often do not know how they are made or how they work. Certain
of them we never even see. There has grown up a separation between how we feel about what happens and our ability to verbalize.
If sometimes we speak out exactly what we feel, we are told, "Hey,
take it easy. You just don't say things like that." When you are
young, the patterns are made. You then grow up with the need

and desire to express what we do not ordinarily express in life, and you become actors with the hope that you can express them, and you then are held back by the patterns that have conditioned you in life not to express.

THE SENSE OF TRUTH

Today many of the young people have a wrong attitude. Because our work offers a way of expression that fulfills the individual talent to a much greater extent than any other process of training or active theatre work, the young person exposed to our work begins to feel that the only important thing is to express himself. It is true that that is one of the important side effects, but that is not the purpose of our work. If you have pain and the doctor gives you an opiate, that also has an effect outside of dulling the pain, but the doctor gives the drug to kill the pain. He is not attempting to induce drug addiction.

A lot of young people somehow begin to think of our work as an end in itself. I get a lot of letters from all over, and all the letters say, "I want to express myself fully. I know that your way of working can give me the opportunity really to express myself, because the work that I have done up to this time seems to me mechanical." There is an element of truth in what they say. But that is not the purpose of my work. Its purpose is to make the actor able to create whatever has to be created. Its purpose is to enable him to share with others an experience that he is creating for them at that moment. Its purpose is to permit him to create truly, by means of imagination, experience that is most of the time not there on the stage. We refer to objects and sense memory. We have a lot of special words. But all of these things exist only to help the actor to be of service.

By "serve" I really mean that the actor proceeds in the same way as a scientist. For instance, a scientist sometimes makes a certain deduction, and everybody says, "You're crazy." The scientist says, "I'm sorry. I've worked it out, and this is the way it comes out. I'm sorry. I can't help it." The scientist is not asserting his own genius. He is only saying that the logic he worked with dictated that the conclusion should come out that way. The scientist is stuck with the result, whether he likes it or not. The scientist is in that sense serving that particular thing that he is investigating.

It is not too much to say that every artist works the same way. I remember once having a discussion with the young pianist William Kapell, who is now dead. We had a few people over to the house, and afterward he stayed on and we got into a discussion of his work. I happened to have some Schnabel records which he had been looking for, so I played them for him, and then he started to bemoan the criticisms of his own work, that people described his work as too personal and subjective. So he sat down at the piano, and he said, "Schnabel plays it this way," and he played it Schnabel's way. Then he said, "But, you see, Schnabel doesn't hear what Mozart is really saying when he plays it that way. This is what Mozart is saying," and then he played it his way. As it happened, I too didn't like his way, but he was stuck with that answer. He was sharper, a little more mordant, a little bitterer than most people are. He wanted to play that way, and therefore a lot of his music was too bitter. The audience did not like it as much as if he had tried to play the music sweetly and romantically, which would have resulted in a blend of his color with what the audience heard in the music. He was stuck with his answer.

In acting being stuck with the result means being willing to go where the acting will lead you instead of to wherever you think it should take you. Often the actor perceives something in his mind. He may have an idea as to how the part should be done, and he uses a particular thing, an object or an affective memory, because he thinks it will help him to accomplish the "how" that he sees in his mind. However, this particular "thing" turns out to have different properties from those he has envisioned—but he is unwilling to leave his mind behind and say, "I will go wherever this 'thing' will carry me." He insists on pushing ahead in the direction he unconsciously thinks he wants to go. He thinks he is doing the right thing; actually he continues to do the wrong thing.

In *My Life in Art* Stanislavski says, "A lot of actors started to make use of my ideas, but actually they continued to do exactly what they had done before." The style of acting didn't change. They said, "All right. I've got an object," but they were unwilling to go where the object might lead. And that's what I mean by serving—that you go where the object leads you. If at the end you find that you don't want what you have, you rub it out. You tear it up.

In the actor—unlike the writer—the process of creation and the process of correction have to take place at the same time. The actor cannot say, "Okay, I worked tonight, and I'll get up in the morning and look at the work and see what to correct." At the moment when he is most impelled, part of the actor—what we call "the sixth sense" and what Stanislavski called "the sense of truth"—must remain active and say, "Hey, you went too far there. Oh, that was phony. You thought it was real, but it wasn't. Watch it! The concentration is going now. You're losing yourself. Now, take it easy!" In the movies the sound track and the picture go through the projector side by side. In the same way the actor's sixth sense goes on during the acting.

The sense of truth is the last thing that the actor develops. Although some of the exercises lead to its development, it cannot be directly trained. The sense of truth is the sum total of all the experiences that the actor has had and can therefore develop only as a result of experience. He has to serve. He has to have the willingness really to go with the object he is creating. Very few people serve that fully—but that is what makes for greatness.

CHAPTER VIII

Problems: Exploration

A LARGE part of the training of Studio members is—directly or indirectly—exploration, work that extends the individual's range of imagination or expression. Opportunity to explore is perhaps the most important facility provided by the Studio. The stimulus to explore is one of Strasberg's most important contributions.

Acting technique is never abstract. What the actor can do and how he does it are closely bound together. Exploration tries to open new galleries and tunnels in the unconscious levels of the instrument, where most actors' creation takes place. It attempts to mine levels never before employed. Thus as he extends his range, the actor also extends his technique.

Conditions at the Studio are especially favorable to the creative functioning of these unconscious levels. Strasberg's insistence that the will be strengthened leads the actor to reach out to try new things. Strasberg's constant encouragement to improvise tends to free the actor from obsessive concern with production results: without that freedom, the actor rehearses only what he has already done. Finally, unless the actor explores before an audience, he can never be sure of his ability to repeat what he has found, a basic requirement of acting: Strasberg's demand that Studio members be professional observers has created a discerning, yet sympathetic, audience for the exploring actor.

Actors of widely varying background become Studio members. Often Strasberg must make a new member aware of what he is doing and how he accomplishes it before he can explore new areas of himself. Often habits of tension, cliché, or inexpressiveness must be broken down. But more often the actor must summon up resources of will and courage to attempt new things.

Nowhere does Strasberg's teaching show to greater advantage than in exploration. He makes the technical processes of acting exciting. Here his full repertoire of incitement, challenge, stimulus, cajolery, logic, anger, sympathy, and insight constantly operates. Here his capacity to strike straight at the heart of an individual's difficulty receives full play. Here his work with actors reaches an intensely personal level.

He also shows the actor that there is a technique for exploration. This technique has three essential elements: to take time, to keep going, and to improvise on a theme. Some actors must simply take sufficient time to allow their imaginations to function. Others must be made to keep going no matter what happens. And the actor who professes willingness to explore, but who unconsciously refuses to deal concretely with any object or situation, must be faced with his own vagueness and generality.

This chapter displays the gamut of Strasberg's moods, which are, in fact, varied strategies for approaching individual actors. No actor can begin to explore until he is convinced of the need to do so. In this work Strasberg must be diagnostician, guide, and gadfly.

CONVICTION OF NEED

Conviction of need is the prerequisite to real exploration. Actor X worked at the Studio for a number of years before he began to make real progress in exploring his instrument. Over these years Strasberg stimulated him to keep moving beyond the immediate tasks and attitudes to which he gave himself. X worked to eradicate local speech patterns. He fell into just "being natural." Ego drove him to seek effectiveness in "big" roles. Strasberg—in such moments as the following—pushed him steadily beyond these concerns into learning "to go with himself," so that in the last few years X's work has had "fabulous results."

To Actor X: Here at the Studio we try to get the actor to make progress rather than simply to give production results. In production, results are usually accomplished even when the actor is not working properly: a person is picked for a role because he has a certain kind of voice and looks. Here, we try to differentiate between what the actor gives for the play and his individual development and progress. The actor always finds the key to his talent in extending himself beyond what may be merely enough for the play.

The people who come into my private classes don't have to pass auditions as you do here, and I don't get too good an initial impression of some of them. Sometimes a person who seems nice and sensible and intelligent comes to me. I don't see very much in him, but I don't like to hurt him, so I say, "Okay, come into the class. We have a place." I assume that in a short while he will drop out by himself. However, I am not satisfied to let people go on doing what they are already doing. I keep sticking pins in them. I say, "It's not happening. Come on. Come alive. Do. Work. Think." Suddenly we find that we have opened a vein. We see blood flowing. We see excitement we never saw before; and then we realize that there is talent in the person, but the talent had been blocked. There was a lot of moss on top. But we had searched on the assumption that there might be more there: "I don't know. You're not doing your best. I don't know what your best is, but this is not yet the best. Your faculties are not yet working." Thus, by stimulating intensity and effort on the part of the actor, I have been able to lead people to results that I must honestly say flabbergast me.

To Actress U: There was a theatricality here we have never seen before. You are worried that you become unreal or unconvincing when you get theatrical. Instead you must experiment to see, "Will it, or will it not happen?"

We sense that there are elements of yourself that you have not used before. These elements, which you have been afraid of, which you have thought of as hammy or external, must be trained and used, must be put under the direction of the wonderful reality and conviction that you have, so that they permeate every part of you—not in a light and casual way but in a completely dramatic and completely theatricalized way.

A fine actor, which means an actor who actually experiences on the stage, to whom things occur which do not necessarily occur to any other actor, has the essential responsibility of learning the laws of his own instrument. You must learn what makes you respond. You must learn why at certain moments you respond one way and what at other moments you do not respond to at all. You must learn why certain thoughts can be used and other thoughts cannot be used. You have to find these things for yourself.

It is time for you to stop temporizing. You have a greater reservoir of imagination than you use. You have a greater reservoir of knowledge about what takes place in acting than you use. Somehow you have a tendency to hold back. Why? I don't know. Perhaps fear of yourself or worry about being hammy or about interfering with natural processes—but you have seen from the things you have done here that there is no need to fear. We are not at all upset by your theatricality. It is not hammy. It creates wonderful richness. Your voice today was quite different, your behavior quite different from anything we have seen. We wish to see this different kind of thing in your acting.

To start fooling around with this in a production is difficult. That is why having a place like the Studio is important. Here you can be observed by people who comprehend what you are working toward, people who have sympathy when your work doesn't go a certain way but who are also able to point out where it went off and why.

This is a place for you to experiment with yourself—not to do what we tell you. Find your own method. You have knowledge. You have conviction. You have imagination. You have a sense of things taking place. Be your own Stanislavski. After all, he didn't come down from heaven. You have the same sensitivity he had.

There is no reason why you cannot find these things. You must find them, as part of your responsibility toward your own progress, toward your career, and even more toward your talent, which, as you know, we all love, but because we love it, we wish to see it constantly refreshed, developed, and expanded.

To ACTRESS DD, *who had just become a star on Broadway when she made her first appearance at the Studio in a part quite different from her starring role:* We are just glad to see you work here, because we know how much courage it takes, especially for people who are functioning professionally and are therefore concerned that we may say something here that will contradict the professional judgment. We all understand what it means to get up and do a scene for the first time.

The statement you have just made to us was a wonderfully clear statement of something we all recognize to be a very real and pertinent problem to the actor. After all, you are working in a play. You are getting paid. What are you worried about? Why are you so upset? *Why do you worry that you can't do another kind of part?*

You feel that you have found out how easy it is to be attractive in an unattractive part, but now you have begun to wonder whether you can be attractive in a part which definitely calls for you to be attractive. That feeling is not unusual among actors. We all understand what it means to face a part in which personal qualities have to be obvious. That is a professional problem. There a lot of us lose courage, but today you faced that problem professionally. You also said that this is important for you personally, and I think we understand that, but most of us are afraid to face it. We prefer to live in the hope and in the dream rather than to try to solve the problem in reality. The fact that you were willing to face this problem in your first scene here and to solve it as well as the comments of the people indicated shows a wonderful attitude.

We know how difficult this whole problem is. We know that in the American theatre excellence in one part unfortunately has the tendency to lead to a repetition of itself. You would like to do something else, but you know what the audience already likes. And you begin unconsciously to wonder, "Can I ever do anything else? Will they ever accept me in anything else?" For you to face that problem in your very first scene at the Studio and to face it as honestly and simply as you did is very wonderful. We can only encourage you, because out of that attitude comes the real exploration and the real progress that an actor makes.

It is very good for you to realize that the part you are playing on Broadway is not the only part you can play. You can play unattractive parts attractively, and you can play attractive parts attractively. You have talent, not just type. Your type helps you to compete on the open professional market, but the thing you really have is talent. You are here because of the talent. You are an actress because of the talent. And the only reason for our being here is to explore talent. That is the service we render to professional actors.

Although the actor cannot know until he has explored what he will discover, the results can often be predicted by another person. Strasberg usually avoids such prediction because of the danger of binding the actor further rather than releasing him. But occasionally he does render important aid to certain actors by confirming their possession of personal qualities of which they may be aware but which they exclude from their acting. He does this in diverse ways, sometimes subtly, sometimes humorously, sometimes so inconspicuously that the actor does not know what is being done, and sometimes through direct statement of the problem.

TT is "an actress of talent and experience." She is a star on Broadway, in the movies, and on television. "The audience accepts her as capable. Yet she hasn't learned to use herself." Strasberg thinks of "her as untouched, unused. The real things within her, the real imagination, the vital elements of her being have not quite been involved in any of the parts she has done. The problem is to stir these elements, to push them, to encourage them. She has great possibility."

To ACTRESS TT: As you went on, I got the sense that this scene can be done quite differently and much better than I have ever seen it done, so that I wish I could see the whole play done as freshly as this approach suggests is possible. But I'm not primarily concerned with the approach. I'm concerned with what the work does for you.

Actor A here mentioned, and two other people suggested, what I think is very important. Today you did look and seem different. That's what they meant by "qualities." There seemed today a different texture to your presence on the stage. It was a softness that you have and which you used once before in Juliet.* Do you remember? Your assumption that you cannot make a certain impression on us physically is actually untrue, but both on the stage and sometimes in life it makes you drive, drive, drive, on the assumption that *that* will make the effect. And when you stop doing that, then you get exactly what you think you do not have, but which you have in plenty. Today, purely in looks, you were more attractive. You looked sexier.

But in that area you did not go personal enough. You give us a general and abstract picture of yourself. But you are a human being, alive, living, pulsing, and you must be true and real to those things in yourself, so that you fuse the living human being with the abstract one.

Now, I must say that the quality of softness continued throughout today, and with it came a kind of ease and the presentation of—I don't know how to put it—of an attractive stage image, of a sexy stage image, to put it simply. And that is something that some of your stage parts have not permitted.

Your first professional part did not call for that at all, and therefore, you developed in that first part a line of strength and clarity and distinctiveness, even aggressiveness of a certain kind. And when that first part was successful, you played a lot of other

---

* TT is "tall and mature, but she had wanted to play Juliet at the Studio," despite the fact that she was not the conventional Juliet type, and she did so "quite wonderfully."

parts on that line even when they didn't need it, because that was the part in which you had been successful.

Today I agree completely with A and the others that there were totally different colors. I shouldn't say "totally different," because I have seen that in you, so it isn't for me so much of a surprise. In a part like Maggie in *Cat on a Hot Tin Roof* that quality is of first importance, but I remember that when we saw you do Maggie it was missing. In that play the girl, no matter what she is, has to be attractive; otherwise the play becomes unpalatable. The girl cannot be just generally attractive. She must be deliberately attractive, a woman who can make herself attractive to a man, who *is* sexually desirable, so that the problem in the play is placed where it belongs, on the man, not on her. We are attracted to the girl, and therefore the man should be. If that isn't possible then there is no drama. When we saw you working on that part, it was approached from the point of view of some realities, which were wonderful, but the work lacked this particular quality of a girl wanting to be attractive, feeling herself to be attractive, and making herself attractive—as you did here today by the choice of simply thinking about what you call the hip bones.

You have other bones, not just hip bones, you see, and those bones are good, so you don't have to worry about it, but you do have to use it. And you have not used it. On the contrary you've almost—you sit on the stage very straight. The energy is usually very strong and definite. And this soft quality, which before today we have seen only in Juliet, and which then shocked us a little bit because it surprised us, we have not seen on the stage.

Frankly, this quality is essential for your progress, acting-wise and career-wise. Because you have it. Huh? I mean, when you sit there, as you sit there now, you have it. That's right. I want to see your legs and I want to see your body this way. Usually—I don't know—but usually in life—I forget; I don't want to make you too self-conscious—but, as I remember, you dress differently. You present an image of capability, an intelligent, no-nonsense kind of thing, and we—how should I say it?—we admire that, but we don't like it. I'm overdoing it just to make the point, but you understand.

These elements have come from the simple fact that you are afraid to take time. Yes. You are afraid of what you will thus reveal about yourself. Yes. You are afraid of what we will see or think about you. Yes, that's right. And that is why the technical process is essential for you. There is simply no other way of getting to that quality. A good director can help you give a little more reality, but this quality you have to bring yourself, because nobody makes your instrument on the stage except you.

This approach today was very much in the right direction. It was a wonderful thing for you, because you did look different. It has been a real pleasure just to see you sitting there. As you sat, the line was good.

It is true that you picked certain things for your concentration which I wished could have been approached a little more sexily. I wished you could have permitted yourself, as some of us do in private when we're taking a bath, to loll over yourself more, so that you could have become more personally involved in the task. I wished that thus you might have brought the entire instrument more fully alive.

You have seen how people change here at times when they start to concentrate. You have seen how the face becomes clear and the shape of the body somehow begins to appear as more than a shape in space. The body stands there. There's a sort of unconscious tension in the face, but we think the person looks perfectly all right. Suddenly that person concentrates, and transfiguration takes place. The face becomes more open. It shines with a kind of inner meaning. The body begins almost to loom in space because somehow it has—we call it faith; we call it confidence; we call it belief—somehow the body belongs. We look at it, frankly, quite differently. It is very attractive, and it is, I think, part of the thing we call sex.

To put it again very sharply, I know women who do not look

as well as they might, but they have it terrifically. They're sexy. And a lot of other women say, "What do people see in her?" Well, I don't know what people see in her. I don't know what I myself see in her. All I know is that something comes over which is sexy, which has an attractiveness, because the body—or the instrument, as I call it—is not just a body in itself. It seems to have a resonance. It is like a wonderful piano that has been well tuned.

Actor A has been a member of the Studio from the beginning. In April 1963, Strasberg described him as a "successful" actor who "has not as yet made full use of himself. His success has not come to a point of no return. He can go on indefinitely on that level." Yet Strasberg feels "a greater talent. It's not a matter of greater success, but of greater talent. He has a wider range than people today think. There is nothing to criticize; what he does is very good. But he has to be led not to settle for something which uses only his skill.

"He's already told me he's working on Richard. I told him that until he works on Richard, he will not be an actor. I didn't really mean that. I don't care whether he works on Richard or not. I meant that until he goes beyond just using himself on the likable level which the audience desires and which he usually conveys to the audience, he will not really be acting. We will see only an extension of his personality, not the use of his talent.

"He prefers to play within a sphere that is simple, that comes easy to him, where he doesn't have to face too many difficult problems. He keeps on saying, 'When I started, I started as a Shakespearean actor,' but he hasn't lived on with that. When I told him to play Richard III, I wasn't trying to bring him back to Shakespearean acting. I was presenting him with problems that appear in their best guise in Shakespeare's plays. Those roles demand and offer depth and intensity of reality and experience that has to remain within the domain of reality and yet be brought to bear on various kinds of theatricality. He hasn't so far done that. He will now, I think, begin to do it."

Almost a year earlier, in May 1962, on one of the occasions when Actor A worked at the Studio, Strasberg had issued to him this challenge:

I want you people to remember today, because I hope that A will from now on engage in a very interesting experiment. I have permitted myself recently out of love for A and out of respect for what he ultimately can do, to be somewhat critical in things I have said to him. I have done this in order to stir within A the incentive to do something I perceive him capable of doing.

It takes effort for an actor to move out of the entire pattern of acting incentives which he has acquired as a result of his experience. He now uses these incentives unconsciously. He carries them with him in the same way we carry mannerisms, habits, and behavior of which we haven't the slightest idea, which we don't mean to do, and yet which we do.

I am not concerned with the goodness or badness of the acting. I am not interested in whether the scene is done the right way or the wrong way. I am interested in establishing within you a reliance on those things which you have *but are not aware of,* so that you push and work in areas where you need not push and work. But I am even more interested in awakening in you the incentive to work for and explore things that I think you have but which you will not easily get unless you do work for them. I am interested in having you work in what is for you the right area.

From that point of view—not from an interpretative or any other point of view—I don't like this interpretation. I don't like your need to use things to hide yourself. I don't like it that when you have to use yourself, you use only those things that are most charming. There is more than that in a human being.

I am concerned to awaken the basic, actual, automatic, unconscious responses that feed your real creativeness. I would like to take away all those actor's ways of somehow propelling a scene. I do not want the thing that comes from the head in order somehow to protect yourself. I want the really wonderful ideas that you have in your heart, in your mind, in your soul, and in your imagination—which are more than those other things—to begin to work.

At the moment I am aware of your goodness, which I would certainly accept on the stage, but here I do not wish to settle for goodness, and I do not really wish to settle for it on the stage, because I feel that it limits the things that you do. You depend on the conscious one-tenth of your mind which sends you into wonderful areas that you don't need to work on. The things you think about come from what you have learned, from what you know, and from what you know that you know. You don't search for the other nine-tenths which you don't even know that you know—which no artist knows that he knows. Look at van Gogh's strokes. He didn't say, "I'm going to make van Gogh strokes." They came from what he had. If he had tried to be safe and sound, whatever he wanted to do would never have come to fruition.

I don't like the criticism the people here gave of the scene. That criticism assumed that the scene was not good. If we saw the scene on the stage with a few little things fixed up, we would applaud it. I do not speak of this scene as not good or not good enough. Unfortunately it is good. Unfortunately it would be accepted. Unfortunately people would applaud it. I am trying to get at something I perceive as opening for you a completely different range of parts. I can see you in the classic parts. I can see you in the Molière parts. I have not seen any other actor who has the Molière face that you naturally have. I don't know where it comes from. You have it. The sweetness and the sadness and the strange sentimentality and the desire to be comic and the desire to please. That's all Molière. He suffered, and he wanted to please. In order to work on these things, a different approach is necessary.

I would like you to remember what we say today. I may be wrong. It may be that you will be able to criticize me and hold me to account. I am looking forward to a great adventure, the kind of thing that makes for a different kind of experience. I'm very glad that you've got the nerve and courage finally to do that, because till now, whatever the reason may have been, you didn't have the courage. And that courage in itself already implies the beginning of what I think will be a very wonderful thing.

TECHNIQUE FOR EXPLORATION

The three techniques used in exploration—taking time, keeping going, and improvising on a theme—are, of course, not separable from general acting problems of insecurity, nervousness, tension, and will. Problems that stop imagination or block expression naturally inhibit exploration. For example, during one of Actress TT's early appearances at the Studio in which she worked on a scene from *Macbeth*, Strasberg called her attention to certain difficulties that prevented her from taking sufficient time on the stage:

One of the things that now confuses you is the assumption that your difficulties come from the nature of the scene. Because *Macbeth* has certain problems which *The Skin of Our Teeth* does not, you pushed yourself into doing certain things which you previously did not do. No. Technically the actor's approach to any scene should be the same.

Your problem is that you push yourself by means of your mental ideas or your wonderful actor's fantasy too quickly—before the instrument is actually ready. If you continue in that direction, you will generate in yourself even worse fear. Your sense of responsibility to the scene, your feeling that "I have to do certain things," will continue to function, but it will function suicidally, because it will tie up your instrument before your fantasy has worked to the extent that you are actually able to carry out the things you perceive in your mind's eye. Therefore, it is essential to establish in *Macbeth* exactly the same process that worked for you so well in *The Skin of Our Teeth*—even if it means waiting.

You have built up waiting as a fear that something's not happening. That cannot be permitted to continue. You must realize that you do not just sit around waiting. You wait for something. When you wait for nothing, nothing happens. But when you wait for something, and the something is clear to you, one of two things may happen. Either the something will appear, or it will not appear. If it appears, fine! If it doesn't appear, you will then have eliminated one thing and can go toward something else. You have gained either way.

The whole point in waiting is that you offer unto your imagination something that will entice it to begin to work. And you then wait for it to work. If you don't, then you do what you do with a car when you get upset. You start pushing the accelerator, and you flood the engine. The gas is flowing. Everything that should be happening is happening. But the gas and the motor are not coming together so as to release energy to make the car go. When the actor gets upset and starts pushing, he floods. He cannot go. So many things are going on that it is impossible for the instrument to come alive.

When you are a good driver, and you have flooded the car, you know that there is only one thing to do: take it easy. If you have difficulty waiting, count. If you get nervous and hysterical, count. Do something to help you restrain your nerves. The nerves will only send you in the wrong direction, and you will never start the car even though your entire purpose is to get the car started.

You have to absolve yourself of the terror which the actor has when he waits and feels, "I'm not doing anything. I'm empty. I'm mute. The whole audience sees it. What the hell am I doing here?" You must free yourself from working in panic. You must not let yourself be rattled by the nature of the scene or the height of the problem or the depth or difficulty of the problem. Rather you must continue the approach which seemed to us so wonderful in your last scene and which gave such wonderfully new results.

Keeping going—the second technique of exploration—implies the willingness to follow imaginative impulses wherever they may lead, not merely continuing to do things on the stage. Otherwise—as Actor UU, Actress H, and Actress G demonstrate in the following episodes—the actor never leaves the rehearsed or conventional ways of acting that he regularly employs.

ACTOR UU: I think I made the wrong choice.

STRASBERG: I don't think so.

UU: My impulse was to go with myself, but since the bed was over in that corner, I felt it wasn't right to say the speech on the bed. So I chose to say the speech over here, which was technically the wrong choice.

STRASBERG: No, that's not a technical choice. That's a conventional choice. I have nothing to say about choices made on technical grounds. There are times when judgment of that sort is necessary for the actor. It is good when the actor says, "No, no, no, I'm not going to do it when I'm kneeling. I'm going to get the thought just as I'm getting up. That will be much more dramatic." That kind of judgment is fed by theatrical imagination. A choice like that shows the actor's sense of when a thing will be better. But your choice came only from convention. You said to yourself, "Throwing myself on the bed has nothing to do with the next line. The next line doesn't say anything about the bed. If I throw myself on the bed, they'll think I'm just pampering myself. I'd better say the speech center stage."

Actually we often evoke the meaning and color of the lines much more by trusting what we are creating. Only after we have done it should the analysis start. Then in redoing it come the moments of choice. You should leave analysis and choice out this first time you explore a scene, especially when you are really going with yourself and are making an effort to go even further. You have too many things within you, which you haven't yet dealt with in this scene, for you to start worrying about making choices. There is more emotion. There is more expression. There is more craziness. There is more honesty. There is more drama. There are things that you don't yet know. There are things you are unwilling to tell yourself. There is a lot more. And there is no way of getting at these things in ourselves except by going with it. You don't know where the river will carry you except by jumping in and finding out. There is no other way to be an explorer.

ACTRESS H: May I ask a question? If I should do this scene again, I haven't the faintest idea what I should do.

STRASBERG: That is the state in which you must now go on the stage. If you are a scientist and insist that you already know the answers, you will obviously never make really great discoveries. If anything, you will only rediscover what someone else has already discovered. The true scientist knows how to go about finding things. He knows how to set the problem. The answer he does not know. Today the scientist is more of an artist than the artist. The scientist is not afraid to use his imagination. He's not afraid to adventure. He's not afraid to ask himself questions to which he doesn't know the answer.

It is true that the scientist's means are much more susceptible to testing than the actor's. The scientist's means invariably work. He can have confidence that they will give him scientific conclusions. But it is also true that here we have found ways and means of working which lead to certain results, and yet too often we are unwilling to accept that evidence. We have found that knowing the answer in advance completely ties us up, but we are too often unwilling to set problems here to which we do not know the answer. Therefore you should be glad that you don't know the answer, because now you can go on the stage here and say, "I'm really exploring. I don't know the answer, but if I find something, it'll be wonderful!"

To ACTRESS G: We see that your work today is being fed by one "reservoir." But since our previous observation has shown us that in you two "reservoirs" exist, something must be happening to the water in the other reservoir. Maybe that reservoir is locked and must be tapped. Maybe something else is the matter. What we will get when we tap both reservoirs we do not know for sure. All we know is that it will be a richer thing, a muddier thing maybe, but nonetheless a richer thing. We know that reservoir must be there somewhere, and yet it is not flowing into the mains.

Why? What is happening to the water in the second reservoir? How can you get it where you want it? How can you put it to use? You must try to find out.

I'm not talking just about the stage. That is the way we judge things in life. Remember what happened once in New Jersey? They read the meters of the water works and said, "A lot of water is being used. We don't know where it is going." So they had to find out. People said, "Well, the meter is wrong. Don't worry about the water. The meter can go cockeyed too." So they checked all the meters, and the meters still said, "Millions of gallons of water are going somewhere." So they checked the mains, and still they couldn't find where the water was going.

Then logic entered in. The logic said, "This amount of water siphoned off would usually lead to a flood. There is no flood. No water has appeared on the surface. There is no canal of any kind. We have checked all the cellars. No subterranean place has been flooded. Obviously the water is being siphoned off into an area that does not flood. An area that does not flood can only be a river." But when they checked some of the outlets into the river, they couldn't find the water.

So what did they do? They had to do a deliberate thing. They checked a thousand feet at a time. That's the only way they could do it. They closed off each thousand feet of pipe to see whether or not the pressure stayed up. If the pressure stayed up, they knew the trouble was not in that thousand feet. And that they did, section by section, and they found the leak. They followed the logic of natural law. They knew the water in the reservoir was going somewhere. They knew there was no flooding. They simply assumed that the water must be going somewhere, and step by step they were able to find it. That is the kind of attitude we bring to bear on this kind of acting problem. And, as you can see, some of it is a little ticklish, because it is difficult to think of ourselves as being that—how should we say?—logically instructed.

G: I would like to start out with the first thousand feet. What should I do?

STRASBERG: The "first thousand feet" means that each of the things you do should be explored as fully as you can explore. Now you are pushing too quickly in the wrong place. The first thing we want is, "No need to move." You sit there, and you don't care whether you move or not. You work only for this object, whatever it is, as fully as you can. If it's being on the beach, you roll yourself in the sand until the sand is in your eyes, until it's in your nose, until it's in your hair. If you're going to work with that, work with it! Let's see where you get to! When you feel like moving, *move!* Don't care whether you roll! Don't care whether you bounce! Don't care whether you jump! Don't care whether you laugh! Don't care whether you scream! *Yell! "I'm great! Great!"* I don't care. Anything. Screech. Yell. Tumble. Anything. Use whatever you have—but without worrying.

> The need to improvise in order to explore is usually clear to the actor, but frequently he attempts—consciously or unconsciously—"just to improvise, just to see what will happen." Successful exploration demands that there be some concrete element to focus and clarify what the actor is doing. Strasberg points out that "when you tell a pianist, 'Improvise,' he immediately asks, 'What do you want me to improvise on?' He knows so many things he can do that he finds it difficult to limit himself to one thing. When you say, 'Chopin,' he then takes a phrase from Chopin and improvises. Improvisation is very difficult to do without a theme. There must be something given as a problem."
>
> Any work on concentration, even on the most elementary level, is, in a sense, exploration. What the actor really explores is the object. In simple concentration exercises the actor develops his beginning ability to create objects and to go with them. However, as soon as he starts working with several objects, the elements of situation—previous circumstances and character and character relationships—begin to manifest themselves. Technically speaking, the elements of situation are merely different kinds of objects. In improvisation the actor always explores a situation. He may emphasize any or all of

its elements, but the essential requirements are that he give himself to the situation and that he leave the sequence free.

J illustrates the kind of actor who needs the security of a predetermined sequence so strongly that he precludes true exploration by unconsciously developing and following a sequence even when he uses such inchoate material as Hart Crane's "White Buildings."

To Actor J, *following his attempt to explore a situation suggested by* "*White Buildings*": You are telling us a story. You made up a scenario, and then you tried to act the scenario for us. Is that what you mean?

J: Well, I used certain definite things, the mirror and the writing and the window.

Strasberg: Yeah.

J: And the music.

Strasberg: Yes.

J: Outside of that I didn't consciously try to follow any definite story line.

Strasberg: Except the one you've just described. Somebody starts to write. He can't write. He then thinks of where he has to go, and the clock tells him where he has to go and how much time he has for that. As a result he starts to examine himself in the mirror, and when he examines himself in the mirror, he thinks of himself and the woman he was in love with, and he still can't write, so he puts the music on and lets the music affect him. Well, that's a scenario. Isn't that what you tried to act?

J: I tried to act the person, not necessarily the story.

Strasberg: No, you didn't try to act the person. You tried to act the sequence. To act the person means that *you* are this individual. *You* come in here. When you try to drink, *you* drink, and you see what effect it has on *you*. You continue drinking until you as this individual feel that the drinking either has had an effect on you or has not had an effect. You do not *act* the effect. You take this imaginary drink, and you try to make it as real to yourself as you can. You try to see whether it functions for *you*. If it doesn't work for you, then what the hell is the matter with the drink? Why doesn't it work? If the drink does work for you, fine! Then you either want to drink more, or you want to stop drinking. You go with that—as the case may be.

Then you perhaps decide that you're not going to write. Nobody has said that you have to write. You haven't got a story. You've only got a person. And *you* as that person try to decide for yourself. You have whatever time there is between being here and going away. What do you want to do? Do you want to write? Do you want to go to a movie? Do you want to turn on the radio? Do you just want to lie there? You follow along the line of the person and find out what he thinks about himself. What mood leads to certain happenings? What things that you do lead to certain other things happening?

That was not what you did. You knew what you wanted to happen, and you tried to act that, just as you do any other scene. You came in, and you sat down to write. But the whole problem is to try to find out how you build yourself to a point where you want to write. In other words, you are trying to find out what is for you the reality of what we call in a writer the creative moment. If you ask a writer, "Well, have you worked today?" he says, "No, I feel lazy," or "I'm bothered, I'm disturbed." And yet often when he's feeling like that, all of a sudden something happens, and he wants to write. What is that thing that makes the writer want to write? That is what you are trying to explore. You want to find within yourself the kind of thing that leads an actor or anyone to want to create something. That is probably what you meant when you said you used the music to try to want to do something. But you didn't follow through. The whole purpose of exploration is to see how something really happens, but if it doesn't happen, that, too, is fine. Then you simply say, "I haven't found the key yet. I have not found the kind of mood or behavior out of which this type of character and this type of event emerge." And you go on exploring.

All I see now in your work is a search for the sequence you will act. Your manner of setting a problem always rushes to a concern with what *should* take place, as if you as a human being had no other awareness. And we suggest that the human being has a much greater degree of knowledge than that which comes only from the mind.

You yourself have moments of despondency, of not knowing whether you can act, of not knowing whether you can get an acting job, of worrying whether you should get some other job, of being worried about what the hell is the matter with you. And we say that the actor can somehow share these moments with the character. We say that this kind of life can be brought alive within you, the actor, and that you can thus bring it alive within the character in the scene who is not an actor but a poet. We say that when you have succeeded in bringing alive this kind of creative moment, you don't have to worry about what you will act—writing or dancing or anything else—because you can then do any scene involving that kind of moment. If it is a writing scene, you will be able to write. If the character is someone who wants to dance, instead of doing a definite dance and giving an obviously exhibitionist and performing value, you will be able to allow the music to affect you in some kind of rhythm that retains a human value because precisely what movements will happen from it are not known in advance. This kind of response does not posit a knowledge of dance and the acting out of the music for the audience.

The same thing was true of what you did with the mirror. There was no real effort to ask yourself, "What happens if I really look at myself in the mirror? Do I see any of the thing that Hart Crane saw? Do I have any of this thing that Hart Crane had? He calls it a dual-sided thing? Do I have a dual-sided thing? What is a dual-sided thing?" I saw no effort to keep thinking until something occurred in you that might have been a dual thing. In fact, if a dual-sided thing had occurred to you, I very much doubt that you would continue to look at it in the mirror. Once that happens to you, you are going to be carried into a totally different area of yourself. You may go to a different part of the stage. You may come back to the mirror, but you will not see in it the same thing you saw before. You will see something inside of yourself. There will be an inner logic as well as an outer logic.

Moreover, if seeing this dual thing makes you remember a personal thing related to it, something will happen emotionally on the stage that we will see, and it will not be simply a matter of what you do outwardly and physically. It will be an actual experience that is at that moment created. Then it may well be that the logic will lead you to a conclusion completely opposite to anything you could anticipate. You will not then need the music to roar you up and rile you up. You will need the music to calm you down. You will put on the music and let it play because you like this music. And the mixture of the music and these other things may then lead your thoughts into a new rhythm and into the creative moment that you are really trying to find. In that way you will really be trying to explore a person.

> To some actors exploration of a scene from a play presents special difficulty because the playwright's words offer a ready-made sequence to which rigid adherence is virtually automatic. Actor VV "wasn't well trained to begin with. He has severe problems of pattern, particularly of conventional behavior and verbal pattern. He has severe speech problems, technical problems of tension, problems of breaking through emotionally. He is a kind of clever actor who has had to be induced to go further, and in fact he has worked very hard on these problems." Actress WW, with whom VV attempted an exploration of the closet scene from *Hamlet*, is a "capable actress who doesn't do what she thinks she's doing and doesn't really create in a part what she might create."

To VV AND WW, *following the scene:* Personally I am willing to accept any negative or positive results of exploration. I am willing to accept your idea of how people behave when there's somebody dead in the room. I am willing to go with you as long as I see that exploration is really being done.

In a lot of what you people call exploration I see on the stage only conventional thinking about the problem, but no solution, no effort, no real thought. Let us say you decided that Polonius' body is there and that people behave in a certain way under those circumstances. I might be willing to accept all of that, but you ignored something that comes before the problem of the body and which cannot be ignored. In order for Gertrude to be able to respond emotionally when Hamlet starts to speak, there must be clarity and conviction about whatever experience she had at her husband's death that led to the quick second marriage. That clarity and conviction must be present so that what he says to her in this scene can hit ground prepared to receive it.

Maybe she has lain awake at times and wondered whether there was something strange. She's married to one brother and then so very quickly to another brother. She loves this brother. Maybe she's too sexy. I don't know. People think of all kinds of things. I don't mean just in the head, but in terms of experience, of the things that have happened to them. If you think about this situation that way, you can then have at your disposal experiences, not thoughts but experiences of your own, which are either called out or contradicted by the scene. When these experiences do not come into your work, exploration does not take place. Exploration is then merely a discussion about something. There is no real exploring.

A good deal of what you called exploration today was on the mental level rather than on a real level. What do I mean by "a real level"? Look at her, VV. She is your mother. Yes? Now, if she is your mother, what is rather odd and unusual? What?

VV: She's so young.

STRASBERG: That's right. This woman always wants to be young, and she is young, and she thinks of herself as young. So what if a year had gone by before she married again? She wouldn't have been so old. What did she have to lose if she mourned one year?

But she's so amorous. Okay. But there's not a wrinkle. The whole tragedy didn't even affect her. Not one thing is changed.

It is all very well for the actor to read the long, learned treatises that psychologists and critics write on the possible relationships of a son to a mother, but I think that the actor who is exploring Hamlet will also find it worth while really to try to find out in himself the kind of impulses that affect one in the relationship with one's parents. What are hindrances? What are incitements? What do some of us have great difficulty in getting over? Obviously, if you wish to work ultimately toward the emotional realities of this situation, then you must make this kind of real search.

Some of these things the actor does as homework. He watches to see what happens in his own environment. He thinks about the reality of people he knows where there are close family relationships between mother and son or daughter. He tries to see what are the peculiarities of such a relationship and how it shows itself consciously and unconsciously. And he seeks to find out how this real knowledge manifests itself on the stage. Then you are really exploring. But the way you explored today was only a negative way. You simply avoided doing the obvious things. Otherwise you clung to the exact sequence and words of the author.

An actor seldom has difficulty with only one technique of exploration. True exploration involves the employment of all of them. Actress XX—a leading performer in movies and television—illustrated this multiple difficulty in a scene from "Return to Kansas City" by Irwin Shaw:

To Actress XX: What have I seen you do? One scene? We can't really judge quite yet, but this seemed better in the sense that it was much more continuous. It did not seem to be a sequence of separate moments in a play. Even at moments when your partner was talking, we felt that you were continuing. If he had said, "Come on, tell me what you want," at that moment you could have told him. You seemed to have a desire to say and do more than you were literally doing; whereas usually the actor is satisfied when he accomplishes what the author intended him to do or implied what he should do. He does it, and then he's finished.

Continuity is important for your work. It has been too low in awareness of your own capacity and in concern for the scene itself. There has been only more or less of an awareness of where the scene is going. You have supplied intelligently the necessary things that any intelligent good actor is able to supply, but settling for that is fair neither to your talent nor to the scene.

Today I saw a beginning effort really to deal freshly with tasks in the scene, and that effort did pay off. You were able to continue a kind of color that is very difficult to maintain. It is that kind of color, half-nagging and half-crying, which is so difficult to carry off on the stage without becoming lachrymose and uninteresting. However, within that color you were able to keep alive and to keep going and to keep changing and to make the work continuous. There was much greater facility than I have seen in your work before.

XX: It's the first time. I always needed the courage to be able to take my time. That's something I'm not used to doing. And I keep wanting to.

STRASBERG: That's right. An actor has no courage to take his time because he's afraid that if he takes his time, he will not have anything to do. He thinks there's nothing to do. There's only the words. If you don't get to the words, then what have you got to do? However, when you begin to think a little bit differently so as to supply unto yourself motivations for and belief in the things happening on the stage, then you can take your time, because there is always something to do.

Even if you are just sitting quietly, you are not doing nothing. You are continuing to be involved with or to be concerned over or to imagine or to dream or to plan the continuity of the scene. After all, this scene could be written completely differently. It might be written with fewer words or more words or different words. But when the actor is prepared to do it, he can do it. He can do the whole scene without a single word. You could sit for half an hour just thinking and doing and making little sounds and noises and could still build up the whole sense of the conflict between you and him. You don't need the author's lines to tell us that. You only need the author's lines to come in and tell the audience what the actors can't tell them, what the conflict is about, what the two people actually want from each other.

Today the work was still limited to the area that was going to be talked about by the two people in this scene of the play. You did not touch upon other things not mentioned in the words which exist between them. These you must take the time to create. These are part of the actor's whole character contribution to the scene. If the actor creates these things, he doesn't have to worry about having nothing to do. For instance, what is this girl really interested in? Is she really interested only in going to Kansas City?

XX: No. She wants to be admired. She wants to be petted. She wants—

STRASBERG: Exactly! She's a young girl, twenty-one years old. She's just been married. She has a little baby. And she thought that when she got married, she would have dresses, New York, a champion, everything like that. She likes to go out dancing. She's been out with fighters, you see, and she knows how they live. She thought he would take her to night clubs and that they would live the kind of life you read about in the columns.

There was no indication of that in what you did. There was only negative indication in that the girl complains that she doesn't have anything. At only one moment did I think you were going to start something. You went over and started to put on a little ribbon. But she's a girl who loves life. If she is not life-loving and anxious to enjoy herself, there is no scene between them because he would drop her like hotcakes. He is very desirous of her. He is very anxious to make time with her, and she is equally anxious. But it has begun to pall. He cannot give her the time she needs. He cannot give her the other things she needs. So she's a very vibrant, alive little girl on the loose. We saw the nagging, but very little of these other colors.

XX: The script says she was dancing with the radio, but I just felt so miserable I didn't feel like it.

STRASBERG: Not only dancing. After all, at this moment—to put it very simply—you want to get him. You want to get something from him. What is the simplest and best way that you have to get something from him?

XX: By shouting at him?

STRASBERG: By throwing yourself in his way! If he's already taken her to Kansas City four or five times, obviously she's got what it takes. We didn't see that except in the natural sort of way you supply it just by being yourself. And therefore, because the play and the author did not make the point at that moment in words, you were left only with one color. You came in prepared to play only this scene. We advise, "Build for yourself the scene and the situation so that you could play the drama. Do not prepare just this scene. The characters do not know that this scene is going to be played. Prepare the character for many aspects of his behavior, not just those referred to by the verbalizations."

A PERSONAL TECHNIQUE

The greater the talent of the individual actor, the more he needs to find a technique commensurate with that talent. The mediocre actor does not have much difficulty understanding what he does and how he does it. But great talent is often as much a mystery to its possessor as to other people. Accordingly, it is more easily frustrated and even destroyed than is talent of the second-rate. Great talent is potentially far more self-destructive than talent which is obvious and therefore easily controlled. It is more open to banality than the safe, middle-of-the-road talent, but likewise it seldom descends to real badness.

In all of Strasberg's work with Actress U it is apparent— whatever he may be specifically concerned with—that his fundamental concern is to lead her away from superficial and mannered acting to an understanding of the deeper and more intense levels of her being and talent. He never suggests a technique to her as an end in itself, but always as a means through which she can further explore and understand and control, and thus avoid the dangers—personal and professional —to which talent makes her prone.

To ACTRESS U: You have had a hard road, and you will earn everything that you will get. On the other hand I have a feeling that you are lazy with yourself. You have been undisciplined in external things. You are unwilling to treat yourself as an actress. You want to be treated as a sincere person. And in the area of deep emotional problems you still stop short. When you find things that are right to do, and you do them once, you then will not face the problem: "How do I do that again? What sets this off?"

This, for the fine actor, is the real need of technique. Only by technique can he preserve those things that are most precious in acting—the moment of revelation, the moment of experience, the moment when something happens most fully and completely on the stage. Actors in the past had no technique. Acting came to them accidentally, by inspiration, by the chance hitting of certain colors within themselves. And today the mediocre actor is quite good. In fact, he's always capable. He seldom suffers. Only good actors suffer. The good actor is sometimes good and the next night not so hot. Half the performance may be good; the other half not so good. Performances of really good actors go up and down.

One of the great tragedies in the modern theatre is an actor who has given the greatest single performances of our time. Stark Young would corroborate that. The performance of Jacob ben Ami in *Samson and Delilah* was the greatest single performance that I have seen. And yet this actor is at times today so ordinary, so pedestrian, that you look at me and say, "What the hell is he talking about?" This man does not have technique for the thing that is greatest within him. That which made him vivid and great, the inner imagination, he is not always able to control.

I saw him give a great, brilliant performance of Dostoevski's Idiot. I remember very clearly and vividly one moment when he discovers a dead body, and I remember the "Ohhhh! Ahhhhhhh!" The startle! The howl! People talk about Moissi's howl, "Oh, that's brilliant," but ben Ami made you start. It was wonderful, it was literally startling. But this man has no technique for the very thing that makes him great.

And just now you actually said the same thing. You admit that at the moments when you have somehow found what you want, some revelation or some understanding of the part, you have a tendency to go away from that discovery. But it is precisely that kind of moment that you must work with and grapple with. All we are asking from you is that you should live up to your own talent. We cannot give you talent, but we are going to force you to live up to the talent that you have. I would like to see a real grappling with this problem: "How must I explore so that this thing that I have found and that I feel to be true to the role can be done with at least part of the fullness and part of the vision and part of the experience at each performance?"

CHAPTER IX

Approaching the Role

STRASBERG: The Actors Studio does not stand for a choice between extremes. We do not represent a separate wing of theatre. We are the only ones in the theatre today who appreciate all theatre. We appreciate English acting when it is well done by Gielgud, but not when it is badly done by someone else. We appreciate the French approach when it is done by superb French actors, but not when it is imitated by actors who happen to come from the Comédie-Française. We appreciate Brecht and Meyerhold. Everybody else criticizes Meyerhold, but we say that he had a wonderful theatrical imagination. His work was not realistic, but it was a great contribution to theatre.

To us all theatre that comes from a creative impulse, that is not imitative, is good theatre and has a rightful place. In good theatre, as Granville-Barker says, the actor does not start out to imitate another actor. He starts out to imitate a character. If he wants to imitate—fine! Let him imitate a character. When a playwright writes about a character, he imitates a character. He does not imitate another playwright. In any art form on any level that kind of imitation can only lead to degradation.

The easy assumption that one approach always leads to good results and another approach always leads to bad results is simply not borne out by the facts. I wish we could stop this senseless opposing of one approach to another and begin to seek real values within each possible approach. Every approach has such values so long as it is not mechanically but artistically followed.

There are, for example, psychologically two kinds of actors. Some actors can go on the stage and always be themselves, and by being themselves they can be the character. Duse was always herself. She was never anybody but herself, and yet she was, by being herself, always the other person. Chaliapin, Paul Muni, Stanislavski himself, are examples of the opposite kind of actor: in order to act fully on the stage they have to feel that there is a mask. When they feel protected by that mask, they can then do anything they want to do, and nobody will think it is them. Both approaches are perfectly plausible. It is not necessary that one should be considered right and the other wrong. The rightness or wrongness of the approach depends simply on the psychological needs of the individual actor.

There are many ways of approaching a role which do not involve jumping to far-fetched or extreme solutions. And while it is true that complex situations and characters cannot be portrayed with complete truthfulness by conventional or cliché means, it is also true that the actor can often come to grips with these difficult and complex acting problems on a simple plane. But he cannot do this by merely following general approaches that are theoretically capable of solving any role or problem in any play. He can do so only by seeking the avenues and processes that are peculiarly capable of helping him as an individual, by following an approach that is valid for him personally.

Some actors seem to feel that what is in a role is so distant from their personal experience that there is no avenue into it for them except one of making a substitute reality that will be convincing enough to make them go on with the scene. But very often simpler, more immediate, more obvious and external solutions can help, even before these actors need to seek complicated solutions —which may not, in the doing, really arouse their belief anyway.

The simplest approach is, of course, to concern oneself solely with speech. It is true that when one does so, judging by the experience we have had, one ordinarily winds up with melody, a kind of chant, a sing-song quality which unfortunately does not make the speech clear. If it did, we would use it, but it does not.

But the simple willingness, the simple effort to say a word, and to mean just what the word means without being concerned about dramatic meanings, is itself of importance. Let us say that an actor is talking to us about exercise. Well, he can pick up a book to illustrate his point, and he can say to us, "To do the exercise you first pick up the book. Then you put it down. Then you pick up the book again. Put it down. Pick up the book a third time. Now, watch this. Extend the muscles of the chest against the book. Do this a few times every day, and it will lead to health, wealth, happiness, and many children!" All the actor has to do is make a simple effort to transmit to us the importance of those words. And their importance is just exactly what they say. You lift it up. You throw it down. You lift it up again. You complete the simple physical task of actually telling the audience with the words what you mean, and to make deep, deep meanings out of that is not necessary.

The simplest thing that an actor does is to speak. The author has already made a kind of logic in the lines. Often the actor need only do the simple carrying out of tasks and the simple conveying of the meaning of the words.

In production, when good actors sit down to read a play the first time, they are just like other people reading something for the first time. When you read a novel the first time, your heart pounds, and you weep, and you laugh, and if somebody comes in, you say, "Go away!" You really get involved and interested and excited. Actors need not even make an effort to read the lines well. They need not have a knowledge of the ending. If they make a simple effort to read the lines and respond to them naturally and sympathetically as in conversation, you are amazed at the extent to which they come alive, the extent to which response rises and drama actually grows. At the first reading actors can give you such wonderful results that the problem becomes, "How do you keep this?"

The actor helps himself not only through the simple use of words, but also by means of simple physical activities. Harold Clurman once saw Lucien Guitry in a scene where he had very little to do. It was a plot scene in which the character finds out that his wife is having an affair, and it could have been a very uninteresting scene. At the beginning Harold wondered why Guitry was putting on his boots. Then he began to watch him putting on the boots. After a little while he found he couldn't take his eyes off those boots, because Guitry, while he was talking, was putting on those boots with such great concern and with such great care that the spectator became utterly absorbed and fascinated by a perfectly ordinary and everyday process. The audience was drawn completely away from the obviousness of the plot.

Sometimes the actor finds such physical tasks in the play, and sometimes he finds them simply to fill his own need. In any case they are ordinary physical tasks. It's a simple problem to do them clearly and carefully and individually. And by doing these things very simply, often you find that you begin to evolve a scene, and sometimes a character. Especially is this true where the author himself has evolved an interesting sequence of objects or logic. Then you merely have to do it.

Some English actors use excellently the approach which tries to make real meaning out of the individual speech. We understand what should be happening. We understand what Shakespeare meant by those particular lines but we have no comprehension or understanding of the entire character or the play. We understand the story, and in Shakespeare the speeches themselves are so moving and so valid and so exciting that they alone encourage us to think that we are seeing a play, when actually we are only witnessing the performance of arias. The speeches are said for meaning, but they are unrelated to the event and the situation.

We have recently seen yet another approach wonderfully illustrated in Sir John Gielgud's *The Four Ages of Man*. He read the speeches for meaning, but the meaning was washed and pervaded by a sense of the emotion and of what is happening, and that gave an excellent definition of the scheme of the scene. We understood what was taking place in the scene.

However, the approach which has been characterized as that of all great acting, not only in Shakespeare but in any play, is the approach in which the actor tries to add to the lines not only what the lines mean, not only what the character is feeling and is aware that he is feeling, but also, as Clare Eames once put it, "the emotions or experience of the character, which the character himself is unaware of, but which the actor must be aware of in order correctly to expound what is transpiring." This leads to the true creation of character. It is the approach to a play that all great actors have exemplified. Whether it was Garrick or Kean or Mrs. Siddons, the brilliance of the acting was not founded on the melodic or rhythmic reading of the lines. All those great actors were invariably criticized for their reading of lines. Other actors living at the same time were thought to read the lines with much greater melody and rhythmic feeling.

Those great actors were brilliant in their approach because they created a character, and people seeing their performances came away with a sense that the person in the play was different from the conventional idea of that character. When Kean played Shylock, the essential element of his performance was a different sense of the character, a sense of Shylock as a young man, a sense of a man impelled by motives and events and characteristics and emotions different from those commonly indicated in the playing of that character.

Great actors also display another element that leads toward character and yet does not seem to start from character. Many people in Garrick's time took exception to his playing of Lear because they felt it was too realistic and thus did not sustain sufficiently the classical level of Shakespeare. And yet this served to make Garrick the greatest actor of that period. The important thing in Garrick's Lear was not simply the character element in it. His Lear did wind up being a character, but the descriptions seem to indicate that the way Garrick acted the scenes was a truer and more convincing portrayal of what *had* to take place than was given by any other actor of his time. When Garrick acted the madness of Lear, there was no vague moving of the hand and staring of the eyes and broken rhythm of speech. Garrick broke with the theatrical tradition of his time. He went beyond the mere creation of character. Through character he revealed truths about the life of man.

It is significant that when Garrick was asked where he got this new believability and truth, he described how he watched a real person who was demented. And he found out that in this real person there were no sudden theatrical starts and fits and stares. He found that the behavior was mostly quiet, and that when this person was quietly and sort of meaninglessly playing with his clothes and seemingly not quite aware of where he was, suddenly he would be impelled by the memory of what had taken place when he had accidentally dropped his daughter's child from the second story and the child was killed, and he would begin to relive that event. He would begin to play with the child, and then he would start to cry, and Garrick said that he learned, from watching these moments of aberration in this person, how to play King Lear.

Everything any good actor does has its appropriate place. We emphasize that the place should properly be in a process and in a sequence, but we also emphasize that such a process must be fundamentally imaginative. For example, you don't get up in the morning and comb your hair and then go into the shower. That would be ridiculous. You comb your hair after you come out of the shower. To do it the other way is weird. And yet on the stage we might have to comb our hair first for the sake of character. And it would be the task of the actor to do this illogical thing not with a superficial imitation of reality, but with all the conviction that we bring to the carrying out of logical tasks in life. It is a paradox of theatre that things are done on the stage in response to a logic that says, "A thing is done through creating an imaginative process of which it is a part and which makes the actor capable of carrying it out."

All Stanislavski's work and all Strasberg's work have been directed toward helping the actor create such an imaginative process as he approaches the role. Each man's almost frantic insistence that he cannot be imitated, that he offers no "system" which can be mechanically copied, that going through the motions or paying lip service accomplishes less than nothing, arises from a profound understanding of the individuality of creation. Pure logic can establish a process of training or of creating a role with relative ease. Different processes may have validity. But any process is meaningless if it does not engross the actor's imagination at each stage of training, rehearsing, and performing.

The principles of the actor's art as enunciated by Strasberg not only have been arrived at empirically and pragmatically, but demand an equal pragmatism in application:

The approach to the role depends on the kind of acting one wishes to create. A formal approach to acting is self-defeating: it leads obviously to cliché or convention.

If the actor's imagination is working, do not disturb it. But if something does work effectively on the stage, the actor cannot assume that such an accidental result is again attainable.

The technique of the trained actor is a means of controlling his personal resources. Without training, technique is impossible. Methods successfully employed in training or in solving problems are equally applicable to the work of creating a role.

The actor must learn to exert effort through exercising will and discipline in order to lead himself into the creative mood and thus to the creative carrying out of the tasks that are set for him.

If the actor has a problem, it must be faced, or it will poison his entire organism of creation.

No actor is ever finally trained. Even trained and experienced actors should periodically subject themselves to pure training work in order to refresh and extend their instruments.

These principles easily emerge from Strasberg's comments to Studio members, and they are implicit in training work, in the solving of problems, and in exploration. However, a rather more detailed process of approaching the role can be described. But—

as always in the theatre—the validity of this process comes not from itself but from the ability of the actor and director to abide by its underlying premise at each stage of work. This premise is that while the actor must grow gradually in intellectual and imaginative awareness of the playwright's creation, this growth must not proceed so quickly that it exceeds and therefore stulti-fies the actor's ability to bring himself alive in the character. Nor must the actor become so absorbed with bringing himself alive that he neglects to work in accordance with the logic of the script.

This process therefore seeks to fuse the reality of the script with the reality of the actor. Neither talent alone nor aware-ness alone nor any mechanical mixture of the two leads to a true performance. Only the ability to discern what is actually taking place as between the actor and the script at any particular moment can enable the actor and director to define what must be accomplished at that moment so that the role may truly grow and develop. And, actually, more than discernment is required. The actor and director must have the courage to abide by such judgments. Otherwise, they merely go through the motions and probably accomplish less for the play than if they had adopted a frankly mechanical, imitative approach at the beginning.

Both Stanislavski and Strasberg insist on the importance of the actor's first impression of a role. Since the first reading often stimulates the actor's imagination more than any subsequent stage of work on the part, the actor must be alert at this time, not only to guard against prejudice, anticipation, and cliché, but to be aware of the creative stirring of his imagination, to discover the nature of his responses so as to recapture them as he works on the role.

In the second stage, the actor must begin to analyze the role and bring himself alive in it. The analysis tries to arrive at an outline of the inner and outer sequences of the part and the logical connections between them. The actor thinks about the meaning of the lines in these terms. At the same time he tries to find objects that awaken his concentration and excite his belief.

In this work of analysis and bringing the imagination alive,

pretense and unconscious self-deception are the actor's greatest
enemies, as Strasberg has emphasized a number of times by the
following story:

Fifteen or twenty years ago I was teaching at the Labor Stage,
where they were trying to create a theatre, and a girl brought in
a scene from *Golden Boy* that she intended to do. With the scene
she brought in a ten-page analysis of how she had worked on it.
I looked at it. I knew the play, I had seen the play, and her analysis suggested a wonderful, brilliant production, and I was amazed.
I could not have thought of the things she had written. They
were not on the stage, of course, but on the page they were
wonderful.

So I said, "Now, you say here that when you were five years old
your father did this and this and this and this. What did you do
in the scene as a result of that?" She said, "Oh, no, that happened
twenty five years ago." I said, "Oh, I see." Then I said, "Well, you
say here that when you were twelve years old your father left your
mother. Now, what did you do on the stage as a result of that?"
"Oh," she said, "that didn't happen now. That happened when I
was twelve." I went through this whole essay. All of it happened
"then." None of it had any effect on what she was doing now.

That kind of analysis is what people think we go in for here
at the Studio, but it is the exact opposite of what we go in for.
We don't care how much the actor knows here (*points to head*).
We only care about how much he knows here (*points to heart*).
We only care about how much he can really live out and how
much he can experience. Knowledge which is not really experience at this moment, is not really being made use of at this moment, is of no value to the actor.

I arrived at that conclusion many years ago in the first years of
the Group Theatre, but I was interested to learn that Stanislavski
arrived at that point only at the end of his life. In the initial stages
of rehearsal of his productions there had always been a great deal
of analysis and discussion which he called "rehearsals around the

table," but toward the end of his life he said, "It's no good. The actors have a tendency to talk a lot, and then they don't do anything, but they think they are doing a great deal because they have all discussed it. I don't go in for that now. I try to make the actor immediately show me what he wants and what he means to do. We do not rule out the stage of analysis of a play, but when we do it, we do it in a very definite way: we block out the major portions of the events in the play and thus give the actors what the director thinks is happening, so they can immediately begin to work on it."

However, when things are told to the actor even to that extent, often all they do is to constipate him. Unfortunately they do not really help him, whereas some small thing, like looking at himself in the mirror or putting on his make-up, often has much more importance. Extensive analyses often do not affect at all what we essentially try to bring about in the actor—his ability to believe, his ability to experience, and his ability to behave.

> Most of the objects used in this second stage of work should be imaginary: otherwise, the actor only falls into a sequence. He must rather begin to concern himself with the subtext, the inner life of the character; he must avoid an overconcern with words and cues. This stage of work must awaken the beginnings of experience in the actor. The actor must fish in every puddle to see what he will find. If he cannot find means to arouse experience in himself, work on the role cannot and should not go forward.
>
> However, once a real relationship to objects and fellow actors is awakened, these elements must be colored and qualified by a sense of what is to take place in the play. In this third stage the actor must begin to create an outline of actions and a sequence of the part that derive from the given circumstances of the play. The actor seeks the past and future of what is transpiring.
>
> Here actors often make unwarranted assumptions. The girl at Labor Stage imagined that intellectual analysis would pro-

duce concentration and conviction. Actress T supposed that since she was like the character in some respects, she was like the character in all respects, and therefore could omit analysis of the role. And Actor M, a very undisciplined individual, assumed that concentration and belief could substitute for the work of analysis, that an active and spontaneous imagination was sufficient for acting the part.

To ACTRESS T: You said that you found out, as you started to think about the part, that you aren't really as much this character as you originally thought. Yes and no. What you mean is that physically you could be the character. In fact, you didn't change yourself physically in the scene. But mentally and emotionally and in terms of environmental behavior you are right. You have none of the things that this character has. If you had been born in her environment and had done the things she did, you could be, with your looks, what she is. But to be what she is you would actually have had to participate in the activities she participated in, been concerned with the things that she was concerned with, and have developed her attitudes.

It is always important to find out as much as possible what would have had to take place for you to be the character. Even if you *are* like that character, the defining of those areas that differentiate you from the character will lead you to a clearer idea of the tasks that you have to present to yourself, to your concentration, to your imagination in order to draw from yourself the behavior which is necessary, but which you will not do unless you define it that clearly, that precisely. Otherwise, you begin to live out these situations as *you* really are, and in most plays that is not quite what the character is.

To ACTOR M: It is dangerous for you to continue the spontaneous freedom, because there seems to be in you a resentment at routine of a certain kind. Thus, there is a danger that, if you continue to be free, the freedom will make it impossible for you to repeat a role. It bothers me that you can come here after you have worked out a certain procedure by means of rehearsal, and that here you do not follow that procedure. It bothers me that you can describe how something happens to you here but that you don't quite know why. That bothers me, even if the thing that happens is good.

M: Well, I know why.

STRASBERG: Why?

M: Well, I think I have a natural propensity to play this character a little coarser than I am, a little rougher, and I thought as a result I felt like an uncle of mine.

STRASBERG: You felt you did that today? And not before?

M: Well, I felt it before, but not as completely.

STRASBERG: That quality should be done fifty times more. In other words, the author suggests that this character is bitter, that life has hardened him. Your partner says to you, "Why don't you smile?" Yet you permitted your own unconscious smile to come through constantly, so that her lines made no point.

M: She felt I should get more of myself into it, likable, warm—

STRASBERG: I am not interested in yourself or not yourself. I am interested in a scene and in work on a scene. I might have said, "Yes, there was more of yourself in this. That's right." But in this particular scene I would only want to use part of yourself and a great deal more of other things. Unless that distinction is made, there is a danger. The danger is an excess of the Stanislavski approach which asks, "What would *I* do in this situation?" And I don't care what you would do. I care what the character would do. Otherwise you make hash out of the play. The actor has to work along a given path. Without that path, freedom is chaos— not freedom. Freedom for the actor is always freedom within defined areas. The actor has freedom to travel on the road, but not just freedom to travel. Just having freedom to travel means that if the car wants to go off the street and up into the apartment house, you bang through the door and demolish the steps.

M: Did I really give you the impression that that's what I think freedom is?

STRASBERG: In the work that I have seen from you and in what I have heard about your work, there seems to be an unwillingness to face the problem of a definite choice. Sometimes that choice can be made by you, but sometimes in professional production that choice is not made by you. In that choice lies the actor's freedom. That is a problem, and the actor faces that problem not by disagreeing but by accepting, and within that acceptance doing the best of which he is capable. Otherwise, it actually means that parts you should play, parts in which you would be good, you refuse to play because what is decided does not quite agree with your ideas. In a production that is impossible.

The analysis that takes place during the third stage of work is of two kinds. One kind—a general analysis—deals with the play as a whole and is directed toward a definition of the main idea, or superaction, of the play, the ruling concept by which the particular elements of the role can be defined. A second kind of analysis is special: it breaks the role or play into sections, each of which has some separate identity. The actor divides the role into these sections so that he will be acting not generally but in terms of discrete units, each of which will have a significance, a tangible value, on which his concentration can be placed.

But, Strasberg warns, the purpose of such analysis is to inspire artistic excitement and enthusiasm; mere mental exploration has little value:

Analysis permits you to enter the fold of the role, to study its separate elements, its nature, its inner life, its entire world. Analysis consists in seeking to understand the outer, external elements and experiences in so far as they affect the inner life of the role. But analysis also attempts to find the comparable feelings, emotions, experiences, and other elements in oneself by means of which one will get close to the role. In short, analysis finds the material essential for the individual process of creation.

But how does the actor enter the "fold of the role" when that role is apparently very far removed from his experience? A good example is a role of a man suffering from insanity, since it can scarcely be presumed that the actor has ever himself been insane. However, says Strasberg, there are a number of things the actor can do to enter even the world of insanity.

First of all, an insane person behaves very logically in relation to the thing that makes him insane. Insanity cannot be equated with any peculiar way of behavior such as old-fashioned actors tried to indicate, the fits and starts which Garrick was the first to break with in his famous performance of Lear. The public still thinks that insanity is strange, although actually they have within their everyday environment plenty of evidence to contradict that idea. Everybody has known people who have behaved perfectly plausibly and yet have suddenly done illogical things, but have done those illogical things quite really and quite truthfully. They do not behave strangely. They behave with complete reality and conviction, but their behavior is founded on some idea or attitude that is not true, and that is what makes them insane. There is not actually much difference between a sane person that kills and an insane person that kills. Both will give you a very logical reason for the killing, but the sane person's reason is founded on an actual happening.

In the second place, the principle Stanislavski used to approach a great variety of difficult parts should be suggestive. This is the principle of looking for the opposite. Thus, when you play an insane person, you do not look for the insanity. You look for his rational side. You look for the thing that makes him a sane human being. Then, of course, you find the thing that makes him insane, but you do that insane thing with full belief and full reality.

For example, Leonidov was a famous Moscow Art Theatre actor, and he was a very good actor, but he would get hold of some element of characterization and just worry it to death. I once saw him give an extraordinary performance in *Yegor Bulichev* in which he was supposed to be incurably ill from his first entrance until his death at the end of the play. Well, through three acts he kept dying in such a way that you felt your mind would go at any moment because you just couldn't watch somebody go on being that nervous and that jittery. You wanted him either to get it over with or to forget about it so that he could pay attention to what was going on. But this strange capacity to catch one idea and keep going on it also enabled him to catch the almost traumatic passion of a character like Dmitri Karamazov. He made up his eyes to emphasize their smallness, and his hair stood up a little bit, and he caught the taut face and the continuity of passion that are not easy to maintain.

Stanislavski was once working with Leonidov on the part of a miser, and he wanted to keep the actor from too close an adherence to the miserliness. So Stanislavski said, "Don't worry about playing a miser. Try playing the man as if he really wanted to do everything possible for everybody. When a man comes into your place and you have to say, 'I'll give you something,' try to look around and find what you could give him. Really try to find something to give him, but discover that actually you can't find anything that's good enough to give him, so that you end up by not giving him anything." Thus, Leonidov got away from obvious miserliness. There was something that made him miserly, but at the same time, if someone accused him of being a miser, he would say, "What do you mean? You're crazy," and he would be perfectly justified in his own thinking in combating the idea. By searching for the opposite color, Leonidov not only obtained the desired result and found a basis for his own belief but also found a reality that was commensurate with the complex nature of reality in life.

Also, it frequently happens both here and in my private classes that an actor works on a part and discovers one little thing that he doesn't understand and therefore throws that little thing out of his consideration. And invariably I have been able to demonstrate that that one little thing which somehow doesn't coincide with his conception of the rest of the play or his approach to the part is in fact the key to the part.* If the actor cannot find the reason for something that seems to him insignificant, invariably that is the key to the character. If you ask the actor, "What does that one line mean?" and he says, "Well, that's the one thing I couldn't understand. Everything else makes sense," the explanation of this one line is always the key to the character which the actor has not yet found. In playing an insane person, the actor should be particularly careful to search for the special logic or experience that conditions in this particular person the behavior that we call insane.

And, of course, another approach is simply to use observation. That is one of the most valuable ways of approaching something that you do not understand. You have to find out. If you are playing the part of a doctor, you try to go someplace to see how doctors behave. You observe how doctors handle certain things, and you try to teach yourself to handle those things so as to look as expert as the doctors. If you are trying to play an insane person, and you're not able to find the answer by analysis or by finding the opposite or by searching out a key to the role, sometimes you can find the answer very simply by looking at or finding out about people who are actually insane. I remember I had a friend who was interning at Kings County Hospital. We went up to visit him, and he took us around. I must say that I had always had the right idea, theoretically speaking, about insanity, but even so I was flabbergasted by the behavior of the insane people that I saw, because it was so totally different from the behavior I had previously thought of as insane.

The actor should not be too ready to assume that any of these unusual parts is so far away from any of us. He should assume in the instance of insanity that in all of us is an element, some element, which when it goes haywire leads to that behavior we call insane. Assuming this, the actor can say to himself, "Now, wait a minute. I have noticed that at certain moments people have

* See Strasberg's exchange with Actress XX, pages 275-78.

said to me, 'You're crazy. What's the matter with you? You must be crazy to act that way.' Well, what did I do at those moments? What made them say that?" Sometimes you will find out that it was an insistence on believing a certain thing which they said couldn't be so. Sometimes you will find it was a tendency on your part to say certain things or to behave in certain identifiable ways. Thus, you will little by little begin to find out more about insanity when it has not yet appeared as insanity. Insanity is a process that develops. At the beginning it is not at all obvious, but it grows from elements that every normal person has. Every human being has within himself some elements of what every other human being has. There are times when we are kings and queens and paupers and murderers and insane people. And therefore the actor should never assume that there is anything in life that is so far away from him that he could never possibly create that in himself.

The actor in the fourth stage proceeds to a deepening of his involvement in the role's given circumstances, with the aim of intensifying the creative feeling and working for the emotional elements of the part. The earlier stage of working with objects concentrated on arousing reality and conviction, on bringing the imagination fully alive after the initial stimulus of the first reading. Now concentration goes toward creating the basic elements of emotion that analysis and other work up to this point have revealed.

This emotional work in turn opens the way to a search for the inner meaning or truth of situations and events and given circumstances. This should lead the actor even more deeply than has any previous work into the past both of the character and of himself so that a final and comprehensive understanding of the problems of the role emerges.

This understanding leads to the last, or fifth, stage of work on the part, which deals with motivating and justifying the actor's behavior. He has now found many things to do. He must now be sure that these things are in fact part of "an imaginative process which makes the actor capable of carrying them out."

He must make certain that a real, rather than a formal, logic enables him to answer the question, "Which circumstances in my inner life would make me, myself, the human being and the artist, do what I have to do in the play?"

The actor must never do something merely because the character does it. He finds a justification for doing it and behaves accordingly. He makes what he is doing his own. And in order that this essential final work of approaching the role be carried out, every effort should be made not to let the performance harden and become fixed. Until the final stages the actor should be kept free and creative.

This process of motivating and justifying the actor's behavior requires constant testing and adjustment. It must remain fresh. It must be kept alive. Its vitality during public performances must be constantly re-examined. If things which previously activated the performance no longer really do so, they must be changed—though the large outline of the role remains the same.

One of the most persistent sources of difficulty for actors is the mistaken assumption that a performance must be either fixed and therefore mainly external, or free and therefore necessarily accidental. We fall all too easily into parroting, "The actor has to learn to repeat," and forget to ask, "What does the actor repeat?" We assume that, since he repeats, he must repeat everything, and that the more exactly he imitates his preceding performances, the better actor he is. We ignore the possibility that an actor with inner technique can be both fixed and free, that he not only can plan to be spontaneous but can actually control his spontaneity on the stage.

Theatre captures life directly, literally, in almost a pulsing process. More than any other art, theatre can create the process of life. The price that theatre pays for this gift is that theatre has the same quality that life has. Life lives and dies. And so the theatre too lives and dies. Theatre is born at each performance.

With the actor, the more unpremeditated things are, the more premeditated they are. The things that are most unconscious in the character are the things that can be done by the actor only if they are most conscious. Those things that are obviously suggested by the lines are easily done. But who knows to do those things which the lines do not suggest, which the character is doing but does not know that he is doing? Only the artist knows what is going on in the character which the character does not know.

The basic difficulty in all acting is that the actor must create on the stage, almost as much as in life, the sense of spontaneity. In all great acting that is done. In all great acting there is the element of spontaneity within a performance that yet keeps a shape and an outline. In great acting there are constant improvisational elements that come through. The performance varies, but the outline remains the same.

Both the spontaneity and the outline have to be accomplished by the actor, as by any other craftsman, deliberately. That is the fundamental purpose of craft. Stanislavski put the idea into a phrase that sounds high hat and highfalutin—"from the conscious to the superconscious." What he meant was that the thing that happens spontaneously in life must on the stage be created by the actor so that he knows he is creating it. It must be spontaneous and yet under the control of the actor. He must be aware and yet caught up in it. That is the peculiar nature of the acting art.

In this respect comedy acting is no different from the acting of serious parts. A scene can be done differently on different nights and still be funny and amusing. The actor need not permit the kind of fear that directors build up in him when they say, "Unless you do it this way, it's not going to be funny. Either do it my way, or it's not going to get the laugh." It is true that you will get the laugh if you follow the director's way. There is something in timing. You do learn to catch the audience and hit it a certain way, but you will get just as much of a laugh by doing the line in other ways.

There is something the actor must be concerned with that is much more essential than getting the laugh, because this is an element that may not be in the performance every night unless the actor consciously works to bring it there. The reason for maintaining the shape of a scene is not that the scene will not be funny if you veer from that shape. Maintaining the shape of the scene leaves the actor free to create the experience and the aliveness that only he can create. Descriptions of great acting of the past as well as a vast theatrical experience in our own time show us that this is possible. It is made possible by maintaining a basic setup in the scene which has been established by blocking it out in sections.

The working out of these sections derives to a considerable extent from a sense of what is taking place. Obviously marking sections will always make for greater logic, because you mark out a section through seeing that something new occurs in that section as opposed to the preceding one. A sense of the transition from one section to the next creates a continuity in the acting; whereas, when you are not aware of the transition, words referring to the new thing are said, and they don't make any sense.

Sections or units are marked out by things that limit them. Within the section no exact sequence is established. The section is continued until the predetermined limit is reached. For example, when I come in I throw the tantrum, and I continue to throw the tantrum until he says something. His saying something marks the limit and brings me back to trying to explain to him. I go on trying to explain to him until he says something else, which marks the limit of that section, and I then go back to the first thing. I go on with the first thing until I reach the limit of that section. In this way it is possible to fix a play in its essential nature so that the basic things in the play remain the same, but within that design the actors are free in their movements and in their behavior. Certain important positions within a section may be set. The actor may know that he will sit in this chair and not that chair. Beyond that the actor is left free to attend to creating the life of the performance.

I am not just talking in the future. We carried this approach to such an excellent conclusion in the Group Theatre that nobody ever knew we were doing it. The productions were very clear and very precise and very definitely staged, and yet each night they were improvised, and therefore each night it was possible for the actor to retain his aliveness. Otherwise it is impossible for the performance to remain spontaneous.

I remember a big moment of improvisation in the first play that we did. Somebody went off stage and killed himself, and Franchot Tone was left sitting alone on the stage. Then he had a moment in which what had happened had to strike him, and then he had to run. The improvisation was very clearly defined, and so were his reactions to it, but exactly when he would run was never set. He had to run whenever the fact of the death would hit him. We also told him that he had three alternatives, because the problem was that he had to run toward the door through which the body would be carried a moment later, and we didn't want the stage to be left empty in case he ran a little soon. So we told him that if he got as far as the door, even if he got as far as to start out of it, he should always come back because he sees the body being carried in. If the actors carrying the body should start late in relation to his running, he should start out, see the body, turn back, and wait for it. However, if his running should be late in relation to the carrying in of the body, he would then have nothing to worry about, because the people carrying the body would push him back from the doorway. It made absolutely no difference as to when he ran, but his being impelled by the proper belief and logic at the moment when he ran made a great deal of difference. When you try to tie sections like that down too precisely, you greatly increase the chances of a mechanical performance.

If an actor is attracted by the prospect of creating a role that is both designed and free, set and improvised, externally correct and yet alive, he often neglects a very important part of the process of creating the role in that way. He wishes to be left free to improvise, but forgets that he must provide resources from which he can improvise. In acting—as in all human endeavor—

something does not come from nothing. Even the technically trained actor, who has a battery of devices for impelling his imagination, often does not realize to how great an extent improvisation in performance can rest on prior improvisation done during the rehearsal process.

Mrs. Fiske is an actress obviously not connected with the "Method," nor is she commonly thought of as a conscious actress, and yet she found her way to very sound methods. This is illustrated in the very interesting statement she made about her starting to work on Ibsen. She had previously worked with much simpler material, parts into which she fitted very easily. And she said that when she came to Ibsen, it was like going into a world of shadows. The Ibsen plays had connotations and depths which the other plays she had worked on had not possessed, and she found that work on these Ibsen plays could not be limited simply to learning the lines and doing what the lines suggested.

An Ibsen play is usually about the last moment in the life of a character, and obviously this last moment is conditioned by everything that has created this last moment. So Mrs. Fiske felt that her work on Ibsen had to be almost entirely improvising rather than rehearsing. During the year she started work on Ibsen she went on a trip, and everywhere she went she tried, both in her mind and by locking herself in a room to improvise, to act out events involving the various characters in the play, so that later in performance, when certain moments arose, there would be associations with these previous moments that had actually taken place in improvisation. In life we constantly are subject to associations from our past experience; but on the stage the author gives the actor only the finished material, the end result. Therefore, when the actor comes to these finished moments of the character's life, he does not have the natural automatic responses of a human being from his own real past. For that reason we have often suggested to actors that they improvise in preparing a role, in addition to working with the actual lines and sequences.

People commonly associate characterization with the mannerisms of the character or the actor. But in the case of the really talented actor, these are the least important part of that talent. It is the really unusual part of the talent, even the strange part —perhaps those human elements that even in life sometimes do not have opportunity to blossom—which provide the answers in an Ibsen part or a Strindberg part. The actor finds these answers deep within his unconscious, within associations of odd and peculiar things of his knowledge and experience. The unfolding of these things may lead to odd and peculiar results, but unless the actor finds these answers in himself, either unconsciously or consciously, he does not really know the significance of what he is doing, and therefore he begins to act out conventionally the things that the author demands. The purpose of improvisation in working on a role is to explore what makes human beings behave in this particular way. Otherwise it has no value.

To ACTRESSES DD AND O, *after they had worked on Strindberg's "The Stronger" improvisationally:* No matter what else you did with this scene, no matter how you finally staged it, even completely differently and including the laughter at the beginning that you used last time, you have already achieved the kind of tension which this scene never has on the stage. I'm sorry! I don't care who plays it. I don't care how well it is done. Invariably the audience pays lip service to the tension. They say, "Isn't it good! Look! She's sitting quietly. That's difficult. Look at that! She has to sit quietly and not say anything. Gee! they're doing it very well. Boy! it's so tense!" You see? It is always a tour de force of acting, but it never has the real tension that comes from catching what is inherent in the play.

Today the scene had intensity, and I don't just mean intensity as tension or clash, but intensity in terms of reality. You had reality. That's right. We were scared of what would happen. It had real excitement. It wasn't just a "Strindberg" play. It was not something we were merely listening to and enjoying. It was something that we were watching with a totally different kind of consideration, with our mind going to this reality and to the play and to ourselves, and there is no other way of evoking that kind of consideration except by this type of improvisation.

There is no way of getting into this scene the kind of Strindbergian antagonism, the kind of primitive, down-to-earth antagonism between men and women and women and women except by improvising, except by exploring in a way that may go far afield, just as a painter making sketches may go far afield, but from those sketches he will get part of the quality he will put into the finished painting. The fullness and the terrific intensity that you got could not be gotten any other way than by just sitting at that table and thinking and exploring and exploding some of the elements that you—and a lot of us—keep hidden.

Regardless of what would be done with the scene from here on in, certain fundamental attitudes, experiences, relationships, and adjustments were found which you would now have to try to maintain. Even if we said, "In the actual scene, we don't want the fight," you could still say to yourself, "I fight. I fought the last time somebody said that to me, and *she* knows it." Nobody knows better than she does that you fight! In this way improvisations really become equivalent to the realities of life. One of you really knows something about the other, so that even though she may be sitting quietly *this* time, when she gets up, you instinctively back up, because you know what she did last time. Improvisation creates and conditions reflexes in the same way that we gain experience in life. Here today on the stage a reality has occurred, and in the future you can respond as a result of that reality in the same way that you would respond if you had had this character's actual experience and behavior. This "life" knowledge is vastly different from the mental knowledge that we usually have of the characters in a play.

These five stages of approaching the role can thus be differentiated fairly clearly, but this differentiation is valueless except as a guide to what must actually be accomplished along the road toward performance. The role must grow as a tree grows, not as a piece of apparatus. A machine does not work until it is finally assembled. An actor must "work" at each stage of development in the part, or he runs the danger of falling into a mechanical result at the end.

Strasberg and the Studio attempt to avoid the sterile dilemmas into which much talk about acting falls. They suggest that the highest art results from an organic approach to the playwright's material, whether that material be serious or comic, naturalistic or highly theatrical. They call for a full use of the actor's resources. They demand a constant, objective appraisal of the actuality of the actor's situation.

Perhaps the greatest stumbling block to the attainment of these ideals in the contemporary theatre is the demand for "style," which premises that "style" and "realism" are somehow opposed. In so far as the actor attempts to satisfy this demand he is driven to an extreme that negates the approach of Strasberg and the Studio.

Rightly understood, "style" is not opposed to realism. "Style" refers to the fact that true expression truly mirrors the almost infinitely varied relationship between reality and the individual artist. "Style" is a measure of expression, not a part of expression. In the correct sense there is no valid "Shakespearean style" or "classic style" or "Greek style." There is only the best expression that the actor can give to a reality that he has explored and understood for himself.

A lot of people are permitted to attend here at the Studio. They don't have to do anything, so they take things for granted. "This is The Actors Studio, but a lot of the work that goes on here, what the hell is it for?" "Kazan works on Greek plays, but what does he come up with? A lot of nonsense." And usually the younger these people are, the more they make these easy judgments. The less experienced they are, the more they know exactly how a Greek play should be done. Mind you, in all the two thousand years of theatre experience that the world has gone through I know of not one example of a production of a Greek play that has satisfied my idea or the world's idea of how a Greek play should be done.

Until I saw Franco Zeffirelli's production, I could not point to an example in the entire history of the last three hundred years of a *Romeo and Juliet* that was fully satisfying—or even mostly satisfying. Fine actors play Romeo or Juliet, and we say, "They got away with it." In Othello or Shylock or Richard young people have come up and have *hit* the first time. Actors have made careers out of those parts. I cannot mention an example of the same thing in *Romeo and Juliet*.

We all sort of pay lip service to the idea that there is ultimately a way of acting any classic play and that this ultimate way was followed by the Greek actors in the old times and by the Elizabethan actors in Shakespeare's day. Well, I would question that, not too argumentatively, but just on the basis of the facts we know.

We have, for instance, some statements of Greek actors. One school said that the other school acted like monkeys. One famous Greek actor prided himself that when he spoke on the stage you couldn't tell any difference from the way he spoke in life, and there were always two schools in regard to speech of that kind. One school didn't like it, and the other school did like it. We have the example of a Greek actor of the fourth century who was playing a scene in one of the Electra plays in which the sister comes out to bemoan her brother, and we have the testimony of that actor who claimed that the lament was very difficult to do. And he said that, in order to help himself, when he came out on the stage bearing an urn in which were supposed to be the ashes of the brother, he actually carried the ashes of his own recently deceased son.

The Greeks had the same problems and disagreements that we have, and there is no evidence that they were able to solve them any easier than we do. If they were good actors, they possessed the qualities that belong to good actors of today or of any other period. If they had difficulties, they were our difficulties.

If we judge by the evidence of Hamlet's speech about two opposing schools of actors, Shakespeare thought that there were not only a lot of Elizabethan actors who couldn't act his plays, but a lot who couldn't act at all. He thought they didn't deserve to be called actors even though they were, as he says, highly successful.

We are trying to find here something that has not yet been found. Maybe we are going about it in too subtle a way, but we are trying to bring a sympathy and an understanding to the basic problems of Shakespearean theatre. We have an awareness that in the Shakespearean theatre there were elements different from our own. We would like to maintain and keep and use those elements. But we would also like our actors to create the behavior with a modern sense of reality and conviction that is at the same time right for the play.

We are not wasting time if we work on problems that in three hundred years have not been solved. The problem of Shakespeare is a valid problem. It is an important problem. It is a problem that Stanislavski did not solve. It is a problem that not one of the great directors of modern times has solved. Actors here and there and now and again have solved moments and parts of it, but as a whole it has not been solved.

So, let us not fall easy prey to this common assumption that if we could only find the secret in the past, we would then be on easy street. If they had any secret, it was no more than the secret of talent. If Michelangelo was great, it was not because he lived in the sixteenth century. He had talent. And if you have talent today, you also can be a Michelangelo—if you live as long as he did and work as hard. Never mind the art. To work on the Sistine Chapel ceiling from a high ladder with back-breaking effort for two years in order to paint those fantastically wonderful figures takes talent, but it also takes excruciating labor. Talent is in that sense universal. Labor is not, and if you do not expend the proper time and effort, you will neither make use of the talent that you have nor solve the problems that you perceive.

I never wish to discourage you people from working toward

something in the back of your minds that may be different from my idea or anybody else's idea. I am only concerned with the process whereby you go about carrying out your own conception. I never wish to discourage your basic effort to make your acting simple, easy, and natural. But I very definitely wish to discourage the idea that when you find this naturalness you will always find the drama.

Very often I see you people following the Stanislavski formulation—as opposed to the Vakhtangov formulation, which I happen to favor. The Stanislavski formulation states, "Here is a girl who falls in love. I have been in love. When I am in love, what do I do?" That is the way Stanislavski formulated the acting problem; therefore, he never solved any of the basic problems in any of the classic plays that he did outside of the Russian repertoire.

Vakhtangov rephrased the approach. He didn't say, "If I was so and so, what would I do?" He said, "If I am playing Juliet, and I have to fall in love overnight, what would I, the actor, have to do to create for myself belief in this kind of event?"

Stanislavski did very interesting things. When an actress would attempt Juliet, he would say to her something like this: "Now, look, darling, you're a young girl. You've been in love. When you are in love, what are you really concerned with? Don't give me this crap that you're worried about whether he's a Montague or a Capulet. In fact, Juliet says, 'Who cares about that?' What are you really concerned with? Now, I don't have time to go into that, so I'll just give you an answer to show what I mean. You are really concerned with whether you are good-looking enough to get him. You are concerned with whether he really noticed you. Was he just acting? Was he just playing with fire? Did you really stand out? What happens to a girl when she's concerned with her good looks? You tell me. I don't know that. This is something that's feminine and youthful. Don't give me the words. Shakespeare has already given the words. We will get the words. You tell me what a girl who fantasizes at a moment like that is *really* concerned with." Stanislavski often tried to find this kind of precise reality, but with Shakespeare he was not able to do it successfully.

When I say that I believe in the Vakhtangov formulation, I do not mean that I was born on Vakhtangov's side. No. We have tried both approaches, and we have found that in certain circumstances the Stanislavski approach does not work. The Stanislavski formulation often leaves you high and dry in something that is natural and easy and simple but is just not what is needed by the play. The Stanislavski formulation often does not lead the actor to seek the kind of reality which the author conceived and which underlies the lines he wrote. It becomes almost a way of bringing every dramatic thing down to a naturalistic level which cannot support the drama. Stanislavski's formulation will then only help the actor by accident.

We should begin to be aware that theatre in the twentieth century is totally different from the concept that lingers on among intellectuals and is essentially the literary approach. The modern concept of theatre art stems from people like Gordon Craig and Adolphe Appia. It recognizes theatre art as a combination of words, sound, sight, movement, and action. Theatre art is a combination of all the elements that go into it. Often these elements taken together can make a play which purely verbally has no meaning into a great work of art. I saw Duse in third-rate folk melodramas, and I saw her in Ibsen, and she was as superb in one as in the other.

At the same time our modern sense of how a play has to be looked at has not from a theatre point of view been fully clarified. We realize that there is something in a Shakespearean play in addition to its literary form, something in its theatrical nature that makes it the great play that it is, but we still have not really come to grips with the mystery of what makes a play great except on the stage. We cannot define a play before the fact in the same way that we can define a scientific thing. To that extent we can still demand that there should be a greater penetration and knowledge of Shakespeare based on an understanding of his plays as works of theatre art.

Shakespeare's mastery of theatre art is found, for instance, in his knowledge that things take a certain amount of time to do and that that is never real time, but stage time. Often in Shakespeare a character gets up at night, but in a few minutes' time it must be daylight. Shakespeare doesn't say, "Just turn the lights up," and leave the problem to the poor actor. He does not leave him stuck with a few picayune lines, so that the audience sees the passage of time as imaginary and unrealistic. Shakespeare is always careful to give the character something to do so as to make it convincing. If he has the actor get dressed on the stage, he gives him wonderful lines to say, so that the audience will not pay attention to his getting dressed. And he gives him enough lines to say so that a skillful actor can easily get dressed, and throughout the lines he provides little phrases like "Tighter here," or "Not so tight" to mark the progress of the dressing. And at the same time Shakespeare uses this business of dressing to get from two o'clock at night at the beginning of the speech to six o'clock in the morning at the end by inserting in the lines little comments like "The stars are fading," and "Look, the moon is gone," and "Oh, dawn is rising," until at the end the character says, "It's early morn, and we must to our task." Shakespeare creates time on the stage.

Stanislavski in approaching Shakespeare through his peculiar formulation was a little too deliberately realistic in the use of time and consequently broke the fabric of the wonderful constructions that Shakespeare created. The scene of Othello's arrival at Cyprus is designed to show that husband and wife have not been able to stay apart, that they are anxious for each other. The boat docks. Othello leaps off and says, "Oh, my love," and he has a long speech with Desdemona. That is the reality of that scene, not the realism of the scene, and when that fabric is broken and a different type of time established, the reality of the whole play is broken. In that scene Stanislavski inserted an elaborate improvisation with the boat's being brought into dock with chains clanking and all the other details being realistically correct. Then he said, "When a boat docks, it doesn't just dock so that an actor can get off; the freight comes off first." So he had extras with freight coming off the boat first. Then he said, "When the governor appears in Cyprus, he doesn't just come to appear in a Shakespearean play. He has to have a delegation to welcome him." So Stanislavski invented a long ceremony of welcome. In the meantime Othello and Desdemona stood around and had nothing to do except be concerned with this naturalistic behavior.

I'm sorry. That may be Stanislavski, but it is not Shakespeare. It has not the slightest value or significance. Who the hell cares? The people have been waiting for Othello to arrive, and he immediately rushes toward his wife, and when Stanislavski at that moment gets involved in the unloading of a boat he is concerned with something in which Shakespeare had not the slightest interest. And Stanislavski's productions of Shakespeare were not successful. People blamed the "Method," but to me they were not successful only because Stanislavski had this strange tendency to stress such superficial or naturalistic details.

People have the impression that we are not interested in the classics. They do not realize that our trepidation in the face of the classics comes from a recognition of the greatness that the classics contain. The greatness and significance of experience and meaning in the classics holds us back from going to the classic plays with the same ease with which we approach ordinary contemporary plays. Great plays are great experiences, not just great words. The great words of these plays are outlines of great events which people experience deeply, whereas in contemporary plays the people who experience are often lesser than ourselves. In these great plays there is no limit to the sensitivity that is demanded or to the grasp of experience that is demanded.

The Shakespearean characters are great people, and no matter how wonderfully well they are done, no matter how much Eliza-

bethan gusto we give them, no matter how much logic and directness we bring to bear, no matter how wonderful the personal
qualities that we employ, the approach that is merely the sum
of those elements will not solve the Shakespearean problem.

In our theatre today we are not just in a rut so far as facing
the problem of Shakespeare and most classic plays is concerned.
We are in a real dilemma. On the one hand we feel, "No. We
lack style. We lack form. We cannot move and cannot talk as
actors of these plays should act and talk." And when you tell
me that, I agree with you. I, too, believe that to be able to act
and talk like Shakespeare's characters, which means to have intelligence and wit and emotional facility and mercurial emotion and
the ability to maintain emotion over a long period along with
words that pour out quickly and fully and intelligibly, is very
difficult. After all, there's only been one Shakespeare in the entire
life span of the world. But when on the other hand it is assumed
that in order to learn to act and talk like Shakespeare's characters
you have to imitate English actors, then I am sorry. Shakespeare
was not imitating English actors. He made rather devastating
comments about some of the successful English actors of his day.
And yet the other side of the dilemma is that we are being
pushed very hard to conceive Shakespearean character in terms of
the formal externals of speech.

Caught as we are in this dilemma, it is important for us to remember that the approach to Shakespeare can only be in terms
of Shaw's statement that classic characters are classic because they
are the kind of people who created our arts, our sciences, our
politics, and our wars. They are people dealing with large problems
of life. They come to these problems with deep sensitivity and
deep intelligence. And therefore, no matter how alive the actors
may be, no matter how much the tone rings out and the words
clatter easily and intelligently along, if they play a scene from
one of Shakespeare's histories so that I can't somehow believe
that these were the people who created the great English empire,

to me it is not Shakespeare. To me it is an imitation of other good actors rather than representation of life.

Because we are aware of the strength of the verbal pattern, we are sometimes fearful that we will get caught up in the Shakespearean phrase, but there is really no need to fear. The phrase, after all, is the embodiment of the thought. One thought can have fifteen adjectives, depending upon the author's ability to find adjectives that are expressive. One of the keys to Shakespearean language is that in his time minds worked a little more quickly and a little more actively than nowadays. In Shakespeare's time you didn't have machines to do your thinking for you. You had to do everything, and the same person who wrote poetry was also a good swordsman and also a guy with the ladies and also finally lost his head on the block. Those people lived the kind of life of which they wrote. Shakespeare himself was at times very close to dangerous things. Marlowe was arrested for being a spy. Ben Jonson was a soldier and killed his man between the opposing armies. People at that time really lived the kind of life that we see in the plays. Therefore, when we know what we are saying and where we are saying it, we need have no fear to say it.

And it is true that today we are in a period that is nonvocal and nonexpressive. Today we feel a lot of things we do not have words to say. Our English is literally poor in quantity as well as quality. We don't have a wide enough vocabulary. Today you find much greater vitality in ordinary speech than in intellectual speech. Bums have a very rich vocabulary. The concept of good speech today implies impersonality and politeness, whereas the Elizabethan concept embraced vividness of thought, of feeling, of sensation, of expression and behavior. The ability to dance and to sing and to fence was necessary to the classes of people with whom Shakespeare came into contact. We need not be afraid of that. I understand the fear of getting caught up in the vocal or verbal pattern, but keeping the thought going with Shakespeare's words through all of Shakespeare's phrases is the key to a lot that Shakespeare says.

In Shakespeare's time the language of the court and the common language came together for the first time in English. People were inventive in language, and they were adventurous in language. Shakespeare's language is not that of a man searching for words, of a man trying to find words for something that he doesn't fully understand. In Shakespeare there is the fullness of sensation that resulted from the fact that in his period things were being said fully.

It is true that the long speeches in the early plays of Shakespeare are still couched in the classic literary tradition and copy the conventional tirades of his time, but there are also one or two scenes in those plays that indicate that Shakespeare had an actor in his company who was able to do certain things, because he wrote scenes for this actor in each play. For example, in *Two Gentlemen of Verona* there is Launce's scene with the dog. It is obviously a scene written for a clown with a dog. This actor evidently had a dog and was able to make a very amusing dog act.

We must always be careful that we do not lose the reality which the author made, and in this scene the reality that Shakespeare made was, "This is a performer." That reality demands far more than a simple, natural quality, no matter how authentic. There must be the sense of a performer performing. The scene obviously is a funny scene, and the dog helps to make it funny. The dog has this wonderful quality, you see, that he, without having read Aristotle and the Greeks, is himself. He knows how to be himself. He has learned the Stanislavski method from himself, and when he comes on the stage he is true to himself, and he looks and moves and watches truly. The actor in working on a scene like this must not be afraid to be tricky, and the tricks have to be both well done and interesting.

It is an act. It is a performance. Yes, it has a character, but we also get in scenes like this the *commedia dell'arte* influence. In the *commedia* there was this wonderful breaking through of the classic form where people speak with objects and to themselves and become characters, and the whole thing happens on the stage rather than in the speeches of the author. In a scene like this there is a real sense of improvisation on the stage, of an act being done before the public to earn its approval. The actor must not hold back from being as quick and as skillful as any clown by conventional ideas of being natural.

There *is* a classic tradition in acting. Just reality is not classic. Just theatricality is not classic. The classic tradition combines the sense of theatricality with depth and strength of feeling. Theatricality plus reality characterizes the classic tradition in acting.

Trying to bring the characters in such a play as the First Part of *Henry IV* down to a kind of human level has a value in so far as it helps the actor to feel that he can logically share that kind of reality and individuality, but it also has a danger. The danger is that unconsciously, but actually and specifically, the actor will set out to demean the great. He will imply that greatness does not exist and that the greatest person is only an ordinary person like any of us.

When we see a character like Prince Hal, we know that he was an historical figure. We know that Shakespeare's history plays were written about important events in eventful times. And we know that somehow we must get from the play and the characters in the persons of the actors the feeling that we have when we see such medieval sculptures as the famous Naumburg Cathedral carvings. Those people are so alive! I happen to have photographs at home, and everyone is flabbergasted that they were created in the twelfth century. The people live. A princess named Uta is so fantastically alive that she cannot be described. Her husband has a face like a Dürer portrait. It is literally and figuratively hewn of rock. This was a man who carried the sword!

You get a sense of people when you look at the people of Michelangelo, when you look at the pictures of da Vinci. They seem real, and they are real. Today they still live. You want to know, "Who was this?" These were people who somehow de-

served to be part of the epoch-making events that the great painters described. Even in German painting and in the painting of
the Low Countries in the fourteenth and fifteenth centuries you
begin to get a sense of reality. In painting historical events they
use faces and characters of people they actually knew, and yet
somehow these actual people deserve to be in those historical
events that are pictured. They look as if they could actually have
performed those tasks. That is the essential thing in the classic
play. We have to feel that this character is capable both of doing
the things that we know he did and of saying the wonderful
things that Shakespeare gave him to say.

By trying to parallel ordinary life too closely in playing these
great figures we make an even more serious mistake than we do
in using an artificial style, because the artificial style, bad as it
may be, still is an admission that there is something in the play
that must be dealt with on its own terms. And sometimes our
effort to demean that something, rather than to rise to it and to
fill it with meaning and significance and reality and conviction,
is worse than trying for the greatness and not bringing it off, because we deny the essential nature of the art we presume to fulfill. These are monumental characters. They have swayed armies.
They made and ruled countries. They brought a country up from
one period of civilization to a new historic level. Therefore, I
bemoan the artificial or purely vocal approach because it will
never really come to grips with greatness of soul and thought and
feeling and wit. Only the tone becomes great—and often only
large and beautiful and melodic—and you do not understand what
is happening on the stage.

Classic plays deal with these great people, but even the small
people in classic art have been seen not by an ordinary person but
by a Michelangelo. He filled them with his passion and his vision
so that they seem somehow more than ordinary mortals, and we
must never permit ourselves to fall into simply bringing these
people down to the ordinary level of reality in order to make them
human.

Don't forget that even in ordinary plays I bemoan that approach. The purpose of this work is not to make everything casual and ordinary. On the contrary, our purpose is to fill everything with the utmost possible significance, to bring out the most important and fullest and most dramatic responses of the human being. Any actor can bring out what is casual and conventional. Sometimes a person off the street can do what is ordinary better than the best-trained of actors. But to create the leap of the soul and the leap of the imagination that brings one into these classic situations and environments and to create that as fully as the ordinary little things the actor does, requires an inner technique that is equivalent to what a painter does when he paints from an ordinary model a character that is somehow different. When you see beggars painted by Brueghel or by Rembrandt, you know that they are beggars, but the fullness of vision and imagination and of life contained in that painting is terrific because it was seen by a great artist.

Plays like the Restoration comedies or George Bernard Shaw's comedies or Noel Coward's comedies are difficult because we realize that they are not like Tennessee Williams', and accordingly they are played with an approach entirely different from that employed with Williams, an approach called "style"—though with no awareness of what style is or what it comes from. Consequently, some scenes are very funny, but other scenes die. A lot of scenes in those comedies are not intrinsically funny. Rather, they're sardonic; they contain some social criticism. Those scenes die because there is no connection between one type of scene and the other. By amplifying the humor and saying, "This should be played externally or just stylized like a charade," the actors are able to solve the problem of the basically funny scenes, but in the bitter or satiric scenes they are lost. They can't quite do it really and they can't quite do it externally, and it doesn't go.

We have seen scenes from that kind of play done here at the Studio in which the actors did not try to be funny but simply carried out a preparation for what presumably the characters should be prepared for; nevertheless the scene was funny. And during the scene, along with all the intrinsic fun and people laughing and the purely theatrical happenings, we would get a sense of what was involved in the play. This sense was outside the comments the author was making. These were moments in which the actors supplied the qualities of real human beings in relation to each other. The actor would give us the strange romantic quality of a man who *could* be intrigued by the woman, and the actress would give us a woman who *could* intrigue men. These qualities were not important for the scene itself. The scene could come across just as well for the audience by being played for pure farce. The audience would laugh, but the play would appear thin, because it would not have any of the values that the actors supplied.

What happened was that the actors appealed to us on a variety of levels, which every play has. Usually we talk about a "Noel Coward comedy" or a "Shaw comedy." We assume that their plays are written on one note and cannot have any other notes or levels or elements. That is not true of any art. It is not even true of abstract art. In the process of creation abstract art is definitely connected with elements of reality.

Chagall in his little autobiography describes his early years in Russia. All of Chagall is a little cute, but his pictures have a kind of charm and nostalgia. And yet some of them have puzzled me a little bit. He has people flying, and a person with his head turned almost off his neck. I'm always curious. What makes a painter paint like this? And in his book I have just found out why. When he was a child, he would be sitting in the chair near the table, and he would smell the fish being prepared by the women in the kitchen, and he says that his head would fly off to the kitchen to take in the smells. That's what he paints. He has a picture of the bride and bridegroom flying around in the air, and he says in the book that they are in the room but not in the room. Their thoughts are flying around in the room, because for the first time they have transcended poverty and are in heaven in their own thoughts. That's what he paints when he paints the bride and the bridegroom. They are flying on a carpet into *A Thousand and One Nights*, while down below remain the green table and the poverty.

In Chagall the things we commonly think of as purely formal, as seeming to derive from a purely formal striving, are the exact opposite. They try to give expression to a thought or to an experience which cannot be expressed any other way. How would you describe visually "I sit near the table, and I smell the fish, and my head flies away" except in the way that he does? You would have to come to that kind of solution in one way or another. Therefore the seeming search for style is really, to me, always a search for content.

The demarcations being made in the theatre today are deadly. "This is a real play," and "This is an historical play," and "This is a French play," and each has its style. No. They come out of different contents. They come out of different backgrounds. They portray different manners and customs. They show different behavior. They have different patterns of rhythm and of sound and of habit and even of theatre. But there is never just a different style or form whereby the French play is in the French style, and the English play is English style, and Shakespeare is Shakespearean style. The essential thing that combines all the elements of theatre and that goes through all the history of theatre is the human being and his living presence. This has not changed in the five thousand years of human endeavor of which we know.

These theatrical demarcations are dangerous when they apply to the end result we wish to achieve. Yes, a French play does have something that is different from an English play. But that something is not done differently. You do not play a French piece on one violin and a German piece on another. You play both on the same violin. We seem to make these formalized differences almost because we don't really perceive the intrinsic differences that stem from meaning, from content, from experience, from what the author was getting at, from the world that the author was part of, and from the theatre that the author worked in.

When the actor has too definite an idea of what we call style, at the best that leads to good skill. Very rarely does it lead to more. He develops tricks that are skillful. And yet, though the great clown has the tricks, it is not the tricks you notice. When you see Chaplin, you don't think of his tricks. You laugh. You cry. You say, "The timing is wonderful," but you don't notice just that. You notice what the timing serves. You notice what it is used for. The tricks we are accustomed to call style are used only in the service of the actor, not in creating whatever texture or quality there is in the play.

A WOMAN IN THE AUDIENCE: I gather that you are interested that the classics should endure, and yet in commenting on productions of the classics you say that these plays should be allowed to die. Would you as a teacher of actors say how American actors can be trained to re-create and perform the author's original intention in the style of the historical moment?

STRASBERG: I am not interested in re-creating the style of the historical moment. If Shakespeare wants to be reborn and do his plays the way he did them, he has full liberty to do so. Obviously, if Shakespeare were alive today, he would do his plays as we do plays, as if he were a modern man.

A classic is a classic only when it is alive and not when it is dead. I do not say that classic plays should be allowed to die. I say that it is better that they should die than to be performed as they are today. Classic plays are plays that have caught images and experiences of man at certain periods. But a classic is not a classic just because it has caught a local historical moment. A classic is a play that, coming out of its own time, has caught something that lives on for all time, that has a universal meaning and content.

The first work that is done for the actor in training him for classic plays is the first work that is done for any actor in training him for any play. The basic craft of the actor is the ability to incorporate a character on whatever level is required. That craft is basic to all characters, Greek, Elizabethan, Spanish, *commedia dell'arte*, whatever you wish. That is not the kind of thing commonly thought of as classic acting, but it is the kind of thing that is thought of as great acting under any circumstances and under any conditions, classic or modern.

The additional work the actor needs for training in classical acting is the development of such basic skills as are required for moving like the characters. Notice that I say "moving like the *characters.*" I don't want you to mistake my meaning. Many classic actors today move like actors of the seventeenth century, not like characters of the seventeenth century. I assure you that characters of the seventeenth century are closer to characters of today than they are to the portrayal of them by classic actors of today. People in the seventeenth century were people, and they behaved with logic and conviction in the context of their time. They wore the costume of their time, and this costume sometimes made them behave differently. But they did not behave in the phony, stylized manner which the classic actor thinks of as classic acting, and which is nothing but classic acting. It is not the creation of classic characters.

There are many approaches to the theatre, but the basic approach to a classic play should be such that the production achieves a sense of style without going into the stylization which is common to classic acting and classic production today. That is the approach for us here in America, not the antirealistic, theatricalized kind of thing that is today boosted up as the theatre theatrical or the theatre of nonsense or the theatre where anything goes, where nothing matters but color and lights and movement. I am not taken in. To me that is nothing more than emptiness. If the audience is taken in, it is only because its life is so empty that it will be taken in by anything. Don't forget that this is the same audience—of which, thank God, I count myself a member—that gathers to see the Macy's Thanksgiving

Day parade, which it finds just as theatrical as anything on the stage.

Theatre basically is meaning. It is experience. It is an image of human beings. It is somehow or other an image of the thing the author has in mind. Obviously there can be differences as to what the author has in mind, but unless you bring back Molière and Shakespeare from the dead, there is no way to settle those differences. The only thing you can go by is the integrity of the individual. You go toward the classic play or any play with the intention of trying to find out what the author wants. You will make mistakes; but there is no achievement anywhere without mistakes.

PART THREE

The Actor and Other People

CHAPTER X

The Actor and the Director

THE Actors Studio's ideals and purposes extend beyond individual training. Strasberg's discussions of the actor's relationships with those elements of the theatre outside himself—particularly the director, the audience, and commercial managements—are an important part of his activity as Artistic Director of the Studio. The formation of The Actors Studio Theatre was the culmination of the Studio's attempts to lift American theatre to a position commensurate with America's eminence in the other arts. The new theatre has grown in a very real sense from Strasberg's continual efforts to define the actor's position and the position of American theatre today in terms of what he admires and what he dislikes, in terms of tradition as well as the contemporary world—actors of the past such as Duse, Grasso, and Chaliapin, and the world theatre of today in France, England, Italy, Germany, and China.

Whenever the actors in a play are good, the director gets credit. Whenever they are bad, he gets bad credit. The strange antagonism that often exists between actor and director grows simply out of a lack of knowledge of each other's problems. The director, being part of the theatre, should know the problems of the actor —at least as well as he understands the problems of the scene designer. When the producer tells the director, "This scenic effect that you have in mind will cost ten thousand dollars; it's too much," the director gets what he means. But when the actor says, "You are forcing me in my instrument, and you are hurting," the director replies, "I don't care. I'm the director, and you'll do it my way, or else." The director understands ten thousand dollars, but the needs of the actor he does not understand.

If twelve musicians decide, "We are now going to learn to play this particular composition," they also have to decide, "Somebody's going to conduct." If twelve people play together, they cannot follow twelve different opinions—even if all the opinions are good. There must be a conductor, and, when the conductor has been picked, the players must follow him. When he wants to work on tempo, they work on tempo. When he decides to work on tone, they work on tone. Unless the players follow the conductor's wishes, the group will never learn to play that particular composition with any logic or significance.

When the Philharmonic Symphony Orchestra played with Toscanini, they were a totally different orchestra than they were under any other conductor. What happened? Did their technique suddenly become better when Toscanini took over? No. Somehow, because of demands that are made and problems that are set and because of the *way* these demands and problems are presented, something happens to musicians—as to actors and other artists—that concentrates all their activity into a unity. That is the function of the director. And when the director best appreciates this problem, he is like a good jockey riding a horse. In racing, the problem of pacing is very important. If you let the horse out at the wrong moment, it will run itself out too soon and will be beaten by another horse that comes on with a rush. Knowing the right moment to let out the horse is the skill of the great jockey. After all, anybody can get on a horse and ride. But the jockey has to know horses and horse racing, and he has to know this particular horse. Some horses start slow and wind up. Some horses start fast and peter out. The jockey who wants to win has to have a sense of the horse, but all too frequently the director who wants to put over a production has not the slightest sense of the problems and needs of the actor.

At the end of the second or third year of the Group Theatre, I summarized the work of that season, and my summary was not very well received by the members of the Group, although I thought it was cogent and logical. You see, conflicts were naturally developing within the unit after two or three years, and I didn't care. I honestly didn't care, but the people were worried that I wasn't worried. What I tried to make clear was that when two people love each other and hope to get married and only see each other once a week, it is natural that they should want to see more of each other. They call each other up. They can't wait. When they're married, the problem is the other way around. They want to get away a little bit. They see each other too often rather than not often enough. That, too, is natural. It's not terrible. It has a logic, and people should recognize that logic and behave accordingly.

When people do not recognize that logic, problems arise. When the Group Theatre was a dream, everything was ideal because nothing had yet been done. As soon as you bring the ideal into the arena of activity, some things work, but other things do not work. Some things you like, but other things you do not like. The ideal never works out exactly as you thought, and therefore there are natural disagreements. These disagreements should be seen as part and parcel of what makes for creative work, not only in the theatre but everywhere. But such disagreements happen especially in the theatre, because theatre work can only be done by people working together.

A writer can argue with his publisher. He then goes away and does his real work by himself. A painter can argue with a critic. He then goes away and does his real work by himself. An actor may argue with his director, and he may even leave the room, but he still has to come back and do his work when the director is there. The actor knows the playwright is watching, and he sees the director whispering to the playwright, but he still has to go ahead. I'm sorry. That is the theatre. That is the way things happen in the theatre. And unless the actor grows up to an awareness of the difficulties and responsibilities that the nature of theatre imposes on him, professional theatre activity is impossible.

In turn, the director can do a lot of things, depending on the nature of the individual actor, without having to worry the actor about them. Then the actor does his work, and the director does his work, and from that a certain fusion comes about which is the totality of theatre art.

A director should argue with an actor only if argument will enable the director to accomplish what he wishes to accomplish. If the actor has a wrong idea and that idea helps him to do what the director wants, the director should not care. If I want a man to go to Times Square and buy me a paper, what the hell do I care if he calls Times Square Madison Square Garden? We could get into an awful hassle. He would say, "You're crazy," and I would say, "You're crazy." The whole point is that he means what I mean, so why shouldn't I say, "Okay, go to Madison Square Garden"? What does that take out of my hide? Do I really agree with him just because I say that? He then goes to Times Square and gets me a paper. He thinks that he went to Madison Square Garden, but I got my paper just the same.

Ego and purely mental victory too often become essential to a director, but actually a director's victory over an actor doesn't mean a damn thing. My teacher, Boleslavsky, said, "Look, tell the actor whatever he wants to hear. What do you care as long as he does what you want him to do?" It's true. What difference does it make who wins the argument when it is usually only a philosophic discussion based on questionable premises? I have seen productions hindered and performances hurt by the director's insistence on ideological or verbal or philosophic agreement. I tell the actor, "Show me what you mean." If what he does is good, why should I argue? If what he does is no good, then I don't care whether he agrees with me or not. Obviously agreement alone will not help me or him.

However, the actor has to have enough ego to recognize the work he has to do for himself. He has to realize that sometimes the director does not know how the actor accomplishes that work, and therefore is not willing to give the actor the time for it, even when it is being done before his very eyes. Then actors must learn to do as the director does when he fools the actor into doing what he wants: he must learn to keep the scene flexible so as to take the requisite time to make things come alive for himself on the stage.

By leaving himself free at rehearsal to do his necessary work, the actor comes up with a lot of material to solve the scene. Out of five rehearsals he will find some things that recur. He does not have to worry about them. He will also find things that come and go, and some he desires that do not come at all. Because certain things happen once and do not happen again he thus discovers what it is he has to create or re-create or reinforce.

The actor often leaves this search out of his professional work. He is so concerned with the end results that he omits the very things that his sensitivity should produce as a basis for the scene, no matter how it is going to be directed. It is very important for every actor's professional career that he learn that a scene may be done in many different ways. The director will insist that the actor do this or that, but he also wants a basic aliveness and sensitivity. The director has to point the way to the finished results, but he also assumes that the actor will fill in for himself the motivation and the experience.

In professional production some actors tend to be completely subservient to the director's demands for finished results. These actors sometimes seem to be very opinionated and egotistical individuals, but in their professional work they are the exact opposite. They give up. We see a little of their ideas, yes, but of themselves we see nothing. They seem to subordinate themselves completely. These actors must sometimes tell themselves, "Wait a minute. The wine needs aroma, but the aroma comes from allowing the wine to stand and mellow." In acting, aroma comes from material that can only be engendered by the actor, and no director—no matter how insensitive he may be—means to rule out its creation.

The director may not know how the actor works. Or he may

take it for granted that the actor will fill in the part and make it his own. And since most actors don't have too much with which to fill in, there is not too much difference between their goodness and their badness. This approach works well enough for the director. When these actors are bad, they're only a little bit awkward. When they're good, they are easy and accomplished. And since most actors are picked as types, nobody notices that anything is missing.

On the other hand there are actors who do not fit a definite type. They can play many and diverse characters. They have sensitivity and imagination. They have talent. It is important for them to realize that the work at the Studio is not intended just to make them free here. It is intended to suggest that in the early stages of professional rehearsal they can afford to work in such a way that they will feel alive in the scene. Although very often they may settle for just doing things to get the immediate results the director demands, they must remember that working to keep alive in the scene will ultimately make it possible for them really to experience on the stage.

It is true that actors sometimes separate the logic of what they do for a director from their own sense of belief. Their unconscious attitude is that anything given them by a director is unreal, and anything coming from themselves is real. No. Both things must be done the same way. The actor must take the time to create both, with the same reality and conviction that he employs in a simple concentration exercise.

There are many possible interpretations of a play. The actor is often called on to carry out an interpretation which does not at all coincide with what he thinks of the play. What can the actor do? If he persists in his own understanding, he will harm himself. But if he follows the director's idea, how then does he act the play? He can get out. Or he can involve himself and the director in a pointless argument. Or, if the actor is powerful enough, he can get rid of the director and risk performing under a director who is subservient to his actors. Or he can surrender and settle for a superficial portrayal. Or he can play the play by setting objects and problems for himself which are able to evoke in his imagination the incentive and the desire and the ability to act out the various kinds of experiences which the director has called on him to create. This is, in fact, the essential problem that we set ourselves here most of the time.

But too many times the actor's idea of a scene is in terms of how the play was staged on some previous occasion. We forget that a play can be staged in different ways and yet remain exactly the same. And we also forget that a play can be staged the same way technically in separate productions and emerge in totally different interpretations. Some years ago we were given a demonstration of this fact when Kazan's production of A *Streetcar Named Desire* was redirected for the road by Harold Clurman. Clurman's production was a different interpretation, and in the leading part there was a totally different interpretation, and yet the external business of the play was not changed. For the actor, staging is not the measure of what really goes on. The actor measures what goes on in a play in terms of experience, which means that what happens in a play is not a meaning and not a word, but an event.

The work of interpretation can be done for the actor by a director, but the actor needs more than that. The director tells him many things about the play, and they may all be right, and still the actor has to find certain things for himself. Suppose the director has told him, "This is a character who is both naïve and direct." But the actor may still need to find out, "Am *I* in this scene sufficiently naïve and direct? Do *I* possess both colors, or only one? Which color comes across? If I lose naïveté when I do directness, will I have to work for naïveté because directness is easier for me?" At this point legitimate confusion too often arises, because the actor then goes to the director and merely asks, "What should I work on?" and this drives the director haywire. He has told the actor about the play. He has told him about the character. He doesn't know what the actor should work on. He only knows the results that he wants the actor to give him. It is the actor's responsibility to avoid these confusions, and he can do so very simply. All he has to do is say to the director, "I see that the scene bothered you. Was I naïve enough? Was I direct enough?" The director can then give the actor a definite answer, and the actor can then tell himself, "Okay. I have to work on that thing more." The question of agreement or disagreement does not have to arise.

In fact, the actor must be concerned with the director's problem, which means with the problem of obtaining results for the production. We stress, however, that the actor should not be too concerned with this problem too soon because of the processes he needs to complete for his own conviction, reality, and behavior. But if the actor doesn't concern himself with production results, it means that he lacks a sense that every artist dealing with space has to develop—the sense of where he is. The actor has to be aware of visual and spatial elements because these are as valuable in the finished production as the inner and personal things.

STUDIO MEMBER: If I have a partner in a scene, do we really need a director?

STRASBERG: You are really asking, "Isn't it so that directors accomplish good results, and therefore to accomplish good results must we have a director?" Yes, but you are not sufficiently aware of the extent to which the actor by himself can achieve staging results that are not only good, but which literally flabbergast directors, so that they say, "I never would have thought of staging it that way."

In one of my classes recently we had a private-moment exercise. It was a rather short private moment, and it was very moving, and it gave me a wholly new idea of how to stage the sleepwalking scene in *Macbeth*. The actress started the private moment with some strong feeling. I don't quite know what it was, but it was strong and emotional. Then, with a kind of strange impulse, she put a candle into a candlestick, took it over to the table, and lit it. For some reason—I don't know why—the emotion was so vivid that she sort of reeled to the table, and then, having lit the candle, she put it down and sat down on the floor. And she started to pray. And as the emotion got the better of her, she slowly keeled over in the movement where the body buckles in on itself. It was wonderful stage movement.

I have always been puzzled by the sleepwalking scene. I have seen performances. I have thought about it. I think I know what work I would do emotionally and dramatically. But I had never before *seen* it. I had never seen what I would want to place on the stage so as to convey to the audience visually, which means directorially, what I think is going on. I had never been able to visualize it as the "march to the scaffold," which is usually pictured in books and acted on the stage. I had always in my mind's eye seen Lady Macbeth reeling at the beginning of that scene. Perhaps I have been influenced by Gordon Craig's wonderful sketch in which she appears with her dress torn as if from writhing in the bed and with hair streaming like a witch. I have always thought of her as somehow reeling with the candle. That part I have seen. But what the hell do you do with her when she gets into the middle of the stage? You're stuck. You've got an aria— no matter how you slice it. You can make it emotional. You can make her walk around. You can say, "Well, I'll put in a pillar and make a picture." Everything comes out as just theatricality. So when the girl in my class put the candle down and then sat down on the floor, I said, "That's my staging. That's what I've been waiting for all these years." She put the candle down, and she sat on the floor, and she started to pray, and the effect we got was that of prayer together with very strong emotion. And it was perfect for Lady Macbeth. Do you see the point? From the actress we got not only expression but staging.

Up to this point I have been talking about the kind of problem that arises between actor and director because of the inevitable difficulty of artistic collaboration. But another kind of problem which arises between them may be the result of personal problems in the individual, yet professionally it should not be a problem because it is a matter of the actor's discipline. In the professional theatre there is too much of this thing: whenever anything is difficult, the actor says to the director, "But this is difficult to do. What do you want me to do about it?" Now, if it was easy, why the hell would we need an actor with an Equity card and with training to do it? Anybody can do an easy thing. Today there is too much of this attitude of wanting convenience on the stage rather than of overcoming difficulties on the stage and of the joy of doing so.

I have been mortified that in some of the things Studio members are connected with the most important lines are the ones that are dropped for reasons of naturalness, actually because the actor likes to say his line comfortably, and when he's asked to say it differently he doesn't feel comfortable. I have been shocked at the extent to which actors in professional production tell the director when he asks them to do something, "Well, this is difficult," or when he asks them why they did not do something, "Oh, I forgot about that. That's right." There is no excuse for this. It is just pure slipshod ignorance, idiotic laziness, but of a fantastic kind which I simply cannot countenance here by the slightest suggestion that we have any sympathy for that in acting. I not only don't have sympathy; I have very definite unsympathy. I am insane on that subject. I have no desire to share an actor's need to be comfortable at a certain moment when the director is asking for some essential thing to be done and the actor says, "But it's difficult for me to do this and at the same time to do that."

Some of the young people who are members of the Studio have on occasion created a wrong impression of the work of the Studio by trying to use in professional production technical approaches that they can't yet do at the Studio in simple exercises. These young actors hear us talk about the work here, and therefore they think they can do it. They get up in professional rehearsal and mean to do these things and immediately assume they are carrying them out. "I'm doing it. What's the director crabbing about? I'm using the 'Method,' and he says—" No. The fact is that these young people have often not yet reached the point where they can create and control—physically, emotionally, mentally, and sensorially—the things that the fully trained actor is able to create and control on the stage at will.

The training work here at the Studio is to a degree haphazardly done. Inner work is done, but outer work is not done. Not sufficient work of either kind is done. When the technical training is done, work on analyzing and playing the role is not thoroughly enough done. But even if all the actor's training has been accomplished, when he comes to production he still encounters problems. The "Method" does not solve every problem.

But these young people face an additional difficulty in these matters that is characteristic of many young Studio members, but which outsiders don't understand. You young people start to work in the professional theatre. You haven't any professional experience. You have come from a college. At the Studio your quality quickly changed when you began to act the right way. Very quickly, when you started to use real concentration on the stage, something strange and personal, something we would often never have imagined, started to happen. You made good progress, and you then began to get jobs in the professional theatre, and that's when wrong impressions began to be created. These young actors are desirable on the professional stage because they bring with them a kind of excitement and inner belief and an ability to share that experience with the audience which not very many actors possess. Usually only very experienced actors can permit themselves to create the kind of excitement that our young people are able to create. Because of their talent they are considered for parts for which ordinarily they would not be considered, and they often wind up playing parts for which technically they are not yet ready.

In the old days an actor went to the provinces, acted in stock, did too much, got into bad habits, but nevertheless acted. In that acting, in the observation of other craftsmen, colleagues or traveling stars, he would begin to make up his own mind. Thus, the process of training would take place unconsciously. Once he got a job, the actor of the past continued, traveled, played all kinds of parts, had an opportunity to work out his acting problems on the stage with other people and at the same time to permit his imagination and ideas about different parts gradually to come into focus. Today, unfortunately, it's the exact opposite.

Nevertheless, despite the sympathy I feel for the young actor faced by the professional difficulties imposed by our theatre today, I cannot permit myself to sympathize with certain attitudes. To say that something is a difficult problem and to go home and work on it—that I understand. To come back and try to do it— that I understand. But for the actor to absolve himself of the doing simply because it is difficult hits me with a shock of exasperation. If he doesn't want to be an actor, he shouldn't call himself an actor. I frankly don't know what label to put on any actor who would accept it as logical that he can plead his personal comfort to a director, as if asking for the director's understanding and sympathy in an area where the director can have no understanding and no sympathy whatsoever.

> Actress HH is a "very mixed-up girl, a girl with talent, but obviously undisciplined and with strong personal problems. Only continuous work would achieve results. It is almost impossible to deal with her difficulty in the Studio because the work there is not systematic and continuous enough."
>
> Following Actress HH's work on O'Neill's long monologue, *Before Breakfast,* which was one of many occasions of Strasberg's attempting to help her, he makes clear his intolerance of her lack of discipline:

To ACTRESS HH: Obviously you have problems in acting. These are not difficulties we have created. They appear when you work here at the Studio because you have them to begin with, but we try to help you with them. Here, for example, I do not care whether or how you have prepared a scene. I only care whether you do it well, because that indicates to me that you have talent, and when talent is given an opportunity to function, I know it will do so.

The professional stage puts greater problems in your way than these personal acting problems you have worked on here. Not every director has been trained by Lee Strasberg. There are directors who will say to you, "Go over the scene. Do the first part here. In the second part keep screaming longer. In the third part you just stood there trying to fix something up. Next time go over there, but try to find something before you go." And when you encounter a director like that, you will be a wreck, because you will face carrying out the things that director tells you to do, but you will not have any knowledge of how to make yourself do them. You will have no knowledge of how to discipline yourself, to do things that you are obviously capable of doing, because you now put in your own way every possible hindrance to acquiring that essential knowledge.

What is the point of explaining to us that something that you wanted to do here, and that you had rehearsed to do here, you could not do because there were not enough props? My daughter, Susan, comes home every night from the show she's working in and tells me that something unexpected happened. In the third act Susan was supposed to be ill and shivering, and the actor who was standing in the wings waiting to enter got so preoccupied with watching her that he forgot to come on and say, "Oh, you're still here." So she came to that moment—and no line and no Prince Albert—and she didn't know where he was, so she just walked off, saying "Good morning, Prince Albert," and stood in the wings and waited for him. On the stage those things happen, and if you lose your nerve, or if you say, "He's got a cue, and I don't know where I am," you are gone.

We do not make those problems. The stage makes those problems. Those are the conditions under which actors work. Not only do your lines go; other people's lines can go. Not only do you not have props because you haven't brought them; sometimes when you've brought them, the stage manager doesn't check them, and you arrive suddenly at the point where you have to pick up a prop and go over and kill somebody and the prop is not there. What the hell are you going to do? Are you going to stand there and say, "I'm so sorry, audience," or go into hysteria? Those are problems of acting, and they can only be solved by facing them —and that you somehow stop yourself from doing.

We of course add to the individual's difficulties here at the Studio. We keep the public away, but we take away your crutches. We urge you to take your time. We leave you free. We push you to absolve yourself of excessive concern with anything that prevents your dealing with your problems. But those problems have to be faced, and the difficulties we impose are designed to help you face them. But you do not face them. What is the point of explaining to us that this scene is the climax of a series of events and that therefore you could not really carry it out? What if you had to do one of those plays that start with a woman killing her husband, and then the whole play is flashbacks? Would you have to go off in a corner and play a whole act all by yourself for an hour before the curtain went up in order to do that first scene? Obviously you have to learn to do such things from a standing start. And if you can go on the stage and do them, I have nothing further to say. I then don't care whether you work my way or Joe Schmoe's way. But when you tell me, as you did today, "I somehow could not really work on this scene, because I have to have a whole play and a full production in order to work up to this part," then I say that your attitude is a very dangerous one, because in reality you will never have that. In some plays whatever you have to do will occur at the beginning. In other plays it will occur two minutes after the beginning. But wherever the actor's work occurs, he has to face the problem of doing it.

On the stage the only things anybody is concerned about are problems that are actually problems, but you make problems that are not really problems. You worry more than we do. We tell you, "If you don't know the lines, go ahead and play the scene." We do not stop you. You stop yourself to tell us, "I can't go on, because the props are gone." But if you can create a logic that enables you to continue the sense of a woman getting up in the morning, we are perfectly willing to go along with that sense no matter how many props you don't have. Today you did not carry out fully the sense of getting up, and I thought you hadn't even tried, and I was going to tell you, "Don't worry about it," and I was shocked to hear you tell us, "I did try, but the props weren't there." It must surely be perfectly obvious to you that you have a problem which you are not facing, and what that problem is.

This scene started off more clearly and was clearer than previous scenes. There was less running around the stage and trying to make yourself busy. There was more concern with things that *you* are interested in, whereas in some previous scenes your whole effort was to pick things that would please me. I felt today much more desire to do things that would coincide with what you think and feel and imagine. I saw a much greater simplicity and directness. Much less bemoaning and pleading for pity and forgiveness of your bad acting. At the end you couldn't help yourself and still told us it was bad, but at least you continued to the end of the scene. In all these areas there was improvement, but I still think you have an essentially wrong attitude toward yourself and your work.

All we are trying to do is to help you to work with your talent, within the professional requirements that we face on the stage today. These are the same requirements that the actor has always faced, to follow out the line he has set for himself, and within reason to be able to do a certain thing at a stated time. Some directors will tell you, "Count ten, and then scream." Other directors will say, "Well, it's a difficult scream. Do it your own way when you feel like it." You will work with both kinds of directors on the professional stage, and therefore that is a problem with which you actually must concern yourself. Instead, you do things like surrounding yourself with a lot of props that have nothing to do with professional production. If professional actors actually rehearsed that way, we would work that way here. But you would not be permitted to use this amount of props in professional rehearsal.

HH: Not use *this* amount of props?

STRASBERG: No, because in order to have these props, a property man has to be on the show, and the property man doesn't come on the show till the last week. It's crazy, but that is what we have to deal with, and that is what we have always had to deal with. A lot of times you will not even have this amount of props at the dress rehearsal. They will not start collecting these things until you are in New Haven, and you will go over to pick up the teakettle in performance, and it will be so heavy you can't pick it up. And you will try to pick up the teacups, and they won't have handles. But they will always promise you, "Don't worry. By the time we get to New York, everything will be all right." But when you get to New York you won't have it either. In New York you will have the promises, but in New Haven you don't even get promises.

You have to be willing to face actual problems. When, for instance, people have a problem with memory, they know there is a reason, and they do something about it. They put things on the stage to remind themselves. When it is really a terrible problem, they hide their lines in books and newspapers and letters in case they get stuck. There is nothing terrible in that. It is a way of dealing with the problem. The terrible thing is that when you have a problem with the lines, you just stop and say, "That's all. I'm having trouble with the lines."

HH: I didn't want just to go on talking.

STRASBERG: That's right. You can't just go on talking. You have to make an effort to get back to the scene. You have to face the technical problems that *you* have, not those that somebody else has. When things don't work for you, you have to know what to do to arouse yourself. You have to know the steps and sequences to follow to make the thing convincing and believable. In this area I saw a certain amount of improvement. I even see improvement in the way you are able to sit here and talk about the scene, but you still push problems into the back of your mind with a naïveté that is almost too much to tolerate. I mean, when you say things like, "Not use *this* amount of props?"

HH: Well, I know—

STRASBERG: That's right. You know. Obviously you know. But here we are not concerned with production. We don't care that you do everything exactly on cue. We only care whether you can adhere to what *you* have set. We presume that when a director asks an actor to do something, the actor will take that and make it his own and find a way of doing it and set it. Therefore, we ask you to do the same thing here—to abide by what you have set for yourself to do. It is absolutely essential in your case that in this area of discipline and technique—

HH: I have to abide by my own decision.

STRASBERG: That's exactly right. Otherwise the talent you have will not be used. Today after I told you to go on, you did go on without a whole emotional storm. Then the scene got more relaxed and had a simple believability, and showed certain interesting colors. But in future scenes there has to be conscious work. *You* have to find a way of going on. *You* have to find a way of developing. *You* have to find a way of correcting the errors that you will be asked to correct. Without that kind of technique not even a star can get by in the present-day theatre. Today very few stars, by themselves, drag in enough at the box office to make it worth while to put them in a show. Today the star must be part of the play. If the actor today is not part of the play, it does not go. Therefore, the things that you have to work on are *your* lack of discipline and the needs of *your* technique—not somebody else's discipline and technique.

HH: But, Lee, that's where I'm having trouble, because—I go sideways.

STRASBERG: I don't care whether you go sideways or backways or anyways. Just saying, "But, well, I go sideways" does not help. If you have to go sideways to solve the problem, then go sideways.

HH: But suppose you do work sideways, and some director

wants you to do over and over again the beginning of two different acts, but you don't work that way—

STRASBERG: Well, then you have to be able to work that way. If that is the way theatre work is commonly done, then that's the way you have to learn to do it.

HH: But how do you keep your imagination alive and still go plodding through the play?

STRASBERG: Here at The Actors Studio you find out what *you* have to do to keep *your* imagination alive while you plod. That director only knows what results he gets. He can't depend on your God-given genius because he hasn't seen it yet. He can only depend on what he sees. If you give him a great performance at the first reading, he will expect you to go on with that. He will only work with you to keep you from losing the great performance that you have already gained. But the time has gone forever when the director has to do it your way. In the old days great stars, great geniuses, were able to work that way. The star had the part all worked out, and he arrived at the stock company, and the other actors didn't know what they were going to do, and they all did it the way the star wanted. That time is dead and buried.

HH: What I meant was that on a particular day we may come to a scene in rehearsal that I just don't get. I don't understand it, and I tell the director I don't understand it, and yet he keeps going over and over and over a scene that I don't get. And no matter which way we go, I can't—

STRASBERG: No, no, no, he will not do that. You confuse the difficulties you have with difficulties you make up. If you tell any director, no matter how poor or slovenly, "Please, if you possibly can, let me go through the movements, but don't make me do it now, and I promise that in the morning I will," he may say, "Goddammit, how the hell did I get stuck with another actor like this?" But if you come in tomorrow, and you really do do it, he will say, "Gee, wonderful! I did that. I let her work properly. I helped her." You are assuming that if they will only let you alone, the work will be easy and you will do it properly.

Well, we are letting you alone here. We don't care how you work here. But we have seen you here when your concentration went and you weren't able to remember lines and to walk on the stage and to stand still when you wanted. We have suggested certain ways of solving those problems, but we don't care if you solve them in other ways.

HH: But directors just seem to want to run through plays. They don't really understand what I'm trying to do, and I don't understand what they're trying to do.

STRASBERG: If the directors knew they could depend on your mañana, they would let you go, but there is too much mañana in the theatre that never gets there at all.

HH: But if they don't know whether I can do it tomorrow, how can they find out if they won't let me?

STRASBERG: That's right. Your talent has not yet been worth it. Why should they?

HH: Well, why shouldn't they?

STRASBERG: You are a young person just starting in, and you want to work as only a finished actor has the right to work.

HH: Right. But should I have two methods? I ask the director, "Can I do something?" And he doesn't like that. He just says to do it again.

STRASBERG: Darling, I don't want to get involved with any experiences you may have had, but I will tell you this, since you are speaking personally. You make such a bad personal impression that no director could possibly have any faith in you.

HH: Do I really?

STRASBERG: Yes. And you know that because you know the difficulty that you're— Oh, darling, you know the difficulty you have had here.

HH: No. I don't know what you're talking about.

STRASBERG: You know how many times you have stopped in the middle of scenes here?

HH: I've only stopped twice in the middle of scenes here.

STRASBERG: I haven't kept count, but I have seen you in scenes where you stop and plead and go on and stop and look around and go on. Ask the people here. If you are unaware of the impression you make, ask the people. There's a lack of discipline, a veering away, if not a literal stopping, a discontinuing of what you are doing and saying, "Well, the hell with it. I don't know what to do." That has happened in almost every scene you have done here. Despite that, we have always been high on your talent. We have tried to make you aware that the talent is worth struggling with. You have been telling me now for six months, "I understand. I will make an effort." Yet you come in and make the effort, and there is such a vast difference between the actuality of what goes on on stage and what you imagine that I am literally flabbergasted.

HH: Well, I don't understand.

STRASBERG: Well, it's immaterial, darling. If the difficulty is really that much—

HH: Am I supposed to work—am I supposed to work like I work in stock? (*Weeps. Throws something. In a tantrum.*) Like in *Gramercy Ghost* and all those plays?

STRASBERG: Now, what makes you say what you just said?

HH: Because I don't understand what you mean.

STRASBERG: Why don't you listen?

HH: I am listening.

STRASBERG: And did I say that you should work here like in stock?

HH: No, but you're talking in a way that makes me think that that is the only thing I know that corresponds to it.

STRASBERG: I don't care what you think it corresponds to, darling. My experience in the theatre and my reputation is such that you should have sufficient—just a moment—sufficient knowledge to understand that what I represent is not stock-company acting. And therefore—just a moment—if you think that I represent stock-company acting, you are making such a fantastic mistake in listening to me that the difficulty is yours and not mine.

HH: That's what I mean.

STRASBERG: That's right. And yet you refuse to accept that difficulty. You refuse to accept my statement that you cause these fantastic difficulties for yourself, that you do not listen to people, that you do not know what goes on.

HH: What should I do, then?

STRASBERG: You have to see the objective nature of the problem. If you go to a doctor and he says, "Take this," and you say, "I don't like it. I hate it," he will say, "I'm sorry. Don't come to me. I only give you what will make you better." The way you now work is to say, "Doctor, it will not make me better. I hate it."

If you cannot work in the theatre as it is today, if you resent the attitudes you encounter in the theatre to such an extent that you find it impossible for your talent to flourish in that theatre, then you will do what a lot of people have done. You will leave the theatre. I can't help that. I am not here to make you work in the theatre. The only thing I can do to help you is to try to show you ways and means by which you can solve problems that you yourself face.

You are not bothered here. You rehearse the scene yourself. You rehearse it your own way. And you yourself are the one who goes up in your lines. You yourself stopped in this scene. If I had followed my own impulse at that moment, I would have said, "The hell with it! If you stop now after all the work we have put in you, I have not the slightest interest in you from this moment on." Fortunately I was able to retain my patience sufficiently to say very quietly, "Why are you stopping?" But in a show I was directing I would have fired you straight out. If I had worked with you in a show for two weeks as we have worked with you here for years on this problem, and you had stopped as you did, I would have said, "That's enough. Obviously she's going to go on that way. I give up." Instead, out of my years of patience I had enough patience left to say, "Why are you stopping?" and that was enough to make you go on and finish the scene and get the response from some of the people that you did get.

There is this strange unwillingness to follow through a logical sequence in order to learn how to work for yourself. I don't care whether you drink milk before you work or whether you take sarsaparilla. There must be a way of work that guarantees me, the director, that you will give me what you say you will give me. But on the other hand, when we do not see you giving what you say you will give, you cannot ask of us any leeway. Even the professional work that you do well, you do differently each time. The director doesn't know where he stands. The other actors don't know where they are. We are not asking you to do something different each time, and we are not asking you to work in stock-company ways. We are only asking you to look honestly at yourself, to realize the difficulties that you as a young actress have a right to have but which somehow, for some strange psychological reason, you refuse to face.

CHAPTER XI

The Actor and the Audience

STRASBERG: It is difficult to talk about acting simply in terms of audience enjoyment, because a lot of things go into an audience's liking or disliking what they see. If a girl is very attractive, I will like any scene that she does. Until a few years ago Betty Grable was my favorite. Frankly I didn't care what she did when she got on the screen; I enjoyed watching her. I would go to see every Betty Grable picture. The point is that I am not immune to the varied effects to which an audience is subject, but I do not react to and affirm artistic results in acting unless those artistic results are actually present.

I can like a scene and still make strict judgments on the goodness or badness of the writing, the acting, and the direction. I may just happen to like that kind of scene.

In the theatre the audience is the final arbiter, but only when it is given a chance to choose from among all possible alternatives. The audience will go on being satisfied with what it is accustomed to see if that is done ably, and with a certain amount of stage energy and a certain amount of faith. Even if what the actor is doing is wrong or bad, the audience accepts it easily because imagination supplies things the actor may not actually be giving. Nonmusical people may listen to music and enjoy it very much. They honestly do not care who plays it. They like the music. Musicians tell them, "Ah, but you should hear Toscanini play it," but they still don't care.

In a way, the audience should never be concerned with technical acting problems. But the actor should always be aware of these problems because his enjoyment of what he sees in the theatre is a test of his own technical facility in professional observation and judgment, not a test of the audience. What the trained actor enjoys proves how well he is able to differentiate the reality from the nonreality of the performance he sees.

Today, generally, there is no real seeing in the theatre, because *seeing*, even for highly skilled people, demands constant return. In the old days people went to see performances more than once, as they now go to music and museums and opera. We think nothing of returning again and again to a particular picture or piece of music, particularly if it's a new piece of music. With these other arts there is constant desire to create the kind of milieu out of which real observation can stem. But even theatre people do not go back to see performances, and so they do not have an opportunity, through a process of comparison, of arriving at opinions that are really worth calling opinions, and are not mere reactions stimulated by the personalities of the performers or the type of play. That situation can change only when you have a theatre that keeps doing the same plays year after year. You will then see that your reaction toward a play and a production changes.

In the theatre today we overemphasize aesthetically the word that we hear, as if hearing the word means that everything done on the stage is thereby vitalized, and not hearing the word means that what is done on the stage cannot be judged. Actually a lot of the times when you do not hear or understand the word, as happens when you go to foreign-language plays, you are by that very fact able to observe one definite area of work and to see what you really get from the actor. A good deal of the time what we think we get from the actor actually comes from the words. When we are deprived of the words, we then depend on real observation.

It is true that the actor's energy in general must be fuller on the stage than in life. It is true that this fullness of stage energy must include the vocal energy. And it is true that the vocal area is particularly important, because an audience becomes very disturbed when it misses something that is said. But certain vocal problems can be dealt with separately from other acting problems. For example, I can sit here and talk to somebody very quietly, and I can do exactly the same thing on the stage. There would be only one difference. What I do here quietly and privately would have to be done on the stage so that the audience could hear and see me as easily as you people hear and see me. Actually people can see me talking half a block away, but they cannot hear me from half a block away. This means that the projection of vocal tone must be a separate energy that is separately controlled. In making the extra effort to be heard on the stage, the actor makes an effort that he does not make in talking quietly to someone here. Nevertheless, the making of that extra vocal effort cannot involve making a tone that is unreal or artificial. The tone must continue naturally and normally. There should not be any loss of the sense of casualness and ease that marks the ordinary conversation. The energy required to reach out to the audience must not drive out every other energy.

> Once, following a scene, a playwright-director in the audience complained that he could not understand the actors. He said that he had never been able to understand all the words in scenes at the Studio, that he did not believe in ignoring technical demands for the sake of finding truth and reality, and that Studio actors were accustomed to making no attempt to be heard, which tended to limit them greatly on the stage.

STRASBERG: When an individual actually has the problem of being understood, we are very concerned with that problem. The trouble with a lot of actors usually is that they can be heard, they can be understood, and yet you don't know a damn thing about what's going on on the stage.

PLAYWRIGHT: Well, you certainly can't know a damn thing if you can't hear.

STRASBERG: I beg your pardon! That does not happen with our people. It does not happen with the people who come from The

Actors Studio. They never have any problem of being heard. Mention the names, and we will go down the list.

PLAYWRIGHT: I'm not going to go into personalities. My experience is that it is a great problem in rehearsal with actors from the Studio.

STRASBERG: It is a great problem in rehearsal with actors from the Studio. Exactly! Because in rehearsal they are working, and you don't wish to give them the privilege of working. You only wish to give them the privilege of performing. No director who is properly trained has difficulty with this problem in performance. In rehearsal the actor is concerned with many, many other things besides the problem of being heard. It is true that sometimes a young and not fully trained actor cannot fulfill a number of tasks —including being heard—at the same time. But ordinarily, when it is demanded of the actor in rehearsal that he be heard, the problem is not that he cannot fulfill the demand. The problem is that if he fulfills the demand he must at that moment give up another phase of work which may in the long run be to him— and to the playwright and the director—actually more important than being heard. A well-trained director knows the actual technical problems that are involved in acting and therefore is able to allow the actor to work at each stage of rehearsal on the problems peculiar to that stage.

There is, for example, the problem of learning lines. A lot of Studio people, especially the directors, are very free with the learning of lines. During rehearsal they do not worry too much about lines. Why? They're not concerned with lines? Kazan is not concerned with lines? I as a director am not concerned with lines? That problem never arises in any one of our productions when the production is *finished*.

PLAYWRIGHT: I had a play directed by a theatre director from the Studio and with many people from the Studio in the cast. You could not hear them in performance, nor did they know the lines. What's more—

STRASBERG: Wait a minute!

PLAYWRIGHT: I am in extreme disagreement with you, and I think encouraging people not to be heard—

STRASBERG: Please, don't be so much either in complete agreement or complete disagreement with me. You see, I can quote you instances from three hundred years ago of this exact problem. It has nothing to do with the approach. These are basic problems in acting. I am not saying that we should not be concerned with them. I am just a little bit aghast that out of all the possible things that you might be concerned with—and there are hundreds of things that I am concerned with—you are concerned with something that is on the whole easily solved.

For instance, Jack Gould in a review of a television play took exception to the speech of a young actor and held up that young actor as an illustration of bad Studio acting. In that same review he gave a wonderful notice to a Studio actress whom he did not identify either by name or as a Studio member. That young actor is now a star on television, and when he came here the first thing we told him was, "You have to speak clearly. You have a good acting quality, but you have to work on speaking clearly and precisely." You have heard us say that to K, because that is a problem with K. Where that is not a problem, we do not make a problem out of it. Where that is actually a problem, which means that the actor is either unable to be heard even when he tries, or that he is psychologically unwilling to be heard, then it becomes an acting problem here.

I am by no means one to minimize problems. I minimize only the peculiar emphasis on details of acting that after a while becomes nonsensical. The statements made are not real. They are not true. These difficulties do not affect "Method" actors alone. They affect many, many actors of different kinds. Stars do not become stars just by speaking up.

A number of you people came around last week and asked me if I read Mr. Olivier's article criticizing The Actors Studio. Everybody was very concerned that I should read the article and become as concerned as they were with his criticism of the way we work.

Well, I am not concerned because I think such criticisms are non-sensical. For instance, I only read the headline of Mr. Olivier's article, but on the following day I did happen to read the *Variety* article on his new production. Now, as you all know, *Variety* is the voice of the Studio. (*Laughter.*) You see, *Variety* must obviously be a "Method" paper, because if you read the review of Mr. Olivier's production, how else could you account for the reviewer's statement that the people were walking around with movement that had no relation to what they were doing, that the people were talking and being heard but that nobody knew what was the relationship between the words they were saying and what they might have been talking about? I was dumfounded to read this "Method" criticism of Mr. Olivier in *Variety*.

If this question of being heard were actually an important problem in production I would be very much concerned with it in general—as in fact we often are concerned with it on an individual basis. The actress here today will, unfortunately, never have that problem. Her problem has been that she speaks up, that every word she utters is heard, but that her ability to use herself has been comparatively nil. Has anyone ever told you that you couldn't be heard on the stage?

ACTRESS: No.

STRASBERG: Of course not. What we are concerned with here are those things which the actors must do for themselves. These are things which neither the playwright nor the director nor the scene designer nor the choreographer nor the voice teacher nor anyone else can do for the actor. Not Mr. Kazan nor even Mr. Stanislavski can turn on "the fire in the actor." That is the actor's own central problem.

Speaking loudly or speaking clearly is achieved by practicing. At those precise moments in the scene when the actor actually cannot be understood, he is told so, and he speaks up. But this problem, which is usually simple to begin with, is, as you say, unnecessarily and unpleasantly emphasized in rehearsal, so that, by the time the show opens, false emphases and false oppositions have been built up. If the director would only wait until the play is really going and the actors are really beginning to work properly and then say, "Look, I can't hear you throughout," or, "I can't hear you here and here and here and here," you would be surprised at the easily achieved results. There is then no argument. No big point is made. Unfortunately, what too often happens is that the director from the very first time the actor reads the play makes an issue of being heard, and then human emotion causes a conflict to arise, but it is a made-up conflict. Obviously the actor wants to be heard, but out of pure ego he then begins to oppose the director, not only in this area, but in matters of interpretation as well.

PLAYWRIGHT: Well, I don't think it is just a matter of speech clarity. It seems to me—

STRASBERG: I'm sorry. I'm sorry to disagree with you, but from my experience with hundreds of actors I can only assure you that being understood is sometimes an emotional problem and sometimes a purely technical problem such as the difficulty of regional speech. We work on the cause—whatever that cause may be in each individual case. But there is no problem at all if the director waits until the actors are already doing the scene and then tells them to speak up. The problem never occurred with the Group Theatre people. It never occurred in my productions outside the Group Theatre. It never occurs in Kazan's productions. Plenty of people who do not come from the Studio cannot be heard. You have worked with some of them. You know the names as well as I do. And you also know that these people argue with you about the play, about changing words to make things easier for them, about changing the play because they "don't like this," and they "don't like that," but actually because with the best intentions in the world they do not know how to carry out tasks that their talent actually qualifies them to do.

In all honesty this question of being understood has arisen in the theatre since time immemorial. This whole opposition of "Method" and "non-Method" is just nonsense. As if, before the

"Method" came, acting was superb; productions were great; per-formances were convincing and real and alive; actors were heard; interpretations were brilliant. And then the "Method" actor came, and suddenly you don't hear, you don't understand, acting is terrible, productions are horrible. I'm sorry. I can't agree with you because my entire experience and the experience of other theatre people leads me to the opposite conclusion. But insofar as the problem does exist, I do not minimize it.

In time the actor develops the capacity to extend his effort in any necessary direction. Sometimes the extension is in a mental area, sometimes in an emotional area. Sometimes it is in a purely physical area, sometimes in the vocal area. When the actor is working properly, he often fears that the impulse will disappear if he extends himself. Nevertheless, we have found the exact op-posite to be true. All the things he is doing become fuller, more expressive, more vivid, more dramatic, and more real. In fact, un-less he does extend himself, the actor is always carrying his impulse and his response like a glass that's full to the top. He walks as if he is walking on eggs.

A technician, a craftsman, tries to distinguish the things that go into the creation of results, because that kind of analysis enables him to work with other craftsmen. Otherwise, he is able only to work with the audience, and if the audience doesn't like what he does, he is stymied. You can explain from today until tomorrow that this is Stanislavski acting and that you are acting the right way, but if the audience doesn't like it you will get nothing from them.

Here in the Studio differences of opinion about acting are valuable because they mirror the differences that exist in audiences, but we must constantly remind ourselves that people in the audi-ence of the commercial theatre may not be as skilled as we are in technical perception. Anyone who wishes to work in the theatre professionally must recognize that every audience member sees with his own eyes and that each "eyes" is different. The ideas that you bring to a production must be clear to other people, not just to yourself. If they are not, your insistence that you are right is valueless in the theatre.

In the theatre, to say, "I don't care whether anyone sees it or not," leads only to committing suicide in public. In other arts, to say that is a matter of courage. In the theatre it is idiocy. In other arts the work remains, and is not subject just to the opinions of your own generation. But the art of the theatre lives and dies with the audience, and therefore there should be constant give-and-take between the work you do here and the audience for whom you may be trying to perform. If that audience does not get what you are doing, something is not quite right—no matter how convinced you may be of its rightness.

I was once telephoned by somebody in San Francisco who was starting a theatre. He was asking theatre people various questions about their experience and tape-recording the answers. And he asked one question in such a way that I felt sure he expected me to answer "No." The question was, "Do you believe in compromise?" I said, "Oh yes, of course I believe in compromise." And then I heard the people at the other end laugh, and I didn't know what the hell they were laughing at, so I said, "Now, wait a minute. You must understand what I mean. If you mean giving up something you wish to do and doing something that you do not wish to do, that is not compromise. That is giving up. But if two people are walking straight toward each other, and each says, 'I'm not going to compromise,' they will collide head on, and no one will be alive to tell the tale. In order to keep walking in the direction he wants to go, each has to compromise a little. Compromise in the theatre means to continue what you wish to do, but to be aware of the conditions under which you are working, to be aware of the various needs that exist in the theatre, to be aware of the level of the audience you are dealing with, and to continue what you wish to do so that it will make connection with that public. Otherwise, what you wish to do is never fulfilled."

Throughout this statement I heard people laughing. I did not know what they were laughing about. A month or so later I was speaking to Franchot Tone, and he said, "Oh, did some people call you from California?" I said, "Oh. Yes. They did. Why?" "Well," he said, "they spoke to me because I had been in the Group Theatre, and I told them various things, but one thing I really drove home to them. I told them that the only man in the American theatre who never compromises is Lee Strasberg." So at least I understood what the laughter was about.

I hope you understand that I do not commend the general kind of lollipop compromise. A studio is not a school and is not a theatre. A theatre is pledged to production. It does not present the ideas that generated the production. It does not present the ideas with which the director excited the actors. It does not present the ideas that led to the choice of the play. A production is something which in the face of the audience must be understood by the audience without any explanation whatsoever.

CHAPTER XII

The Actor and
American Commercial Theatre

STRASBERG: I have just read a description of the Russian theatre in the time after the Revolution by a man who was part of that theatre. There was no heat, so to keep warm you burned part of your furniture or your books and magazines if you had them, and he says he had a wonderful library that served to keep him warm. There was almost no food, so you ate strange things you had never eaten before—frozen potatoes and herrings from which you had to cut the tail and the head because otherwise they would stink too much. And the thing that was really difficult was that they had no light. But he said that was a time when people dreamed the dream of theatre more than at any other time. The entire Russian people became imbued with theatre as if it was their only salvation; he described it as a mass mania. They had dramatic groups in the Revolutionary armies. Every troop had a dramatic cell. Teachers were invited to come to the front to teach dramatics.

Under those conditions perhaps we too would work that way. But what about Vakhtangov? It is true that he knew he was dying, but the people that worked with him worked just as hard as he did. His schedule was fantastic. When he got up in the morning, he had to go to the Moscow Art Theatre and work on the production for that night. Then he had to go to his studio. Then he had a rehearsal for a new show. Then he had the evening performance. After the performance he started work with his studio,

357

and they stayed up till morning. Then he would catch some sleep, get up at eight o'clock, and be ready to go back to the theatre.

At the Moscow Art Theatre they complained that he gave too much time to other theatres, and he had to defend himself. When they raised the salaries of the other people, they didn't raise his salary, and he wrote a wonderful letter in which he denied that he was taking any time away from them. He said that he gave them all the time that anybody else gave. Nobody could complain that he came to rehearsals and gave less than others. But, he asked, didn't he have the right to do these other things that he thought so important for the theatre and the young people? He was not taking any time away. Why should he be attacked? And when I read that letter—I realize that those were strange times—I began to realize how slothful we are.

The American theatre had no artistic history until modern times. It has had only a commercial history. The traditions of theatre art were founded abroad. The great actors who have performed here—even in our own lifetime—have been mainly foreign actors. American theatre started as a purely social activity. In frontier America and rural America, in mining camps and small towns and even in cities, the theatre had no purpose except entertainment, and American theatre still continues that tradition, a tradition created by people whose sole need was to be amused. Only in modern times has America developed an artistry in theatre that has rightfully taken a place in the theatre of the world.

Nevertheless, the American theatre has remained primarily devoted to the interests of entertainment and commerce, and it was for the individual actor who must work in that theatre that the Studio was primarily created. The Directors' purpose was to make a place where professional people, people already working in theatre, people whose talent was already well founded, could continue the kind of work that an artist-craftsman needs to do on himself.

Every actor is driven into the theatre by some need for self-expression. Every actor feels that somewhere there exists a kind of skill and perfection worth struggling for because of an inner recompense completely different from the reward for work that is good only from the audience's point of view. But the circumstances of production in the commercial theatre today are terrible. They are in no way related to the creative needs of the actor or of any other creative individual in the theatre. The rules and regulations of the commercial theatre do not derive from the needs of an actor or a director or a playwright; therefore, when the actor gets caught up in commercial production, the process of his growth as a craftsman almost invariably stops. The Studio was created to give that kind of individual sustenance which every creative individual needs. From that point of view the role of the Studio in the commercial theatre will always be necessary and important.

Somehow the American theatre has been very backward in affirming the best tastes of its most outstanding practitioners. Not even people who are independent in production, like Katharine Cornell, have been able to create for themselves the kind of material they desire. They sit and wait for the material to come to them, and the material does not come. In fact, the more distinction the actor achieves, the less material is available to him, because then both the actor and the outside world are driven to believe that only the topmost material is suitable. The outstanding actor's material becomes more and more confined. Every actor who has assumed an outstanding position in the American theatre has inevitably suffered this closing in.

The work we did in the Group Theatre in the thirties was sufficient to show our intentions and to indicate a little bit how our ideas could be carried out, but scarcely any of these ideas is thought about in the American commercial theatre today. Only the most salable part was caught up and used. Yet these ideas are more essential to American theatre today than they ever were.

The conditions we faced in the late twenties and the thirties have changed. Then the theatre was burgeoning. When we criticized, we were in a minority. Our artistic ideas were minority ideas. The commercial theatre was successful. Many productions were done, and there were a lot of successful plays. Every year there were a lot of hits and a lot of actors employed throughout the year. Then an irreversible change started.

Because of movies and television the commercial theatre will never go back to the way it was in the twenties. The basic setup has changed. Movies and television have taken over a good deal of what was previously the work of the commercial theatre, and they can do this job better than the theatre can. I was a little startled when a dramatic critic complained, "Where are the westerns we used to go to in the theatre?" I have three television sets for professional reasons; sometimes I am engaged in running back and forth from one to the other in order to keep up with a western that I like to watch and also with a couple of other shows that I have to watch professionally. That is where westerns have gone. You do not even watch westerns in the movies any more. You watch them on television. Even now there are still three or four good western serials that you can watch religiously—or, at least, that I can watch religiously. (*Laughter.*) Spectaculars have taken over the function of vaudeville. Television comedy is the equivalent of stage comedy in the twenties. Almost every kind of theatre that was popular in the twenties will ultimately be taken over to some extent by these other media which are much more capable of wide and efficient distribution than is the living theatre.

Only one aspect of living theatre cannot be taken over, and that is living theatre done not for commercial gain but for artistic purposes.

Theatre as an art plays a very, very important role in life. It is a need of mankind. The story of Vakhtangov and the Russian theatre shows that when life becomes difficult we become all the more aware of the role of art and the need for art. You tend to get caught up in life when it's easy. In America there is still a sense that art is an embellishment. I don't wish to appear to be making theoretic pronouncements. I am not saying, "Well, art is superior." It is a fact that when you go through the history of all the arts you find that art is not an embellishment at all. It is a real activity. It started with the earliest civilization we know of, and means much more to man than mere ornamentation. Those things that Americans too easily think of as accessories are part of the thing that makes man man. People have not only been willing to live for the arts, they have been willing to die for art, and they have died. We forget that in the American theatre. We forget the artists who have said, "No, this is the way I'm going to paint. I'm sorry. If you don't want to buy my picture, the hell with you! A thousand years from now they'll buy my picture. I'll starve." And they do. And their pictures are not bought until after they die.

The ignorance about theatre that has been permitted to continue in the American commercial theatre must in some way finally be broken. And it can only be broken by theatre people who take up the challenge and make themselves heard. I am appalled that almost every individual who has a position of importance in the theatre and whose opinion is therefore requested on various theatre problems starts off his statement by saying, "Well, of course, I don't know anything about this subject," or, "Of course, I have never done this," and then hauls off into a repetition of all the common and stale phrases that he has used for the past twenty years. I am appalled that there is never on these occasions any coming to grips with the fact that theatre experience is going on now. We need not continue to be ignorant of the work and the intelligence and the suffering that properly goes into theatre. Through our greater present knowledge of the functioning of the actor and the director and the other elements indigenous to theatre, I know that we are able to understand the theatre of the past in a way that till now has been literally impossible. And I am emboldened to hope that that knowledge is not just an intellectual preoccupation of mine, but that it can be an essential part of the functioning of American theatre in the next twenty years.

Decisions being made today will have influence over the entire coming theatre generation. It is about time theatre people demanded that these discussions about theatre should not be left to businessmen—whether of the theatre or of the world outside the theatre—and not to critics and other such people who are valuable and necessary to theatre, but who unfortunately haven't the knowledge that can only come from participation in the *making* of theatre, not just in the *business* of theatre.

CHAPTER XIII

The Actor and the Theatre
in the World of Today

STRASBERG: Today there is an aesthetics of theatre. Today *theatre* is an art. In the nineteenth century a play was done only in terms of the nineteenth century, but today we are able to approach any play, Greek, Shakespearean, or modern, so as to come to grips with making clear what is in it. Building on the past, Adolphe Appia, Gordon Craig, Stanislavski, Meyerhold, and others have laid the basis for theatre work far more comprehensive than in any theatre of the past. Today there is a sense of *theatre* wider than any historic style, a sense of the entire concept of theatre. There is appreciation for all theatre of the past, and yet that contemporaneous vision which every artist contributes is retained.

Today the theatre—all over the world, not just in America—faces the need to take this comprehensive understanding and put it to work fully, on the highest level, and with the best resources available. But at the moment no other country has the potential for solving this problem that America possesses.

I do not feel—as a lot of critics do—that American theatre is dying of realism. I do not feel that theatre is dying because actors are convincing. My impression is the opposite—that most theatre, American and foreign, has settled for a kind of superficial paying of lip service to realism, that the purpose of realism, which is to see life whole rather than sentimentally, plays virtually no part in theatre today.

Do not forget, too, that what is commonly complained of in

363

American theatre is a subject of complaint all over the world. People say of American theatre, "Well, it's just a financial problem," but that problem exists in different forms everywhere.

I am at times pessimistic about *people* in the American theatre because they do not sufficiently differentiate between these financial and artistic problems. But I am never pessimistic about *theatre* in America. Our potential is great. In all honesty I would not care if we had only four theatres in New York. If we had four great theatres in New York, would that be less than having eighty bad ones? Who wants theatres that have a lot of productions that nobody wants to see? I'm sorry. I may be quixotic. I may be stupid or a little cuckoo, but I cannot look with trepidation on the possibility of four theatres in a great city like New York, each with an established company and with a repertoire that lasts through the years.

I would look with great hope and excitement to a time when we had four real theatres in this city and other equally fine theatres across America. Now we have theatre buildings in New York, and in the rest of America we have the second-rate theatre that we are graciously willing to send out of New York "in order that the American theatre should be brought to life." Broadway magnanimously sends out second-rate companies so that "the great hunger for theatre should be satisfied." To me that is typical and completely erroneous and phony theatre thinking, the kind of thinking that would not be accepted on Wall Street in selling a product, but which is accepted on Broadway as sound, down-to-earth thinking, box-office thinking, practical American thinking, thinking that will save the theatre. I am not pessimistic about theatre, but I am at times profoundly pessimistic about that kind of attitude.

Most people are aware that the twentieth century marks a decided advance in politics, in science, in industry, in social life, in cultural life. Most people have a sense of decided change, an opening up of new energies in certain art forms, music and painting. But most people do not think of theatre in the twentieth century as having advanced. Only if we look carefully do we perceive the vast change in technical realization that has taken place. This knowledge has scarcely percolated to theatre people, and it has not in any way affected the general public's attitude, although the attitude of the audience is more important in theatre than in any other art. Someone can stand before a Klee and say, "I don't get this." Fortunately his reaction has very little value; the reaction of the entire world over twenty years will decide the place of Klee. But in the theatre the audience participates more directly, vitally, and actively than the audience for any other art, and its ignorance of the possibilities of theatre at its best—a theatre in which the great actor takes his place in the ensemble —is one of the major obstacles to the solution of the problem of world theatre.

For example, Chekhov's *The Cherry Orchard* was performed on television. I was appalled that at least three reviews were head-lined, "Actors Triumph over Weak Play," and that another re view said that although it wasn't much of a play, the actors almost put it over. Such appalling lack of knowledge of this play and its characters actually has very little effect on Chekhov's status in the theatre of the world, but it is one of the many unfortunate signs of the insensitivity and ignorance and, in fact, degradation of mass opinion.

I feel very keenly that one of the crucial developments of the world today is the mass sharing of culture. In the past, culture was the prerogative of a select group. It is now possible for great masses of people to share our untold cultural wealth. This is an inevitable part of the process of modern history, but there is great danger that the public, in coming unready to this culture, will appraise it on its own level. The great public will assume that its own level is the only level because it does not know that there is any other. The danger here is not that the public cannot be appealed to. The danger lies in the fact that, either accidentally or deliberately, the public is actually *not* being appealed to, and therefore that mass distribution of culture will only lead to a spiral of mass degradation.

I consider myself fortunate that I lived in a period in which I could still see actors who had enjoyed a continuous and a consistent development. I saw great actors who had played the same parts for many, many years, so that in seeing them I witnessed the culmination of a lifetime of work. I saw people like Duse and Grasso and Chaliapin. I saw the Moscow Art Theatre in 1923, when Stanislavski still played the early plays with all the great actors that were still alive. From that time I have carried in my imagination a sense of the greatness of which the actor is capable. I have moments of real experience, not just theories, for all the things I describe to you.

Unfortunately these great moments in theatre are only sporadic. You see here a performance of Duse's and there an ensemble of the Moscow Art Theatre and some other time a production by Vakhtangov. You see the great and terrific efforts of Meyerhold, but when you put all of these things together they still do not make up the totality of which the theatre is capable. They show only the possibilities of theatre. Put together the genius of Duse and the ensemble of the Moscow Art Theatre and the vision of Vakhtangov and Meyerhold and the concepts of Craig and Appia, and you will have some sense of what theatre might achieve.

For a twenty-year period after World War I various factors— the work of those individuals, the revolution in Russia, the state of world theatre—produced sudden examples of what could be done, but in every case some inhibiting factor prevented the artistic consummation of these tendencies of twentieth-century theatre. The Moscow Art Theatre carried with it the heritage of the past. Stanislavski remained in vision a nineteenth-century man. Vakhtangov died at thirty-eight. Meyerhold removed himself from the influence and inspiration of the Moscow Art Theatre, and his work stood isolated on a mountain peak of terrifying theatrical vision, unsupported by the kind of actor's reality and conviction that the Moscow Art Theatre had so profoundly developed. Duse was a hundred years ahead of her time.

About 1935 the hazards of war began to destroy the progress

that had been made by the work of these few great figures. Not until after World War II do we get again in the productions of Brecht a major contribution that is capable of arousing the world to a sense of theatre. And I think that to some extent we can say that concern with the "Method," even though it has involved misunderstanding and vilification, has also led to a concern for theatre.

If peace comes to our world in the next decade, perhaps the work that was interrupted in the thirties can be continued. It has sort of been kept alive in the Studio. The ships have gone down, but we have kept ourselves alive on open rafts. We have saved ourselves. We have kept the spark of life and the sense of creative continuity going. We have possibilities once more of theatre on a wide scale. Theatre can go on—but only if the proper conditions and circumstances are created. Otherwise we will simply settle for our present commercial values and for what can be done under our present conditions, and we will simply put up a sign over that activity: "This is Art." I am not worried that theatre will not continue. The unfortunate thing is that it will continue. It will become even more popular. It will make more money. There will be more television, more jobs, more superficial skill, more everything. There will be more and worse theatre, but we will then confuse what can be done with what is being done. We will ask, "What more is there?" But if we no longer see the possibilities of greatness, how can we dream of it?

What Eleonora Duse contributed in the theatre still lives to-day. Duse represents, perhaps more than any other individual in the last hundred years, the creative nature of theatre, the sense that the actor's medium has always to be struggled with in order to accomplish on the stage what the actor desires. Some of Duse's comments were mordant. She said that if theatre was to remain alive all the actors in it had to be killed. She was not speaking from antagonism to individual actors, but out of realization of what the theatre demands from the actor. She was deeply conversant with the way in which the actor must learn to lose the conventional, imitative parts of himself so that from this burning away might arise the phoenix of a new being, creating from his own impulses, honest with himself, honest with the audience, seeking applause as a necessary part of success, but not being willing to accept success in lieu of what he wishes to create.

In Duse's own life, appearing on the stage entailed extreme suffering. It was a terrifying experience. She always had a sense of being naked, of revealing the innermost parts of herself, and she liked this feeling as little as any human being does. It is the most difficult thing the actor is called upon to do. The essential revelation of the actor is done with his own body and his own real emotions, and with his own body and emotions functioning at those very moments when the audience is watching most intently. Duse—more than any other actor of whom I am aware—suffered from this basic difficulty, but somehow through that suffering her performances not only summarized the search for inner and outer truth which the theatre has been making for hundreds of years, but actually went a step beyond that because each moment on the stage was designed. Yet each moment was designed in terms of the reality of a human being. Her artistic sense enabled her not only to *act out* the reality of a human being, but to *reveal* a reality which would not be seen by the ordinary eye observing that human being. Perhaps this came from her Italian background—I don't quite know—but it added to her acting a Michelangelo quality, a classic quality, the ancient Greek sense of the body's speaking. Very, very few actors have done that.

Duse achieved a fusion of the inner and the external which we have not arrived at in our theatre. The emphasis in the theatre today seems to be on one or the other. The work in the Studio has tended to be on the inner phase of this work. It has not encompassed the actor's sense of the external as part of the creative process, wherein the external elements themselves become heightened, and the human being thereby becomes a more wonderful instrument of expression and therefore responds, like a rare violin, more deeply and truly to the dictates of the inner technique. The theatre will require the next hundred years to deal with what Duse represented in this area. She was an isolated example. Few actors can be as inwardly intense as she and as outwardly expressive in a way that was beautiful, but with a beauty that always served the dictates of what was transpiring. The beautiful things she did were never used because of a pure beauty of their own.

You saw gestures in Duse that were not copied gestures, and which were not completely theatrical gestures as Bernhardt's were, but which were fed by a sense of great Italian art. Duse actually went to museums and watched sculpture and tried to find what made the sense of movement in a statue and yet preserved its nature as art. You saw in her an almost terrifying relaxation; she had the willingness and ability just to stand. And yet in her films we see that she deliberately maneuvered so as to hide her face. But her movements were strong. When she took something, she took it! When she hit the wall, she hit it! And yet she is commonly described as Duse of the beautiful hands. But it was the *expressiveness* with which they related to the object and the *sensitivity* with which they were able to evoke the flickering reality and responses and suffering of the individual that made her hands truly beautiful.

She had a scene in a film in which she took care of and prayed for her dying child. As she prayed to God, her hands over this child were beautiful. It is quite true that almost the nearest thing to it is the flight of birds. Her movements somehow conveyed the sense of mysterious grace and power that is ordinarily found only in nature, and yet the flutter of the hands was not done just to create a sense of beauty. What came out of the hands was her extreme vulnerability, her desire to do something for the child and at the same time her inability to do anything, and consequently her need to call on the mysterious power of God to help her. It was not pretentious, external fluttering of hands. It was not rhythm or music. It had meaning and reality and conviction, an expressiveness of all the elements which the human being possessed.

In this film of Duse you can see that at the very moment when her hand is still it seems almost more alive than when it moves. It seems somehow to cling. When the man lets it go, the hand itself does not move, but it has terrific sentience and sensation. At other moments in the film she takes the child and almost poses, and at still other moments she takes the child in a way that is very concrete and real. But with that reality there is somehow a sense, not as if "I'm taking a child," but as if "A child is being taken." She had that sense in every part that she did.

Duse's voice was rather high. When she was young she had to train her voice for strength and fullness, but it remained the high Italian kind of voice. In fact, when I heard her in 1923 in the big Century Theatre, I thought her voice was a little too big. I was seated in the back of the orchestra, and I had no difficulty in hearing. Her voice had a strange quality which I have never heard in any other voice. You were never aware of expenditure of effort. The voice came out easily. It was somehow on a stream of breath. It seemed to float. It simply left her and went on. It traveled, and yet you had the sense that it was the same easy voice wherever you might hear it in the theatre. It was a voice that had no difficulty, perhaps because of her uncanny ability to relax.

When you compare Duse to Bernhardt, you see that it is not impossible to have a strong theatrical sense and yet to make the theatricality completely a part of character.

Duse could act whatever problem was set for her. The whole problem of playing Ibsen, as I've often said, is to play what happened before, and one of the critics described Duse in Ibsen as playing the things between the lines. She called that the third dimension in acting and ascribed the possession of that particular quality to great acting. Still, she was always in a way more Duse than the character, though what she played through Duse was not so much the character as the play. She played the significance, the meaning, and the reality of each play through herself. She had the ability to be most herself and yet highly theatrical.

When I saw Duse in *Ghosts*, I walked out of the theatre with a sense of "Well, this is good, but is this great? What's great about it?" I wasn't swept away—but I couldn't get rid of what I had seen. I kept thinking about it and saying to myself, "Gee, isn't that wonderful? She came on the stage, and she didn't do anything. She was dressed in a black dress, and in the whole first act she just leaned back on that elegant couch and talked." That's all she did, and yet you watched; then suddenly something happened, and you knew it happened. The only thing I remember her *doing* in that play was a gesture. It was the great moment when she saw her son making advances to Regina in the next room. At that moment she was just standing at the table. She looked into the next room, and suddenly it was as if the water came up and encompassed you, rolled in upon you so that you had to fight your way out of it. You seemed to be enmeshed in something very fine like cobwebs as she spoke: "Ghosts." She did not become hysterical. She saw something, and it had an effect on her, and that was all. But she created, finally and ultimately, a sense of what was going on, a sense of the character, a sense of what the play was about, and in realizing this, I suddenly realized the greatness of her achievement.

Giovanni Grasso was one of the really great actors, and one of the greatest emotional temperaments of our time. Duse had a greater continuity of temperament, but it never reached the almost physiological state of emotion which I have seen Grasso generate. He gave a sense of the real, old-fashioned virtuoso. You have never seen such pure physical reality on the stage. I do not mean external acting. His was a reality in which emotion and body are tied together. Even in Duse reality was not that way. Duse was very pure. Her acting was like an essence that had been abstracted from reality. It was like orange juice. The rind and the pulp are gone. You drink it. It goes down easily and softly. It is pure orange juice. Well, watching Grasso was very different.

He was a stocky, heavy man with kind of thin legs, and he was very out-going. He used to stand outside in front of the theatre until five or ten minutes before the curtain went up and watch the people go in. He enjoyed people and society, and he stood there. He wasn't showing off. He wasn't waiting for anybody to come up and take his autograph. He just enjoyed the fact that he was in America and that all kinds of people were coming to see him.

I went to see him in *La Mortá Civile*, which was a famous old Italian play about a man who has been thought dead and comes back to find that his return creates difficulty for his wife, so he commits suicide. Before the last act I went backstage with other people, and he didn't understand English, but he embraced everyone, especially if it was a pretty girl, and he would hug them and kiss them. He would listen to what they were saying without quite comprehending, and he would smile. He was alive and easy. Then we went back into the theatre, and the curtain went up for the last act. I will never forget the shock, because, when the curtain rose, there was the same man we had seen only a minute before, and he was sitting there, pale, tense, emotional. His face was white. He was literally shaking inside. He was a man ready to commit suicide, and you said to yourself, "Jesus! When did this happen? I just saw him." He was a man who loved to act.

The Italian approach, which I have also seen in some of their companies, especially the Teatro Piccolo Milano, is excellent. To the Italian, acting is bread. The Italian actor doesn't ask for explanations. He doesn't ask what the motivation is. He doesn't ask why he should act. He only wants to act. When he gets on the stage he wants to act, and he does whatever he does with the fullest faith and the fullest confidence. He throws himself into everything with great conviction. If he has to work, he is no good. If he has to create a psychological core, it turns out to be not right and not necessary. His body is so alive, and his way of talking and behaving is so theatrical and vivid on the stage that to begin with you get something that is quite believable. It is never "realistic," but it is real because of the actor's belief in what he is doing.

They do not puzzle too much: "Well, wait a minute, should it be hot? Should it be cold? Should it be tired? Should it be this way or that way?" They add these things quite easily as a result of what goes on in the scene. They are easy in their responses. They accept the things that are happening, and they get believability and a wonderful theatricality. Behind this kind of acting is always a sense of the actor's being an actor, but loving to perform because "If I didn't, what the hell would I be doing?" Very few of us have that sense.

Grasso was a Sicilian, and I saw him do extraordinary parts in which he had to do the Sicilian fighting with knives. He would play in one-act plays, ordinary, corny westerns which always had scenes with knives, and he loved to do them. It was wonderful! He didn't just say, "How is it done? Wait a minute, why am I doing it?" He would ask the other fellow, "You want to fight?" and the knife would be out. He was passionate. The sense of immediate conviction was terrific. He always played the sort of man who is not loved, but who loves the woman and protects her.

I once saw Grasso do something that I have literally never seen another actor do. Something had to happen to him in just a moment on the stage, the audience had to see an actual change take place, and yet the actor could not use physical action. Grasso was playing a runaway prisoner, and he comes into an inn, and the girl gives him bread and wine. He takes the bread and the wine, and he looks at her. And at that moment you saw this man fall in love. He was not acting big. He had no words. You saw it happen. How I don't know, but there was no question of it. The emotion remained inside, and yet you saw it. I still remember a detail of the business, and to this day I don't know whether it was stage business or real. As he looked at the girl, he started to tear off bread and to stuff it in his mouth, and then the moment of love came. He stopped stuffing the bread. The bread crumbs stuck in his throat, and he tried to dislodge them. Then he slowly chewed and swallowed what was in his mouth, and this was so perfectly expressive of the love that you could not tell the reality from the acting. You only knew that it must all be acting.

I also saw this man, at a time when I had brought some friends to see him act, go through half a performance, and nothing happened. He got a little annoyed, not too much, but as if he knew that one night it happens and another night it doesn't. He had very sparse hair, and he would run his hands through his hair when he was a little annoyed and just walk around the stage and play the scene. Then he came to a moment when he had to go over and handle a woman. I saw him do this in a number of scenes, and he would always touch the woman's hair. Naturally this was the third act of a triangle play, and he was the jealous husband. His wife was sitting on the side of the bed, and he walked toward her. He was just as he had been all along, unmoved, untouched; the performance wasn't going very well. He put his hand on her hair, and suddenly you saw something happen. He was disturbed. His eyes were distended. And he pulled her up by the hair. And then I held my head up, and I sat back, and I turned to my friends and said, "You see?" Here was a man capable of this great emotional excitement, but he had no conscious technique with which to control it.

I doubt that the ability to make acting and sound and singing coincide on the stage has ever been greater than in the case of Chaliapin. A singer's tone has to come out full and resonant, and yet it must carry whatever emotion the singer wants it to have. Moreover, the tone is part of a musical progression, and the emotion has to keep pace with the music. In my lifetime only Chaliapin, and, to a lesser degree, Maria Callas, Lotte Lehmann, Ezio Pinza, and a few others, have been able to do that. Most singers simply color the tone and make believe that something is happening.

Chaliapin had the acting impulse very strongly. He played parts that would be difficult only to act and he played them superbly, but at the same time he sang them superbly. Character was visualized as character, and the music was realized as the dramatic event to an extraordinary extent. Chaliapin carried out both character and event completely.

One of the great acting lessons I have had was to see Chaliapin play the same role in two different operas, the devil in *Mefistofele* and the devil in *Faust*. He created two totally different characters within an area of characterization that seems very conventional. The character is a devil, and you must be reminded of a devil. The devil in *Faust* was French and a cavalier. Even the sound of the voice was a little nasal, although Chaliapin couldn't speak French very well. He completely created the cavalier's quality and movement. The devil in *Mefistofele* was Miltonic. When Chaliapin came on, he was the opposition to God, the enemy of God, and the equal of God. The two characterizations were entirely different.

That was a great acting lesson to me, because Chaliapin not only showed that it could be done, but that it could be done in a sphere as circumscribed and classic in its demands as that of opera. The demands of opera are, after all, more precise than those of Shakespeare or the Greeks, but that did not stop creativity in Chaliapin's acting or prevent a completeness of characterization that used the music for the expression of a deeper and stronger and more vital intensity than the human being could utter by any other means. Classic speech, too, is speech that comes from fullness of emotion. In classic plays the emotions, not the speeches, are big. The speech in Shakespeare or in Sophocles comes from the strongest feelings of the greatest individuals in life. And to see that Chaliapin was able to create the reality of such persons in an even more formal expression than is found in the classic plays was one of my first acting lessons. I was making twenty-five dollars a week, and I paid seven dollars for a ticket to see him. That was a high price to pay for an acting lesson, but I enjoyed every minute of it.

(*March* 1961:) We would like to say hello to the members of the Comédie Française who are here. We are sorry that we cannot do it with greater formality. We in America are perhaps much too informal, but our informality does not hide the admiration and, if I may say so, the envy that we feel for a theatre that can look back upon a great tradition. We in America envy that very much. Sometimes we are proud, because we feel that we have talent. Sometimes we feel that in playwriting we have even more talent than others may give us credit for. What we do not have is the sense and tradition of theatre. What we lack in America is the sense of responsibility toward the art of the theatre which was brought into the world theatre for the first time by the Comédie Française. The Comédie Française played the great role of being the first theatre in the world arena to subordinate the individual actor to the entire production. It was the first theatre to make the actor feel that he owed a responsibility to his art and to the theatre rather than to feel—as we commonly still think today—that the theatre owes him a living. That kind of tradition we do not have enough of anywhere.

We are honored to welcome you. We hope that sometime we can repay the visit by sending you a company of our own. Unfortunately that is the very thing we envy in you. In America we have no companies that we can send. So at the moment we can only express our delight at your being here, our envy of what you possess, and our hope for the future, that someday we will be in the position of returning the favor that you have brought to us.

In the summer of 1961, while en route to spend a month observing the Berliner Ensemble, Strasberg visited Italy:

My first experience was unexpected. Some people came to interview my daughter, and when they found that I was there they wanted to interview me. When I am abroad, I usually don't give interviews, because I travel for purposes of changing myself. I am not in the mood to tell people what I find amiss about myself, and to talk about it is something I prefer not to do. So when they started asking questions about myself that I am usually perfectly willing to answer, I suddenly turned the tables and asked, "Where are your Italian actors?" There was a dead silence. Then they said, "What do you mean?" And I said, "Well, the Italian theatre has serviced the world theatre on a number of occasions with a great reservoir of acting talent that has revivified the theatre and given other people an example of acting at its highest level. That took place on at least two occasions historically. I went through the period of Duse, and I know how much it meant to see an example of a person dedicated to the art of the theatre who could show us the far reaches of theatre possibilities. We were able to examine our own work and progress in terms of her. Where are your Italian actors now? I cannot believe that there is no talent in Italy. The talent must be as phenomenal as ever. Italy is a naturally theatrical country."

The easy answer to my question might have been that the Italian actors are all in the movies. Unfortunately, the Italian movies have no actors. They have wonderful directors and wonderful-looking women, but hardly anything that can pass for acting. It is not acting in the sense that we are accustomed to think of acting. Certainly it is not acting that is comparable to that of the great Italian actors—Salvini, Rossi, Zacconi, Novelli, Grasso, and, of course, Duse—all those actors who have made up the great tradition of the Italian theatre.

The interviewers did not answer, but in putting the question I myself suddenly realized something about The Actors Studio. If there was an organization like The Actors Studio in a country like Italy, the results would be phenomenal. You cannot tell me that Italy does not have as much talent as it ever did. Yet this talent is not searched out; this talent is not nurtured. And talent needs nurturing more than any other commodity.

In any country, a place like The Actors Studio has a great role to perform—even if it does no more than trouble the waters. It seems to me that in every country today there is a strong need for organizations dedicated to searching for talent and to arousing some kind of interest and attitude and feeling about the theatre. This can of course be done differently in different places, but it must be done. In every country of the world I find a great hunger for theatre, and in most countries, including our own, I find the satisfaction of that hunger very small.

A few years ago I happened to read an article by Harold Hobson in the London *Times* in which he was commenting on a highly regarded American actress who had performed in England. In his article he stated that, although this actress may think she is great, she is after all only second-rate; whereas England has at least five great actors. Now, great actors are my love. I would give anything for a great actor in any language and of any kind—comic, tragic, anything. Five great actors at one time is something that has never occurred in the entire history of the world. When you have one great actor in ten years, that is a great thing in the history of the theatre. When you had two great actors, Mrs. Siddons and Kean, within a few years of each other, it was one of the great periods of English theatre. When you had during eighty years five great Italian actors, that was called the Italian movement in acting, and it made a terrific impression on the entire world. To believe that any country has at the same moment five great actors is sheer insanity. That attitude of resting on one's laurels is a chain around the neck of the English theatre. We ourselves are at times very dogmatic, but that kind of ego-stubbornness hurts the English theatre, because they are capable of better and different work which would not in any way ruin what they now have, but they cannot get at that work so long as that attitude is maintained.

The young people I have met in England seem to feel the need of a new stimulus. I was very impressed by the young people there. They have wonderful talent. There was a young actress there, for example, that I liked very much. I thought she had a wonderful quality, that she could go places, so I told one of the important actors that I was impressed with her. He said, "Oh, I don't like her voice." This was an actor whose idol happens to be Edmund Kean, and Edmund Kean's voice was such that the critic who wrote that he hoped Mr. Kean would get over his cold by the next performance was forced to write two weeks later that he was sorry, that it wasn't a cold but his natural voice. For an established actor of talent and perspicacity to be that offhand in dismissing a young talent that had given evidence of ability to do unusual things is wrong, and is an example of the stultifying attitude that pervades so much of English theatre.

Not that the English theatre is bad. It is simply that the English theatre represents an outdated style. There is an English tradition in acting, but the English theatre now only holds onto the externals of that tradition. What is now created on the English stage is not humanity, not people, not reality, not even conviction. It is acting. It offers the best that acting has and therefore also the worst. It is worth watching. We can learn some things from it. I love the environment of the theatre in London. I do not like the theatre.

When we see certain performances of Olivier we sometimes tend to say, "Well, it's a little superficial." Why are they superficial? There is great imagination in them, more imagination than in a lot of performances which are more organic because Olivier is giving of himself more completely at each moment. Is it that his idea of the part and the play is not clear? On the contrary, it is marvelously clear. You know exactly why he is doing each little detail. In his performance you watch an actor's mind, fantastic in its scope and greatness, working and understanding the needs of the scene. He understands the character better than I ever will. I don't even want to understand the character as much as he does, because I think it is his understanding that almost stops him from the completeness of response. The only point that we could make to Laurence Olivier would be that he does not create on the stage to a full enough extent the reality and the conviction of what he understands.

If we criticize Larry Olivier's performance, it is only because it seems to us the outline of a performance. It is not a performance. Olivier has a fine talent, but you get from him all of the actor's thought and a lot of his skill and none of the actual talent that he has.

And, mind you, I am not one of those who goes around saying that about Laurence Olivier. I am very tough and very harsh, but I do not say that, because he is one of the people that I most admire in the theatre today. To me Larry represents something that nobody here in this goddamn America has. There are a lot of people here in America that I think have talent. They have as much, and even more, talent than Larry has, and, I'm sorry, I could kick them in the behind, and it wouldn't make a bit of difference to the American theatre whether I did or whether I didn't. Larry has theatre courage of a kind which is utterly amazing and utterly fantastic; it is almost more important than the actual talent that he has.

The English theatre of today is not a development from the Elizabethan theatre. When the English theatre resumed at the Restoration, it was a combination of humanist and classical traditions and Italian staging. The principles of Elizabethan theatre were not rediscovered for another two centuries. Stanislavski never recognized the Elizabethan principles in the structure of Shakespearean drama. They were not brought to the attention of the world until William Poel's productions did so in the nineties.

The extent to which Poel's discoveries have interfered with the development of English acting is not yet commonly recognized. By the end of the nineteenth century English acting was on the way to solving the Shakespearean problem. It made the plays more real by use of the ensemble, but also many merely good actors were beginning to approach the character acting that had previously been the province of only great actors. But just as fine actors like Forbes-Robertson and Mrs. Pat Campbell were finding the way to a fusion of the character approach of modern acting and the demands of the Shakespearean temper, the influence of Poel caused a reversion to the production techniques of Elizabethan staging. Acting began to be tied to a process of archaeological reconstruction. The full texts were restored. The slowness of realistic staging was speeded, and the actors were made to run along rapidly. These influences, while of great value, interfered with the natural development of English acting, and when the English theatre came back after World War I it came back paying lip service to the great tradition of English acting without any actual recognition of the accomplishments of the Garricks and the Keans that English actors pride themselves on following.

I heard before I left for the summer [1960] that the Chinese classical theatre was going to appear in Canada, and so out of curiosity I thought I would see it. A little of my old youthful concern with theatre still remains, so I considered the possibility of going up, but the summer went by, and I did not do anything about going. If some people had not kept after me, I would not have gone. Well, we did go to Montreal finally, and it was a tremendously inspiring experience.

I cannot say that we were tremendously enthusiastic, because we were critical. We did not like everything. But one of the inspiring things was the discussion with the actors which showed that they were aware of their problems and were concerned with finding solutions to them. In fact, without saying so directly, they were willing to recognize that in the work we represent lie some of the solutions that they are seeking.

Never in my life have I seen actors' technique as thrilling as I saw in these performers. That was what primarily excited me. I have seen the Japanese theatre. You may remember that I was very temperate in my reactions. I enjoyed it, I appreciated it, but

I saw in it only training for a particular style. I could not share in it. I was not very involved.

I had read quite a good deal about the Chinese theatre, so I was not unprepared for what I saw, but the actual experience was utterly thrilling. In one scene a girl wants to get to her lover, and she has to cross a river, and she calls the old boatman to take her across. There was no boat on the stage. There was no scenery. There were two actors, and they acted out the life of a boat. I pride myself that I am not easily fooled, but I saw that scene from the balcony the first night I was there, and I swear the stage rocked. That boat was rocking. I rocked with it. I have never seen anything as fantastic as that scene.

I saw a scene in which two men try to kill each other. One man has stolen into the other man's room to kill him. The stage is lit, but the room is supposed to be dark, and the two men supposedly cannot see each other. The acrobatics in that scene literally flabbergasted me. I have never seen acrobats who could do what those actors did. Acrobats build themselves up to the leaps they make. These actors from standing still could jump around, sideways, overhead. Never have I seen acting that combined so much ease and skill and security. I saw a scene of amazing virtuoso handling of swords, and in the midst of the scene one of the women began to have pains, and she acted out with marvelous reality the whole process of childbirth. And I saw a second boat scene in *The Legend of the White Serpent* in which four people cross a river in a boat and in which a girl and a man fall in love, but this time the action was not done just to exploit the skill. The love was very tenderly and subtly suggested.

In Meyerhold's school, the kind of training these Chinese actors undergo hardened into a style. I was very much impressed when I visited Meyerhold's theatre. The acrobatic training was interesting, but it was one-sided, because it made the actor ready to act without at the same time making him a good actor. I have always thought that that kind of acrobatic training was the best physical training for the actor, but it was not until I saw these Chinese actors that I realized its wonderful possibilities for combining realism and theatricality. In other theatres these results have been abstract, but the Chinese theatre leads me to believe that an approach to classic production that runs not just on the rail of physical dexterity and theatrical flair and not just on the rail of reality and inner conviction, but on both rails, could be of decisive importance.

In the summer of 1956 Strasberg saw the Brecht Berliner Ensemble in London. Then, in 1961—just after the East Germans built the wall across Berlin—he spent more than a month observing the work of the Ensemble in their home theatre in East Berlin.

(*October 1956:*) Discussing theories is suicidal unless it is based on what you see on the stage. I flatter myself that I have as much knowledge of theatre as any theatre person. I have read everything there is to read about the theatre of Brecht. I have had long discussions with some of my friends who are experts on it. I met Brecht here many years ago, and from that acquaintance I derived some idea of what he stood for. But I had always been at a disadvantage, because I had not actually seen the Brecht theatre. So I was very curious to see it simply in order to evaluate what I thought I already knew.

The experience of actually seeing Brecht's theatre was totally different from what I had expected. It is nothing like what I had read or been told about. The Brecht theatre fundamentally has nothing to do with the theory about which Brecht has written. The intellectuals have, in fact, given such a totally wrong impression of Brecht that the English critics' impression of the actual manifestation was strangely vitiated. Their reviews were odd. All the favorable reviews wound up by saying, "Well, it is good, but what is the shouting all about? When it is good, it is just good, and I am moved, and when it's bad, it's bad. Where is all the theory that says I'm not supposed to be moved?"

The fact is that when people go to a Brecht play and they do not like it, they say, "It's just a Brecht play." When they go to a Brecht play and they do like it, they say, "This is good. I was moved. I was touched. What the hell is all this talk about? I had the same kind of experience with this particular play that I have with other plays." There are a number of Brecht's plays that do not come over, precisely because they were written in terms of the theory, and about these plays you say, "Well, I get it. I understand it. But who cares?" But when a Brecht production comes over, it comes over with the same sense of reality as in any other good production.

Brecht was intelligent enough to realize this. Fortunately, before his death, he said, "The theory doesn't matter. There are some people who understand me and don't act the right way. And there are other people who don't understand me, and they act the way I want."

When I was in Russia in 1934, I read an article about the "Diagonal Method of Meyerhold," and I said to myself, "Gee, I've been doing that for the last two years, and I didn't even know it was a method." Similarly a theatre technician can watch the Brecht theatre and can see that they are making certain emphases and doing certain things out of regard for Brecht's theory, but these are things that people do here without having a theory. I could not see that the theory played any important role in any of the good Brecht productions.

Mother Courage could have been done more impressively and excitingly, but I found it interesting. *The Circle of Chalk* was one of the finest productions I have seen in my entire life. It ranks with productions like Vakhtangov's *Turandot*. But the theatricality of these productions is very difficult to describe. It is not an obvious or a mechanical theatricality. The acting is extremely simple and natural, but it is directed very obviously toward the audience. Two people sit and talk in easy tones. There is no "acting," but both are turned outward. There is no attempt at completeness in the physical staging, which consists entirely of selected details.

In a scene in which there is supposed to be rain, the actors come in wearing clothes to keep off the rain, but there is no rain. The clothes do not drip. There are no complicated effects. The actors just come in and stand. Nobody tries very hard to act wet, so I thought, "Well, they just don't go in for that sort of thing."

Do you remember the scene in which Mother Courage sells chickens? Well, I have seen that scene done here, and the actress acts an event. She makes contact with the object. She uses a particularization. She prepares herself. Well, Mother Courage came in with the chicken and sold it for a high price. It looked like a first-class job of prop-making, but after she sold the chicken she sat down and took the chicken and started to pluck it. It was a convincing chicken because it was a real chicken. She plucked real feathers, and those real feathers flew all around the stage.

In another scene the cook is sitting on the stage cutting carrots. And, mind you, when we do what is supposedly a propaganda play we pretend that the carrots are not just carrots, but society or man's fate or the depths of the universe, and we cut up the carrots to suggest the message of the play. No. In *Mother Courage* the cook used a very sharp knife, and he peeled the carrots and then sliced them very neatly and very definitely, and each slice fell into a pail with water in it—real water. And as each slice dropped, you watched the water squirt a little bit. And when he threw the last piece in, you saw the water squirt all over the stage, but nobody on the stage paid any attention. It was just real, and for this kind of reality in the Brecht productions I was totally unprepared.

Other moments are completely stylized. At one point Mother Courage's son dances, and the dance was not Chinese or Japanese but a strange dance that didn't resemble anything in particular. And, frankly, this was one of the moments that the audience did not care for too much.

But the audience liked very much the moment in which Mother Courage tries to decide whether or not she should run away with the cook. He asks her to go away with him, but to leave her mute daughter behind. They are standing outside a house, and the man is singing for food, and she is trying to help him out, and it is terribly cold. Mother Courage is wearing a very long and heavy peasant's coat with a high collar. There is no snow, but quite simply and believably they show that it is very cold. Mother Courage cannot make up her mind, and as she stands there, now and then coming in on the end of a song, she is so cold and so miserable that little by little she sinks inside this enormous coat so that she is completely hidden. That was a moment of wonderful mood. It was a real mood and a real cold. It was not done with props. It was not done with theory. It was not Stanislavski. It was not Brecht. It was a great moment of acting done only as a very good actress can do it.

But at another moment Brecht deliberately avoided an emotional response. When the body of Mother Courage's son was carried in, the situation is such that she has to say she doesn't know him. Mother Courage merely sat down, cramped her hands together, and there was a moment of absolute stillness, and finally the curtain came down. I personally wished that that scene had been made more emotional, and this was only one of a number of places that I felt should have been made more impressive by a stronger handling or a bolder and lustier treatment. In this respect perhaps the theory held them back a little too much.

The Circle of Chalk is the old story of the judgment of Solomon. At the end, a princess and a peasant girl both claim a child. It is actually the child of the princess, but during a revolution she had been so concerned with her own well-being that she forgot the child, and it was saved and brought up by the peasant girl as her own. At the end a judge decides that the peasant had acted as the true mother. Thus, the play is a fantasy and does not demand too great an emotional response, but it does demand good acting, sometimes very real, and sometimes very theatrical, and great theatric skill. The acting was, in fact, very good, and the sets and costumes were flabbergastingly colorful and theatrical.

The entire production was superbly done with the most extreme kind of subtlety.

The peasant girl was played by an actress who is not at all the star type. She is a rather plump girl, and she played very honestly, simply, and naturally. It was straight. There was no effort to act. When she sang, she sang. When she did physical things, they were believable, but not impressive. There was no forcing. There was no attempt to affect the audience too much. But the great thing was not the absence of an effort to be emotional; it was the fact that she made no effort to act.

On the other hand, many of the characters were played in a semi stylized manner. There was so much pure theatrical delight in the costumes and appearance of the court characters that you literally held your breath. All the actors wore wonderful half-masks. In the masks there was no attempt at theatrical effect for its own sake, but each mask captured the psychological core of the particular character. The half-mask does this better than the face can, because it enables the actor to give his face a more emphatic characterization without destroying his ability to act or the outline of his humanity; the lower part of the face is made up to coincide with the mask. The princess was played by Helene Weigel, who was Brecht's wife, and she had a chalk-white face, dark eyes, a red mouth, and her hands were white with silver fingers and gold nails. Whatever was not done simply and naturally in the production was stylized, but it was not unreal. It was not unconvincing. It was professional. Each moment and each gesture was chosen and composed. Every detail was just so. Everything—including the reality—was part of a composition. That is what stylization means in its true sense.

The outstanding scene in *The Circle of Chalk* takes place in the peasant girl's home village where she is living with the child. Everybody assumes that the child is illegitimate, so her family has to marry her off. Her brother goes to the mother of a man who is dying and pays for permission to marry the dying man to the girl. The village people are invited to the wedding, but even the priest doesn't know whether it's a wedding or a funeral. The setting is divided into two very small rooms, and in one we see the dying bridegroom, red-haired, red-bearded, and covered with a blanket. In the other room all the villagers crowd in until to get any more in you literally have to kick somebody out. And at one point someone does force his way in, and suddenly somebody else finds himself outside and doesn't know how he got there. It is a brilliant crowd effect and equal to what Vakhtangov did in *The Dybbuk.*

In the midst of this highly stylized wedding celebration, they take out two long loaves, like yellow corn bread, and they cut them up, and they pass the slices around, and everybody eats it, and the crumbs fall all over the stage. They literally stuff themselves. Nothing could be more real. Then some musicians come in and say, "We have to celebrate because the war is over," and suddenly the dead man sits up and says, "The war is over?" He had been shamming, so he chases everybody out, and the poor girl finds herself married to this man. And then the curtain comes down and goes up, and we see him sitting in a barrel taking a bath. His shoulders are naked. There is no water. There is no soap. It is her duty to be scrubbing his back, but she's shy; she's his wife, and she doesn't want to be a wife. That is the whole scene, but an entire situation is shown brilliantly. Brecht was triumphantly successful at combining real elements like the corn bread and the bath and a fairy-tale atmosphere, because in every case the real elements are exactly right for establishing the entire mood and believability of the scene, but do so in a terrifically theatrical way.

None of the actors in the Brecht theatre does anything that he cannot do well. If an actor can't dance, he isn't called on to dance. They match what they wish to accomplish to the capacities of their people. Sometimes they create a fairy tale, but when they want to use reality it is really real. And the totality has theatricality of the utmost simplicity and extreme guile, guileful in such a naïve way that the result is literate, poetic, and really professional.

(*November 1961:*) We arrived in Berlin at a time that was not good for the Brecht Theatre. The closing off of West Berlin had caused them to lose a number of actors who lived in the Western Zone. This seemed a calamity, but it turned out that seeing them under these conditions was the best possible introduction, because we saw them rehearsing at a time when they could not afford to put on any kind of act to impress us. They had to put a number of actors very quickly into a number of productions, and therefore we were able to tell what is of paramount importance to them, because that is what they would emphasize at such a time. We could see the theatre in terms of its real intentions, which are much more significant of a theatre than its theories or even its finished productions.

I was surprised by the ease of the people in rehearsal. The actors did not separate themselves as human beings from what they did on the stage. There was no getting into character or changing to a kind of heightened theatrical behavior. This was true of the stars as well as the extras. In fact, we had difficulty telling the extras from the other people because the extras at times were the most interesting people on the stage, and this came from the very simple fact that the extras were not actors.

The extras are all people like students who were earning a little extra money. The Brecht Theatre does not like to use actors for extras, because they have to get rid of the mannerisms learned in dramatic school. They claim that it takes three years to get rid of the bad things that actors have when they come to them. They prefer to use ordinary people who will do what they are told, behave as the director wants, and yet look like real people. And they do look like real people!

One of their best extras is the head technician of the theatre. I remember that particularly, because when I saw him I said to myself, "I know him. I have seen him in a very important part." And finally I asked Miss Weigel, and she said, "Oh, he's the head technician, but he plays little parts. He loves to play, and he is always the most impressive individual on the stage. He looks magnificent, and when he has some extraordinary costume to wear he enjoys it so much that he looks more distinguished than any king."

For years everyone has read that the Brecht Theatre goes in for something called "alienation," which means that the audience is encouraged not to be involved or to believe in the play. The intention supposedly is to make the audience see the production simply as a theatrical performance. Well, I waited for "alienation" to be used in rehearsals, and I was rather shocked because the first thing that the directors said to the actors was something like this: "Now, please, make it realer. A little realer. What the hell are you doing there? Don't make it so stylized. Don't do all that theatricality. Drop that actor's tone. This is the real thing. Just tell it to him." And then they would explain very simply and try to show the actor how to speak very naturally.

Their acting was the simplest acting I have ever seen in my life. I would not have the courage to permit actors to be as simple as these people demand that their actors be. The acting is stripped of all mannerisms, of anything whose purpose is to show the actor's skill or his special talent. It is character acting in its simplest form. The actors are usually well chosen. The character is clearly stated. The actors then with the utmost simplicity and at times the utmost lack of theatricality—which in itself comes across as a kind of theatricality—act out the events and the situations in the play.

I stayed on to see one play, because people had told me that the Brecht production was a great production, but I could not believe that any production, no matter how great, could make much difference in this play. *Galileo* is not such a bad play, but I could not believe that anything different from what I imagined could be done with it, and I could not imagine anything that would make it really work. I had been impressed by many other of the Brecht productions. I had seen *Galileo* in a very good production here, but when I saw the Brecht production I was astonished, because I had to admit that it really did make the play work. It was totally different from the New York production, not by being more stylized but by achieving a theatricality through being simpler and realer.

The setting, costumes, and props were simple, but gave such an extraordinary sense of the period of Galileo that they can only be described as great. The set was three walls apparently made of a wood with a rich Renaissance texture. However, we discovered afterward that it was actually a very light hammered copper. This gave a sense of the opulence of the Renaissance that I have never seen equaled by the most magnificent painted sets. The costumes were historically correct, but they avoided the brilliant colors of Renaissance painting. The tones were rather neutral, but for that very reason they seemed to fit the individuals and to take on an individual coloration. The props were fantastic in their accuracy and reality. The scientific instruments were made of wood and metal, built to scale, and they worked. Even if a prop was not handled in the play, it worked. Nothing in a Brecht production is ever treated as unimportant or superfluous, and this absolute reality of the physical objects made them really live on the stage.

Brecht has been built up into the archapostle of antirealism. We must realize that Brecht's theatre is not anything like that. Brecht called his theatre the theatre of epic realism. Everything on the stage is real. Everything on the stage is natural. Theatrical elements are used only when something has to be done which cannot be done as well any other way.

In *The Circle of Chalk* there is a scene in which the soldier the peasant girl loves comes home to find her married, and the two stand with an imaginary brook running between them. They speak simple lines to each other, and then they sing the thoughts of love they cannot speak. That is the simplest way to express that idea on the stage. How else could you show what goes on inside a human being? Broadway would use some complicated mechanism. The lights would go down. Odd music would play in the background. Voices would come over loudspeakers. The scenery would light up, and you would see the inside of somebody's brain, like a commercial for headache powders. No. Brecht did not search for theatricality in order to create a formalized stage. Brecht's theatricalized form derives from the simplicity and content of his material.

The acting in *Galileo* was so simple that you cannot describe any details. There was no moment of which you can say, "Ah, that was terrific!" You can only say, "What he did at that moment was so utterly simple that it could not be any simpler." But the production as a whole, the terrific compression, the sense of reality given by the background, and the high significance of the selected details of reality, both physical and in the acting, all these came together to lift the actor—not to a level of formalized or merely stylized theatre—but to what Brecht calls "historic reality." Brecht tries to show you that if you were there, "this is what you would see." He wants you to be fully aware of the significant thing that took place at this particular historical moment. It is historical reality. Details that have no meaning are stripped away. I have never seen on any other stage as much eating as goes on on the stage of the Brecht theatre, real eating, and not just in performance —in rehearsals! But people eat on the stage there, or perform any other task, only because it is an essential part of a particular historical moment.

The last moment in *Galileo* begins with his saying good-by to a student at the front of the stage. And then Galileo turns and walks all the way up to the rear of the stage, which is very deep and slanted up to where a table, not ornate but authentic and very real, stands, and he sits down to eat a very real meal. He has now given up what he could have fought for in order to live a certain kind of satisfying mundane existence. He has settled for the good things of this world. And as he begins to eat, the lights very slowly begin to fade. There is no lighting magic. There is no spotlight. There is no effort either to conceal the lights or to impress you theatrically. There is only an effort to inscribe indelibly on your consciousness: "This is what a man gave up for. Watch him eat. Watch him." And the eating goes on—one minute, two minutes, three minutes. It is very undramatic—and yet it is more dramatic and more poignant than if you acted your head off. All Brecht did was to isolate the simple event: Galileo gave up for this; this *you* remember.

When I left America late in July of this year, my mood was a peculiar one. I did not feel that the work we had done here was at an end, but I did feel that we had reached a point where something new had to take place. I was willing to face the possibility that some of our work is not perhaps as essential as it has been in the past. I was quite willing to suppose that work might be going on in the theatre of the world which would make necessary a revision of the kind of work which the Studio represents.

When I returned to America, I was asked, "Are you glad to be back?" and I said, "No, I am not glad to be back." I did not mean that I was not glad to be back in America or that I was contemplating leaving the American theatre. I meant that I had had a touch of what theatre can be by being privileged to watch a theatre at work. I realized what it meant to have a theatre. What I saw on the Brecht stage is the most outstanding theatrical achievement of the last twenty years. It is the greatest contribution to the theatre of the post-Stanislavski period. And yet most of the people of the Brecht theatre are not very good actors; only a few are good actors. The extras are not even actors; they are not talented people. It is the vision which is talented. It is the intention which is great. It is a theatre, and therefore what is done on the stage is not just done to impress you. It is done to make the play clear, to bring alive an original author's intention and experience and to have the audience share that intention and experience.

Brecht has made an inspiring contribution to world theatre, and he has done that in a world in which most of the theatres are hollow and sterile and looking for a way out. What is done at the Brecht theatre is not meant to hide hollowness. It is meant to fill hollowness with meaning, with purpose, with intention, with significance. The costumes, the masks, the actors—everything on the Brecht stage subscribes to this basic purpose.

Brecht's theatre has been accepted and its reputation has grown in the same years in which the Studio has become known all over the world. I assume that the reason has been partly the same in each case. Each organization has done something to fill the emptiness of the theatre, and therefore people feel that in each organization there may lie some answer to the crisis that the theatre faces today. It is true that theatre faces a crisis every year, but in recent years the feeling has grown that the crisis is of major proportions, that something is basically wrong with the state of the theatre.

Unfortunately there is no Brecht theatre in America. There is no theatre here that could work through a crisis the way they have continued to do. There is no theatre here that can do and redo and maintain productions over a period of time. There is here no ensemble theatre working honestly and soundly in order to bring the audience some sense of the image which real theatre people hold.

The theatre of America and the world faces a major crisis today because demands made upon it are of a kind that never existed before. World political conditions are opening the doors between peoples on an international scale, and with the opening of the doors has come a feeling of emptiness. The doors open to nothingness; there is no understanding and no appreciation of one people on the part of another; literally we have opened the doors, but to whom we have opened them we do not know. The people of the East do not know us; we do not know them. The political conditions that have opened the doors have actually heightened the misunderstandings between peoples. These misunderstandings demand a sharing of cultural life between peoples, because without it there can be no real living on the international plane. If you live on the international plane only economically and politically, you only kill each other. Wars are bound to continue. Only through the arts, which enable us to look at life a little more objectively than is possible solely through politics, can we begin to appreciate what goes on in our own life and therefore become susceptible to what goes on in the lives of others. The crisis lies not in the fact that the theatre is worse off today, but that theatre today is called on to fill a need of a totally new kind.

I do not get very excited about this talk of crisis in the theatre, because we foresaw it thirty years ago when we started the Group Theatre. The Group Theatre was not founded out of any ideological interest or out of a desire for social drama. It came out of the firm idea that no true theatre can emerge from a group of actors who work together for a few weeks because they have been hired for a production. What we foresaw was that a theatre as a unit can have the same kind of artistic development that one individual has. We proclaimed at that time that a theatre demands the kind of coherence and unity and selflessness in which all the selves become a larger self, but a larger self in which each individual finds his own true expression within the unity of this intention. True theatres do not rival each other. On the contrary, the existence of one true theatre encourages and makes possible other theatres, different from the previous theatre in their intentions, but equivalent in technique and ensemble and artistic purpose. That is what we perceived thirty years ago when we said that the future path of the American theatre must lead to the growth of true theatre, which is ensemble theatre, because that is the only way that truly creative work in theatre can be done.

EPILOGUE:

The Actors Studio Theatre

BY ROBERT H. HETHMON

The organization of The Actors Studio Theatre clearly marked
the beginning of a new era for the Studio. When the Lincoln
Center for the Performing Arts refused to make the Studio
one of its constituent units, the membership resolved to form
a new theatre. It was formally inaugurated in June 1962.

Within the Studio there had been, from the beginning, hopes
of forming a theatre, and the possibility was an annual topic of
discussion. No group of actors can remain fruitfully in association for an indefinite period without the motivation and goal
of public performance. Robert Lewis resigned after the first
year because of a difference of opinion on precisely this issue.

These hopes were brought into sharp focus—beginning about
1956—by the Lincoln Center corporation's invitation to discuss
the Studio's becoming part of the new project. During the next
five years the Studio found itself in a peculiar position. It could
not ignore a vast new force in American theatre. On the other
hand the talks dragged on and on, and, while the Directors
hinted that "something wonderful was going to happen," no
agreement was reached.

The differences of opinion between the Studio Directors and
the Lincoln Center corporation were in fact fundamental, but
this was not recognized for some time. Strasberg felt that the
proper way to start a gold mine is to find a vein of gold and
then form a management to mine, purify, and sell the gold. The
Lincoln Center corporation felt that the best way to start a
gold mine is to form a management, hire mining engineers, dig
a tunnel, and then raise money to buy gold to put in the mine.

Discussion began with Kazan's writing a statement outlining

the Directors' ideas for a theatre that would be an extension of The Actors Studio. This produced no concrete result except that Kazan, who had previously been unsure about his personal participation, decided that he would be willing to participate in such a repertory group.

Next, the Juilliard Foundation brought in Michel St. Denis to advise on the formation of a theatre school. This, Strasberg has said, was "the first indication that Lincoln Center was not receptive to the idea of an indigenous American theatre movement." Kazan threatened to resign from the Lincoln Center committee, but the Directors had early agreed to give Lincoln Center all possible leeway, so he decided to "stick it out." Two other indicative happenings followed. Robert Whitehead was announced as organizational head of the new theatre. Then the late Mrs. Vivian Beaumont, who had given money to build the Lincoln Center repertory theatre and for whom it is named, announced that she was giving it in the hope that it would never house the plays of Tennessee Williams. No official voice of Lincoln Center protested. Accordingly Cheryl Crawford, who had in 1950 produced Williams' *The Rose Tattoo* on Broadway and was to produce his *Sweet Bird of Youth* in 1959, resigned from the Lincoln Center theatre's advisory board.

The next development was an invitation to Kazan to join Whitehead in managing the new theatre. Strasberg and Kazan decided that he should accept, hoping the Studio's ideas might thereby have some chance of adoption. For two years thereafter Kazan continued to make various proposals for Lincoln Center's utilizing the talent that had been developed in the Studio. None of these was accepted, and when Kazan told Strasberg that he nevertheless planned to continue in the new theatre Strasberg decided that he could have nothing further to do with the Lincoln Center project.

The situation was at this stage in June 1961, when Strasberg told the Studio's membership, "We are now at a dead end. Whatever I hoped for in the Lincoln Center seems fated not to be fulfilled." Strasberg admitted that at the moment the future was unclear and that the members would have to make their need for the Studio strongly apparent in order to counter the drift that seemed to be setting in.

In late summer 1961 Strasberg returned from a European trip amid rumors that the Studio would not reopen, but it did so in October. The classes continued normally.

But there were unresolved problems. In early December it was announced that only enough funds were on hand to keep operating until the end of January. Finally, on February 16, 1962, Cheryl Crawford informed the members that promised contributions had not been made and that the Studio would run out of money in two weeks; she stated that the Directors were putting the problem up to them.

An emergency committee was formed. Within four days more than fifteen thousand dollars was raised. More importantly, a Committee to Secure the Long Range Financial Stability of The Actors Studio was established, composed of representatives of the three units and three members appointed by the Directors. This Committee began to examine the Studio's history and to assay Studio opinion. Suggestions were solicited. A special meeting was held on March 6 to allow any member to voice his ideas.

On April 2 this Committee recommended to the Directors— legally the membership has no authority; it can only suggest —certain actions for gaining financial support, including establishment of a fourth unit devoted to production. On April 4 the Directors gave the Committee approval and authority to implement their recommendations.

The Committee, which then began to call itself the Members Committee, set to work; subcommittees began a general appraisal of Studio policies and practices. On May 11 the formation of The Actors Studio Theatre was publicly announced. During the week of May 21, first William Fitelson and then Elia Kazan resigned from the Studio's directorate on the grounds of possible conflict of interest. Finally, on June 12, the Committee's plans and reports were submitted to the final meeting of the 1961-1962 season. The formal existence of The Actors Studio Theatre dates from that meeting.

Major changes in management had taken place. Two Studio members had been nominated as new Directors by the Members Committee and elected by the Board. A Production Board of eleven members, including Strasberg and Cheryl Crawford, was formed. Strasberg continued as Artistic Director of The Actors Studio. Miss Crawford was appointed Executive Producer and Roger L. Stevens General Administrator of the new theatre.

The passage of two seasons has in fact seen considerably more achievement than the mounting of the first auspicious productions of The Actors Studio Theatre. The Members Committee has become a permanent body, serving as a liaison between membership and directorate, and with provision made for rotating representation based on annual spring elections. New membership policies have been instituted for the Playwrights and Directors Units, and many new life members have joined the Studio. The Production Board meets continually. However, the most significant development—and the one holding the greatest potential importance for the American theatre —is the agreement signed by an overwhelming majority of the Studio's life members, many of them stars of the top rank, to give their services for at least four months each year at salaries substantially below those that many could ordinarily command. It is fair to say that The Actors Studio Theatre is the only modern theatre of potentially world-wide importance that has sprung from and is the common property of its actor members.

TECHNICAL TERMS AND TOPICS

Action, 136-38, 308

Affective memory, 102, 107-14, 131, 138, 160, 233, 250, 306

Animal exercise, 104-105

Anticipation, 113, 135, 179-84, 288

Art of acting, 63-87, 209

Audience and actor, 48, 66, 80-81, 84, 94, 99, 115, 122, 139-40, 161, 175-76, 178, 181, 185, 190-91, 205-209, 222, 226, 242, 244, 249, 252, 261, 265, 284, 299, 318, 321, 325, 338, 347-56, 365, 368, 384, 387, 390, 394

Belief (confidence, conviction, faith, trust), 78-80, 84, 86, 89, 94-99, 101, 116, 118-19, 122, 129, 131, 133, 140, 142, 146, 149, 154-55, 165, 167, 170, 174, 177, 187, 189, 199, 204-207, 217-18, 220, 230, 243, 245, 247, 255, 260, 274, 276, 282, 286, 288, 290-92, 294-95, 297, 301, 307-308, 316, 330, 335, 340, 347, 382-83

Casualness, see Literal acting

Character, 65, 67, 69, 98, 103-104, 106, 120, 122, 124-26, 128, 138, 173, 178, 180, 190, 197, 203-204, 207, 215-16, 226, 243, 247, 269, 271-72, 277-78, 281-82, 284-86, 288, 290-91, 294, 296-99, 302, 304, 311, 315, 321, 331-32, 366, 370-73, 375, 379, 381, 387, 389-390

Chinese theatre, 9, 55-57, 325, 381-383

Classic plays and acting, 9, 63, 263, 285, 305-306, 308, 311-12, 315, 317, 320-22, 368, 375-76

Cliché, see Conventional reality in acting

Comedy, 299-300, 305, 317-18, 320

Commedia dell'arte, 105, 314-15, 321

Comfort, see Literal acting

Concentration, 34, 54, 73, 82, 84-86, 88-89, 91, 93-105, 110-11, 113-18, 126, 131-33, 141-42, 150, 153-54, 156, 159, 161, 165, 167, 170, 173, 185, 193, 198, 200, 203, 205-206, 208, 222-23, 226, 243, 246-48, 251, 260, 269, 284, 288, 291, 293, 297, 330, 335, 339, 343

Confidence, see Belief

Conventional reality in acting (see also Faking; Mannerisms; Verbal pattern), 33, 46, 64, 71, 80-81, 86-87, 105, 114, 116-17, 133-34, 136, 175, 185-86, 189, 201-202, 204, 210-22, 245, 253, 266, 273-74, 281-82, 285-88, 294, 303, 312-15, 317, 321, 331, 363, 368, 371, 375, 379

Conviction, see Belief

Direction, 45, 48, 63, 136-38, 174, 180, 182, 194, 227, 230, 247-48, 260, 288, 290, 299, 307, 325-47, 350, 352-53, 356, 361

Discipline, 20, 39, 143-69, 193, 279, 287, 307, 334-46

Dramatic faculty, the, 64, 68-72, 197, 309, 393

Dual nature of the actor, 34, 46, 75-81, 152, 155-57, 164-65, 171, 180, 193, 209, 227, 299, 368

Ease, see Relaxation

Elizabethan theatre, 44, 248, 306-307, 321, 380-81

Emotional work (see also Affective memory), 35, 41, 66, 74, 93, 100-102, 104-105, 107-20, 133-34, 148-149, 160, 171-74, 184-92, 199, 208, 212, 214-15, 217, 219-31, 233, 235-40, 242, 246-47, 255, 266, 273-75, 279, 284-85, 291, 293, 297, 312, 332-34, 354, 371-375, 386

English theatre, 281, 284, 312, 319, 325, 378-81

Ensemble theatre, 15, 64-65, 364-66, 376, 380, 394-95
Event, 69, 98, 100, 104-105, 120, 128-30, 167, 173, 178, 186, 190, 197, 203, 244-45, 247, 271, 284, 297, 311, 331, 375, 385, 390, 393
Exploration, 44, 73, 102, 109, 131-132, 152, 175, 192, 197, 199, 203, 216, 252-80, 287, 303-305
Expression, 65-69, 80, 85, 88-90, 93, 101, 116-19, 133, 152, 155, 161-163, 165-67, 173, 177-78, 202, 210-53, 264, 266, 305, 313, 319, 333, 354, 369-70, 374-75
Expressiveness, *see* Expression

Faith, *see* Belief
Faking, 78, 140-42, 174-77, 226
Fear, 203-206, 226, 241-43, 248, 260, 264-65, 276, 313
Fear of being carried away, *see* Emotional work
Fear of not being carried away, *see* Emotional work
Forcing, 152, 177-78, 200, 208-209, 211, 222, 244-45, 258, 264-65, 325, 387
French school of acting, 80-81, 116, 145, 200, 281, 319, 376
Fusion, 81, 111, 114, 119-20, 140-141, 154, 166, 184-85, 211, 219, 229-30, 245-49, 258, 272, 288, 328, 368, 371

Gibberish exercise, 213-15, 222
Given circumstances, *see* Previous circumstances
Greek theatre, 44, 305-306, 321, 363, 375

Hysteria, 83, 166, 173, 265, 338, 371

Ideal training of the actor, 55-57
"Illusion of the first time," 77, 167, 299, 301
Imagination in acting, 31, 35, 56, 79, 82-86, 94-142, 148, 150, 152, 160-61, 167, 170-212, 218, 228, 241-42, 244, 249, 252-53, 255, 257, 263-65, 267, 270, 286-88,

291, 297, 302, 317, 330, 336, 342, 379
Improvisation, 56, 64, 102, 105-107, 116, 137-38, 160, 181, 213-15, 226-41, 252-53, 264, 266-67, 269-279, 298-304, 315
Impulse (and/or response) 45, 65-67, 80, 85, 88, 90, 91, 94, 100, 105-106, 108, 112, 115, 120, 134, 143, 147, 152, 155, 158-59, 162, 164, 166-67, 169-72, 174, 179, 185, 188, 194, 199, 203-204, 210-13, 215, 219, 222, 226-27, 229-30, 232, 240, 243-44, 255, 262, 265, 275, 283, 288, 354, 369, 373, 380
Individual acting problems, 5-6, 11, 16, 18-19, 31, 43-54, 90, 115-19, 145-47, 153, 156-62, 170-280, 287, 306, 336-37, 345, 349-54
Inexpressiveness, *see* Expression
Inspiration, *see* Impulse
Involuntary expression, 155, 162, 164, 206, 210-11, 220, 224-25, 240-43, 264-65, 292
Italian theatre, 325, 372, 376-78

Japanese theatre, 44, 55-56, 133, 244, 381-82
Justification, 293, 297-98

Keeping going, 152-53, 155, 173, 207, 224-25, 228-30, 232-38, 246, 248, 253, 264-72, 275-78, 338-39, 343, 345

Literal acting, 63-64, 66, 93, 101, 187-88, 196-204, 216, 235, 308-311, 314-17, 334
Logic, 45, 65, 120-30, 135-36, 147, 173, 204, 208, 247, 250, 268, 273, 283-84, 287-88, 294-96, 300-301, 315, 330, 339, 345
Looking for the opposite, 294-95

Mannerisms, 165, 177, 210, 215, 217, 242, 262, 302-303, 389-90
Mental clarity, 81-82, 192-94, 199, 211, 217, 226, 235, 250, 263-64, 274-75, 288-90, 293, 304, 379-80
"Method, The," 3, 17, 20, 36, 38-

43, 59, 69, 87, 130, 196-97, 302, 311, 334-35, 351-54, 367
"Moments of difficulty," 42, 120, 130-42, 170
Motion pictures, 28, 30, 58-59, 219, 257, 275, 360, 377

Naturalness, *see* Literal acting
Nervousness, *see* Involuntary expression
Nonexpressiveness, *see* Expression

Object(s), 95-105, 110-11, 113-14, 116, 118, 120, 126-29, 131-32, 142-43, 154, 156, 160, 167, 173-174, 177, 186, 216, 221, 242, 249-251, 253, 260, 265, 269-73, 284, 288, 290, 297, 331, 385, 391
Observation, 54, 80, 104, 200-201, 240, 275, 286, 296
Originality, 135, 204-205, 211

Particularization, 125-26, 131, 135, 138, 154, 176-77, 385
Permissiveness exercise, 213
Personalization, 131, 138
Personal technique, 7, 16, 35, 54, 63, 130, 146-47, 177, 236, 252, 255, 260, 278-80, 282, 287, 341, 374
Preparation, 54, 82, 132-36, 138, 219, 227-28, 248, 317, 336, 338, 385
Previous (given) circumstances, 69, 104, 120, 122-23, 127-28, 137-38, 269, 274, 277, 290-91, 297, 302
Private-moment exercise, 114-19, 159, 184-85, 222, 226-27, 233, 332
Production (scenic) problems, 38, 44, 46, 53, 82, 119-30, 132, 145-47, 153, 163, 175-76, 181-84, 187, 199, 203-205, 212, 228, 230, 247, 249, 252, 254, 256, 262, 264, 276, 281-322, 329-32

Relaxation (ease), 48, 66, 82, 88-94, 111-12, 114, 134, 139, 141, 145, 149, 152-55, 161, 164, 168, 172, 192, 200, 206, 208-209, 211, 216, 220, 222-24, 245-46, 253, 258, 260, 264-65, 273, 330, 341, 369-370, 382, 389

Response, *see* Impulse
Russian theatre, 357-58, 360, 366

Sections of a scene or role, 290, 293, 300-301
Self-awareness (*see also* Truth, sense of), 19, 80, 102, 118, 146, 152-53, 161-62, 164-67, 170, 176-77, 187, 205, 208, 210, 215, 217, 219, 222, 224, 226, 231, 234, 239-42, 252, 273, 276, 288, 292, 345
Self-consciousness, 103, 153, 243, 259
Sense (sensory) memory, 96-104, 110, 113-14, 118, 120, 126-28, 131, 139, 173, 249, 270, 335
Sensitivity, 34, 75, 147, 150, 167, 171-73, 186, 188, 199, 205, 215-216, 227, 242, 255, 311, 329-30, 369
Situation, 69, 98, 103-104, 106-107, 120, 128-30, 178, 189, 197, 204, 215, 244-45, 247, 273, 269-70, 274, 278, 282, 284, 292, 297, 390
Song-and-dance exercise, 161-69, 223
Speech training, *see* Vocal training
Star pause, 245
"Starting from where you are," 103, 138, 242-43
"Starting from zero," 138, 267
Stock-company acting, 335, 342, 344, 346
Style, 305, 312, 316-17, 319-21, 363, 379, 382
Stylization, 77, 317, 321, 385, 387-391
Subtext, 67-69, 106-107, 122, 129, 133, 136-39, 178-80, 183, 199, 201, 213-15, 245, 275-78, 285, 288, 290, 293, 297-99
Superaction (line of a role or play), 258-59, 288, 290, 292-93, 298-99, 339

Taking time, 134-36, 151, 173, 186, 191, 233, 245-46, 253, 260, 264-265, 269, 271-72, 275-78, 338
Technical reality in acting, 69, 140-142, 173-74, 197, 202, 242-49

Technical skills in acting, 9, 148-52, 173, 296, 314, 320-21, 382, 388

Technique, *see* Personal technique

Television, 35, 58-59, 257, 275, 360, 367

Tempo, 211, 244-45

Tension, *see* Relaxation

Theatricality, 65, 73, 134, 188, 203, 220-22, 235, 254, 261, 266, 281, 305, 315, 318, 321-22, 333, 369-371, 373, 383-84, 386-92

Timing, 299, 320

Trust, *see* Belief

Truth, sense of (feeling for truth), 165, 196, 207, 210, 234, 249-51, 299

Vagueness, 155, 161, 195-96, 216-17, 253

Verbal line, *see* Verbal pattern

Verbal pattern, 163, 178-80, 199, 204, 212, 217, 220, 245-46, 273, 275-77, 282, 285, 300, 312-13, 316

Vocal training, 9, 56, 117, 148-50, 223, 253, 273, 306, 348-54, 370

Will (willingness), 35, 49, 83-85, 94, 97, 114, 128, 143-69, 171, 174, 177, 186, 205-206, 215, 219, 222, 225, 229, 234, 240, 252-53, 264-265, 282, 287, 335, 345, 369

NAMES AND TITLES

Abbott, George, 14
ABC Network, 22
Actors Studio, The: admission, 18,
   31–32, 39, 172; building, 1–2,
   9, 27, 59; Directors Unit, vi, 8,
   21–22. 399–400; history, 7–11;
   influence, 19–21; Playwrights
   Unit, vi, 8, 21–22, 47, 399–
   400; "projects," 19, 22;
   purposes, 4–6, 27 36, 193–95,
   202, 207, 209, 249, 255–58,
   325, 352, 358–59, 367, 378;
   regular sessions of Actors Unit,
   2–3, 18–19; relation to
   commercial theatre, 4–6, 10–
   11, 18–20, 27–36, 50–51, 57–
   60, 144, 218, 247, 256–57,
   325, 327, 334–36, 339–40,
   345, 354–55, 357–362, 364,
   367; the Studio stereotype, 36–
   38
Actors Studio Theatre, 8, 10, 21–
   22, 325, 397–400
Adler, Luther, 16
Adler, Stella, 16
All the Living, 16
American Laboratory Theatre, 13–
   14, 23, 104, 144
American Theatre Wing, 16

Anderson, Robert, 8
Annals of the Elizabethan Drama,
   52–53
Anouilh, Jean, 187–88
ANTA Theatre, 8
Appia, Adolphe, 309, 363, 366

Bach, Johann Sebastian, 45
Balloon, 14
Barrault, Jean-Louis, 36
Barrymore, John, 13, 156
Bartók, Bela, 52
Beaumont, Mrs. Vivian, 398
Beethoven, Ludwig van, 45–46,
   52, 105
Before Breakfast, 336
Bellini, Gentile and Giovanni, 221
ben Ami, Jacob, 13, 66, 279
Berg, Alban, 52
Berliner Ensemble, vi, 325, 376,
   383–393
Bernhardt, Sarah, 37, 149, 369–
   70
Big Knife, The, 16
Bijou Theatre, 22
Boleslavsky, Richard, 13–14, 145,
   328
Booth, Edwin, 78
Booth, Junius Brutus, 37

Bourgeois Gentilhomme, Le, 43

Bradish, Gaynor, 8

Brahms, Johannes, 52

Brecht, Bertolt, 281, 367, 383–93

Brecht Theatre, *see* Berliner Ensemble

Breuer, Bessie, 22

Bromberg, J. Edward, 16

Brueghel, Pieter, the Elder, 317

Burbage, Richard, 13

Butterfield 8, 131–32

Callas, Maria, 374

Campbell, Mrs. Pat, 381

Cardinal (Cardinal Nino de Guevara), 51

Carnovsky, Morris, 16

Cat on a Hot Tin Roof, 259

Century Theatre, 370

Cézanne, Paul, 67

Chagall, Marc, 318–19

Chaliapin, Fyodor, 13, 66, 282, 325, 366, 374–76

Chaplin, Charles, 320

Chekhov, Anton, 22, 64, 70–74, 365

Cherry Orchard, The, 365

Chopin, Frédéric, 269

Chrystie Street Settlement House, 12, 14, 23

Circle of Chalk, The, 386–88, 391

City College of New York, 11

Clare Tree Major School of the Theatre, 13

Clurman, Harold, 15–16, 283–84, 331

Cobb, Lee J., 16

Colum, Padraic, 14

Comédie Française, 281, 376

Copeau, Jacques, 14, 76

Cornell, Katharine, 359

Country Girl, The, 16

Coward, Noel, 136, 317–18

Craig, Edward Gordon, 13, 57–58, 65, 309, 333, 363, 366

Crane, Hart, 270, 272

Crawford, Cheryl, 1, 7–11, 15–16, 22, 36, 398–400

Dalberg, Baron Wolfgang von, 198

D'Annunzio, Gabriele, 186

Dean, James, 27, 30

Decroux, Etienne, 9

Dekker, Thomas, 52

Delsarte System, 41

Delza, Sophia, 9, 57

Dostoevski, Fyodor, 280, 295

Dudley, John Stuart, 8

Dürer, Albrecht, 315

Duse, Eleonora, 1, 13, 37, 53, 66, 157, 185, 191–92, 282, 309, 325, 366–71, 377

Dybbuk, The, 388

Eagles, Jeanne, 13

Eames, Clare, 285

Esther, 14

Eurydice, 187–88

Faust (Gounod), 375
Fielding, Henry, 220
Fifth Column, The, 16
Fiske, Minnie Maddern, 302
Fitelson, William, 8, 399
Fitzgerald, F. Scott, 14
Fleck, Johann Friedrich, 198
Fontanne, Lynn, 188–89
Forbes-Robertson, Johnston, 381
Ford Foundation, 10
Four Ages of Man, The, 284
Four Walls, 14
Frank, Waldo, 14
Freud, Sigmund, 145

Galileo, 390–93
Garfein, Jack, 27, 30
Garfield, John, 16
Garrick, David, 1, 65, 144, 220, 285–286, 294, 381
Garrick Gaieties (1925), 14
Garrick Gaieties (1926), 15
Ghosts, 371
Giant, 27
Gielgud, John, 36, 281, 284
Gillette, William, 77
Goethe, Johann Wolfgang von, 3, 209
Gogh, Vincent van, 67, 263
Golden Boy, 289
Gould, Jack, 351
Grable, Betty, 347
Gramercy Ghost, 344
Granville-Barker, Harley, 281

Grasso, Giovanni, 66, 325, 366, 371–374, 377
Greco, El, 51
Green Grow the Lilacs, 15
Group Theatre, 14–16, 21, 23, 66, 105–107, 111, 214–15, 222, 289, 300–301, 326–27, 353, 356, 359, 395
Guardsman, The, 14
Guinness, Alec, 218
Guitry, Lucien, 283–84

Hamlet, 13, 65, 108, 273–75, 307
Harbage, Alfred, 52
Harris, Jed, 29
Harvey, William, 43
Hawthorne, Nathaniel, 208
Hazlitt, William, 192
Heifetz, Jascha, 54, 155, 190
Hemingway, Ernest, 16, 126
Henry IV, Part One, 315
Henry V, 176
Hermes, Alice, 9
Heywood, Thomas, 52
Hirschfeld, Al, 204
Hobson, Harold, 378
Hooch, Pieter de, 72
Horowitz, Vladimir, 44, 178
House into Which We Are Born, The, 14
House of Connelly, The, 14
Hudson Theatre, 10, 23

Ibsen, Henrik, 70, 302–303, 309, 370–371

Inge, William, 8
Irving, Henry, 4, 13, 65
Israëls, Josef, 73

Jonson, Ben, 313

Kapell, William, 250
Kazan, Elia, 7–8, 10, 15–16, 21,
    36–37, 53, 184–85, 305, 331,
    350, 352–353, 397–99
Kazan, Molly, 8
Kean, Edmund, 1, 37, 65, 108,
    192, 285, 378–79, 381
Kemble, Charles, 37
Kemble, John Philip, 1
King Lear, 285–86, 294
King, Tom, 220
Klee, Paul, 365

Labor Stage, 289
Lady from the Sea, The, 191–92
Legend of the White Serpent, The,
    382
Lehmann, Lotte, 374
Leonardo da Vinci, 45, 315
Leonidov, Leonid, 294–95
Lewis, Robert, 7, 15–16, 53, 106,
    397
Liebermann, Max, 73
Liliom, 13, 128–30
Lincoln Center for the Performing
    Arts, 397–98
Loeb, Philip, 12, 14
Lord, Pauline, 66
Lunt, Alfred, 188–89

Macbeth, 81–82, 108, 121, 190,
    264, 331–32
Macready, William Charles, 133, 190
Maeterlinck, Maurice, 12
Magnani, Anna, 192
Malin Studios, 9
Mann, Daniel, 8
Mannheim National Theatre, 198
March, Liska, 9
Marlowe, Christopher, 53, 313
Mefistofele, 375
Meisner, Sanford, 8, 16
Men in White, 105
Merchant of Venice, The, 192,
    285, 306
Meyerhold, Vsevolod, 55, 57, 281,
    363, 366, 382, 384
Michelangelo, 35, 45, 307, 315–
    16, 368
Millionairess, The, 86
Moissi, Alexander, 280
Molière, 263, 322
Mooney's Kid Don't Cry, 178
Mortá Civile, La, 372
Moscow Art Theatre, 13, 65–66,
    72, 74, 294, 357–58, 366
Mother Courage, 384–86
Mourning Becomes Electra, 153
Mozart, Wolfgang Amadeus, 45,
    52, 250
Muni, Paul, 282
My Life in Art, 251

Naumburg Cathedral, 315
New Year's Eve, 14

Notebooks (Chekhov), 71
Novelli, Ermete, 377

Odets, Clifford, 8, 16, 66,
    106
O'Hara, John, 131
Olivier, Laurence, 33, 36, 351–
    52, 379–80
O'Neill, Eugene, 10, 336
On the Art of the Theatre, 13
Othello, 306, 310–11
Ouspenskaya, Maria, 13, 104

Page, Geraldine, 8
Pinza, Ezio, 374
Pirandello, Luigi, 14
Player, The, 20
Poel, William, 380–81
Princess Theatre, 8
Private Lives, 136
Processional, 14

Racine, Jean, 14
Rain, 13
Rainmaker, The, 169
Rebel Without a Cause, 27
Red Rust, 15
Reinhardt, Max, vi
Rembrandt, 45, 52, 317
Return to Kansas City, 275–78
Richard III, 134–36· 219–21· 261,
    306
Riggs, Lynn, 15

*Right You Are If You Think You
    Are*, 14
Romeo and Juliet, 227–41, 258–
    59, 306, 308–309
Rose Tattoo, The, 398
Ross. Helen, 20
Ross, Lillian, 20
Rossi, Ernesto, 377
Rubens, Peter Paul, 50

Salvini, Tommaso, 133, 377
Samson and Delilah, 13, 279
Schnabel, Artur, 250
Seagull, The, 22, 71–74, 188–89
Shakespeare, William, 37, 44, 52–
    53, 63–64, 68, 76, 82, 108,
    135, 245, 261, 284–85, 305–
    16, 319–20, 322, 363, 375,
    380–81
Shaw, George Bernard, 244, 312,
    317–318
Shaw, Irwin, 70, 275
Siddons, Mrs. Sarah, 1, 82, 107–
    108, 121, 133, 285, 378
Skin of Our Teeth, The, 264
Sokolow, Anna, 9
Sophocles, 375
Stanislavski, Constantin, 1, 7, 13–
    14, 23, 40–41, 43, 53, 57, 65,
    74–75, 82, 86–87, 89–90, 95,
    108, 115–16, 119, 130, 138–39,
    165, 180, 197, 210–12, 220, 245,
    251, 254, 282, 286–89, 292,
    294–95, 299, 307–11, 314, 352,
    354, 363, 366, 380, 386

St. Denis, Michel, 398
Stern, Isaac, 190
Stevens, Roger L., 400
Strange Interlude, 10, 23
Strasberg, Baruch Meyer, 11
Strasberg, Ida, 11
Strasberg, Lee: personal history, 8,
    11–16; private classes, 4, 9, 21,
    41, 56, 58, 88, 90, 101–103,
    115, 119, 161, 167–69, 180,
    196, 254, 295; as teacher, 16–
    18, 102, 168, 212, 253
Strasberg, Susan, 337
Strauss, Richard, 52
Stravinsky, Igor, 52
Streetcar Named Desire, A, 331
Strindberg, August, 181, 303–304
Stronger, The, 181–84, 303–304
Students of Art and Drama, 12
Sudermann, Hermann, 12
Summer and Smoke, 122–23
Sundown Beach, 22
Sweet Bird of Youth, 398

Talma, F. J., 76
Taylor, Laurette, 66
Teatro Piccolo Milano, 372
Tender Is the Night, 125
Terborch, Gerard, 72
Terry, Ellen, 65
Theatre Arts magazine, 12
Theatre Guild, 12–15, 23
Theatre Guild Studio, 15
"Three-Day Blow," 126–28
Three Sisters, The, 74, 124–25

Tintoretto, 51
Tone, Franchot, 16, 301, 356
Torn, Rip, 8
Toscanini, Arturo, 35, 54, 326, 347
Townsend Harris High School, 11
Turandot, 384
Two Gentlemen of Verona, 314

Union Church, 8

Vakhtangov, Eugene, 112, 120,
    138, 308–309, 357–58, 360,
    366, 384, 388
Variety, 352
Vegetable, The, 14
View of Toledo, 51

Wagner, Richard, 52
Weigel, Helene, 387, 389–90
Welles, Orson, 29
"White Buildings," 270–73
Whitehead, Robert, 398
Whitman, Walt, 106
Willard, Dorothy, 9
Williams, Tennessee, 178, 317, 398
Wisconsin Center for Theatre
    Research, v
Wolfe, Thomas, 133
Wordsworth, William, 112

Yegor Bulichev, 294–95
Young, Stark, 279

Zacconi, Ermete, 377
Zeffirelli, Franco, 306